CITY ON A HILL

CITY
ON A
HILL

Urban Idealism in America
from the Puritans to the Present

ALEX KRIEGER

THE BELKNAP PRESS *of* HARVARD UNIVERSITY PRESS
CAMBRIDGE, MASSACHUSETTS AND LONDON, ENGLAND   2019

Library of Congress Cataloging-in-Publication Data

Names: Krieger, Alex, 1951- author.

Title: City on a hill : urban idealism in America from the Puritans to the
present / Alex Krieger.

Description: Cambridge, Massachusetts : The Belknap Press of Harvard
University Press, 2019. | Includes bibliographical references and index.

Identifiers: LCCN 2019019803 | ISBN 9780674987999

Subjects: LCSH: City planning—United States—History. | Utopias—
United States—History. | Cities and towns—United States—History.

Classification: LCC HT167 .K74 2019 | DDC 307.1 / 2160973—dc23

LC record available at https://lccn.loc.gov/2019019803

Dedicated to Isara and Isaiah,
and to Anne, partner in life and the more gifted writer

Ten thousand people had "squatted" upon a square mile of virgin prairie that first afternoon . . . . Here indeed was a city laid out and populated in half a day. Thousands of campfires sparkled upon the dark bosom of the prairie as far as the eye could reach.

OKLAHOMA BOOMER, 1889

Utopians traced the lines of the first city.

ANATOLE FRANCE, 1895

CONTENTS

Illustrations follow page 220

PREFACE

CITIES ARE COMPROMISES IN TIME: compromises among efforts to preserve a past, overcome the challenges of the present, and pursue plans for the future. In America, the future has weighed heaviest in this balance. Generations of Americans newly arrived, moving to the West—or relocating to the suburbs, then exurbs, then in some cases back to city centers—have shaped cities with a utopian resolve to build a better future. The traces their dreams have left on our cities are the subject of this book.

Since the first Europeans arrived in America with hopes of finding or establishing an Eden, there have been religious and secular movements aimed at perfecting society. The American Revolution itself has been cast by at least one Pulitzer Prize–winning history as a utopian undertaking.[1] Political and social reformers—from the Revolution through the Progressive Era to the Sixties and beyond—have routinely sought to mobilize support by calling on Americans to live up to the promise of the country's origins, the promise of a self-governing people valuing equality and pursuing happiness. Such rhetoric of utopianism often forms the core of the most anodyne political speeches.

Thumb through *Weekend Utopia: Modern Living in the Hamptons,* or *Smartphone Utopia, Criminal Utopia, Cruising Utopia, Fishing in Utopia,* or *Surrendering to Utopia*—the last sounding rather pleasant. These are among some fourteen thousand offerings on Amazon with "utopia" in their title. Strip out the duplicates, many of them different editions of Thomas More's *Utopia,* first published in 1516 and still in print, and it is still an impossibly long reading list, suggesting a persistent American fondness for utopian ruminations. While you are at it, dip into Frederic Jameson's brooding 2016 essay "An American Utopia"—perhaps while listening to David Byrne's 2018 album *American Utopia*.

Three publications served as my own inspiration for delving into the topic. Leo Marx's *The Machine in the Garden: Technology and the Pastoral Ideal in America* first sparked my fascination with aspects of an American culture that seems to thrive on idealistic ventures. "With an unspoiled hemisphere in view," Marx writes, "the dream of a retreat to an oasis of harmony and joy was removed from its traditional literary context. It was embodied in various utopian schemes for making America the site of a new beginning for Western society. In both forms—one literary and the other in essence political—the ideal has figured in the American view of life."[2]

Marx's two forms of the ideal—*literary* and *political*—compelled consideration of a third form: the *physical*, or how an ideal might become manifest on the land. And that led to the course I have offered at Harvard for more than three decades: *Designing the American City: Civic Aspirations and Urban Form*. This book is a product of that course and the many, many students and teaching fellows that shaped my understanding of American urbanization through their participation.

A second inspiration was *Visions of Utopia: Nashoba, Rugby, Ruskin, and the "New Communities" in Tennessee's Past*, which ends with a disarming thought. Acknowledging that pursuing utopia is a fool's errand, John Egerton nonetheless calls for more utopian ideas, given their contribution to a nation which, as he puts it, "has in its Constitution an idealistic and near-utopian objective: 'to form a more perfect Union.'"[3] Egerton admires, as others have, what Americans have been willing to reach for. I am reminded of a line by Hendrik Willem van Loon, an author of children's books, in his unusual introduction to Lewis Mumford's 1922 classic *The Story of Utopias*: "a Utopia, however strange or fanciful, is the only possible beacon upon the uncharted seas of the distant future."[4]

Anne Mackin, my wife, provided the third inspiration with her *Americans and Their Land: The House Built on Abundance*. It begins with a sentence that could just as well have begun my book: "Nothing has shaped the American character as fundamentally as the sheer abundance of land and resources that met the European colonist, that met the westward-moving settler, and that still appears to meet the American suburbanite pressing into the exurbs."[5] That extraordinary abundance has fueled many a utopian inclination.

Inspiration has been abundant, then, but why the need for another narrative with idealistic aspiration as its point of departure? This book's specific focus is on the strong disposition Americans have to think differently about places to live—their enduring desire to move past perceived limitations, first, of the late-medieval world, then of the early industrial city, and eventually of the enormous, modern-day metropolis. My aim is not to locate utopia. That is best left to philosophers. Nor will I try to show how each utopian muse—every new set of cultural aspirations, really—has advanced social justice, equality, or prosperity. Utopian impulses do not guarantee utopian results.

Isaiah Berlin, a philosopher whose writings are full of warnings about utopia, declared that "as guides to conduct they can prove literally fatal." He was referring to twentieth-century totalitarian and fascist movements and their disastrous consequences. In their wake, many concluded that utopian conjuring was not only foolish but harmful. Yet, what precedes Berlin's chilling verdict is a more optimistic one: "Utopias have their value—nothing so wonderfully expands the imaginative horizon of human potentialities."[6] Americans have aimed at imaginative horizons across the country's history, especially about how to reconceive the places in which they wished to live out their lives.

Ruminations about utopia suggest optimism, which in turn suggests naivete. At the moment, optimism is in short supply, given growing worries over political polarization, climate change and denials of it, racial tensions, acts of intolerance, and increasing economic inequality. Books along the lines of Alissa Quart's *Squeezed: Why Our Families Can't Afford America* appear more commonly than predictions of sunny tomorrows.[7] I hesitate to deliver a Pollyannaish perspective on American culture and urbanization, aware of the histories that have been and must still be written about many of the nation's dystopic features: the near-complete destruction of indigenous cultures; the horrors of slavery; the extreme nationalism of such conceits as Manifest Destiny and American Exceptionalism; the political and corporate restraints placed on social and economic equality; and the despoiling of the environment in the name of progress. To varying degrees, misguided idealism has been part of all these histories, validating accounts of conquest as opposed to the realization of paradise.[8]

Some may find it ill-advised to attach the word *utopia* to any aspect of American urbanization. My argument that the suburb has utopian origins might be cited as such folly. The typical metamorphosis from model garden suburb to generic suburban sprawl, however, only emphasizes the contingent nature of utopian ventures—one generation's aspirations becoming a subsequent generation's commonplace, or burden requiring reevaluation. As microbiologist Rene Dubos writes in *Dreams of Reason: Science and Utopia*, perhaps echoing Isaiah Berlin, "it would seem that utopias can exist as realities only if they die shortly after being born, to be reborn with new shapes."[9] Theologian Paul Tillich adds: "It is the spirit of Utopia which conquers Utopia." But he also acknowledges that "cultures which have no utopia remain imprisoned in the present" and that "the fruitfulness of utopia [is] its ability to open up possibilities."[10]

This book follows the opening up of such possibilities. It focuses on experiments in creating settlement, efforts both compelling and naive, successful and problematic. It presents Americans' desire to move beyond the imperfect cities inherited from prior generations and to embark on improving life in new urban patterns. The idea is to offer an interpretation of patterns of settlement and attitudes toward urban life that are characteristic of American culture. It also seeks to reveal the processes, ambitions, dreams, plans, designs, and actions that have influenced American urbanization, often leaving traces of their idealism. These advanced in concert with insights stemming from the European Enlightenment and, soon after, in reaction to the explosion of urbanization brought about by the Industrial Revolution.

I have already made heavy use of the word *city*, and it will appear again often in the pages that follow. The word will refer to places we conveniently understand as cities, such as Boston and Chicago, but this book is not only about them. *City* will be used in its ancient connotation—an area inhabited by citizens—from the Latin *civis*, for citizen, and *civitas*, for the social body of citizens.

Because America was built by arrivals, the process of creating settlements was continuous. Cities being made anew heralded the arrival of the modern age, and the notion of a modern age is key to appreciating them. French theorist Jean Baudrillard expresses this with halting admiration: "Imbedded in the idea of America is the idea of the modern age: they are synonymous." Inadvertently he was echoing a proclamation by Thomas Paine in the appendix to *Common Sense:* "We have it in our power to begin the world over again."[11] Both recall John Locke's oft-quoted statement from the seventeenth century—"In the beginning all the world was America"—an observation to which we will return.

Landscape is no less important a word for this narrative. The modern metro-politan environment is a landscape, a complex and quilted one. Traverse any large metropolitan area and this is evident. Anne and I have had the good for-tune of building a retreat in New Hampshire, about sixty-five miles from our home in Boston. (Guardians of urban compactness could accuse us of being weekend sprawlers.) Moving between these two domains, we experience diverse territories of settlement. From the bustle of downtown Boston we cross a cen-tury and a half of peripheral urbanization, through remnants of the New Eng-land countryside and its old Puritan-covenanted towns, some of these enduring as quaint villages that draw summer people and tourists. We travel past old farms now advertising organic practices that appeal to urbane sensibilities, and past mill towns reborn as havens for tech entrepreneurship. One senses an urban-to-rural "transect," but not in the linear, sequential pattern that New Urbanist apostles illustrate. John Stilgoe, the distinguished historian of land-scapes, tells of the word's multiple references and ancient roots, but reminds us that landscape is ultimately a human invention.[12] Trying to create landscapes for desirable settlement—not always cities in a conventional sense—has been one of Americans' great utopian quests.

Coming to America as a child, with parents having endured the dystopia of Europe during and following World War II, no doubt influenced my apprecia-tion for the American inclination to pursue ambitious dreams. I write these lines during a family weekend at a fortuitous address: a hotel on Eden Street, one block from a parallel street called Paradise Drive, in one of our favorite places, Acadia National Park in Maine. The name *Acadia,* a modification of *Arcadia,* was placed on a sixteenth-century map of the north Atlantic coast after a voyage by Giovanni da Verrazzano. That mapmaker gave the coast of Maine the name of an ancient district in Greece considered to be the "idyllic place"—just as others across time and with considerable hope have bestowed similar moni-kers upon places across America.

CITY ON A HILL

I.1 *The Island of Utopia.* Woodcut by Ambrosius Holbein used to illustrate the 1518 edition of Sir Thomas More's *Utopia*. His imagination was likely inspired by stories of the discovery of a New World.

INTRODUCTION:
DREAMS OF A FUTURE IN A NEW WORLD

> Drive through Jerusalem Corners, New York, or Promise City, Iowa;
> pass the freeway exits for Elysian Valley and Arcadia in California; stop
> at the "Garden of Eatun" restaurant in Cozad, Nebraska. American
> place names revive settlers' visions of the New World as earthly
> paradise, dreams about the apocalyptic properties of the American
> landscape first expressed when Columbus claimed to be discoverer of a
> "new heaven" and a "new earth."
>
> DOLORES HAYDEN, 1976

AMERICA IS NO LONGER IDENTIFIED AS a "new earth," much less as paradise. Utopian imaginings do not appear as regularly in literature or lyrics as they once did. Nevertheless, the country's association with beginnings and promise endures. Despite anxiety-inducing turns in national politics, America remains a dreamed-about haven for people around the world. And certainly, those many Edenic place-names across the land have survived.[1]

Columbus's claim of finding a whole new heaven and earth, more than the geographic details he and later explorers mapped, fueled dreams of fortuitous beginnings. The transcendent possibility that the paradise of the Judeo-Christian bible might be recaptured in that new place occupied the minds of theologians, philosophers, and the faithful. For premodern cultures, a return to paradise—the doctrine of millennialism—was not a fantastical expectation. They had inherited the medieval assumption that, somewhere beyond the three known continents of Europe, Asia, and Africa, Eden must exist.[2] Might a new world lead back to a state of innocence or grace—the conditions assumed to have existed in paradise? Ulrich Hugwald, a sixteenth-century teacher of Aristotelian ethics and publisher of some of Luther's papers, expressed the belief of his era when he said the discovery of the Americas would lead "to Christ, to Nature, to Paradise."[3] An *idea* about America preceded the arrival of those who became Americans. As historian Michael Kammen puts it, "There is a sense in which Americans, from the outset, could not fully control their own destiny because they had a mythology before they had a country."[4]

High expectations led countless inhabitants of the Old World to head for the New, in hopes of finding Eden or at least unshackling themselves from oppression and starting fresh to build a new and better society. The overwhelming (though not unsettled) wilderness they found upon arrival was hardly paradise.[5] Of the original Plymouth colonists, only sixty out of one hundred and two souls survived their first winter on American soil. Every subsequent winter took its own toll. Dreams of social and self-improvement had to wait. Only after the basic struggle for survival was won could settlers turn to the long process of establishing the social norms and conventions by which they wanted to live.

An instinct to look ahead developed, expressed well in a Thomas Jefferson letter to John Adams: "I like the dreams of the future better than the history of the past."[6] Others have offered analogous thoughts. "The Americans love their country, not indeed, as it is, but as it will be. . . . They live in the future, and make their country as they go." So wrote Francis J. Grund in *The Americans* in 1837, two years after Alexis de Tocqueville's first volume of *Democracy in America* made similar observations.[7]

That the New World expanded the frontiers of social and political organization is broadly accepted. It is no surprise, then, that the reevaluation of Old World institutions and values extended to the question of how best to gather spatially in communities. Europeans have often perceived and celebrated the restless, experimental quality of the cities built across the Atlantic. Torn between tradition and the forces of political, social, and scientific revolution, seventeenth- and eighteenth-century Europeans saw the Americas as a pristine world (conveniently overlooking native peoples) where new primary forms of community could be established in line with religious ideals or Enlightenment values. Later, during the nineteenth century, as European cities faced the stresses of industrialization, multitudes arrived with anxieties as much as hope, seeing in American cities the chance to circumvent the chaos, pollution, crowding, and squalor of the age. Emerging seemingly overnight, these cities brimmed with hope, even if it was inevitable they would later fall prey to the same problems as London and Manchester. In the twentieth century, European travelers, seeking an authentic spirit of modernity, caught glimpses of what modernism could bring to the city. (See Figure I.2.)

Consider the impressions of a perceptive European upon his encounter with the American city in 1945. "The striking thing is the lightness, the fragility," he writes about the cities. The city "has no weight, it seems barely to rest on the soil." American cities were "born temporary and have stayed that way." They form "a moving landscape for its inhabitants, whereas our [European] cities are our shells." The dynamics strike him as dramatically different: "We Europeans change within changeless cities, and our houses and neighborhoods outlive us; American cities change faster than their inhabitants do, and it is the inhabitants who outlive the cities." As a result: "For us a city is, above all, a past; for them it

I.2 Opening day at the Empire State Building observatory, in 1931 by far the tallest building in the world overlooking the most unprecedented city in the world.

I.3 **Jefferson's building block for his America, depicted as a bountiful plantation, albeit here with slave quarters spreading down the hillside.**

is mainly a future; what they like in the city is everything it has not yet become and everything it can be."

To the extent that history is present in the cities he tours, it seems accidental: "the past does not manifest itself in them as it does in Europe, through public monuments, but through survivals." In other words, the older parts of a city "are there simply because no one has taken the time to tear them down, and as a kind of indication of work to be done."

"Our beautiful closed cities, full as eggs, are a bit stifling," he even concedes: "once you are inside the city, you can no longer see beyond it." In America, things are different. "Frail and temporary, formless and unfinished, they are haunted by the presence of the immense geographical space surrounding them. . . . You feel, from your first glance, that your contact with these places is a temporary one, either you will leave them or they will change around you." The forward-looking quality of places like New York and Chicago is what most impresses him: "The cities are open, open to the world, and to the future. This is what gives them their adventurous look, and even a touching beauty."[8]

The impressions are those of Jean-Paul Sartre, writing in *Le Figaro*. Echoing European visitors dating back to de Tocqueville, Sartre expresses an appreciation for American cities as sites for reinvention. Understanding what drives such re-invention—such constant experimentation in organizing society spatially—is the purpose of this book's narrative.

I begin with Thomas Jefferson, often depicted as antagonistic to cities, who had the most precise view of what America should become. Joseph J. Ellis, among Jefferson's more perceptive biographers, describes him as someone "who combined great depth with great shallowness, massive learning with ex-traordinary naivete, piercing insights into others with daunting powers of self-deception."[9] It is a near-perfect description of a utopian. Jefferson's ideal-ization of the "tillers of the soil" led him to the homestead as the building block of a new society and the Cartesian grid as a means to partition the lands of post-Colonial America. As long as citizens had adequate access to land, he believed, America would avoid the corruption he saw in European cities and society. Chapter 1 introduces Jefferson's vision of America as a republic of in-dependent citizens occupying and cultivating their own gardens. (See Figure I.3.) Long after Jefferson, in 2002, *USA Today* asked its readers where they would prefer to live if money and current circumstances were not factors. A majority (51 percent) chose a hundred-year-old, ten-acre farm. Less than 9 percent chose a designer loft in Manhattan, even given a palatial four thou-sand square feet.[10]

Chapter 2 investigates an expectation that was easy to sustain when, as in Jef-ferson's day and for decades afterwards, the supply of land in America seemed limitless. This was the assumption that Americans would live in nature, enjoy-ing its sublime qualities while partaking of its resources, and thus constitute a "nature's nation."[11]

A pastoral imagination has inspired generations of Americans, from the New England Transcendentalists forward, and is one reason that America has been accused of having an anti-urban culture. Chapter 3 addresses this anti-urban-ism. While the modern American city engenders awe, for many it also engenders discomfort, sometimes fear, and a sense of insufficient humane qualities. Ameri-can cities tend to be admired for their size and industriousness, for their material wealth, for their lack of exhibited sentimentality toward the past (until recent interest in historic preservation), and for their propensity to accommodate change—but the admiration rarely comes with genuine affection. Imagine a citizen of one of Europe's capitals sharing Henry Ford's conclusion, reached with a particular instrument in mind: "We shall solve the problem of the city by leaving the city."[12] This certainly sounds anti-urban, unless understood in relationship to a differently imagined pattern of human concentration.

Concurrent with the idea of a republic of homesteaders, Americans have been fascinated with the small town, variously called the *hometown* or *country town*. Chapter 4 follows such veneration from the covenanted New England villages of the Puritans, romanticized a century later in Currier and Ives lithographs; through the many communitarian experiments with town-like enclaves; on to early suburban estates and more recent efforts by "new urbanists" to redeploy traditional town models to wean Americans from suburban sprawl.

Settlements organized around industry took root early in the nineteenth century. One inclination was to locate industry away from existing town centers. The reasons were both practical and aspirational. In New England, water rather than coal was the initial means of powering machinery, so it was advantageous to site early factories alongside rivers where the currents were strongest. But there was also a belief that a healthful setting might ensure a more content and productive labor force. A comparable current phenomenon might be the habit of high-tech companies in Silicon Valley to site their campuses at some distance from San Francisco, and stock them with all kinds of amenities and creature comforts—for the workers' well-being, and no doubt keeping them at their terminals longer. The tradition of the company town-away-from-town is the subject of Chapter 5.

Suburban estates, as they were first called, and soon garden suburbs, gained popularity across much of the nineteenth century, before metastasizing into suburbia during the second half of the twentieth. Chapter 6 recalls how appealing these new kinds of environments were, precisely for being set apart from the "rasping frictions" of the constantly changing industrializing city. Early suburbs were not seen as substitutes for the city but as retreats to domestic comfort, places to recuperate from the day's labors and city bustle. Such suburban idealism still surfaces more often than urban pundits believe. As recently as 2018, an account of Serenbe, a thousand-acre development on the outskirts of Atlanta, carried the title "The Seductive Power of a Suburban Utopia."[13] (See Figure I.4.)

Chapter 7 focuses on the dispersal of settlement across America. Within several months in the midst of the Civil War, at President Lincoln's urging, Congress

I.4 **Promotional photo of Serenbe, a suburban community being developed on the outskirts of Atlanta, and described as a "suburban utopia."**

enacted three far-reaching programs. The Homestead Act enabled citizens to acquire public land at minimal cost; the Morrill Act granted land to states to establish public universities; and an expanded program of grants to railroad companies achieved transcontinental connectivity. Around the same time, in a less formal trend, new states began siting their capitals near their geographic centers, perhaps to suggest equal access to resources and to those governing.

The most common street name in America (other than the ordinal ones such as *Second* and *Fourth*) is *Park*. That reveals much about American predispositions about place. As America entered what has been called the "furnace stage of urbanization" in the second half of the nineteenth century, strategies to keep the furnace from burning out of control were urgently advanced. Chapter 8 focuses on the reintroduction of nature into the increasingly unnatural city. The hope was for public parks to serve as an antidote to smoke and dirt, and a civilizing and healing force for city dwellers. A new profession of landscape architecture, led by Frederick Law Olmsted, created exemplary parks across urbanizing America, one of the great achievements of American city building.

Chapter 9 covers an outpouring of utopian literature at the end of the nineteenth century. Social reformers were inspired to better plan, administer, and regulate the city by Edward Bellamy, William Dean Howells, and other writers depicting brighter futures, just as they were moved to action by the urban misery captured in Jacob Riis's camera. The modern profession of city planning would arise as a consequence.

Chapter 10 moves backward and forward in time to review the unusual history of our nation's capital. The United States' founders, while committed to distributing land to citizens in support of an agricultural economy, nonetheless understood the importance of towns for the transaction of commerce and for governance. The case is made in this chapter that the nation's capital required not one but two utopian inspirations, a full century apart, to achieve its monumentality.

Meanwhile, many Midwesterners believed that Chicago would surpass New York to become the largest and most important city in America. Chapter 11 describes why this seemed likely. During much of the nineteenth century, Chicago was a machine for unimpeded growth. The "city of the big shoulders," to quote

I.5   Depression era Resettlement Administration poster, clear in suggesting a preferred realm for life.

Carl Sandburg's famous poem, was a cauldron of production, an immense warehouse and distribution center. Cultural progress was secondary to industrial progress. Chicago was first on earth to assemble the full set of characteristics associated with the modern metropolis.

The democratization of mobility is the focus of Chapter 12. For a pre-twentieth-century mind, the advent of motorized vehicles for rapid personal transport—and that such machines would be affordable to ordinary people—would have been a vision as utopian as any, yet this was realized within a couple of decades. It was a miracle that gave rise to a radical implication: good roads (along with potable water, proper sewage, electricity, and ease of communication) could eliminate geographical limits for cities—perhaps eliminate the need for cities entirely, as they were historically understood. Along came Frank Lloyd Wright and his proposed "Broadacre City" utopia, promoting a complete decentralization of settlement. The appeal of the suburb would no longer be as a place apart for those fortunate to be able to withdraw from the city; now, all Americans could experience the "life by the acre" that a Depression-era Resettlement Administration poster extolled. (See Figure I.5.)

Spreading out is also the subject of Chapter 13, but in the form of recurring communitarian and "back to the land" movements. These have generally arisen in times of cultural or economic change, when people's instincts tell them to pull away from the mainstream. Many eighteenth- and nineteenth-century groups come to mind, some fleeing religious persecution and others seeking secular havens. In more recent memory, the Great Depression saw waves of people opting for a romanticized rural and small-town life, assisted by federal policies including the short-lived Resettlement Administration—and the socially tumultuous 1960s sparked a surge in communes and other experimental forms of group living. This inclination to move away has sent people not only westward across the continent, but to manageable distances away from those chaotic cities.

Chapter 14 considers the age of urban renewal, generally treated by history as a dystopic era. Like all utopian ventures, it began with dreams of substituting a better future for the present. The downfall of urban renewal was that it followed this formula literally, starting with wholesale demolition of old neighborhoods. (See Figure I.6.) This razing was done in the name of "slum clearance" and sometimes worse yet as "negro removal."[14] Virtually all of the effects of urban renewal have long been considered negative. Half a century removed from it,

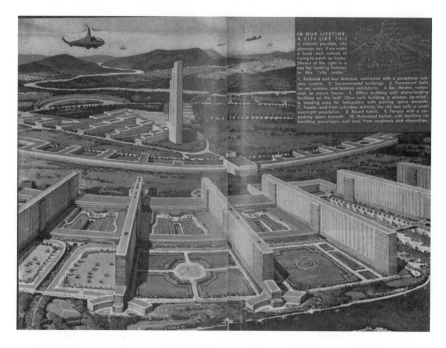

I.6   A modernist dream among the "urban renewers." The description begins: "In our lifetime, a city like this is entirely possible, city planners say, if we make a fresh start instead of trying to patch up decay."

however, one can see how the period and its policies laid the groundwork for the city's identities to be reshaped for the late twentieth century and early twenty-first century.

It may be that I am sometimes too ready to assign utopian inclinations to efforts whose proponents considered themselves realists. Not so in the case of Walt Disney. His experimental prototype city of tomorrow—the EPCOT as he imagined it, not as it was built, much less as it survives—arose from a frankly utopian vision, and at a time when regard for the existing city was at a nadir. In retelling Mr. Disney's EPCOT dream, Chapter 15 also introduces the new towns movement of the 1960s and 1970s. Programs launched under this banner, originating in the United Kingdom with the Garden Cities idea, were intended to demonstrate how to create better forms of cities—better than either those failing "inner cities" being poorly renewed or the expanding suburban rings beginning to be criticized as nothing but sprawl.

The cities of Las Vegas and New Orleans are hardly known for their utopian origins, yet both deserve a place in this narrative. Chapter 16 focuses on what is being learned from this unusual place called Vegas. If the ideal driving the nineteenth-century growth of Chicago was to create a city optimized for industrial processes, the vision for Las Vegas was the urban center dedicated to the maximization of pleasure. That goal may seem trivial to many, but it is no less aspirational. The exaggerated divide between the city's extraordinary center and its miles of mundane perimeter, reveals two distinct utopian strands, marking the city as a harbinger of the future. Cities increasingly compete for residents, visitors, and investors with focused, thematic campaigns—Dubai being the prime international example. They have all taken their lessons from Las Vegas.

New Orleans conjures up different themes, especially that of perseverance. Chapter 17 describes the city's perpetual resilience as it has been battered by the forces of nature. That will strike most as quixotic rather than utopian. Still, the history of the city's phoenix-like recoveries from dozens of disasters reflects another American instinct: the stubbornness to go on. Perhaps it is another legacy of settling a new world that turned out not to be paradise, and so required perfecting.

Chapter 18 turns to a current utopian vision, caricaturized by supporters and critics as "e-topia." Its proponents claim with regard to virtually any problem related to urbanization that solutions will come from analysis of terabytes of data generated by electronically networked infrastructures, producing so-called smart cities. This fresh form of utopian confidence has captured imaginations at an opportune moment, as memories of mid-twentieth-century urban decay fade and suburbs have become too commonplace to foster much conceptual enthusiasm (except for those intent on urbanizing them). Concurrent with this e-topian evangelizing has been a partial return of Americans to the heart of the city from the places formerly seen as more hospitable to modern life. (See Figure I.7.)

Finally, in a Postscript, I offer musings on present-day concerns. The growing calls for more data-rich "smart cities," environmentally "resilient cities," and socially "just cities" speak to ambitions as Elysian as any prior, and no less illusive. Utopias are generally imagined in a pastoral environment, no doubt due to the influence of the biblical paradise. Poignantly, utopians from Plato to Thomas Moore to Edward Bellamy envisioned the good place as an ideal city. Now that

Greenway Rings
Fountain, July 2016

I.7   The Rose Kennedy Greenway in Boston, created on top of a highway rebuilt in a
tunnel. The greenway reconnects districts that were severed by the original 1950s
elevated highway. See Figure 14.5. The nearly two-mile-long park, a rare physical
rebuttal to an old (and remaining) concern; "to the few the great city gives all, to the
millions it gives annually less and less." Observed by Clarence Stein in the same 1925
Survey Graphic in which Lewis Mumford declared the future of cities dismal. Both Stein
and Mumford were founders of America's Garden City movement.

there are seven billion seekers of good places—and soon eight, then nine billion—an urban setting will have to be that good place for most. How to continue to perfect cities, allowing them to remain, in Claude Lévi-Strauss's memorable phrase, "the human invention par excellence" is the challenge of this still young century.

1.1 Over Nebraska: citizens' homesteads contained by the grid of the Continental Surveys, remaining evidence of Jefferson's agrarian republic.

1

JEFFERSON'S BLUEPRINT FOR AN EGALITARIAN REPUBLIC

> Democracy [is] born of free land . . . American Democracy was born of
> no theorist's dream. . . . It came stark and strong and full of life out of
> the American forest.
>
> FREDERICK JACKSON TURNER, 1893

> The winding road is the pack-donkey's way. . . . The straight line is a
> reaction, an action, a positive deed, the result of self-mastery. It is sane
> and noble.
>
> LE CORBUSIER, 1922

WHEN Frederick Jackson Turner wrote that American democracy emerged from the land, he was echoing Thomas Jefferson and many of Jefferson's fellow founders, for whom freedom and land were intertwined. And while the farmer in Jefferson was unlikely to be as dismissive of pack-donkeys as Le Corbusier seems, he certainly believed in the sane and noble aspects of the straight line. Jefferson was convinced that America's vast territories, divided into ample citizen homesteads ruled by a surveyed line, would form the foundation of an

1.2   Chicago's street grid stretching beyond the horizon and unto the prairie.

egalitarian republic. His advocacy manifested itself in land-distribution policies that left a permanent mark on much of the country.

To fly over large segments of America, whether urban or rural, is to see a grid below. A Cartesian order prevails, as if a giant piece of graph paper were laid over the land. Think of Manhattan or Chicago, Kansas City or much of the rural Midwest, where the precision of the rectilinear grid dominates. (See Figure 1.2.) The majority of such partitioning of the land took place during the nineteenth century, when Americans spread across the continent establishing cities away from the east coast. But the origins of this land-subdividing tradition date back earlier, to the last third of the eighteenth century, and to an ideology that anticipated a dispersal of citizen-farmers over the territories recently liberated from the British.

Before there were towns in the New World, much less cities or suburbs—before there were strip malls, subdivisions, big boxes, power centers, edge cities, perimeter highways, and far-flung exurbs—there was an unimaginably vast supply of land. And there still is. For arrivals from European societies, the promise of this bounty of land was manifold. They saw, first, the opportunity to dwell in, harvest, hunt, mine, and reap the land's resources. More intoxicating still was the prospect of possessing portions of them. It was a dream to make a small part of the New World one's own, to achieve self-reliance and independence from the feudal, oligarchic world they had left behind, and ultimately to prosper from ownership. Desire for land, and the quest for a society minimally constrained by centralized authority, shaped much of the pattern of American settlement and, more broadly, American culture.

Framed in a less romantic way, the discovery and settlement of America unleashed one of the most potent economic forces of the post-feudal West: the idea that land might be owned and traded as readily as, say, livestock. It was a revolutionary idea that land could be a common commodity of economic exchange—that property was a source of wealth and status for the average citizen, not just for the landed gentry. A whole economy came to be based in no small measure on expectations of land's ever-increasing value, on a continent of dispersed homes on small rectilinear lots—the social and environmental consequences of which would take nearly two centuries to fully materialize. (See Figure 1.3.)

The chief polemicist for such an egalitarian distribution of land was Jefferson, part-time farmer, drafter of the Declaration of Independence, third president, and America's representative in the pantheon of Enlightenment philosophers.

1.3 By mid-twentieth century Jefferson's promise of 160-acre homesteads had become eighth-of-an-acre suburban lots.

"The small land holders are the most precious part of a state," Jefferson explained. "It is not too soon to provide by every possible means that as few as possible shall be without a little portion of land."[1] His friend and fierce rival John Adams agreed: "The only possibility then of preserving the balance of power on the side of equal liberty and public virtue is to make the acquisition of land easy to every member of society; to make a division of land into small quantities so that the multitude may be possessed of landed estates."[2] Both Jefferson and Adams did, however, hope to minimize the accumulation of wealth among a few, and neither fully anticipated the land-speculation economy that would follow.

Jefferson's gift for oratory and writer's instinct for the memorable phrase gave the Declaration of Independence the famous phrase "life, liberty, and the pursuit of happiness." Earlier drafts, much debated, contained the phrase "life, liberty, and the pursuit and acquisition of property." Variations of this early wording found their way into many of the original state constitutions, where they remain.[3] In revising the original phrase, Jefferson was hardly relinquishing a commitment to property rights. That right was not under debate. A century earlier, John Locke's *Treatises on Civil Government,* much admired by Jefferson and other founders, had established that a right to work the land was a fundamental right. Locke invoked an older authority, quoting scripture: "The heavens, even the heavens, are the Lord's; but the earth hath he given to the children of God."[4] For Jefferson, happiness would come as a consequence of owning a part of America.

The Cartesian grid was thus a crucial tool to advance an equitable subdivision of land, perhaps even to guide a fair distribution of happiness. Jefferson put it to use for a national survey, for demarking state boundaries, and for laying out towns and cities of all sizes, including the nation's capital. As we will see in Chapter 10, he insisted that Pierre L'Enfant, the capital's designer, combine the grid with the radial street pattern that L'Enfant, inspired by André Le Nôtre's Versailles, felt more appropriate for the capital of a nation on the rise.

Deploying a continental grid might assure a republic of citizen farmers. "Those who labor in the earth are the chosen people of God, if ever he had a chosen people," Jefferson famously wrote in *Notes on the State of Virginia,* his sweeping commentary on the nature, history, and potential of his native state, and by extension the country overall.[5] He imagined a citizenry cultivating its gardens (he did not distinguish between gardens and farms in quite the way we do today) on an idealized landscape set between the forces of civilization, not always benign, and the bounties of nature. Such a republic, he believed, would be spared the cyclical waves of repression, conflict, and conquest he considered common in Europe.

To understand Jefferson's ambition for his new country, the grid and the garden must be explored as metaphors—along with a third concept, that of a "middle landscape," geographically positioned between nature and civilization. Each of these was important to early American settlement, and each still influences how Americans spread across their metropolitan landscapes. The metaphors of grid, garden, and middle landscape are intertwined, but each warrants its own introduction.

The Sane and Noble Grid

A grid arises from the desire to measure and control. It is a means to divide and subdivide items on a page, over a territory, or across a continent. It establishes mankind's presence on the land. A grid creates a regular and predictable pattern, allowing the possibility of an equitable distribution of land for a republic of landholders. Ready access to land would, for Jefferson, prevent citizens from being beholden to others or oppressed by authoritarian forces. He wrote somewhat arrogantly to a French aristocrat: "I think our government will remain virtuous for many centuries as long as they are chiefly agricultural; and this will be as long as there shall be vacant lands in any parts of America. When they are piled upon one another in large cities, as in Europe, they will become corrupt as in Europe."[6] To ward off corruption and crowding, a spatial concept was needed to help allocate land to the many. Here the grid proved useful.

Jefferson helped draft an ordinance in 1784 that, modified and ratified a year later by the Continental Congress, would become the generative force in establishing the grid as a dominant presence across America's geography. Following the settlement of western land claims at the conclusion of the War of Independence, two competing interests demanded a national land policy. On one side were land companies eager to purchase and organize settlements on the frontier, the income from which would replenish the nearly empty coffers of the fledgling federal government. On the other side were the citizens wishing to acquire farm plots, whom Jefferson was determined to satisfy. The Land Ordinances of 1784 and 1875, the survey of western lands, and the Northwest Ordinance of

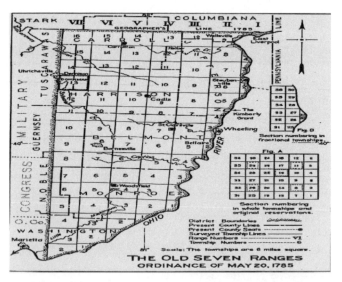

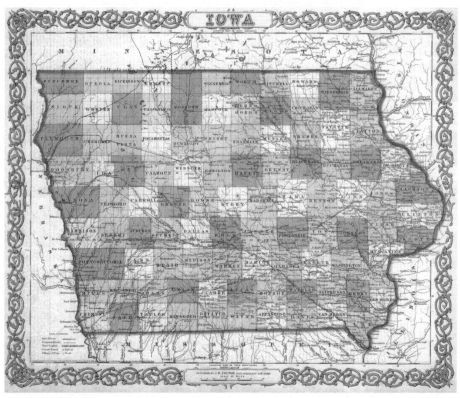

1.4a (top)   The initial survey, of what became the seven ranges of eastern Ohio: the beginning of the public land survey system from the Land Ordinance of 1785.
1.4b (bottom)   The continental grid demarking 99 geometrically ordered counties of Iowa.

1787 resolved this conflict by dividing the land into townships that could be sold whole or as individual lots.[7] (See Figures 1.4a and 1.4b.)

Instantly, the new country's need for a land policy was translated with mathematical precision into an orderly definition of a vast wilderness. Enabling that vast land resource to be dealt with as a commodity would have consequences, ultimately, which Jefferson could not have anticipated.

Gridded plans have existed throughout history, deployed by almost every civilization that has reached a certain stage of development. In agriculture-based societies, the grid has aided efficient planting, irrigation, and land reclamation, as in the cultures of Mesopotamia, the Indus Valley, Egypt, China, and pre-Columbian Peru. During periods of empire building, it has proved conducive to establishing military order and ease of colonization, as in the cultures of the Assyrians, the Greeks, the Romans, the Incas, and the Spanish-held territories of the New World. The grid's advantages are manifold: it is a simple device with which to survey, subdivide, and therefore control territory. It makes for easy record-keeping, census-taking, and taxation. It facilitates clear orientation and movement. At certain historic moments, as in America's early decades, its use and precision becomes a key to cultural identity. In *The Idea of a Town,* Joseph Rykwert postulates that "divine law" was as potent a force in the gridded layout of ancient towns as utilitarian surveying techniques. "The Roman who walked along the *cardo* knew that his walk was the axis round which the sun turned, and that if he followed the *decumanus,* he was following the sun's course." Thus, Rykwert concluded, the educated Roman had a sense of a universe and felt at home in it.[8]

In a later chapter we will encounter another such divine law, that of the Mormons, who accepted an ecclesiastic mandate to use the grid—and the fact of the continental survey—in laying out their many gridded towns throughout the west. Gradually the grid began to acquire a yet broader ideological connotation, connected with its basis in regular, equal divisions. Various American commentators, observers, politicians, and polemicists, from Jefferson on, began to associate qualities such as democracy, economy, morality, rationality, and pluralism with the grid, as they relied on it more often, and eventually more indiscriminately, in laying out towns and cities.

These new communities did not, however, become bastions of equality. As it turns out, the Cartesian grid also facilitates land speculation and expedient development. As nineteenth-century Americans began witnessing the effects, Frederick Law Olmsted, America's great park designer, came to refer to the grid as "the epitome of the evil of commercialism."[9] Today's metropolitan America, with its miles of suburbs, exurbs, and their attendant commercial and corporate sprawl, reflects a process perhaps worthier of Olmsted's disdain than Jefferson's imagination. It is a legacy of distributing land less in the cause of egalitarianism than as a commodity of economic exchange. Yet it was true in 2007, just prior to the Great Recession, that fully 69 percent of American households owned their homes, mostly on independent parcels of land. They were no longer farmers, to be sure, but it was a statistic that would make a modern-day Jeffersonian proud. Coincidently, 70 percent of American heads of households were landowners at the time of the American Revolution (although there was a significant catch: no women, Native Americans, or slaves were eligible to own a piece of America).[10]

Cultivating Gardens

Each space delineated by the grid can become a domain nurtured by a citizen or family. The grid thus enables the creation of many gardens. "I have often thought," Jefferson wrote in a letter to a friend, "that if heaven had given me choice of my position and calling it should have been on a rich spot of earth, well watered, and near a good market for the production of a garden. No occupation is so delightful to me as the culture of the earth."[11] Heaven served Jefferson well in this regard, as it has many American landowners. The word *garden* stands for far more than growing vegetables for one's kitchen.

Since Eden, we have thought of gardens as places where people and nature come together, usually under human stewardship. The garden is a place of sustenance, delight, and hard work. Each garden, whether owned by a Jeffersonian farmer or a suburban homeowner armed with a lawn mower, expresses personal or family preferences or values. American settlement has been profoundly shaped by the desire to possess a piece of land, to cultivate one's own domain, and to fulfill the promise of independence and prosperity. "A man's home is his castle" goes the common proverb, but in Jefferson's terms, a citizen's parcel of land registered his freedom and self-worth. Walt Whitman would concur. Half a century later, just prior to the establishment of the Homestead Act (described in Chapter 7), he wrote that "a man is not a whole and complete man unless he owns a house and the ground it stands on."[12]

1.5 Looking to the East Hill in Providence, Rhode Island, and its silhouette of individual, proud homes.

1.6 Thirty terraced homes, built between 1767 and 1774, their individual identity suppressed to form a Royal Crescent and define a large public space in Bath, England.

For Jefferson, a garden was the domain of the freeman, while all of America was a continental garden there to be cultivated. Together, then, grid and garden—the collective web and the individual's domain—created a network over the land, connecting people and separating them, establishing a balance between society's constraints and the individual's purpose and expression. As people cultivated their individual gardens, they collectively cultivated a nation of free, self-sustaining citizens.

A new form of city would thus evolve. The overall shape of the city traditionally evolved out of some collective priorities, often walled off from the countryside for safety and defense, or ordered around formal geometries expressive of

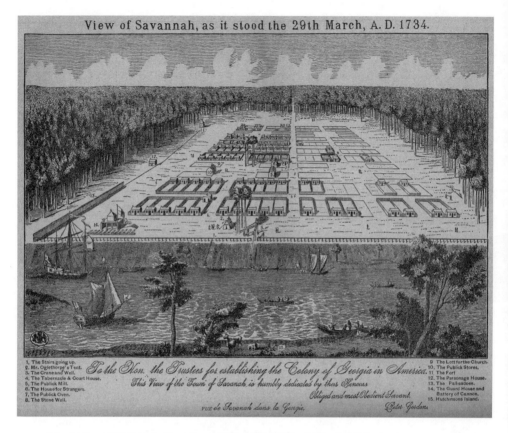

View of Savannah, as it stood the 29th March, A. D. 1734.

1, The Stairs going up.
2, Mr. Ogiethorpe's Tent.
3, The Crane and Well.
4, The Tabernacle & Court House.
5, The Publick Mill.
6, The House for Strangers.
7, The Publick Oven.
8, The Stone Well.

9 The Lott for the Church.
10, The Publick Stores.
11 The Fort
12, The Parsonage House.
13, The Palisadoes.
14, The Guard House and
Battery of Cannon.
15, Hutchinsons Island.

To the Hon. the Trustees for establishing the Colony of Georgia in America.
This View of the Town of Savanah, is humbly dedicated by their Honours
Obliged and most Obedient Servant,
Peter Gordon.

VUE de Savanah dans la Georgie.

1.7 A view of Savannah, Georgia, as it stood the 29th of March, 1734.
The canonical view of the plan of Savannah at its founding.

authority. In America, settlements emerged more often on a foundation of individual lots and structures. Compare two late eighteenth-century urban environments: a street in Providence, Rhode Island, and the Royal Crescent in Bath, England. (See Figures 1.5 and 1.6.)

In Providence, the silhouette dominates: each house stands separately, rising freely from its own garden. The grid of streets then serves as a sort of collective umbilical cord to join those proud, individual houses. In Bath, the Royal Crescent is also made up of homes, but it is the overall facade defining a public space that is clearly of first importance, not the thirty individual houses of which the crescent is composed.

Or examine a canonical image of early city-making on American soil, the 1734 plan of Savannah, Georgia, which preceded and inspired Jefferson. (See Figure 1.7.) It shows a clearing in the forest and a collection of houses with fenced gardens. Savannah's founder, James Oglethorpe, sought to create a town for the "worthy poor," while helping to secure the British colonies against northward encroachment by the Spanish from Florida. His plan—a grid organizing groups of forty houses and their gardens into wards around a common—made for an endlessly reproducible system and proved the powers of grid and garden operating in combination. In 1850, a visiting Swedish novelist, Frederika Bremer, described its success: "Savannah is the most charming of cities. . . . It is an assemblage of villas which have come together for company."[13] A few years later, another visitor wrote: "If four-and-twenty villages had resolved to hold a meeting and had assembled at this place. . . . The result would have been a facsimile of Savannah."[14] Two more poetic descriptions of an American town would be hard to come by. In Savannah, the repetition of wards containing identical formations of independent houses, private gardens, and common spaces showed Jefferson how the grid could balance individual aspirations with a larger communal order, all with the cultivation of nature at its heart.

Dwelling in a Middle State

American intellectuals, and city builders for that matter, have often mused about the benefits of living in a setting between nature and civilization. The roots of such an attractive balance date back to the discovery of America, as Europeans became intrigued by the prospect of a New World apparently untouched by civilization. The Enlightenment and the Romantic movements put their own inflection on this idea of a middle state. In the eighteenth century, Jean-Jacques Rousseau began to argue that the very processes of civilization bred artificialities and social imbalances, stresses that periodically had to be overcome. Might there be a state of innocence against which to gauge the process of European civilization and especially its faults?[15] Ideas about the need to balance instinct and intellect flourished. Many thinkers argued that primitivism (or innocence), as exemplified by the cult of the noble savage identified as the American Indian, might somehow combine with Enlightenment rationality to produce the best human condition.

As such ideas spread, the New World was seen as a setting for the pursuit of such balance. Thus, the British moral philosopher Richard Price wrote in the mid-eighteenth century that "the happiest state of man is in the middle state between the savage and the refined." He could cite the evidence: "Such is the state of Society in Connecticut, and some other of the American provinces." A statement in the 1797 edition of the esteemed *Encyclopedia Britannica* seemed to concur: "It may in truth be said, that in no part of the world are the people happier . . . or more independent than the farmers of New England."[16] Reading such would have given Jefferson much satisfaction. Certainly, it underscores the Enlightenment lineage of much of Jefferson's thinking about the proper basis for a modern nation.

Were Americans as blessed as the *Encyclopedia Britannica* claimed? What about the hardships of eking out an existence amidst the harsh New England wilderness and its equally harsh climate? And what about the deprivations caused by isolation from the old world? The paradoxical answer was that, in taming the wilderness, the American farmer was cultivating a garden. In discarding colonialism he was freeing himself from the wretchedness and corruption of European urban society. A new state was being realized on a landscape occupying this middle position between innocent primitivism and the achievement of civilization. The ideal of a middle state could now be extracted from the realms of literature and philosophy and given a physical and social reality, manifested by independent citizens as they plowed their gardens.

Agrarianism, a philosophy proclaiming the superiority of rural life, had been part of the cultural tradition since before the age of Jefferson, especially in England. Interest in antiquity during the Renaissance revived the praise of husbandry found in the works of Virgil, Hesiod, Cicero, Horace, and their imitators. Contrasting the innocence of bucolic existence and the moral decay of city life was commonplace in Elizabethan literature. By the middle of the eighteenth century, Samuel Johnson could make this observation: "There is indeed scarce any writer who has not celebrated the happiness of rural privacy."[17] An idealized, if naive, image of the farmer emerged: he was someone content with his simple life, without envy of wealth, possessing high morals by virtue of his toil on the land. To this, however, the agrarian and economic reformers of the eighteenth century (Adam Smith and the French Physiocrats prominent among them) added the radical idea that agricultural yield, the productive use of land, was a primary source of a nation's wealth.[18] Husbandry attained a new status.

The yeoman, no longer just a peasant content with his lot, emerged as symbol of the freeman.

Back in the colonies, the urbane Benjamin Franklin, a prolific agrarian pamphleteer, declared that the "great business of the Continent is agriculture" carried out by "the industrious frugal farmer." Historian Henry Nash Smith summarizes the philosophy of many of the founders: "Agriculture is the only source of real wealth . . . every man has a natural right to land; labor expended in cultivating the earth confers a valid title to it . . . the ownership of land, by making the farmer independent, gives him social status and dignity, while constant contact with nature in the course of his labors makes him virtuous and happy."[19]

Could it be possible, intellectuals asked, to settle an unspoiled new world in a way that would minimize the extremes—the loneliness and fear of the wilderness and the corruptions of the city? Could a domain be established where only the best attributes of both nature and civilization could be permanently enjoyed?

Over time, as settlement proceeded, the contrast was less between untamed wilderness and the city than between "the country" and the city, with a vague pastoral condition identified as the desired middle ground. Ralph Waldo Emerson expressed this as a profound lament: "I wish to have rural strength and religion for my children and I wish city facility and polish. I find with chagrin that I cannot have both."[20] Such chagrin merely intensified the search for a life with access to both city enterprises and the splendors of nature.

In Jefferson's day, the French-American farmer and writer J. Hector St. John de Crevecoeur wrote about where Americans should look to achieve this balance. In 1785, coincidently the same year as the Continental Survey, he published *Letters of an American Farmer*, which was much-read on both sides of the ocean. Crevecoeur described an America evolving into three realms: a string of pioneering outposts pushing westward across the continent; a realm consisting of an expanding region of prosperous farms; and a developing region of coastal cities patterned after European society. He wrote that the latter produced undesirable social conditions, while the pioneering outposts were harsh and uncivilized; the middle realm, therefore, provided the best setting for virtue and happiness. "What should we American farmers be without the distinct possession of that soil," he wrote. "It feeds, it clothes, us: from it we draw even a great exuberancy."[21] A century later, Frederick Jackson Turner cemented his reputation as a historian by postulated a virtually identical theory, concluding that it was in the settlements near the frontier, rather than at the frontier itself or in the established cities back east, that a truly distinctive America would evolve.[22]

Jefferson referred to himself as "a savage from the wilderness of Virginia."[23] He fought arduously for the interests of the freehold farmer and pushed for cultivated landscapes to form the social and economic basis of the young republic. But neither his vision nor his life was consistent on these matters. The realist in him understood that the concept of a permanent rural society was merely a "theory," and one that "the servants of America are not at liberty to follow."[24] The simplistic vision of Crevecoeur, after all, implied a static, unchanging society. Experiencing the transition of the eighteenth century into the nineteenth, Jefferson anticipated (with some reluctance no doubt) the fundamental changes that industrialization would inevitably bring. His hope, as Annette Gordon-Reed and Peter Onuf explain in a recent biography, was that the shift from self-sufficiency on homesteads to "having to rely on wages provided by others" would evolve slowly.[25] Nonetheless, Jefferson wished to demonstrate a desired state of being. This would require that his artistic sensibilities combine with his intellect to create two idealized environments.

Architecture Is My Delight

"Architecture is my delight," Jefferson told a visitor, "and putting up and pulling down one of my favorite amusements."[26] For him, great architecture was itself a civilizing force. An enlightened society, he argued, required a population educated not only in the realm of ideas, but just as importantly in the arts—including architecture.[27] Were Jefferson's contribution to American culture merely that of an architect, and not also as drafter of the Declaration of Independence, president, and force behind the continental survey, he would still be a major historical figure. He was an architectural connoisseur and innovator. Inspired in his own efforts by the artists of the Italian Renaissance, he also championed and learned from the first generation of American architects, such as Benjamin Latrobe and Charles Bulfinch, architects of successive phases of the US Capitol Building. His own design for the Virginia State Capitol was among the very first to incorporate the form of a classic temple as the front of a government building, something that became virtually synonymous with all manner of public buildings—state capitols, courthouses, post offices, and financial institutions—well into the twentieth century.

1.8   Jefferson's homestead, Monticello, with the Mullbery Row gardens at right, managed by scores of slaves.

With two remarkable designs he moved beyond architectural ingenuity to produce archetypes for the kind of environments that represented his ideal of America. On one gentle hilltop of his beloved Virginia he located his home and farm, Monticello, and on another he placed what he called an "academical village," establishing the University of Virginia.

Inspired by Renaissance country villas designed and championed by Andrea Palladio, Monticello seems to at once command and cradle its hilltop. (See Figure 1.8.) Considerable topographical manipulation was required, yet it appears as if the situation was always so. It enabled the service wings of what was, after all, a farmstead to be at a level below the formal residence, conveniently accessible to the vegetable gardens. The roofs of these service wings form a grand, two-sided veranda, inwardly defining a calm, private lawn to which the rear of the home opens up, while enabling views over the gardens to the broader Vir-

1.9 Engraving of the "academical village" at the University of Virginia, with Monticello depicted in the background at the very top of the hill.

ginia landscape. Pavilions anchor the ends of these two verandas, as if they were miniatures of the main house, framing an axis from home to nature. Palladio would have applauded, admiring both the elaboration upon his own villa compositions and Jefferson's temerity in placing his villa on the very top of a hill— something attempted only rarely by Palladio.

Jefferson fussed with his Monticello for forty years, tearing parts down and rebuilding to perfect the place for his own use, and to serve as a model of what an independent homestead—his idea of a building block of the nation—should be.

Not without irony, however, this iconic American homestead was managed by scores of slaves. In an early draft of the Declaration of Independence, Jefferson called slavery "a crewel war against nature itself," and variously referred to slavery as "moral depravity," and a "hideous blot" on a nation created in support of human liberty. Yet, to his everlasting dishonor, he could not dispense with the usefulness of that "hideous" institution, any more than could the other owners of plantations or more humble farms.[28] He has often been called the most enigmatic of the founders, and this is one reason. As one of his many biographers puts it, only "a disconcerting form of psychological

1.10   Detail of the colonnade that defines the great lawn at the University of Virginia.
Five pavilions sit to either side of the lawn, each a classroom dedicated to a subject to be
studied, the professors' residence above. Connecting these houses of knowledge are
rows of student rooms, still among the most desirable accommodations on campus,
reserved for honors students, despite their sparseness.

agility . . . would make it possible for Jefferson to walk past the slave quarters
on Mulberry Row at Monticello thinking about mankind's brilliant prospects
without any sense of contradiction."[29] The complex relationship between Jefferson and his slaves has gradually been shared with visitors to Monticello,
culminating in the summer of 2018: a modest exhibit was dedicated to Sally
Hemings, a slave with whom Jefferson fathered six children, four of whom
survived into adulthood, became free, and produced many descendants with
DNA linked directly to him.

A home and farm, Monticello was an individual's contribution to society.
What about a representation of community? This, Jefferson achieved at the University of Virginia. (See Figures 1.9 and 1.10.) An axis is even more powerfully felt
here, anchored at one end by the great edifice of the campus library, both symbol
and storehouse of human knowledge, stretching in the other direction to the free

and verdant hills of Virginia, to the endless bounty and promise of the continental garden. Student and faculty residences and classrooms are located to either side of this axis, midway between the library—civilization's repository—and the open vista to the west, organized in a grid fronting a common lawn with gardens behind. That open vista was unceremoniously closed off by a later campus building.

Much has been written about Jefferson's inspiration for the layout of his academical village. Some see aspects of Roman Fora, others are reminded of certain medieval monastic compounds or more "modern" eighteenth-century institutions, such as the Royal Naval Hospital near Plymouth, England, or the plan to expand Union College, designed just a few years earlier. There is a strong resemblance in layout (paradoxical in light of Jefferson's republican commitment) to the Chateau at Marly—built by Louis XIV, the Sun King, and visited by Jefferson during his years as ambassador to France. All of these and others may well have served as artistic inspiration. Jefferson also sought advice from two architects he admired, William Thornton and Benjamin Latrobe. But the academical village was ultimately an expression of his own intellectual and artistic powers, remarkably produced during the last decade of his long life. It was further demonstration of how Americans might organize themselves in communities, perpetually residing between the realms of the intellect and that of nature. It is also an exquisitely beautiful place. (See Figure 1.10.)

Aspirations and Consequences

The Jeffersonian blueprint of grid, garden, and pastoral (middle) landscape is felt physically and metaphorically at both Monticello and the University of Virginia. Nature and humanity encounter each other in both places, as they must. Jefferson's intent was to create a mediated encounter, not a confrontation—an orchestrated embrace of one realm by the other. For Jefferson, this embrace was one of humankind's noblest achievements, signifying a new society being formed at a point of conversion from wilderness into garden, using the wise tools of the intellect. The ongoing reenactment of this conversion by the efforts of each citizen would represent the particular promise of American civilization. This was but one of his soaring aspirations for the nation he helped shape, the product of an intellect able to reconcile complexity and naivete.

A less favorable assessment of the Jeffersonian blueprint might peg Jefferson as the inadvertent founding father of privatization and metropolitan sprawl, creator of a land speculator's paradise and the inspiration for an endless array of "poor man's Monticellos" (fortunately, without slaves). Such a critique is not so easy to dismiss, since, as later chapters will show, the earliest suburban experiments were just as motivated as were Jefferson's aspirations by dreams of incorporating nature into the creation of a new form of settlement.

Anne Mackin, in *Americans and Their Land,* offers a yet harsher criticism of the Jeffersonian insistence on land ownership as social equalizer. The idea that citizens must continue migrating to more abundant and fruitful lands at the periphery of existing communities, she argues, encourages escape rather than solutions to the problems of society.[30] The ease of spreading outward, which to Jefferson and the subsequent adherents of Manifest Destiny symbolized egalitarianism and liberty, may have led instead to a diminishment of civic responsibility and a reduced interest in the common purposes of community. Escaping to make a new and better place might have absolved citizens of concern about, and responsibility for, the places left behind.

2.1a (left)   Kindred Spirits, Asher B. Durand, 1848. Depicts the painter Thomas Cole and journalist/poet William Cullen Bryant (of "Go West" fame) enjoying a Catskills scene.

2.1b (right)   Places of awe remain: A family enjoying a Grand Canyon overlook.

2

A NATURE'S NATION IN THE GARDEN OF THE WORLD

> We are still in Eden.
>
> THOMAS COLE, 1836
>
> It's mostly us now.
>
> BILL McKIBBEN, 2005

JOHN LOCKE'S FAMOUS DECLARATION that "in the beginning all the World was America" was written with regard to property rights. Locke was asserting that humanity had begun in a world not yet owned, with property therefore being a natural right, not a concept requiring government authority. He also saw property facilitating the products of human labor; it was a key concept to the capitalism of Adam Smith, to Jefferson's agrarian republic, and to the socialism of Karl Marx.[1] But Locke's phrase also invoked the image of a pristine New World, innocent and untouched by civilization. To be sure, this ignored the civilizations that Native Americans had been building for thousands of years, and the harshness of the wilderness that confronted the colonists. Nevertheless, the desire of settlers and later immigrants to experience the majestic scale of the continent and to cultivate its abundant resources has been a driving force in American history. A Jeffersonian sensibility might express it strategically: by embracing and adapting nature into a continental garden, using the tools of an enlightened civilization, a nature's nation would flourish.

Ideas, reveries, and mythologies about nature have been ongoing across American intellectual and popular history. Today, however, few would embrace the idea of a nature's nation. Misgivings about the consumption and plundering of the environment to the point of altering the climate render the notion naive. The idea of an unchanging, permanent nature against which the temporal activities of humanity are measured seems quaint, a concept of a more innocent age. We are more likely to worry that there is no longer a natural state left anywhere on the planet. It has been three decades since Bill McKibben wrote *The End of Nature;* four since Ernest Callenbach's novel *Ecotopia,* in which a revolt against "bad air, chemicalized food, and lunatic advertising" leads a group of Americans to secede from the country and establish an ecological utopia; and more than half a century since Rachel Carson's *Silent Spring* brought home how human activities were damaging life on land and in the oceans. Carson did not mince words: "How could intelligent beings seek to control a few unwanted species by a method that contaminated the entire environment and brought the threat of disease and death even to their own kind."[2] *Silent Spring* caused a turning point in awareness, because Carson made it clear that we were poisoning ourselves.

It is instructive, then, to return to the Romantics of the first half of the nineteenth century. Still living with the idea that America could be Eden, their concern was not the depletion of resources but the sense of losing touch with the redeeming aura of nature. Perry Miller, who has done much to chronicle the role of nature in American intellectual history, puts it this way: "The more rapidly, the more voraciously, the primordial forest was felled, the more desperately poets and painters—and also preachers—strove to identify the unique personality of this republic with the virtues of pristine and untarnished, of 'romantic,' Nature."[3]

This differed from Jefferson's association of virtue with cultivation of the land. It was more about the ennobling effects that come with the appreciation of nature. The references to "preachers" and "romantic" nature are both significant. Liberalization from strict religious doctrine was in the air. "To be enlightened," the historian Carl Becker writes of this period, addressing one of the precepts of the European Enlightenment, "was to understand . . . that it was not in Holy Writ, but in the great book of nature, open for all mankind to read, that the laws of God had been recorded."[4] How best, then, to interpret and live by this book in light of the approaching forces of industrialization, which seemed determined to consume nature?

The Romantics sought an antidote to this materialism and utilitarianism in the form of direct contact with nature. Holding fast to nature was essential to guard against the "artificialities" produced by modernization. Nature, not the mechanizing world, had to remain the source of wisdom, spiritual insight, and moral virtue, and only it could light the path to beauty. Unlike old Europe, where romanticizing nature could at best provide some intellectual respite from an already "corrupted" civilization, America could offer continuous contact with uncorrupted nature and keep the forces of artificiality in check. Nature's proximity might even enable reconciliation between those anxious about civilization's progress and the agents of modernization. The Romantics sought, again in Miller's words, a world "between forest and town, spontaneity and calculation, heart and head, the unconscious and the self-conscious, the innocent and the debauched.[5] This was another evocation of the middle landscape ideal introduced in Chapter 1.

To achieve this reconciliation required that the whistle of the locomotive join, but not displace, the beloved sounds of Henry David Thoreau's forest. In a melancholy chapter called "Sounds" in *Walden; or, Life in the Woods*, Thoreau seems to accept the inevitability of the railway's arrival, and even its importance to society, yet he nonetheless objects: "I will not have my eyes put out and my ears spoiled by its smoke and steam and hissing."[6] Once that piercing whistle abates, the sweeter sounds return: "At evening, the distant lowing of some cow in the horizon beyond the woods sounded sweet and melodious." If only the train's purposes were noble. "If the cloud that hangs over the engine were the perspiration of heroic deeds," Thoreau muses, "or as beneficent as that which floats over the farmer's fields, then the elements and Nature herself would cheerfully accompany men on their errands and be their escort."[7]

The painter George Inness sought to find the resemblance that Thoreau could not. In *The Lackawanna Valley*, which portrays a locomotive and nascent industry in a verdant valley, the puffy "clouds" rising above the engine and from unseen machines behind the railway roundhouse and church steeple could suggest heroic deeds. (The painting, not coincidentally, was commissioned by the president of the Delaware, Lackawanna, and Western Railroad.) But the felled forest in the foreground, though it might have been for a hay field, would for Thoreau be an ominous sign. (See Figure 2.2.)

Whether as pessimistic as Thoreau or as hopeful as Inness, the Romantics considered it vital to achieve a harmony between nature and the advance of civilization. The term *Transcendentalism*—applied to Thoreau and other New

2.2   George Inness, *The Lackawanna Valley*, 1855.

England Romantics—captures something of the utopian and spiritual dimension of this quest. The preceding Enlightenment, the Age of Reason, had been associated with a different search—the confident project of explaining the world rationally—and had advanced both the promise and excesses of the Industrial Revolution. Like their European counterparts, American Romantics reacted to these excesses by stressing the nonmaterial. They believed emotion should not be held subservient to reason. They yearned for the unattainable to counter the certainties of science. Henry James characterized the Romantic quest as the search for "the things that can reach us only through the beautiful circuit and subterfuge of our thought and our desire."[8] Later, e. e. cummings would make his own argument for emotion in verse:

> While you and I have lips and voices which
> are for kissing and to sing with
> who cares if some oneeyed son of a bitch
> invents an instrument to measure Spring with?[9]

As long as nature—beautiful, mysterious, spirit-enlightening, and reassuring—remained near, the quest seemed possible. But what if civilization and industry advanced too far? The anxiety troubled many intellectuals and artists, not least the great painter of the American landscape Thomas Cole.

"We are still in Eden," Cole wrote in 1836, extending the claim of the first settlers to the New World. "The wall that shuts us out of the garden is our own ignorance and folly."[10] To expose the dire consequences of this folly, Cole painted *The Course of Empire,* a set of five massive allegorical canvases. Half a century later, when the American course of empire was much further along than Cole would have wished, an event in Chicago provided a physical analog for his allegory.

In 1893, a trolley ride away from the engineering marvels of Chicago's commercial Loop, featuring the world's first skyscrapers, there appeared what the leading architecture critic of the day described as "the most integral, the most extensive, the most illusive piece of scenic architecture that has ever been seen."[11] The World's Columbian Exposition, with the resplendent classicist plumage of the *Cour d'Honneur*—its grand arrival court—captivated a nation.[12] The influence of the Chicago World's Fair on American urbanism and cultural aspirations has been substantial, and it warrants reappearance in several chapters. Focusing on the phrase "the most illusive piece of scenic architecture," I will in this chapter interpret the fair as Cole, Thoreau, Emerson, or Hawthorne might have had they still been on the scene in 1893. For the Romantic-minded, Cole's epic paintings and the course of the epic fair would have seemed startlingly similar.

The first canvas in Cole's *Course of Empire* was *The Savage State.* It shows both nature and humanity in a raw, primordial condition. Here, the wilderness remains the realm of disorder—of the heathen without human cultivation, of humankind battling nature for survival. The mood is ominous and inhospitable. (See Figure 2.3.)

The site selected for the World's Fair was also inhospitable, if less dramatically so. It was a foreboding expanse of low sand dunes, swampy swales, and stunted vegetation. One of the prominent New York architects invited to participate in the design of the fair called the area a "near desert waste." (See Figure 2.4.) Frederick Law Olmsted, whose task it would be to transform it into a park after the fair, acquiesced to the site selection under some pressure. "If a search had been made for the least park-like ground within miles of the city," he grumbled, "nothing better meeting the requirement could have been found."[13]

2.3   Thomas Cole, *The Course of Empire: The Savage State*, 1836.

2.4   Area along Lake Michigan selected as the site for the Chicago World's Fair, c. 1890.

2.5   Thomas Cole, *The Course of Empire: The Arcadian or Pastoral State*, 1836.

Cole's second canvas, *The Arcadian or Pastoral State*, shows the wilderness transformed into a cultivated landscape. This was the condition that so inspired the Romantics: a Virgilian society ideally situated between the extremes of wilderness and civilization, living in obvious and potentially perpetual harmony with nature.[14] (See Figure 2.5.)

The fairgrounds had not existed in a prior pastoral state; the site was available only due to inaction on the part of city officials. Twenty years earlier, Olmsted had prepared a design for a park there, as part of a network of open space and parkways for the south side of Chicago, but his design had never been implemented. (See Figure 2.6.)

The third of Cole's canvases is *The Consummation of Empire*. In its landscape, simplicity and innocence have given way to luxury and architectural magnificence. Nature, so prominently symbolized by a jutting cliff in the first two canvases, is now barely visible. The peaks of humanity tower over those of nature. While the landscape has clearly been despoiled, the scene is sensual and

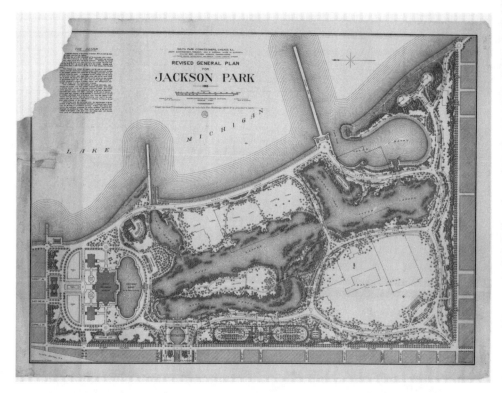

2.6   Revised General Plan for Jackson Park, Olmsted & Vaux. Initially conceptualized
in 1869 as part of a broader park plan for the Southern part of Chicago, the plan was
realized following the closing of the World's Fair. The thin red lines indicate where
the fair buildings were located. The Fine Arts pavilion at left was the only Fair
building that survived, rebuilt in real granite, and remains today as the Museum of
Science and Industry.

enticing, temporarily blinding the viewer to the consequences of a hedonistic
and arrogant civilization. (See Figure 2.7.)

Now consider the Columbian Exposition at its peak. A visitor's initial view
of the *cour d'honneur* must too have been breathtaking and enticing. Cole surely
would have recognized the symptoms. Upon one's arrival, a view of Lake Michigan, the fair's equivalent of the jutting cliff, was itself obscured by a giant peri-
style. The fairgoers, mainly rural citizens of the Midwest, many of whom had
never visited a large city, were simply unprepared for the sight. "Sell the cook
stove if necessary and come. You must see this fair," Hamlin Garland, a writer
known for his stories of Midwest farmers, wrote to his parents in Dakota. But

2.7 Thomas Cole, *The Course of Empire: The Consummation of Empire*, 1836.

2.8 View of the Grand Basin, the most ceremonial and spectacular area of the Chicago World's Fair, 1893.

2.9   Thomas Cole, *The Course of Empire: Destruction*, 1836.

2.10   View of the Chicago World's Fair grounds following its destruction, 1894: "The Republic" statue still in place, visible at left.

2.11   Thomas Cole, *The Course of Empire: Desolation*, 1836.

"the feast was too rich, too highly-spiced for their simple tastes" the son later admitted. "Take me home," his mother had begged on the third day of her visit, "I can't stand more of it."[15] Even Henry Adams, less prone to hyperbole than many contemporaries, reacted strongly: "The first astonishment became greater every day," he recalled in his autobiography. Attending the Exposition, one "seemed to have leaped directly from Corinth and Syracuse and Venice, over the heads of London and New York." It represented a startling break with the past: "Here was a breach of continuity—a rupture in historical sequence!"[16]

Another visitor was equally awed: "What a terrible, annihilating sense of insignificance overwhelms one at the realization of this endless procession of races which have preceded us and shall succeed us! What an imperial destiny it promised to mankind." [17] A still relatively young nation was surely exposing its own imperial ambitions. (See Figure 2.8.)

The fourth step in Cole's tracing of the course of empire is, not surprisingly, *Destruction*. This canvas shows civilization engulfed in a cataclysm of flame and smoke. A headless warrior holds up a now broken shield against the encroaching darkness. Only the jutting cliff is still bathed in light, the one landmark likely to survive the destruction. (See Figure 2.9.)

2.12   A one-third sized replica of the "The Republic," which overlooked the Grand
Basin (Figure 2.8). It currently graces an intersection near the old fairgrounds.
Daniel Chester French, the sculptor of the magnificent 65-foot-high gilded original,
also sculpted Abraham Lincoln for the Lincoln Memorial.

At the end of the fair, it was the World's Columbian Exposition Salvage Company and not mythical barbarians who sacked the fair—in an effort that itself required two and a half years, and the dispersal of many fragments to various parts of the world. But the process of destruction was initiated neither by the salvage company nor by nature's elements—which, given the chance, would have expeditiously reduced the facades made of "staff" (an ingenious mixture of plaster bonded with shredded hemp) to dust. Within months of the fair's closing, a series of fires consumed many of the buildings surrounding the *cour d'honneur*. These were blamed on labor protests which had erupted as a post-fair economic recession momentarily dimmed Chicagoans' enthusiasm about the future. Interestingly, Daniel Burnham, the planning mastermind of the fair, had actually proposed that the exposition be set on fire after its conclusion. Cole's canvases were far from his mind; he imagined a carefully controlled incineration. When, instead, the unplanned conflagrations blazed—and a monument to the triumph of civilization over nature burned to the ground—the symbolism was profound. (See Figure 2.10.)

The final canvas Cole simply titled *Desolation*. The remnants of the once mighty empire are disappearing, evidence of its greatness being overtaken by creeping vegetation. The jutting cliff once again presides over the scene, unperturbed by the passing of civilization. Once more, the mood is tranquil. (See Figure 2.11.)

In Chicago, vegetation of a less primordial sort soon covered the fairgrounds. Shortly after the fair closed, Olmsted was asked to implement his twenty-year-old plan for Jackson Park. His picturesque naturalistic landscape, restricted to a small area during the reign of the *cour d'honneur,* now blossomed. Having never fully accepted the formality of that grand court, Olmsted proceeded to eliminate most traces of it. Where the great axial basin once lay, a continuation of the sylvan lagoon flourished. His only concession to the site's immediate past ("for the sake of architectural harmony") was a geometric lagoon and perimeter drive for the Art Building. The one building to survive, it was rebuilt with durable material to become the current Museum of Science and Natural History. Thus, the Arcadian state bypassed earlier now triumphed, with its own remnants of a bygone civilization. (See Figure 2.12.)

Minimal evidence of the fairgrounds has remained, roughly in this state, for decades, as Jackson Park itself lacks sufficient maintenance and care. With the construction of Barack Obama's presidential library, soon to begin at the edge of Jackson Park, better care will surely come to this historically significant land-scape.

Cole's haunting *Course of Empire* cycle, admired wherever it was exhibited in the nineteenth century, was a painterly argument for life in the Arcadian state, but offered little hope for an American nation steadfastly marching toward the consummation of empire. With the material attractions of empire building so seductive, how were the fourth and fifth states—the fate of Rome—to be avoided? The transformations that the aging Olmsted wrought on the fairgrounds presented one possibility. As we will see in Chapter 8, reformers such as Olmsted were determined in the second half of the nineteenth century to return nature to the heart of the city, as a way of improving or restoring its capacity to host human life.

The purpose of the Columbian Exposition was not, of course, to reenact in three dimensions Cole's moralizing paintings. On the contrary, the fair's primary impact was to herald the arrival of what came to be called the City Beautiful era, dedicated to introducing classic beauty and monumentality to the city. It was a moment of optimism about the future, heralding civic splendor, not airing concerns or literary musings about the assault of industrialization. Untroubled by Cole's worries, the advocates for a City Beautiful believed it was time to display the promise of an emergent American empire, to proudly feature her entrepreneurial and technological prowess, properly adorned with time-honored artistic sensibility. In the words of one prominent American architect, Ralph Adams Cram, it was a time to produce places that were "beautiful in the sense in which things have always been beautiful in periods of high culture."[18]

The Romantics, largely gone by this time, might not have been so convinced. For all their philosophical differences, Emerson and Thoreau, Margaret Fuller and Bronson Alcott, Hawthorne and Melville, and Walt Whitman and Emily Dickinson all believed that intrinsic beauty was to be found more readily in nature than in constructed artifacts. Beauty was "the garment of virtue" for Thoreau. "It is monstrous," he wrote, "when one cares but little about trees but much about Corinthian columns."[19] Emerson believed that the "uncorrupted behavior which we admire in animals and in young children belongs to him, to the hunter, the sailor—the man who lives in the presence of Nature. Cities force growth and make men talkative and entertaining, but they make them artificial."[20] He reinforced Thoreau's point: "Nature paints the best part of the picture; carves the best part of the statue; builds the best part of the house."[21] Cole agreed, as a passage in his "Essay on American Scenery" makes clear:

> There is in the human mind an almost inseparable connection between the beautiful and the good, so that if we contemplate the one the other seems present. . . . He who looks on nature with a "loving eye . . . in gazing on the pure creations of the Almighty, he feels a calm religious tone steal through his mind, and when he has turned to mingle with his fellow men, the chords which have been struck in that sweet communion cease not to vibrate."[22]

A Romantic would have argued that the builders of the fair, and the builders of Chicago and New York, were getting things backward on their march to the future. Human activity is temporal and should be measured against the immortality of nature—not the other way around. A virtuous nation must be positioned amid nature and respect its laws, not seek progress at nature's expense. Consider the image of a fledgling town's main street, an iconic symbol of settlement westward. (See Figure 2.13.) The exaggerated storefronts, the Romantic would argue, attempt to substantiate and aggrandize the presence of civilization, but in truth those storefronts, along with other signs of human presence, are fragile. The monument as in Cole's paintings is the mountainside, certain to endure beyond the imposition of false fronts, a constant amidst vicissitudes of human interventions on the land.

At the turn of the twentieth century such Romantic views held less sway. The nation was hurtling forward into a marvelous future of machines and motion, invention and production, upward mobility and wealth-building. Americans could exploit nature's bounty without concern for its limits. The mountain was there to enjoy, yes, and even to consume, for there were surely other mountains nearby. And regarding Chicago, whatever the fair's lessons, the city was well on its way to becoming Nature's Metropolis, as the historian William Cronon named it.[23] Like a Hydra, like an octopus, it reached out for the vast natural resources of a huge region. Then, having processed these, it exported them back as machinery and fuel (as we will see in Chapter 12) to propel America's journey to the future.

Thus, the nineteenth century featured two distinct sensibilities in the cultivation of the continental garden. There were those seeking spiritual awakening via

2.13   Abandoned buildings along the main street of Eureka, Colorado, a ghost gold mining town, c. 1940.

the veneration of nature, sensing, if yet only subconsciously, that there were limits to nature's bounty. And there were those attracted by millions of acres of fertile lands, eager to make the continent the "breadbasket" and tool provider for the modern world. So embedded was the idea of the continent as a bountiful garden that, well into the twentieth century, one effect of every social or economic crisis was to reenergize a back-to-the-land movement, as if nature could provide the security that society could not. That few city dwellers ever actually returned to the rigors of farming was immaterial. Raised amid the economic and cultural opportunities of city life, Americans nonetheless looked to rural America or the country town for roots and assurances of stability.

The search for nature's laws and wisdom, not merely its accruable resources, took on various guises during the late nineteenth century, with its champions being, at different times, park builders, social reformers, conservationists, decentralists, regionalists, and early ecologists. It resurfaced periodically during the twentieth century—which in its second half more and more resembled

Cole's *Consummation of Empire*—led by environmentalists, who had begun to doubt the immortality of nature. Those post-Romantic champions of nature were not all the intellectual descendants of Cole or Thoreau, but they were similarly determined to mitigate the destructive potential of empire building.

Olmsted, his sons, and their dedicated followers had been at work for decades providing a semblance of nature for city dwellers in the forms of parks and parkway systems. J. Sterling Morton, a Nebraska Territory pioneer committed to farming and forestry management, conceived of a day dedicated to tree planting. On the first Arbor Day, held April 10, 1872, an estimated one million trees were added to the landscape. An annual tree-planting holiday led by public school programs then gained national observance during the 1880s. John Muir, whose activism helped preserve Yosemite Valley and Sequoia National Park and who is often referred to as the "father of the National Parks," initiated the Sierra Club in 1892, and remained its tireless president for two full decades. He helped persuade President Teddy Roosevelt to designate Yosemite as a national park in 1903, and fought for the National Park Service that was finally established in 1916. Appalled by "sardined humanity," the forester and planner Benton MacKaye advocated for large-scale land conservation to protect wilderness areas against encroaching urbanization. Like Muir, he hoped to establish a national ethic for conservation; he was among the founders of the Wilderness Society in 1935 and instrumental in the creation of the Appalachian Trail. MaKaye's decentralist perspective was, in turn, carried forth by a new kind of regional planner during the 1920s, and especially during the decade of the Great Depression.[24]

Robert Park, Ernest Burgess, and their colleagues at the University of Chicago began to study the "nature" of cities. Fascinated by the emerging scientific study of plant and animal ecologies, they drew analogies with societies to found the new field of human ecology. Another founder of the Wilderness Society was Aldo Leopold, who argued for an environmental ethic in terms similar to Muir's and MacKaye's in his *Sand County Almanac*: "There is as yet no ethic dealing with man's relation to land and to the animals and plants which grow upon it. Land, like Odysseus's slave girls, is still property. The land-relation is still strictly economic, entailing privileges but not obligations."[25] Perhaps he thought of Henry George, whose late-nineteenth-century writings from a political economist's perspective had advanced the principle that land and any profit from it should be a public resource, not a means of private speculation.[26]

Supreme Court Justice William O. Douglas's brilliant dissenting opinion in a 1969 case brought by Sierra Club, which had hoped to block construction of a ski resort on land surrounded by Sequoia National Park, argued that a voice was needed to speak for nature itself. "Contemporary public concern for protecting nature's ecological equilibrium," he wrote, "should lead to the conferral of standing upon environmental objects to sue for their own preservation."[27]

It would take the marine biologist Rachel Carson and her 1962 book to make clear that we were no longer living in Eden, and in fact closer to the latter stages of Cole's *Course of Empire*. Not only were we consuming nature, we were poisoning it—and ourselves, too—with pesticides such as the then widely used DDT. With mid-twentieth century science on her side, Carson reminded America about a Romantic insight that had mostly been forgotten: that we must heed nature, not simply admire its scenic vistas while depleting its resources. An annual Earth Day was established and first celebrated in 1970. Still today, however, Carson's entreaty to "follow another road"—the title of her concluding chapter—goes largely unheeded. "We stand now where two roads diverge," she wrote. "But unlike the roads in Robert Frost's familiar poem, they are not equally fair. The road we have been traveling is deceptively easy, a smooth superhighway on which we progress with great speed, but at its end lies disaster. The other fork of the road—the one "less traveled by"—offers our last, our only chance to reach a destination that assures the preservation of our earth."[28] Written more than half a century ago, the passage is truer still today.

An Earlier Voice

Three decades after Thomas Cole wrote of losing Eden, his anxieties would find a new voice in George Perkins Marsh. At the outset of his 1864 *Man and Nature,* Marsh announces his purpose to reveal "the extent of the changes produced by human action in the physical conditions of the globe we inhabit; to point out the dangers of imprudence and the necessity of caution in all operations which, on a large scale, interfere with the spontaneous arrangements of the organic or the inorganic world."[29]

An attorney by training and able philologist, Marsh was pragmatic rather than Romantic, and less widely quoted than Thoreau or Emerson. But in recent decades Marsh has been heralded as a pioneering environmentalist. His concerns were with matters such as soil erosion and deforestation, which he believed would result in widespread desertification. Marsh was among the first to argue that, while human action upon the natural environment was inevitable, its consequences were not. So long as we were aware of what we were doing, we might gather determination and wisdom to repair the impact. Referring to mankind's "destructive power," Marsh believed it was "time for some abatement in the restless love of change which characterizes us . . . [having] now felled forest enough everywhere."[30] Marsh thus bridges the gap between the early nineteenth century's idyllic admiration of nature and the progress-focused positivism of the end of that century. His was a modern recognition that the interactions between humans and nature have reciprocal consequences, and that nature is not merely a garden for man to consume. A century later, an observation attributed to the boxer Muhammad Ali evokes Marsh rather beautifully: "Looking at life from a different perspective makes you realize that it's not the deer that is crossing the road—rather it's the road that is crossing the forest."

The words we use today to describe our relationship to nature—stewardship, sustainability, resilience, conservation, ecology, and even smart growth—may not be those of the seekers of Eden, or remotely resemble the poetics of Emerson or Thoreau. Yet they, too, speak of an aspiration to heed nature, and with an even clearer view of the consequences of not doing so. We now see that the prospect of desolation is nearer than the realm of a painter's imagination.

3.1 *Across the Continent. "Westward the Course of Empire Takes Its Way,"*
Frances Flora Bond, 1868. Manifest Destiny art: The train facilitating the spread
of civilization, while the Native Americans are left in its smoke. An unintended
interpretation would be of civilization polluting the wilderness, the train leading
passengers away from this town to despoil a territory further away.

3

INTERPRETING AMERICA'S ANTI-URBAN BIAS

> The City is the nerve center of our civilization. It is also the storm center.
>
> REVEREND JOSIAH STRONG, 1887

> The hope of the city lies outside itself. Focus your attention on the cities—in which more than half of us live—and the future is dismal.
>
> LEWIS MUMFORD, 1925

> I'd rather be a forest than a street.
>
> SIMON AND GARFUNKEL, 1970

> With all due respect for the wondrous ways people have invented to amuse themselves and one another on paved surfaces, I find that this exodus from the land makes me unspeakably sad. I think of the children who will never know, intuitively, that a flower is a plant's way of making love, or what silence sounds like, or that trees breathe out what we breathe in.
>
> BARBARA KINGSOLVER, 2002

A RESPECTED CLERGYMAN refers to cities as storm centers. The distinguished author of such weighty texts as *The City in History, The Culture of Cities*, and *The Condition of Man* proclaims the future of cities dismal. Beloved balladeers sing of forests over streets. Play on paved surfaces makes a Pulitzer Prize–winning author unspeakably sad. Across all these bits of evidence, a tradition of anti-urban bias may be discerned. "If ever I lived to the hurrying metronome of mortality, it was when I was twenty in New York City," one writer proclaims. "At no time in my life did I know more nervous stimulation; nowhere else was I ever so miserable."[1] Readers of serious books in America are hardly surprised by such passages.

It is important to point out the anti-urban scarlet letter pinned on American culture, given how many utopian departures have sprung from it. One can, however, debate how pervasive this anti-urbanism has been. Barbara Kingsolver's beautiful passage, for example, is not explicitly an anti-city rant; she only wants us to remain in touch with the wonders of the natural world. But embedded in many expressions of preference of nature are implicit rebuffs to the city. Our language supports this, beginning with the derivation of "natural" from nature. Anthropological research supports it, too, finding an innate human preference for greener landscapes, suggesting evolutionary psychology that can be traced to our beginnings on the African Savannah. Meanwhile, we speak of cities as artificial and alienating. This is not unique to Americans. Here is Leonardo da Vinci, around the time of the Columbian voyages, expressing a melancholy sentiment in one of his notebooks about a life spent mainly in Florence, Milan, and Rome: "This is what happens to those who leave a life of solitary contemplation and choose to come to dwell in cities among people full of infinite evil." Elsewhere, sketching hygienic satellite towns around Milan, he notes: "people should not be packed together like goats and pollute the air for one another." [2]

Seeking a new Eden, early settlers to American were not inclined to build prodigious cities—and indeed, there would be no need for prodigious cities for centuries. Paradise is rarely imagined as a bustling metropolis. It is important, however, to distinguish between opposition to the very idea of gathering in cities and desire to reconceive and improve upon the form they take. As an example of the former, consider this declaration: "In substantial measure, the discontents of urban civilization are a function of man's deep seated and fundamental rejection of the city as an idea." This was not a pioneer heading west a century and a half ago, or a southern agrarian suspicious of northern urbanization, but the editor of a book about suburbanization published in the 1970s.[3] This chapter will challenge such blanket conclusions.

The Rise of the City

In the preceding two chapters we saw that neither Thomas Jefferson, dedicated to his agrarian republic, nor the Romantics, seeking communion with nature, were enthusiastic about urbanization. In the early decades of the nineteenth century, America was still predominantly a nation of farms and villages. A number of port cities had grown up along the Atlantic and continued to expand, but most Americans living on their farms or in small towns had no reason to expect the rate of urbanization to dramatically change. In 1809, when Thomas Jefferson retired to Monticello and from public life, the largest city in America was New York: it had ninety-six thousand people, plus another twenty thousand or so distributed across its four future boroughs. It was big for its time, to be sure, but still just a fraction of London's size and smaller than, for example, New Haven today. Philadelphia was next at sixty-one thousand, Baltimore was just shy of forty-six thousand, and Boston was at thirty-four thousand—and they had taken nearly two centuries to get to that size. Charleston, another port city, was not quite at twenty-five thousand, while Savannah hadn't yet hit six thousand. Most others, if we could call them cities, were in modern terms the size of subdivisions.

By the publication of Thoreau's *Walden* four decades later, in 1850, the population of New York had ballooned to 515,000, with its future boroughs adding another 140,000; Philadelphia had doubled its population to 121,000; Baltimore tripled to the size of 170,000; and Boston nearly quadrupled to 137,000. Along the Ohio and Mississippi Rivers, the cities of Cincinnati, Louisville, St. Louis, and New Orleans were also growing. New Orleans had been home to a mere ten thousand or so people at the time of the Louisiana Purchase in 1803, but now stood at 116,000, mainly due to its role at the economic transfer point between the Atlantic Ocean and the Mississippi watershed. Such growth was impressive, but again, it had happened over forty years, much of a nineteenth-century human lifespan. And these cities were the exception. Apart from New York, none had attained the behemoth scale that others would over the next four decades.

London already was a behemoth, having grown from one million residents to an unimaginable two million over those same four decades. Many an English poet, writer, and intellectual—not least, William Wordsworth, who helped

3.2   The chaotic bustle in late nineteenth-century urban America. Mulberry Street, New York, c. 1890.

inspire the Age of Romanticism—was troubled by London's growth and fore-saw "terrible evil" in an urban future like London's. Charles Dickens had writ-ten memorably about the pollution: "It was a town of red brick, or of brick that would have been red if the smoke and ashes had allowed it; but as matters stood it was a town of unnatural red and black like the painted face of a savage."[4] Dickens's savage was not the "noble savage" of the Romantic imagination, the Native American mythologized as the innocent, free-spirited inhabitant of a world uncorrupted by civilization. His metaphor for the savagery of the mod-ern city was a frightening brute. The prospect that Dickens's London would be replicated across the Atlantic, a path that New York City seemed to be on, surely distressed many Americans of the nineteenth century.

Let's move ahead to the decades to either side of 1900, when the coming of an urban age could no longer be doubted. (See Figure 3.2.) A deeper set of con-cerns about the phenomenon simmered. Around 1880, some 70 percent of the population still lived on farms or in towns of less than 2,500 people; three decades later, the 1910 census counted 46 percent of the population as urbanized. Shortly it would exceed 50 percent. A number of American cities were then doubling in population, not every four decades, but virtually every decade. The big city had arrived, its citizens struggling mightily under the strain. Many commentators were alarmed, but the thousands flowing regularly into growing cities were hardly arriving as anti-urbanists. They were arriving for economic opportunity and the better life they expected to find in those cities.

A paradox was developing across the second half of the nineteenth century. Americans were building cities as fast as any prior civilization (though not as fast as China and some other parts of the world are building them today). They were raising their cities instinctively and expediently, at times with noble intentions but more often with a speculator's fervor, and generally without much hesitation. But this explosive urban growth was causing considerable intellectual trepidation. It is not so clear that those concerned sought to reject cities entirely but, in the face of unprecedented growth and change, they understandably pushed harder for reforms or alternatives. In doing so, they were following an already long tradition of city worrying dating back to and beyond the Revolutionary era. And as we shall see, the tradition would grow as American cities developed their twentieth-century complexities.

Intellectuals versus the City

Thomas Jefferson, a dedicated agrarian, is generally considered a canonical early exponent of anti-urbanism in America. Among his memorable anti-city statements are these two oft-quoted favorites: "I view great cities as pestilential to the morals, the health, and the liberties of man." And: "When they get piled upon one another in large cities, as in Europe, we shall become as corrupt as in Europe." [5] He was against replicating the kinds of cities he witnessed during his travels in Europe, as much for the social harshness he observed in the early industrializing cities of England as for the undemocratic governments out of which old European cities sprang.

There was a hint of hypocrisy in this. Jefferson enjoyed the intellectual and architectural stimulations of Paris during his five years as ambassador to France, where, as a biographer put it, "his own pursuit of happiness was at its most exuberant."[6] Notice the qualifiers "great" and "large" in the two quotes above. He was not against cities altogether, but determined to control the scale of urbanization. On the subject of the nation's remaining forever agricultural versus succumbing to a manufacturing destiny, his famous battles with Alexander Hamilton were less about whether the transformation would occur than about its pace. Toward the end of his life he even seemed to acknowledge the benefits that cities could provide. In a letter to William Ludlow in 1824, Jefferson imagines a journey "from the savages of the Rocky Mountains, eastwards towards our seacoast." During this reverse route from west to east, he writes, one "would meet the gradual shades of improving man until he would reach his as yet, most improved state in our seaport towns."[7] These do not sound like the words of an outright condemner of the idea or the purpose of cities.

The Transcendentalists were heirs to Jefferson's urban anxieties, as were the Hudson River School painters, various other pastoral dreamers, and importantly, many religious authorities. In Chapter 2, we heard Thoreau's lament: "The whistle of the locomotive penetrates my woods summer and winter."[8] It was the signal of the inevitable, unwanted, encroachment of modern civilization. We still read Thoreau today, but the complementary, more severe sermons of generations of religious authorities are less familiar. The Protestant preacher Josiah Strong (1847–1916), for example, famously called cities "a serious menace to our civilization."[9] According to a popular nineteenth-century slogan, "God the first garden made, and the first city, Cain." The murderous Cain, of course, stood for moral decay, corruption, artificiality, vanity, lust, calculation, and materialism.[10] This echoed the biblical depiction of cities as centers of iniquity— see Sodom and Gomorrah—created by people wishing to escape God's judgment. Perhaps this explains why not one of the twenty-three American towns named Zion has evolved into a bustling metropolis.

As urban growth accelerated later in the century, city skeptics had ever more reason to worry. Debates emerged on both sides of the Atlantic as to whether cities at the scale of London, Berlin, Paris, and now New York and Chicago were merely flawed in planning or administration, or were inherently unworkable and inhumane. Steven Johnson captures the mood eloquently in *The Ghost Map,* his fascinating account of how medical and social reformers discovered the cause of a devastating mid-nineteenth-century cholera epidemic in London: "A sort of existential doubt lingered over the city, a suspicion not that London was flawed, but that the very idea of building cities on the scale of London was a mistake."[11] Tuberculosis, typhoid fever, infant mortality—all results of crowded, unsanitary conditions—regularly took their toll, making city living precarious.

Urban worries accelerated among diverse constituencies. We see it in proclamations about America's manifest destiny to spread across the continent. It appears in Frederick Jackson Turner's 1893 "frontier hypothesis," linking the health of American democracy to the existence of a frontier as an escape valve from eastern cities. We will encounter it in a subsequent chapter, as Olmsted and his contemporaries sought to return nature back to the city while supporting suburban yearnings. In politics, the "Great Commoner" William Jennings Bryan took up the cause in his famous "cross of gold" speech while campaigning for the presidency in 1896. "Burn down your cities and leave our farms," he exhorted, "and your cities will spring up again as if by magic; but destroy our farms, and the grass will grow in the streets of every city in the country."[12] He was preaching to his political base, fueling the post–Civil War divide between southern rural values (and remnants of the plantation system) and northern industrialization and cosmopolitanism—a divide that remains evident in national politics today. (See Figure 3.3.) In literature, Henry James, whom no one could mistake for a commoner, observed in *The American* that his compatriots possessed "civic instincts" without the need of "forms of a high old civilization," though he evidently missed some of those high forms and decamped to London for lengthy stretches.[13]

Such expressions continued into the twentieth century, with Americans again in dialogue with Europeans. After the First World War, intellectuals grappled with the ideas of the German historian and philosopher Oswald Spengler, whose monumental *Decline of the West* argued that all great cultures were city-born. Many Americans agreed instead with the great Chicago architect Louis Sullivan, who articulated a common opinion in his 1917 *Kindergarten Chats*: "For while the great cities are great battle-grounds, they are not great breeding-grounds. The great minds may go to the great cities but they are not (generally speaking) born and bred in the great cities. In the formation of a great mind . . . solitude is prerequisite; for such a mind is nurtured in contemplation, and strengthened in it."[14]

It was a view that Emerson, Thoreau, and their fellow Transcendentalists would have recognized and embraced. Many were becoming convinced that the physical concentration that seemed endemic to large cities required mitigation. Then there was Lewis Mumford, considered in the mid-twentieth century to be one of the great interpreters of the course of urbanization. "The hope of the city lies outside itself," he concluded in 1925—three years prior to Henry Ford's more direct, and self-interested, advice to simply drive away.

3.3 The Grangers, or "Patrons of Husbandry," emerged as a conservative political organization in the post–Civil War era. Such a chromolithograph poster would hang in member homes, a reminder of (white) agrarian virtuousness, and suspicions about city cultures.

One influential group of literary contemporaries, the southern agrarians, might not have found Ford's technological solution appealing, but they otherwise agreed with him that the future of America—at least its southern part—required leaving the city behind. To see this, one need only peruse *I'll Take My Stand,* a collective plea for resistance against the loss of southern traditions and ways of life penned by twelve southern writers and poets in 1930. In "The Hind Tit," essayist Andrew Nelson Lytle wrote: "It is in fact impossible for any culture to be sound and healthy without a proper respect and proper regard for the soil, no matter how many urban dwellers think that their victuals come from groceries and delicatessens and their milk from tin cans."[15] It was the "tawdry conveniences of modernism" that they rejected and the North's "headlong race for mastery over nature called Progress."[16] Much later, poet Robert Penn Warren, although he recanted a contribution to *I'll Take My Stand* in which he had advocated segregation, still delivered a southern agrarian's perspective: "The past is always a rebuke to the present. . . . It's a better rebuke than any dream of the future."[17] Large cities were evidence of the burdens of progress, the central focus of the southern agrarians' protest.

In the decades following the Second World War the American economy boomed, but no golden age for older American cities emerged as a result. This was clear to the authors of one of the more influential assertions of cultural anti-urban bias in American history. In their 1962 book *The Intellectual versus the City*, Morton and Lucia White trace a strand of anti-urban ideas across the entirety of the nineteenth century and on to the mid-twentieth. They connect the mindset of Jefferson to literary titans such as Melville, Hawthorne, Poe, Henry Adams, Henry James, Howells, Bellamy, and Dreiser, and then to America's greatest twentieth-century architect, Frank Lloyd Wright. The book is well researched and persuasive, but begins with a telling sentence: "The decay of the American City is now one of the most pressing concerns of the nation."[18] The Whites' research and writing was heavily influenced by their time; the 1960s were a troublesome era for the physical and social aspects of America's major cities. City centers had seen little investment since before the Great Depression thirty years earlier. Decay was evident: the urban renewal programs were not proving very helpful, large cities were theaters of civil-rights and soon anti-war demonstrations, and suburban retreat was at full bore.

The unstated implication of their work was that a century and a half of accumulated hostility toward cities had contributed to the sorry state of American urbanism at mid-twentieth century. The Whites had a point. Even worse, many Americans in the 1960s and 1970s thought the problems of the big city were so deep and numerous as to be insoluble. (See Figure 3.4.) Approaching New York City on a trip from his new-age farm, Stephen Diamond voiced a sentiment other Americans have shared: "you could feel yourself approaching the Big C (City, Civilization, Cancer) itself, deeper and deeper into the decaying heart."[19] This reflected then, and still does, a bundle of concerns and discomforts: uneasiness about physical concentration; annoyance with the hassles of getting around; discomfort in engaging people unlike oneself; anxiety in negotiating the thicket of municipal bureaucracies; dislike of the hurried pace of daily life, and the city dwellers' tolerance of unconventional social mores and lifestyles. Yes, many Americans find all of that unappealing about big cities. Big cities are also considered noisy, polluted, congested, and crime-ridden, not to mention havens for big government, begetting dependence rather than reinforcing individualism. Americans have, indeed, been ambivalent about the value of such conditions to their lives, and especially to a place they would prefer to call home. (See Figure 3.5.)

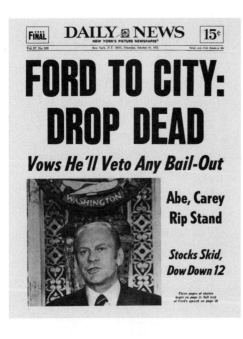

3.4 (left)   Famous 1975 headline reporting that President Gerald Ford was denying New York City's request for federal assistance to avoid bankruptcy. Federal assistance would arrive, but the headline was indicative of a general disregard at the time for older cities.

3.5 (right)   Midtown Manhattan: a scene that many Americans would still consider unappealing as a setting for their lives.

Benton MacKaye, the decentralist introduced in the prior chapter, expressed a common sentiment. "We find ourselves in the shoes of our forefathers: their job was to unravel the wilderness of nature; ours is to unfold the wilderness of civilization," he wrote. "Or are we to be lost in the jungle of industrialism?"[20] Though the words *city* and *civilization* have common roots, for MacKaye, cities and civilization had parted ways. But note, too, that literary culture does not always reflect a whole society's views. Historian David Schuyler makes this point cleverly with regard to the Whites' research, saying that their finding of a deep anti-urban tradition does not "account for the millions who . . . wrote with their feet rather than with their pens by moving from farms or from abroad to the nation's cities."[21]

Scholars continue to present the case that anti-urbanism is deeply embedded in our culture. In *Fleeing the City: Studies in the Culture and Politics of Antiurbanism*, for example, ten essays bring a variety of political and sociological perspectives to bear on the phenomenon and its origins in different cultures across history. Roger Salerno's contribution to the collection begins with a striking sentence: "Before cities there were no poor."[22] It is a rhetorical statement introducing a discussion of how fear of cities stems in part from the presence of poor, uneducated, menacing, and other disagreeable populations in them. This speaks to a real tension in debates over urbanism. To dispel the impression of the big bad city, theorists and planners often project the image of a civilized, enlightened polis, but in trying to civilize, sanitize, and increase the appeal of the city, they ignore or displace those for whom the city is most essential.

Another recent book, Steven Conn's *Americans against the City: Anti-Urbanism in the Twentieth Century*, makes the case that anti-urbanism remains deeply embedded despite evidence of renewed interest in urban living. Conn expresses a not-uncommon view that urban indifference will persist as long as American culture indulges in the fantasy of ultimate personal freedom—privileging individualism and self-sufficiency over the responsibility to the common good that, for Conn, is the essence of urban culture.[23] Such an argument seems persuasive except that, for every real or mythological Daniel Boone heading into the wilderness to get away from the city, there has been a corresponding experiment in communitarian living, as we shall see in later chapters. Of course, Conn might well respond, the concern for a common good in most such experiments is limited to a specific in-group rather than to a general or universal urban constituency.

Qualifying American Anti-Urbanism

Critiques of anti-urbanism provide a reminder of the excesses of that tradition, and the critics are part of the problem. As anti-urban literature fuels additional worrying about cities, the worries become self-perpetuating. What if we reinterpreted America's past, at least partially, to recognize that anti-urban ideas have always coexisted along with hopes of improving aggregate living? Perhaps we would see that the arrival of the modern age, associated with the discovery of the Americas, compelled a rethinking of what cities needed to become, both in a new world and to modernize the old. Could those features of America's metropolitan landscapes often lamented by tradition-minded urbanists be the result of a determination—whether motivated by aspiration or pragmatism—to reimagine forms of human settlement befitting a modern world?

The tradition of seeking to perfect human settlement is older than American expressions of disapproval of cities. Reverend John Winthrop hoped the first settlers of Boston would "bear one another's burdens" on "a shining city upon a hill." Jefferson, although he found no occupation "so delightful to me as the culture of the earth," also sketched idealized forms of settlement throughout his life. When Ralph Waldo Emerson lamented that he could not have both "rural strength and religion" and "city facility and polish" he was dreaming of some ideal balance, not expressing utter scorn for the growing cities of his time. He also understood that "the test of civilization is the power of drawing the most benefit from cities."[24]

Other Americans harbored similar hopes that their cities, new forms of settlement in a new world, might avoid, or at least minimize, the kinds of trauma that came with the social, political, technological and managerial transformations of the prior four hundred years. The instinct has been, as has often been noted by European intellectuals, to rethink the city in light of the ideals arising out of the European Enlightenment, and to make the most of the explosive forces released by the Industrial Revolution. In general, the emerging American culture was deeply influenced by Enlightenment ideals—among them, the turn to *reason* and *science* to produce a secular understanding of the natural world; the pursuit of *personal liberty* and *social egalitarianism;* the recognition of *private property* as a source of wealth and independence; the celebration of *individualism* and *self-sufficiency;* the belief that *progress* would provide continuing opportunities for social and economic advancement; and the pursuit of origins in a new world transformed by all these enlightened values. That these same social and political principles would spill over into people's thinking about how to aggregate in spatial communities should not be surprising.

Perhaps due to the prevalence of today's suburbia, a belief persists that Americans find it hard to accept urbanism as central to their lives and consequently have, more often than not, built cities that are less than urbane and difficult to love. Various surveys and polls over the years do reveal a preference for pastoral or small-town environments, as Chapter 4 will discuss. Manhattan notwithstanding, and overlooking the centers of Boston, San Francisco, and a dozen or so other cities, America has indeed long been a culture of suburbs and small towns. But while the prefix *sub* in the term *suburban* might suggest *less than* or indicate a subordinate role, in the annals of American urbanization it should really be seen as alternative. (See Figure 3.6.)

The same Lewis Mumford who leveled fierce criticism at the modern city nonetheless considered history's first utopia to be not Eden, but the idea of a

3.6   During the 1950s and 1960s developer Joseph Eichler built some 11,000 homes in a distinctive mid-century modern style. The promotional photographs for Eichler Homes, such as by photographer Ernie Braun, even more than the homes themselves, defined the image of a modern family lifestyle.

city. His point was that, at least since the time of the Greeks, the human imagination has played with the notion of an ideal congregation of citizens— "civitas." In ancient times, Mumford argued, the idea of a city was "the closest approach to paradise that one might hope for on earth."[25] He spoke not of the city beneath one's feet, mind you, but of one that was imaginable and worth striving for. Similarly, Michael Cowan interprets Ralph Waldo Emerson not as an opponent of cities but as a man seeking reconciliation between love of nature and urban culture. In Emerson's generation, Cowen writes, there was a profound tension between hopes for a New Jerusalem and longings for a New Eden.[26] Any New Jerusalem would presumably have to be as impressive as the ancient Jerusalem, one of the world's first great cities upon a hill. And as for a New Eden, it would need to be as garden-like as the biblical paradise. Such dual, paradoxical longing did not belong to Emerson's generation alone. It has been felt and expressed overtly and subliminally across American history, and will show up in the pages to come as those utopian traces in American place-making.

4.1 The Town Common in Westport, New York, exhibiting the charm that stirs the small-town ideal.

4

THE SMALL TOWN AS AN IDEAL:
PURITAN COVENANTS TO CELEBRATION, FLORIDA

There was once a place where neighbors greeted neighbors in the quiet of summer twilight. . . . Where children chased fireflies. And porch swings provided easy refuge from the cares of the day. The movie house showed cartoons on Saturday. The grocery store delivered. And there was always that one teacher who always knew you had that special something. Remember that place? Perhaps from childhood. Or maybe just from stories. It held a magic all of its own. The special magic of an American home town.

SALES BROCHURE, CELEBRATION, FLORIDA, 1996

The town is the home from which we escaped yet whose map is etched forever in our memories.

RICHARD LINGEMAN, 1980

TODAY'S GLOBAL ECONOMIES advance with a metropolitan bias, powered by the concentration of innovation-minded talent and entrepreneurial zeal found in the largest cities. This portends badly for rural and small-town America; in December 2018, the title of a *New York Times* feature read "Abandoned America." Rural counties are home to considerably older populations, have higher unemployment and substantially lower median incomes, and continue to experience population loss.[1] Many expect these trends to intensify as the digital revolution is anticipated to reduce the stresses and complexities of urbanization, leading to still larger and "smarter" cities.

Yet, misgivings about the "big city" remain among many Americans as hold-overs from a prior revolution. Generations who experienced the onslaught of industrial urbanization hoped for and imagined more hospitable settings in towns of physical grace, offering proximity to nature, comforting traditions, communitarian civility, and freedom from city burdens. In this chapter, we en-counter the ideal (if not often the reality) of that small town etched in our memories.

Thomas Jefferson may have been keen to partition America into indepen-dent homesteads for his agrarian nation. Upon their arrival to the New World, however, colonists did not head into the wilderness to make their own claims of land. That would have been foolhardy—indeed, suicidal. William Bradford, writing *Of Plimouth Plantation,* remembered arriving on the *Mayflower* and confronting "a hideous and desolate wilderness, full of wild beasts and wild men"—hardly the hoped-for Eden.[2] Of necessity, arrivals gathered in hamlets and villages for communal support and out of religious or secular allegiance, often bound by covenants or terms established prior to their passage. For a time, colonial Massachusetts even had laws barring the location of homes more than a half-hour's journey from a town's common.[3]

The early settlements were primitive, focused on shelter and security, far from picturesque, and not much different in organization from European vil-lages. Over the course of generations, however, some of these places, having ac-quired the grace that comes with age and care, ascended to the status of beloved archetypes. As citizens were lured away from their farms and villages by the better economic and social prospects of the rapidly growing if exasperating cit-ies, many looked back romantically to the idea of the country town as the ideal place to grow up and to live. It is a romance that resurfaces periodically, and in recent decades has been an important feature of the New Urbanism movement.

Seaside

When a small town with the alluring name of Seaside was privately built in the 1980s, it didn't take long to capture the imagination of suburban developers, homebuilders, planners, cultural pundits, and public officials. Set along a mag-nificent stretch of beach in the Florida Panhandle, Seaside was meticulously

4.2   The Town of Seaside, Florida, the design of which helped initiate and give momentum to the New Urbanism movement.

planned and artfully designed. It is an endearing place of several hundred homes built initially on eighty acres (though it has since expanded) and a number of buildings designed by notable architects. A modest array of shops and some civic facilities are included, as well. Hailed as a long-sought answer to monotonous, unsustainable, suburban sprawl, it soon acquired astonishing fame. Seaside has been celebrated at national conventions of homebuilders, in myriad conferences, symposia and books, by the Prince of Wales (who was sufficiently inspired to launch construction of England's own model village, called Poundbury) and by all manner of media, from network news and *60 Minutes* to the *New York Times* and *Travel and Leisure*. Three decades later, Seaside continues to attract visitors from near and far. As one of the most fashionable time-share resorts in the region, it even markets its own resort paraphernalia under the brand of "The Seaside Style." (See Figure 4.2.)

As America approached the end of the twentieth century (and a new millennium), still uncertain about the benefits of the big city and now bored with suburbia, Seaside rekindled old yearnings for the quality of life associated with small towns. A popular history of New England captures that mood: "A village on a hill, white houses facing on a green, tall elms arching overhead, and a little white church spire pointing heavenward: for many Americans this picture represents stability, tradition, national roots, and a retreat from urban stress."[4] It may lack arching elms and a white church steeple, but Seaside still evokes that familiar and alluring image.

Retreat may be the crucial word in the New England town description. In the case of Seaside, it was a retreat less from urban stress (except on holiday excursions) than from commonplace suburbia. As the design and construction of Seaside inspired the New Urbanism movement, many "new urbanist" or "neo-traditional" communities followed. A Congress for the New Urbanism formed in 1993 to codify the movement's goals in a *Charter of the New Urbanism* and further spread them. The opening statements of the Charter's preamble are worthy of reprinting:

> The Congress for the New Urbanism views disinvestment in central cities, the spread of placeless sprawl, increasing separation by race and income, environmental deterioration, loss of agricultural lands and wilderness, and the erosion of society's built heritage as one interrelated community-building challenge.
>
> *We stand* for the restoration of existing urban centers and towns within coherent metropolitan regions, the reconfiguration of sprawling suburbs into communities of real neighborhoods and diverse districts, the conservation of natural environments, and the preservation of our built legacy.[5]

Aspirational and urban minded this would seem, except that the movement's practitioners rarely went beyond planning somewhat denser forms of suburban development, which did not deliver the range of amenities and activities one would expect of an actual town. To reverse "disinvestment in central cities" or achieve the "restoration of existing urban centers" are more difficult tasks. Perhaps "the New *Sub*urbanism" would have been a more accurate name for the movement, but of course that would have been anathema to advocates whose stated goal was to "urbanize" the suburb, not be associated with creating further suburban sprawl. More recent publications, such as *Retrofitting Suburbia* and *Suburban Transformations,* better reflect the movement's focus. The New Urbanists were promoting what they considered to be commonsense alternatives to the problems of sprawl, but an underlying utopianism was also at work.

Sentimental Utopianism

A bedrock faith of New Urbanism is that greater sociability could be engineered through a particular set of physical arrangements and design aesthetics. This is where utopianism entered. By offering an appealing, sentiment-arousing alternative to conventional suburban development, the New Urbanists were able to persuade developers to adjust their generic subdivision layouts. They argued that the ubiquity of sprawl made it harder to foster community, a cherished American goal that many who fled the city were seeking. They asserted that, while the housing industry kept on producing standard subdivisions, Americans really preferred places that were unique—places like, for example, the historic town of Marblehead, Massachusetts. (See Figure 4.3.) A key insight was that conventional zoning ordinances prevented the replication of charming places such as Marblehead. These outdated codes originated (and still operate) in response to the urbanization challenges of the Industrial Era—rising density, squalid tenements, inappropriate mixing of industry and housing, and growing fears that the next noxious factory, or the even more unsavory tannery, would move in next door. Under the resulting zoning codes, it is not possible to produce contemporary versions of a Marblehead, a town that predates the Industrial Revolution. Most municipal ordinances would forbid its mixture of uses, multiplicity of scales, and narrowness of streets, and thus prevent the intricate and intimate weaving of the fabric that characterizes these towns of memory and weekend retreats.

Other insights brought forth by the New Urbanists included their challenge to the Department of Transportation's single-minded concern for the movement of cars. Traffic engineering professions, it seemed clear, ignored the fact that streets are environments that should be designed for multiple users, including pedestrians, rather than engineered solely for motorized vehicles. Ideas for "transit-oriented development" were offered to help wean Americans from dependence on cars. Strategies to reform outdated zoning codes were advanced, in support of producing more diverse environments. The New Urbanists also sought to end the ostracizing of the poor in enclaves of public housing that looked nothing like other people's homes. They worked with the Department of Housing and Urban Development in the 1990s to develop the radical new idea of building "normal-looking" places for those least able to house themselves. Much of the housing built under the Hope VI program during the 1990s was

4.3   A view of Marblehead, Massachusetts. A Pilgrim from the Mayflower arrived in the area in 1626, the first European settled there in 1629, and the town incorporated in 1649. Beloved by tourists in search of New England history and traditional small-town charms.

conventional in appearance, the aim being to destigmatize subsidized housing and erase the scarlet letter that identified a poor neighborhood. (See Figure 14.10.)

These and similar contributions by the New Urbanists have significantly changed American urban planning. Some credit the movement with sparking the revival of interest in cities evident in the early decades of the twenty-first century. The founders of New Urbanism, especially Andres Duany, Elizabeth Plater-Zyberk, and Peter Calthorpe, deserve enormous respect for disrupting America's suburban complacency and fostering a more urban-focused public discussion. Their promise, however, was to revive a sense of community that Americans had lost, and doubts remain about how well that has been delivered.

Celebrating Celebration

By the mid-1990s, public attention began to stray from Seaside. To heap greater praise on it might not have been possible. Its magic, however, was also slightly tarnished as less remarkable copycat developments elbowed in nearby. Its starring role in *The Truman Show*, a 1998 film which concludes with the hero's

4.4   Aerial view of the center of Celebration, Florida, founded by the Disney Companies in the 1990s and named "New Town of the Year" by the Urban Land Institute in 2001.

triumphant escape from a stiflingly perfect town called Seahaven, perhaps did not help. National attention shifted to a new effort, by the Walt Disney Company, to conjure up the Great American Town. (See Figure 4.4.) As an avalanche of media ensued about Celebration, Florida, it focused at first on the irresistible promise of a place sure to be as creatively conceived and expertly managed as Disney World itself. The long-term value of investing in a home there seemed assured. With expectations running high, thousands entered the 1995 lottery for the right to purchase Celebration's first five hundred homes.[6] But there were bemused skeptics, as well. Michael Pollan published a piece in the *Sunday New York Times Magazine* called "Town Building is no Mickey Mouse Matter."[7] Ross Rymer's critique in *Harpers* made a disquieting observation that applied to many other neo-traditional developments: "Celebration is billed as being in the great American tradition of town building, but it is a town whose mission isn't the pursuit of commercial advantage, or religious or political freedom, or any idea more compelling than a sense of comfortable community. Its ambition is, in the end, no greater than to be like a town."[8]

The question inevitably arose: How exactly does "a sense of community"—a favorite New Urbanist phrase—get delivered? Can neighborliness and social cohesion be reliably fostered by a certain arrangement of streets and blocks, pocket parks and plazas, old-fashioned Main Streets, traditional architectural imagery, smaller homes on tighter lots, or other physical attributes? Our small-town mythologies suggest so. Consider how a 1995 article in the *Economist* begins:

> Any American of a certain age can picture the place. Peaceful and picturesque, it is full of houses with porch swings and picket fences. Children play in the streets and grown-ups chat with their neighbors. The place is familiar from Norman Rockwell paintings and countless black-and-white movies. A few years ago Bill Bryson, a writer, described his efforts to find it. "The place I was looking for would be an amalgam of all those towns I had encountered in fiction," he wrote in *The Lost Continent: Travels in Small Town America*. "Indeed, that might well be its name—Amalgam, Ohio, or Amalgam, North Dakota." Or, Celebration, Florida.[9]

Celebration has now entered its second quarter of a century, and it remains a distinctive place for most who visit. Celebration Village, the community's downtown, remains charming, picturesque, and relatively active, aided by the subsidization of its Main Street storefronts, and is still a source of pride for its residents. But it has not evolved into as dreamy a place as many fans of Disney Imagineering anticipated. Its population, under ten thousand—not the twenty thousand originally envisioned—has experienced a variety of real-life setbacks. There were foreclosures following the Great Recession; crises in the quality of home construction; controversies over school curricula; disappointments with amenities and services available along that main street; governance squabbles among home-owner associations and Disney management; and in one grim month, both a suicide and a murder. By 2004, Disney had divested itself of much of the real estate—which had been its intention all along, but perhaps accelerated as dealing with citizens turned out to be tougher than managing cast members or serving tourists eager to be entertained. Peter Rummell, who directed the initial design of Celebration on behalf of Disney, acknowledged some exasperating elements in the community: "Those are the people who go to Disney World eight times a year and think that because Main Street is clean they could extrapolate that to a community and think that it was going to be perfect.

4.5   View of the Main commercial street in Celebration, Florida,
named Celebration Avenue because a Main Street already existed
in Osceola County, of which Celebration is part.

Those are the people who think their kids will never get a B in school and there is never going to be a weed in their lawn when they move to Celebration."[10] (See Figure 4.5.)

Weeds remain rare in Celebration, but life's traumas have in a way been healthy. They have tamped down Celebration's "pixel dust" aspects. One hopes that the annual traditions of dispensing autumn leaves and winter "snow" from containers built into the streetlights has also waned. The intrigue of a Disney-made town persists, primarily for charmed Disney World visitors. Celebration remains under private management, unincorporated, like Seaside. Its residents and proprietors are still subject to the 166-page Declaration of Covenants that outlines do's and don'ts. But Celebration is evolving, as any place does, through the actions and lives of its residents. Andrew Ross, another early chronicler who lived there for a year, predicted that the community many expected to emerge as a product of the town's design would instead be recognized to have been shaped more by the circumstances, adversities, personalities, and characters of those living there.[11] He was right. Celebration remains a good place to live for those who have chosen and can afford to make it their community. "I moved here because I loved Disney—we had such blind faith," one resident told the *New York Times* around the time Disney was divesting. "But this was just a business venture for them, and now it's up to us. Their success is based on financials, and ours is going to be more, 'Are you proud to live here? Do you love your life here?'"[12]

Type "Celebration, Florida" into your internet browser and click on the map that comes up. The town's central plan is clearly discernible, bordered by a golf course greenbelt. Now pull back the view to take in the outer villages and beyond, and observe the morass of regional sprawl spreading for miles through this part of Florida. The same is evident along the Florida Panhandle near Seaside, much of it attracted by the charms of Seaside. Have Celebration and Seaside furnished a meaningful answer to sprawl, yielded a solution for small town environmental stewardship, or provided a model for enhancing neighborliness and community? Confidence in such claims varies considerably.

Housing several thousand residents, even twenty thousand for that matter, on nearly five thousand acres, with another forty-five hundred or so acres held in conservation might have worked for residents of Celebration, but it was hardly a national solution to suburban sprawl. Critics began to caution the New Urbanists about overstating promises and touting panaceas. Some accused such communities—most not as well designed, financed, or promoted as Seaside and Celebration—of perpetuating an obsolete concept. Why prop up the mundane, middle-class notion of "the good life" and why indulge in "designer sprawl" just at the moment when interest in existing urban centers was growing? Other critics noted that neotraditional communities had a habit of morphing into homogenous demographic enclaves—hardly rainbow coalitions. Were these places simply an acceptable form of suburban "yuppie flight"? The 2010 census listed 91 percent of Celebration residents as white, in contrast to 58 percent of the nearby town of Kissimmee and of Oceala County, of which Celebration is part. And what about the ubiquitous vernacular imagery—was it a necessity to marry those aesthetics to the modern domestic conveniences, or just a sophisticated lure? Were the resulting densities too low to support real civic vitality? Did such "towns," most of them unincorporated private developments, represent the triumph of private management over elective local governance? Did they, however unintentionally, legitimize more peripherally located, home-dominated, socially homogenous real estate developments, instead of encouraging more support of existing towns and cities?

In carefully edited, rose-colored evocations of a golden age of small-town excellence, skeptics see a scene from which many Americans have, in fact, been fleeing for a century. They know there is a parallel and quite different history of the American small town, a tale of its abandonment for the lures of the city. We will explore that phenomenon in a moment. First, however, let's visit the earlier era of veneration that created some of our small-town myths in the first place.

Before Seaside

Seaside, Celebration, and their successors rely on a cultural memory of wholesome small towns. Earlier generations critical of their era's course of urbanization turned to similar memories. "Consider the village itself," Lewis Mumford wrote in 1924, "Would it be an exaggeration to say that there has never been a more complete and intelligent partnership between the earth and man than existed, for a little while, in the old New England Village?"[13] Of course, that was an exaggeration. It is also a good illustration of how long we have promoted the small town as the environment that best fosters community and well-being. Opposed to the spread of suburbanization, but fascinated by the British "Garden City" idea, Mumford saw the small town as a necessary retreat from Manhattan, Philadelphia, and other over-stressed modern cities. Throughout Mumford's illustrious career as a historian of cities and ardent critic of modern urbanization, the belief in the wholesomeness of small-town life was rarely far from his thoughts. He was deluding himself, however, that his support for the small town would thwart suburbanization; most suburban developers simply claimed that *their* subdivisions were recapturing the small-town charms he admired.

Mumford was hardly alone. A year earlier, Thorstein Veblen, the man who coined the terms "conspicuous consumption" and "conspicuous leisure," concluded that the country town was "one of the great American institutions; perhaps the greatest, in the sense that it has had . . . a greater part than any other in shaping public sentiment and giving character to American culture."[14] Harlan P. Douglass, one of the many town boosters of the late nineteenth century, saw even more potential in small towns: "Here stands greatness humbly clad; here patriotic labour is involved with charm; here deep social processes are bound up with intimate personal contacts; here especially the high fortunes of the open country are to be centred and inspired; here lies the pleasant middle-ground through which if one will have it so the Garden of Eden merges into the City of God."[15] (See Figure 4.5.)

More prosaically but no less ardently, the founder of a website entitled *Love Small Town America* echoes Veblen, Douglass, and Mumford: "The atmosphere [is] different than the big city . . . People welcomed us with open arms, there was real one-on-one interaction at the schools for my kids, real estate was inexpensive and there was an authentic community spirit that lived among everyone."[16]

Such enviable conditions may indeed exist. The New Urbanists promise to create them by artful design. But the people most eager to promote and take advantage of our attachment to small-town ideals have been suburban developers, and less through design than by association. Thousands of ordinary subdivisions at various scales are deliberately called villages, just as the six villages of Celebration are. The word *village* sells the promise of "neighborliness," no traffic jams, and other freedoms from the hassles, real or imagined, of city living. Adjacent to Boston, the upper-middle-class suburb of Newton still refers to itself as a collection of thirteen villages, and hosts an annual Village Day. There are countless village-sized suburbs, such as humble Meadowlands Villages in Wisconsin with its hundred or so affordable home lots. By contrast, the population of the Village of Hoffman Estates, within Chicago's suburban ring, exceeds fifty-one thousand and is still growing. Also not exactly village-sized are "The Villages" in Florida, home to more than 150,000 people and still advertising small-town charms and neighborliness to attract more retirees.

This dubious naming of ordinary suburban subdivisions to evoke town qualities is rampant. A blogger bemused by this trend recently compiled a list of fanciful subdivision names just in the vicinity of his hometown of Scranton, Pennsylvania, with amusing commentary:

> Blueberry Hill Estates (atop an old landfill!)
>
> Quail Hill (even though quails aren't common there)
>
> Gable Crest (most homes here don't have gables)
>
> Butler Heights (nobody here has a butler)
>
> Wildflower Village (no wildflower gardens in sight)
>
> Saddle Ridge (where's the horses for those saddles? nowhere!)
>
> Glenmaura (just a snooty-sounding name for a seven-figure community)
>
> Laurel Hill Estates (built upon a small mound they call a "hill")
>
> Paradise Park (no park within walking distance)

Insignia Pointe (what's with the "e" at the end of "Point?")

Willow View (no willows in sight)

Horizon Estates (eastern view of Wal-Mart, not the horizon)

Pocono Ridge Estates (not in the Poconos)

Fox Meadows (neither foxes nor meadows in sight)

Highland Hills (if you consider 800 feet above sea level to be "highlands")

River Mist (no "mist" up here)"[17]

One need not be a cynic to conclude that market research, rather than any design ingenuity or topography, informed these naming choices. The New Urbanists might have overstated things by claiming their designs could restore the scale, character, and sociability of the paradigmatic small town of generations past—but pulling such allusions out of thin air? They would have called it irresponsible.

But what exactly was the archetype? What was its relationship to the popular Currier and Ives prints of American life that appeared toward the end of the nineteenth century, or to the nostalgia in plays such as Thornton Wilder's 1938 *Our Town*, or to popular Hollywood films such as the 1947 *It's A Wonderful Life*, with Jimmy Stewart fighting for the soul of Bedford Falls against a heartless mortgage banker?

The Archetype and Its Transformation

In a 1966 book, *As a City upon a Hill: The Town in American History*, Page Smith offered another testimonial on behalf of the small town: "By no means do all American towns bear the Puritan imprint; yet here was the archetype and, muted or modified as it might become in every particular recreation, the earliest New England towns reveal themes which persist to the present day."[18] These New England villages, the first dating from the early seventeenth century, have been idealized in different ways for more than two hundred years. Before describing any idyllic features, it is important to note that they were fundamentally exclusionary. Non-Puritans could not live within their borders. Still, the Transcendentalists in the early nineteenth century would describe them as model communities. From the middle of the nineteenth century, village life would be more broadly romanticized as the rapid pace of urbanization led builders to devise the first suburban estates deliberately emulating small towns. Early in the twentieth century, planners drew on the New England tradition as they advanced Garden Cities. And recently, as we have seen, the New Urbanists— and more superficially those marketing departments responsible for naming suburban subdivisions—have sought to replicate or evoke the qualities of social harmony and physical grace associated with old New England. It is an irony that, by encouraging so many people to retreat from urban centers, this long history of idealization unleashed the forces of suburbanization that proved truly antithetical to the ideals of small-town life.

All this makes it difficult to discuss the early New England towns without descending into cliché. But an understanding of the initial organization of the Puritan village and how it evolved will allow us to better see how the same image of a perfect hometown could be invoked both to encourage retreat from the expanding industrializing city (and so unleash suburbanization), and to offer an alternative to the ubiquitous suburban landscape, as it was by the New Urbanists two-thirds of a century later.

Small groups bound by strong feelings of kinship settled most of the early English villages in New England, starting with the first permanent English settlement of Plymouth, established in 1620. In any new community, the leading male members would sign a covenant (not unlike Celebration's Declaration of Covenants, which clearly harked back to these early agreements) confirming the terms by which village lands would be held and maintained. Typically, modest home plots bordered a Common for grazing, and land cleared for farming beyond the street of homes was allocated to male heads of households based on their wealth or social status. Everyone lived in the town and compactness was, indeed, legislated. Once all the house lots around the Common were allocated, the process of starting another town began. Within a decade of Plymouth's founding, settlers formed two dozen more towns under such covenants. One of them was Boston, in 1630, which would come to be associated with John Winthrop's famous phrase; in a sermon delivered en route to the New World, he called for founding "a shining city upon a hill. "[19]

The binding covenant was a necessity as long as the survival of the community depended on communal effort and associated spiritual kinship. This emphasis on cooperation is where Mumford found his "harmonious balance." Such unity of purpose, however, lasted only a couple of generations. Once survival was assured, liberties beckoned, including the liberty to amass one's own property and material wealth. What Mumford overlooked (and others have since) is that the physical grace of these communities had little to do with their original communitarian purpose. In time, residents would devote attention to the appearance of the town, and create the various physical icons we now associate with traditional towns: the graceful church steeples, the beautification of the Commons, the proud town halls and sturdy rail stations, the trees planted on Arbor Day, and the fastidious domestic facades and front gardens. But these were products of a much later age.

A few of the early Puritan towns blossomed, economically and aesthetically. Others, along with the hundreds of secular communities that followed as America spread westward, began to lose population and economic purpose in the great dual migration of the second half of the nineteenth century—either to the burgeoning industrial city where economic opportunity lay, or to new beginnings further at the western frontier. Village improvement societies formed to make their towns more appealing—more village- or town-like—to keep ambitious and enterprising citizens from leaving.[20] This local boosterism, somewhat out of desperation, amplified efforts at civic beautification, conjoining beauty with sociability, and creating in a few cases those charming places that Americans remain attracted to and nostalgic about, such as Marblehead, Massachusetts.

Two years prior to Mumford's assertion about the "harmonious balance" found in the country town, Sinclair Lewis's novel *Main Street* had offered an opposing view:

> Under the stilly boughs and the black gauze of dusk the street was meshed in silence. There was but the hum of motor tires crunching the road, the creak of a rocker on the Howlands' porch, the slap of a hand attacking a mosquito, a heat-weary conversation starting and dying, the precise rhythm of crickets, the thud of moths against the screen— sounds that were a distilled silence. It was a street beyond the end of the world, beyond the boundaries of hope. Though she should sit here forever, no brave procession, no one who was interesting, would be coming by. It was tediousness made tangible, a street builded of lassitude and of futility.[21]

Lewis's protagonist, Carol Kennicott, is expressing her dismay about living in Gopher Prairie, modeled on Lewis's own birthplace of Sauk Centre, Minnesota. (See Figure 4.6.) For Lewis, the country town represented no harmonious

4.6 A more typical scene among the
many abandoned and near-abandoned
small towns. Compare to the romantic
image of a small town. See Figures 4.1
and 4.3.

balance, only ingrown mores, absence of opportunity, and lack of interesting
people. Earlier in the book he calls it "dullness made God."[22] Lewis's and Mumford's strikingly differing impressions of the small town (formed, to be sure, in
different eras) represent the two contradictory histories—myths, really—of the
American small town. One is overly sentimental and presents it as worthy of
recurring fascination; the other treats it condescendingly and emphasizes the
abandonment and neglect that continue to the present.

Elms, Porches, and Community

There are many ways in which the positive associations surrounding the small
town recur in American culture. Thomas Campanella's history of a single species of tree is a good example. In his beautifully titled (and beautifully written)
Republic of Shade: New England and the American Elm, there are very few
detailed descriptions of towns.[23] Yet, as we read about certain magnificent elms,
we are inevitably transported to old places not unlike the ones the New Urbanists have been promising to recreate. (See Figure 6.11.)

The magazine *Southern Living* placed an image of house fronts in Celebration, Florida, on its cover in September 1997 and devoted a feature article, "The
Power of Place," to singing the town's praises. It was one of dozens of such articles

4.7 Triple Deckers: three-floor, three-unit housing common to New England, with both front and back porches on each floor.

published around the turn of the millennium as criticism of suburban sprawl mounted. "Inspired by the best and beloved towns of the South, Celebration fosters the grace and gentility of a bygone era," the *Southern Living* article began. "It's a sit-on-your-front-porch, speak-to-your-neighbor kind of place."[24]

The idea of neighbors chatting across front porches is always enticing. Going through old files recently, I found *Boston Globe* articles from two consecutive days in 1996 that suggest such congenial images might not capture the whole story.[25] The first day's headline read "Front Porch Fosters Neighborly Charm: Trend Could Help Unite Communities." Like many stories around that time, all supportive of traditional notions of community, the article extolled the virtues of small-town life. It was full of proper porches on proper homes lining proper and sociable streets.

The very next day's *Globe* arrived with a more sober, if also sadly familiar, kind of headline: "Front Porch Shooting Kills One, Wounds One." Somehow, that particular porch did not bring civility to a troubled Boston neighborhood. Ironically, this was in one of the most "porched" sections of the city, given its large stock of triple-deckers—a type of multi-unit housing that New England builders favored around 1900—and the *three* front porches gracing every one of them. (See Figure 4.7.) A drive-by shooter that night had his horrible mission made much easier by the victim's decision to lounge on a porch. Of course, to paraphrase gun lobbyists, porches don't kill people, people do. It may well be true that many neighborhoods would gain both charm and the possibility of neighborly exchange through the addition of a traditional element such as a porch. But we should not exaggerate what an architectural feature can accomplish.

Symbols of attractive lifestyles are useful, but too great a focus on these diverts attention from other factors that facilitate or inhibit community. Comforting though traditions may be, not all realities can be escaped by conjuring up the icons of the great American small town.[26] Isn't it rather obvious that the formation of community requires willing citizens more than form? Evoking nostalgic images of bygone places, organizing a particular arrangement of spaces, or referencing certain small-town characteristics may create a sense of community. But it is the willingness of citizens to partake that makes community real.

Having expressed considerable reservations about New Urbanist claims about the creation of community, let me end this chapter on a supportive note. In the summer of 2014, I attended the twenty-fifth anniversary weekend of the founding of Kentlands, Maryland. Designed by Andres Duany and Elizabeth Plater-Zyberk. Kentlands is part of the City of Gaithersburg, not an unincorporated subdivision, and an early New Urban, neotraditional project. Entering its second quarter century, it consists of several well-designed, reasonably mixed-income neighborhoods on graciously landscaped streets, made up of mostly single-family homes but including some multi-family apartments. And it has a unique Main Street, which looks and functions somewhat as a traditional "downtown" street, with an impressive array of shops and restaurants at ground level and apartments and some local businesses on upper stories. On a Saturday evening it was full of teenagers and couples, apparently from surrounding suburbs, strolling up and down this rare nearby version of urban vitality amid the sprawl of metropolitan Washington. Immediately adjacent, masked from view by one side of Main Street's mixed-use buildings, is a typical suburban shopping center complete with big box stores and plenty of surface parking. One is able to move Alice-like, through the looking-glass, from one realm to the other. Many of the weekend visitors no doubt drove to and parked in the shopping center, and for a shift of experience emerged unto the aura of the Kentlands Main Street.

4.8   Main Street being enjoyed in Kentlands, Maryland.

A certain kind of place attracts Americans, especially when their daily lives lack a lively physical ambiance. (See Figure 4.8.) But the most impressive aspect of the weekend in Kentlands was not its Main Street, but its residents' enthusiasm for the place. Many of them, both young and old, told heartwarming stories during the anniversary programs or testified in other ways to what a good place Kentlands was to grow up in, and grow old in. Small-town life, though its qualities are often exaggerated, does now and then deliver on its promises for Americans—and thus keeps their small towns etched in memory.

5.1 The Ponemah Mills in Taftville, Connecticut, view of a classic New England mill town.

5

THE COMPANY TOWN AWAY FROM TOWN

> I had a lovely view from my window . . . it was neither city nor country
> exclusively, but a combination of both. [It] was like a beautiful picture.
>
> LOWELL MILL GIRL, 1844

> We decided to build, in close proximity to shops [the factory], homes
> for working men of such character and surrounding as would prove so
> attractive as to cause the best mechanics to seek the place for
> employment in preference to others. We also desired to establish the
> place on such a basis as would exclude all baneful influences, believing
> that such a policy would result in the greatest measure of success.
>
> GEORGE PULLMAN, 1894

> Once the campus is open, Apple employees will have relatively little
> reason to leave the building.
>
> APPLE EXECUTIVE, 2014

APPLE'S RECENTLY COMPLETED HEADQUARTERS in Cupertino, California, designed by Sir Norman Foster, has been dubbed the "spaceship." It is a vast, cir-
cular building four stories tall and a mile in circumference. From a distance it
appears to be hermetically sealed, promises to be immune to hackers, and looks
as if it just might be able to take flight in an emergency. A few miles away, in
Mountain View, Google is constantly planning expansions of its "Googleplex"
home base. Titillating architectural renderings promise additional amenities

5.2   The rooftop playground at Facebook headquarters: keeping staff amused and by their work.

designed to keep staff happy at or near their monitors. In nearby Menlo Park, Facebook's new headquarters, designed by Frank Gehry, has been described as "a cross between high art, twentieth-century corporate thinking, and a child's candy-fueled daydream."[1] (See Figure 5.2.) The offices of these Silicon Valley leviathans are the current products of a lengthy American tradition of seeking to perfect the workplace and its relationship with the surrounding environment.

The nature of most work—we used to say labor—has changed dramatically since the onset of the Industrial Revolution. Industries grew dependent on access to the capital, labor, markets, and transportation infrastructure of cities. The rise of the modern city was in turn a direct result of industrialization, requiring a concentration of capital, labor, and markets. Industrialization brought a host of complexities to the city and to the companies clustering there—not least the challenge of how to manage large groups of laborers. Around the turn of the nineteenth century, and periodically since, industrialists sought more controlled environments for their enterprises, and resolved to build their factories and related services outside urban centers. The advantages included cheap land, room to grow, easy access to sources of energy, and the expectation of being able to better manage workers away from the unruly distractions of the city. In such company towns, maximizing productivity was the primary goal, and worker well-being—for reasons benevolent, naive, or oppressively paternalistic—was constantly monitored. It was never an easy balance to maintain.

The tradition might be said to have begun with Alexander Hamilton, first secretary of the United States Treasury, and the most economy-focused of the Founding Fathers. Hamilton's fiscal and business acumen was responsible for the establishment of a national bank, the creation of a system of tariffs for trade with other countries, and a reinitiated trade relationship with Britain. Up until his infamous 1804 duel with Aaron Burr left him mortally wounded, he was also active in efforts to end the international slave trade. Hamilton was less convinced than his rival Jefferson that the destiny of America would depend on the farmer; he instead advocated development of a manufacturing and commercial economy. No doubt also to Jefferson's chagrin, he was among the first to argue that agriculture, too, could contribute more to the nation's economy if it were organized at scale, rather than left to the whims of household farmers.

Hamilton called for "a new morality" based on the "dignity of toil and the spiritual rewards of industry in a healthful environment."[2] In 1791, he formed the Society for the Establishment of Useful Manufactures, along with several like-minded entrepreneurs. They set out to build a factory town along the Passaic River in New Jersey, named Paterson in honor of the state's governor. The venture failed over financing troubles, but its model of harnessing the strongest currents of a river, in proximity to ample natural resources, and near (but not in) a center of population for access to labor, was taken up by the leaders of America's Industrial Revolution. It helped to inspire the mill towns of New England, which housed the country's first large-scale mechanized factories and were, initially at least, committed to providing benevolent environments for workers—especially for that particular class of them called the mill girls. Beyond seeking rushing rivers to power their operations, these mills aimed for physical settings that might produce a content and thus more productive labor force.

Toward the turn of the twentieth century, social concerns about employees' living and working conditions in burgeoning industries led to a new generation of company towns. Among the most notable were Homestead, Pennsylvania, and Gary, Indiana—both massive and long-standing centers for the production of steel—and the short-lived Pullman, Illinois, the dream of railcar industrialist

George Pullman, who set out to provide, as we'll see in pages to come, an all-encompassing and tightly controlled environment for his workers.

Early in the twentieth century, employers built on the ideas of the City Beautiful and Garden City movements to create what they hoped were garden-like industrial communities. Noteworthy towns included Kohler, Wisconsin, founded in 1913 and named after the plumbing equipment manufacturer; Morgan Park, Minnesota (1917), built for a US Steel subsidiary; Tyrone, New Mexico (1917), created for the Phelps-Dodge Copper Mining Corporation; and Kistler, Pennsylvania (1918), built for the Mount Union Refractories Company.[3] All were located on open, undeveloped sites, with the underlying hope that, as a more favorable relationship was established between labor and living, larger towns would grow up around these company-established cores. Such towns became proving grounds for a generation of architects and planners such as John Nolan and Bertrand Grosvenor Goodhue. One result was the professionalization of town planning, a nascent discipline seen as necessary to overcoming chaotic urban growth.

At mid-twentieth century, the immediate predecessors of today's digital-age work environments appeared. These were the sprawling suburban corporate campuses laid out on spacious, well-landscaped grounds away from city centers, though tethered to circumferential urban highways. (See Figure 5.3.) Those campuses, like today's headquarters of Apple, Facebook, and Google, were not classic company towns. With the advent of ready personal mobility, companies no longer felt obliged to provide employees with housing and civic services. But they shared their predecessors' aim to craft environments with qualities adding to job satisfaction (which today include clattering on keyboards within "a candy-fueled daydream"). The goal in all eras has been better corporate performance. We can see some of these similarities, as well as what has changed, if we look more closely at some of the important company towns in American history.

The Lowell Experiment

By 1822, the proprietors of the Boston Manufacturing Company in Waltham, Massachusetts, determined to grow their business, were ready to give up on the feeble current of the Charles River. The company headed north to a more rapidly moving stretch of the Merrimac River near the Pawtucket Falls, with currents strong enough to power multiple mills, and soon an entire town. The company's founder, Francis Cabot Lowell, for whom the town is named, died too soon to see

5.3 A suburban corporate haven characteristic of the second half of the twentieth century. As a century earlier in Lowell for the "ladies of the loom," the suburban corporate campus was seen as a safe and attractive place for middle-class (white) women to pursue a career, though mostly limited to secretarial and clerical roles.

his experiment take shape at industrial scale. But it was Lowell's travels through early English textile-producing centers, and his adaptation of the power looms he witnessed there, that set in motion the initial mechanization of American industry.

Cotton-spinning enterprises had been operating since the 1790s in the Fall River and Pawtucket areas of Rhode Island, where Samuel Slater, an English immigrant, had assembled—from memory—a water-powered spinning frame equal to the ones he had worked on in England, to produce spindles of yarn. But the process to get from raw cotton to actual cloth still required two steps. The yarn produced by the spinning machines, which were simple enough for children to operate, had to be sent to nearby farms where families of weavers would convert it to cloth. Lowell's patenting of an American power loom enabled far more efficient production, all housed on company grounds.[4]

But who would operate these additional machines? Surplus labor was hard to find in farming country always in need of able hands, especially at planting and

5.4 A mill girl at work.

harvest times. Here, Alexander Hamilton had suggested a course of action: "It is worthy of particular remark," he wrote in his "Report on the Subject of Manufactures," presented to Congress in 1791, "that, in general, women and children are rendered more useful and the latter more early useful by manufacturing establishments, than they would otherwise be."[5]

Employing children in factories may have been cruel, but it answered the need for a new pool of labor. Farmers' children and, in particular, teenage girls—not being trained for the plow like their brothers—were only so much use on the farm. But their employment by industry was not uncontroversial. Few young women labored away from home, much less in factories, so it was essential to provide a safe setting for them.

Employers calculated that if they took care of these "Ladies of the Loom," as they were sometimes called, they would win their families' approval to employ them, and at the same time increase the girls' enthusiasm for the work. (See Figure 5.4.) For a brief period in Lowell and in other mill towns across New England, an unusually supportive interdependence was established. In exchange for long hours spent operating the looms, these young ladies earned an hourly salary—uncommon for women usually engaged in unpaid domestic labor—and were also supervised by protective matrons. They were housed and fed in adequate boardinghouses, offered schooling, social activities, and mandatory church services, and given access to a shop or two, plus reading rooms and performance spaces for their scarce leisure time. A literary journal, *The Lowell Offering*, was even published for a while, featuring contributions from these same ladies of the loom. This chapter's second epigraph, penned by the young lady with the lovely view from her window, appeared in an edition of that journal.[6] Describing the lives of these workers, historian John Reps even suggests that "female loom operators found themselves in an atmosphere more akin to a convent than a conventional industrial enterprise."[7] Lowell soon became a regular stop for European visitors seeking to understand the industrial energy of the young United States. After a visit in 1834, the French engineer and politician Michel Chevalier remarked on the probity of the thousands of young women employed at Lowell, as well as on the wages they earned compared to European women: "Lowell is not amusing," he wrote, "but it is neat, decent, peaceable, and sage."[8]

The mutually beneficial relationship between managers and workers did not last long. Working conditions were, in fact, far from healthy; these were twelve-to-fourteen-hour workdays amid horrendously loud and dangerous machines. The ventilation was miserable, causing the air to be filled with choking cotton and cloth particles. By the mid-1830s, a mere decade into the Lowell Experiment, managers' demands for greater productivity were being countered by mill girls' demands for shorter work days, better safety provisions, and more control over their personal lives—a lack of freedom being the downside of life in a convent. When economic downturns led management to reduce wages without cutting hours or improving working conditions, labor strikes followed, and efforts at unionizing began. It was inevitable that the early cohorts of mill girls, now more demanding, would be replaced by more desperate and, initially at least, less demanding new immigrants from Europe.

By the 1850s, Lowell was the largest industrial complex in the country, and there were similarly organized competitors in nearby towns such as Chicopee, Dover, Holyoke, Lawrence, and Manchester. But the idealism behind the "Lowell Experiment" had waned.[9] A dilemma of American industry had been exposed. Financial success and social betterment do not always go hand in hand. As long as Lowell was perceived to be both supporting the mill girls' personal growth and making a profit, the company was praised as an exemplar. But as soon as it appeared that profit depended on oppression, the enterprise was deemed un-American. Half a century later, George Pullman would repeat the mistake. (See Figure 5.5.)

The World's Most Perfect Town

At the 1896 Prague International Hygienic and Pharmaceutical Exposition, a vote was held to declare the world's most perfect town and the winner was Pullman, Illinois.[10] Twelve miles south of Chicago's Loop, this company town had been one of the more popular offsite attractions during the 1893 World's Columbian Exposition, thanks to a rail connection between the town and the fairgrounds provided by George Pullman's railcar company. But the designation of perfection came late. Those for whom Pullman was built hardly considered it perfect by 1896. The aura of the place had been greatly diminished in the few years since by a debilitating labor strike, begun by Pullman employees, which spread nationally before being quelled by federal troops. Two years after the Prague Exposition, ongoing disputes between George Pullman and his workers led the US Supreme Court to order the Pullman Palace Car Company to sell all its non-industrial properties, including the residential properties the company had built for employees.[11] The town that had been constructed to fulfill the utopian vision of George Pullman had been exposed as ill-suited for its em-

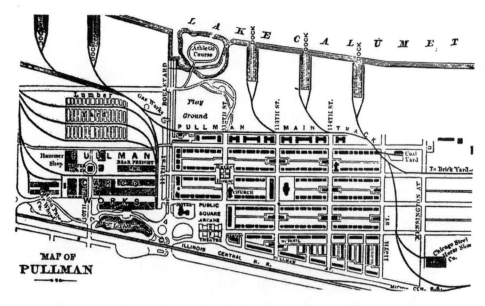

5.5 Plan of Pullman, Illinois: arrival by train at the man-made lake and administration building (which partially concealed the factories beyond), the public square and its shopping arcade leading to the well-kept residential areas.

ployee residents, the very people whom Pullman hoped would benefit from its meticulously conceived design.

Pullman's innovation, the "palace car," made travel by rail comfortable and affordable, and made its inventor wealthy and famous. *Pullman* became a byword for quality, emboldening Mr. Pullman to undertake the design of an entire town. Along with other industrialists of the time, he was concerned about the deplorable conditions in which people worked and lived, not least in his own burgeoning city of Chicago. Ironically, his concern arose partially out of a fear of labor unrest—precisely the problem that would arise from the conditions he created. He set out in 1880 to build a town where his company could grow, and part of the plan was for his workers to remain content and productive by living clean, sober, and moral lives. Multiple accounts from the time and an extensive photographic record testify that he did indeed create a remarkable physical place. It featured many civic and commercial facilities, parks and squares, and residential districts, all arranged as you would find in a long-established town. Part of the town's conceptual appeal lay in how a massive industrial concern seemed to fit within the familiar scale and charm of a small town.

The town was dubbed the "place where everything fits," and carefully planned to show off its ample town amenities. Even the arrival from Chicago was well choreographed. One disembarked from the train into a park-like setting. Across a man-made lake stood the company's impressive administration building with its tall clock tower, its size screening from view the less attractive factories beyond. Through a large glazed area in the administration building could be seen the famous Collis Engine, the most advanced machine of its era, on display to impress visitors with the sophistication and efficiency of the company. Immediately to the right of the lake, a town common was visible. Prominent buildings around its edges invited entry to the rest of the town. (See Figures 4.5 and 5.6.)

The town was perfect in appearance—and appearances were important to Mr. Pullman. He often spoke of "the commercial value of beauty," which for him seems to have meant order, cleanliness, and predictability as much as pleasant aesthetics. Upon the town's completion, he told receptive reporters, "I have faith in the educational and refining influences of beauty and beautiful, harmonious surroundings, and will hesitate at no expenditure to secure them." [12]

Pullman reached for perfection in design, but set out to manage the town "as a strictly business proposition." That would prove its Achilles' heel. In Pullman's matter-of-fact business mind, every aspect of the town needed to operate at a

5.6   Partial view of Pullman at the public square, c. 1890, looking like a real and charming town.

profit—not just the factory producing his palatial cars. Thus, when he lowered wages during an economic slowdown, he did not lower workers' rents—a cause of the infamous strike. At the same time, workers began to chafe under what felt like oppressive behavior control. There were dress codes, regular inspections of homes for cleanliness, and a prohibition on sizable gatherings. Any such loitering might be a prelude to protest. Public speeches or town meetings were not allowed, nor were independent newspapers. A theater was a cultural amenity the town offered, but Pullman himself selected the entertainment to make sure it was appropriately tasteful. Among the most resented restrictions in a town full of male workers was surely the shortage of bars. There was only one, to which foremen had first access and which had prices too high for most laborers, anyway. The town's lone church building was rarely used, because the various congregations could not afford its per-service rent. One minister described Pullman as a "relic of European serfdom."[13]

For a century, historians have debated whether Pullman was motivated by a calculating spirit of exploitation or by naive paternalism. Granting him the benefit of the doubt, he may have simply misunderstood human nature and how much resentment would be stirred up by such curbing of freedom. Business titans prior to Pullman (like the proprietors of New England mills) and since his day (such as the Disney leaders who greenlighted Celebration, Florida) tend to assume that business instincts can serve equally well in the creation and the management of communities. But business interests and community interests are rarely the same, and even less likely to cohere when the former seeks to govern the latter. The history of Pullman, Illinois, proves this, despite the town's impressive buildings—many of which remain standing in what has become a fine middle-class Chicago neighborhood. Ultimately, it was only Mr. Pullman's and not his laborers' idea of utopia.

Other company towns were built in the same era, but none with quite so domineering a personal vision. Soon, a reluctance developed on the owners' side to act as both employers and landlords, though nearby housing was still essential. Many industrialists shared Pullman's self-serving conclusion that it was the scale of urbanization—cities themselves—rather than the scale and processes of their industrial enterprises that proved "disruptive to health and morals." This belief reinforced more pragmatic reasons for leaving the city at the end of the nineteenth century: land became cheaper, assembly lines required horizontal layouts and thus larger property footprints, city congestion increased, opposition rose to the presence of noxious industries in settled areas; and people became more fearful of the "mobs," "slums," and epidemics they associated with life in close quarters. By mid-twentieth century, cities seemed inexorably headed for decline; many companies joined individuals in following the siren call of suburbanization.

Not Exactly an Industrial Utopia

No one ever considered Gary, Indiana, to be perfect, though its prideful founders had called it an industrial utopia. It was founded in 1906, some thirty miles southeast of Chicago, following the merger of the US Steel Corporation and Andrew Carnegie's steel empire, one of the largest consolidations in American history. The town's population expanded to 178,000 by 1960, and then retraction began with the decline of the American steel industry. Since the 1960s, the city's history has been dismal. Deprived of its economic purpose, Gary fell to eighty thousand by 2010 and, like other cities shedding residents, its demographics changed. Today, its African American population exceeds 80 percent. It is also among the poorest cities in America, and a third of its homes are unoccupied and dilapidated.

Not all of this can be blamed on its origins as a company town, though the shortsighted faith in the endurance of a single industry certainly did not help. Unlike in Pullman, and likely due to Pullman's demise, Gary's founders gave little thought to the design of the town. Company engineers laid out streets and blocks in the most expedient way. Few civic amenities were provided and, although a separate company to deal with housing was set up, owners were largely interested in selling lots to workers and speculators. The result was that, apart from some planned areas in the immediate vicinity of the massive steelworks, Gary became a virtual shantytown of poorly built housing for the successive waves of immigrants drawn to its jobs.[14] Though it was an astonishing industrial success (until 1960, that is), Gary never became as iconic a company town as the ones designed to create enviable work and living conditions. It was cheap and dirty, a place with only the loosest connection, if any at all, to utopian dreams. Since the 1960s, it has been an icon of the rust belt—polluted, obsolete, and abandoned. (See Figure 5.7.)

Future attempts at town-making would result from the reorganization of large companies into separate domains of production, research, and management, accommodating different categories of employees accordingly.

5.7   A characteristic view of Gary, Indiana, when steel was still being produced.

5.8   **Partial view of the General Motors Technical Center in Warren, Michigan,
miles away from Detroit.**

An Industrial Versailles

A half-century forward from Pullman and Gary, a new company-building venture captured the imagination of Americans. In the 1950s, General Motors' Technical Center in Warren, Michigan, was designed to concentrate the company's styling, research, and engineering development operations in a location away from Detroit. It was an ultramodern campus more than half a mile long, designed first by Eliel Saarinen and then by his son Eero, both visionary architects with reputations similar to Frank Gehry's today. Beyond its daily functions, the Tech Center—or Styling Center, as it was colloquially called—served for many years as the visual backdrop for GM's annual introduction of its new lines of cars, covered widely on television and in magazines. Just as Pullman's Palace Car became a symbol of democratized, comfortable communal travel, the Tech Center represented mid-century wonder, and the triumph of democratized mobility. (See Figure 5.8.)

As at Pullman, aesthetics were important. But at the Tech Center, the goal was not to produce an image of a town but to directly associate the design of the place with its research prowess and the style of its products. Pullman had promised an alternative to the problematic industrial city. The Tech Center was a means to associate cars with the sort of environment for which they were being made. The Tech Center's location, size, and streamlined expression represented a synthesis of the age—an era of outward spread and suburban dreams, amid mid-century disdain for "the inner city." An architectural periodical dubbed it the American Industrial Versailles.[15] Another enthusiastic writer pointed to Greek and Italian antecedents: "Just as the Acropolis was built to be contemplated by a man standing still, and Venice to be enjoyed from a drifting Gondola, the GM Technical Center should best flash by a Buick window at 35 mph."[16] No need to provide housing or civic functions there, though the location was twenty miles from Detroit. This was no town but a lifestyle manufacturer. Not the Center but its output was the stuff of utopia. Each year's new car models promised a new frontier just a ride away, in an even more streamlined machine.

The Tech Center offered an early example of a new way large corporations were reorganizing. Production and leadership functions no longer needed to be contiguous. Indeed, upper management preferred them not to be, as different classes of workers were involved in them. Among the consequences of this reorganization would be greater separation between "blue collar" and "white collar" labor, and the rise of a new format for capitalism.

Pastoral Capitalism

Louise Mozingo's history of suburban corporate campuses, offices, and research parks traces the modern corporation's move, along with upwardly mobile citizens, to the bucolic suburban landscape.[17] In the decades prior to the rise of Silicon Valley, this happened along Boston's Route 128, for example, heralded as "America's Technology Highway." Along that new highway, actually a segment of an interstate designed to bypass central Boston, Digital Equipment Corporation, Wang Laboratories, Lotus, Raytheon, Data General, Computervison, GTE, and Analog Devices, among others, were spawned. These were the digital-age parents of Microsoft and Apple. A main advantage for these companies was proximity to their labor pool, already nestled in nearby suburban Edens, who would no longer need to commute downtown. Between the mid-1950s and 1980s, Boston's population decreased by some 250,000 people, most of whom moved to suburban areas around and beyond Route 128. Over the same period, the number of companies along Route 128 increased from one hundred to over twelve hundred.[18]

Mozingo describes and illustrates a host of remarkable corporate enclaves set amid lovely meadows, streams, lakes, and woods, first adjacent to east coast cities and eventually across the country. These were impressive places (Leo Marx's *The Machine in the Garden* comes to mind) designed for a particular white-collar (and mostly white), car-owning demographic who wanted to enjoy working sequestered from both home and urban stress. For a future generation, such isolation would become dull and tiresome, but it wasn't to those whose sensibilities had been shaped by Depression, war, and inner-city decay.

For Mozingo, three of the corporate building projects that defined the era were the 1954 General Foods Headquarters in White Plains, New York, some twenty miles north of Manhattan; the 1957 Connecticut General Insurance Company near Bloomfield, Connecticut; and the 1960s Deere & Company Administrative Center in Moline, Illinois. The Deere complex was perhaps the purest archetype, taking brilliant advantage of a beautiful bucolic site, and further enhancing it by a remarkable landscape design and striking modern architecture. The main building actually straddles a ravine and overlooks a lake. In many of these corporate campuses, the relationship between the landscape and the buildings is the most distinctive aspect of the workplace, and often the most appreciated by users. Recall that mill girl's delight of a lovely view, now seen from an office window.

The location of the Deere complex showed that corporate campuses could exist beyond the peripheries of tumultuous, slum-weary, large cities. Moline was a town of thirty-two thousand people at mid-century and hasn't grown substantially since. Today, it is considered part of the larger Quad Cities metro area region, of which the population is only around 360,000. Moline is 60 miles from Iowa City, 150 miles from Chicago, and 260 miles from St. Louis. Deere, a famous maker of agricultural machinery, was first established in Moline in 1848, having located there for the waterpower and transportation advantages offered by the Mississippi River. Over a century later, when it sorely needed new office facilities, it resisted the mid-twentieth century trend of relocating headquarters to the edges of a major urban centers. Having chosen to remain in Moline, however, its president during the 1950s insisted that a truly distinctive design would be required to attract talent to the company, and to brand it for global

markets. Euro Saarinen, already at work on the GM Tech Center, was hired and he retained Hideo Sasaki to design the landscape. Following Saarinen's untimely death, Kevin Roche completed later phases. Such design "A teams" were responsible for installing many of these corporate machines into their pastoral gardens. These bucolic campuses created the counterpoint to the image of modern corporate America: the downtown glass skyscraper.[19] As the twenty-first century unfolds, however, a reaction is taking place and a third corporate image is emerging.

A Partial Reversal of the Corporate Diaspora

Late in the nineteenth century, the standard response to stress-inducing urban concentration on the part of a George Pullman was to move the company away. By the mid-twentieth century, this same impulse led to the popularity of the "business park," or corporate "campus" set in pastoral surroundings. Today, a

5.9 The "Spheres," an amenity for employees and an emerging local landmark at the recently completed Amazon corporate headquarters in downtown Seattle.

move back to the city is underway. Suburban business parks are being vacated as the appeal shifts to urban "innovation clusters." Corporate America has been discovering how hip, dynamic, entrepreneurial-focused, and fun cities can be—or at least select portions of them can be.

As Amazon, for example, gained scale in Seattle, it determined that its headquarters belonged downtown rather than in suburban Bellevue. Its three skyscrapers, and more underway, surround a spectacular greenhouse-like structure that invites staff to descend, unwind, and interact. A *Seattle Times* headline captured the intent: "Lush Nature Paradise to Adorn $4 Billion Urban Campus."[20] (See Figure 5.9.) Staffers can still experience nature, but now they do so indoors rather than in crafted suburban vistas. Timber giant Weyerhaeuser has opted, too, to leave its striking woodland headquarters south of Seattle for downtown digs.

Boston has welcomed General Electric, a move the *Wall Street Journal* reported with an eye to the changing times: "General Electric Co. will relocate its

5.10   2015 Local advertisement in support of GE's decision to relocate its suburban executive headquarters to Boston. The move has yet to be a game changer as GE has struggled with substantial downsizing since its announced move.

headquarters from leafy suburban Connecticut to Boston's busy waterfront."[21] (See Figure 5.10.) It's a representative move; GE's headquarters has migrated several times to reflect the trends we have followed in this chapter. Its leafy, modern, Connecticut headquarters was the result of the 1970s relocation from one of Pastoral Capitalism's early examples, the famous Electronics Park in Syracuse, New York. And that was a 1940s move from GE's massive, concentrated Schenectady Works, an industrial icon from early in the twentieth century. Current business setbacks at the company have, for the moment, stopped the construction of its new urban headquarters.

Connecting Boston's future to its history of textile and shoe industries, athletic shoe giants Converse, New Balance, and Reebok have each committed to downtown offices, the latter planning a move from a corporate headquarters built less than twenty years earlier in the nearby suburb of Canton. Meanwhile, in Chicago, that symbol of the suburban commercial strip McDonald's has similarly relocated its headquarters to downtown, after many decades in Oak Brook, Illinois.

Why such shifts? The CEO of the chemical company Chemours offered a succinct answer: "They don't want to be confined to a building with a cafeteria, and be next door to a shopping center."[22] By *they,* he is referring to today's generation of college-educated, culturally active, aspirational seekers of exciting careers and lifestyles more readily available in urban contexts. A corporate move to a lively city center is thus in a way strategic. GE's move, for example, involves just several hundred executives and supporting staff, not its legions of mid-level managers, much less the rest of its thousands of employees.

In a way, then, things have not changed as much as might appear. As in the mill towns of New England, the desire to find a proper environment for a particularly valued group of workers precipitates near-utopian dreaming. After two centuries in which employers and employees alike sought ideal work environments away from town, the aura of a bustling city center has become this era's idea of a productive environment, at least for executive labor. The long-term demographic implications of this trend have yet to be understood.

The return of a corporate headquarters to an urban location not only helps but also impacts that city, as Seattle is discovering with Amazon's arrival. In 2017, when Amazon announced its intention to build a second headquarters site and said it was open to considering any location, 238 cities submitted their cases for why Amazon should choose them. Knowing that the prospect of up to fifty thousand jobs was awfully tantalizing, Amazon's challenge to those cities was a sort of "what are you offering us?"[23] Confident cities should simply have responded "plenty," and turned the question around: How would your presence, Amazon, enhance our public realm, benefit our parks and open spaces, help reduce and not add to local congestion, encourage diversity and opportunity in careers, and assist in the provision of affordable housing—since such qualities will benefit your employees and their new urban environment as well? New versions of company-dominated towns are not needed. Rather, what would be most helpful to cities would be more corporate commitment to and involvement in expanding civic enterprise.

6.1 A home under construction and a portal to the American dream.

6

"GRACE DWELLING IN IT": THE ROMANCE OF THE SUBURB

> The suburban ideal has always been utopian—presenting an escape
> from the more unpleasant and sometimes noxious aspects of city life to
> a pastoral setting located close enough to urban amenities to enjoy the
> pleasures of the city. With the very best of the two worlds of town and
> countryside, one is not forced to choose to be either a country cousin
> or a city cousin. Instead one can become a suburbanite—a compelling
> new vision of ideal family living that began drawing Americans away
> from the center of cities as early as the 1830s.
>
> GREAT AMERICAN SUBURBS, 2008

SUCH A CHARMING TESTIMONIAL to the suburb as this chapter's epigraph offers is not much heard of late. Having metastasized during the second half of the twentieth century into *suburbia*, the characteristic form of settlement across metropolitan America, it is too familiar and ordinary to be appreciated as something special, much less utopian. As Yi-Fu Tuan put it back in the 1970s, when broader impacts of suburbanization were beginning to be felt: "Suburb is an ideal . . . On the other hand, 'suburbia,' a word of much recent coinage, appears to mock this ideal."[1] Far more vitriolic commentary abounds. Consider James Howard Kunstler's 2001 condemnation: "This nation's massive suburban build-out was an orgy of misspent energy and material resources that squandered our national wealth" and led to "cultural destruction . . . especially the loss of knowledge, tradition, skill, custom, and vernacular wisdom in the art of city-making that was thrown into the dumpster of history."[2]

A far different view—and hope—existed for much of the nineteenth and well into the twentieth century. There were many expressions of affection for the idea of the suburb, as we can see in a sampling of five commentaries, spanning a forty-year period. In 1859, Sidney George Fisher wrote:

> The advantages are so obvious that this villa and cottage life has become quite a passion and is producing a complete revolution in our habits. It is dispersing the people of the city over the surrounding country, introducing thus among them, ventilation, cleanliness, space, healthful pursuits, and the influences of natural beauty, the want of which are the sources of so much evil, moral and physical, in large towns.[3]

In 1866, a resident of Llewellyn Park described it as a near-magical place:

> [where] the occupant can meet, almost as it were by enchantment, the calm quiet of the primeval forest, and by reflection and contemplation. . . . is fitted to wrestle with all the rasping friction and incessant care of a busy city life.[4]

The great park designer Frederick Law Olmsted, in 1869, had high praise and anticipation for the suburb:

> The most attractive, the most refined and the most soundly wholesome forms of domestic life, and the best application of the arts of civilization to which mankind has yet attained.[5]

In 1873, one writer summed things up fairly neatly:

> The controversy that is sometimes brought, as to which offers the greater advantage, the country or the city, finds a happy answer in the suburban idea.[6]

And in 1899, chronicler of city growth Adna F. Weber, was very optimistic about these peripheral developments:

> The "rise of the suburbs" . . . furnishes the solid basis of a hope that the evils of city life, so far as they result from overcrowding, may in large part be removed.[7]

Hard as it might be to accept, today's widespread suburban landscapes, often associated with conventional or boring lifestyles, social balkanization, and environmental indifference, were once considered a progressive, radical idea. They might even be seen as a utopian departure from millennium-old ideas of what constituted a city, how future cities ought be planned, and how they should engage their natural surroundings. The suburb, as its nineteenth-century supporters suggest, was a revelation for those troubled about the long-term viability of the rapidly industrializing city—and being swamped by congestion, coal smoke, human and animal waste, and cholera epidemics. Weber, in *The Growth of Cities in the Nineteenth Century*, quotes what used to be a common belief: "There is then a permanent conflict between the needs of industry and the needs of humanity. Industry says men must aggregate," sociologist Charles H. Cooley claimed. "Humanity says they must not, or if they must, let it be only during working hours and let the necessity not extend to their wives and children."[8]

The Garden City idea, introduced in Great Britain at the turn of the twentieth century, brought further hope that the spread of the suburb could provide reconciliation between town and country. Ebenezer Howard, in a book that would ignite the Garden City movement, describes the "town-country magnet" that must be constructed so that the two can be enjoyed together.[9] (See Figure 6.2.) This belief in a "middle state," or a "middle landscape" as later commentators named it, has an extensive history of its own (as introduced in Chapter 1). In 1921, William E. Smythe portrayed this state in a simplistic yet socially minded way in "Getting the Rural Savor into City Life" (a clue), a chapter in the book *City Homes on Country Lanes* (a second clue):

> Those comfortable folk, who do as they please because they have the price, have decided that the way to achieve the utmost satisfaction is to be *of* the city, but not *in* the city. They are distinctly metropolitan in their business interests, and in a part of their social interests, as well; but they have learned that the way to get the most out of the city is to come to it each morning, after a restful night among the sights and sounds of the country; and that the way to get the most out of the country is to go to it each night after a strenuous day in town, to discover its beauties afresh, with a little shock of joyful surprise.
>
> My proposition is this: If that is a good thing for some of the people, and particularly for those who can have the best there is in life, then it is a good thing for vastly more of the people who would do it if they could. And to make it possible for them to do it is a part, and a very urgent part, of the job awaiting the builders of America.[10]

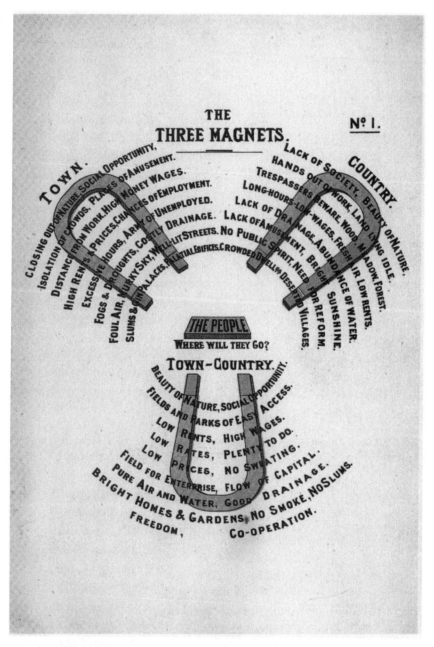

6.2 Ebenezer Howard's three magnets of town, country and town-country, the latter well worth reading as one of the seminal articulations of what later came to be referred to as the middle landscape.

The initial attraction of the suburb was to be this recurring disengagement from the city, a place apart. The appeal was in spending evenings and weekends in a healthful setting amidst nature, away from the toxic air and "rasping frictions" endured during days of toil in the city. According to Lewis Mumford, it was intended for "a self-centered life, in which private fantasy and caprice would have license to express themselves openly, in short, to withdraw like a monk and live like a prince."[11] The economist John Kenneth Galbraith also understood the suburb's appeal and who stood to enjoy it first: "From the earliest days of the Industrial City there was a strong desire by the few who could afford it to escape its smoke and grime and even more its unlovely landscape. So with the Industrial City came the suburb. . . . These settlements had no central function—they did not rule, sell, or make. They were places where people found space."[12]

Ample space, yes, but more important than elbow room or even fresh air, that space enabled citizens to fashion an expanded family nest—perhaps not the 160-acre quarter-section planned by Jefferson and promised to homesteaders, but a home and garden nonetheless. What could be more enticing for crowded city populations? Space, greenery, and a proper home! A family's dwelling, "having a domestic spirit of grace dwelling in it, should become the church of childhood, the table and hearth, a holy site." So preached Horace Bushnell back in 1864, describing an ideal that would ultimately become part of the American Dream.[13]

Bushnell was a Congregational minister, theologian, and a well-known but controversial promoter of religious liberalism. He advocated for a measure of independent thinking outside of church teachings, best nurtured, he believed, through a wholesome family life in a proper place of dwelling. The Congregationalists, originally called "Independents" (having broken from the orthodoxies of the Church of England) were responsible for the arrival of the Separatists of Plymouth Colony and the Puritans of Massachusetts Bay. These were the very groups whose covenanted communities helped inspire the later admiration for the small town, which then served as inspiration for some of the early suburban estates—with these viewed by some today as a model to wean Americans from suburban sprawl. It has been a fascinating progression, as explored in Chapter 4. A home on one's own plot of land has always been the nucleus of the suburban ideal. However, a less noble aspect of the genesis of the suburb was what historian Daniel J. Boorstin calls the intent to "stratify." Early suburbs (and

6.3 A young family in front of their newly purchased Levittown home.

many since) provided islands of homogeneity, where a family, in Boorstin's words, "could hope to live an artificial, antiseptic idyll, untroubled by any not their own 'kind.'"[14] (See Figure 18.5.)

Let's move ahead a full century to the great post–World War II expansion of the suburban landscape, during the construction of the Levittowns and their emulators. Looking at that young family proudly standing in front of its newly acquired, modest home, does not Bushnell's "church of childhood" ring true? Even more so, perhaps, as by mid-twentieth century such a holy site was becoming available to just about all (white) Americans. Within new homes were modern luxuries such as refrigerators, washers, driers, and even televisions— Mr. Levitt sometimes threw them in for free. Americans must have nodded in agreement with young Dorothy clicking her heels in the beloved *Wizard of Oz*: "There's no place like home. There's no place like home. There's no place like home." (See Figures 3.6 and 6.3.)

A Place to Withdraw

Being able to enjoy a respite from town at a comfortable place of retreat has long been an advantage enjoyed by the three P's: the powerful, the privileged, and the prosperous. Roman emperors had their summer villas away from the capital, as did kings and popes away from their seats of power. Landed gentry depended on ownership of country estates for wealth and prestige and town homes for urban pleasure, business proximity, and social interaction. The merchant classes, in their turn, sought country estates of their own, or at least some sort of stake outside the world of commerce and business. And so the modern suburb began.

Settlements at the periphery of the polis have carried positive and negative associations across history. There were those privileged few who owned grand villas outside of city walls with property enough to support country pleasures. But there were also the excluded and the rejected, forbidden from entering the medieval city, clustered in shacks at the base of its walls. In *Bourgeois Utopias,* Robert Fishman cites an *Oxford English Dictionary* definition of "suburbe" as originally meaning a "place of inferior, debased, and especially licentious habits of life."[15] Kenneth Jackson begins his masterful history of the suburb, *Crabgrass Frontier,* with a chapter entitled "Suburbs as Slums," which explains their premodern status outside the privileges of *civitas.* Yet the epigram Jackson chooses to open the chapter, from a 539 BC clay tablet, describes the beauty of a place with the benefit of proximity to Babylon, but free of its noise and dust.[16]

The privileged could partake of town and country, while those with few privileges were kept on either side of city walls. Heathens, itinerant beggars, suspicious travelers, and the diseased were barred from entry, while many poor folks were held within with few other places to go. This all changed with the removal of city walls, and the expansion in the post-feudal era of what we now call the middle classes, who sought the amenities they saw the rich enjoying. If not expansive country estates, they wanted access to healthier, more natural settings— and in time, new means of transportation brought these within reach.

Historians point to the suburb's modern origins not in America, but at the peripheries of London, Manchester, and other dense and dirty cities in the vanguard of the Industrial Revolution in Britain. The extraordinary evolution of the American suburb, and its ultimate distinction, has been in the continuous expansion of access to those who wished to be so accommodated—even to the point, as we shall see with Frank Lloyd Wright's "Broadacre" in Chapter 12, that everyone would be invited to partake of the benefits.

But let's return to the mid-nineteenth-century archetype to more fully appreciate the pioneering suburban enterprises. This warrants an introduction to a remarkable publication. No future account of the rise of the suburb will be free of debt to the magnificent 2014 compilation by Robert Stern, David Fishman, and Jacob Tilove, tellingly entitled *Paradise Planned: The Garden Suburb and the Modern City.*[17] Across 1,079 pages and some three thousand illustrations, the authors present the evolution of the suburban idea with extraordinary detail and optimism.

It is important to note that the specific purpose of *Paradise Planned* is to separate the history of the suburb from a history of suburban sprawl—thus the use of *paradise* and *garden* in the book's title. Here the garden suburb, not the suburbanization that followed, is introduced as the humane planning response to the inhumane conditions caused by massive urbanization across the nineteenth and early twentieth centuries. The value of the garden suburb was lost, according to the authors, under the massive spread of suburbia. So it is critical to recover, they claim, both the original idea and the histories of the communities it inspired. The garden suburb can again serve, as the authors recommend, as the positive component of urbanization it once was. The book's very last sentence positions the garden suburb as holding "the key to the future of our cities."[18] Even if one disagrees with the manifesto to redeploy suburbia's antecedents, or sees the book as just loving obituary for the passing of our suburban century, *Paradise Planned* positively engulfs the reader with appreciation for the archetype.

While there is a tendency to think of the garden suburb as largely an Anglo-American tradition, *Paradise Planned* unveils its global reach. The breadth of examples discussed is mind boggling. One encounters John Nash's Regent Park in London and the French *Le Vesinet*; Beverly Hills and Coral Gables; Ebenezer Howard's diagrams and Hampstead Garden Suburb; Lowell and Manchester in New England, as compared to the later Pullman, Illinois; a host of German modernist *siedlungs* from the 1920s and Italian *città giardinos*; Robert Owen's utopian *phalansteries* (the huge building complexes proposed by Charles Fourier for people to live and work in harmony); Walter Burly Griffin's Australian Canberra and Lutyen's Delhi; Gary, Indiana, and Claude Ledoux's ideal city of Chaux; the "private places" of St. Louis; and of course, Seaside and Celebration, Florida. Among the earliest illustrations is a lovely aerial of the Royal Crescent at Bath, England. (See Figure 1.6.) Among the last is a photograph of Walt Disney in front of a giant plan of his proposed Epcot Center. (See Figure 14.1.) That is enormous latitude to convince the reader of the power and spread of the garden suburb idea.

Let's focus more narrowly here on five seminal American examples, whose utopian traces are visible during a visit even today.

Passing through the gates into the still exclusive environs of Llewellyn Park, New Jersey, one is transported right back to the archetype. (See Figure 6.4.) One immediately feels that sense of retreat from cacophony, no longer from the chaotic urbanism of the Industrial Revolution, but from today's endless northeastern New Jersey sprawl. As Richard Guy Wilson has explained, several rather remarkable, overlapping strands of idealism drove the founding of Llewellyn Park, begun in the 1850s and generally considered the first fully planned suburb. These included Swedenborgianism, Transcendentalism, Fourierism, and the general preference for nature over a too-rapidly urbanizing civilization that swirled among American intellectuals at mid-nineteenth century.

Llewellyn Haskill, a prosperous businessman and member of the Perfectionism sect, or Swedenborgian Church, was fascinated with that swirl of Romanticist thought. Within his social circle were luminaries such as Washington Irving, William Cullen Bryant, Thomas Cole, and Andrew Jackson Downing. He was certainly an acquaintance of Frederick Law Olmsted, whose Central Park project he supported. As founder of these four hundred acres of verdant hills in West Orange, in creative partnership with the architect

6.4   A postcard view of the entrance to Llewlyn Park: the sense of entering a special realm apparent.

6.5   A typical street scene in Riverside, Illinois, with the streets slightly depressed to create the illusion of a continuous lawn from property to property. Frank Lloyd Wright's Conley House is at right.

Alexander Jackson Davis, he sat out to build an Eden for his family—and also those fellow members of his class of businessmen who were similarly enlightened by Romanticism and possessed the means to enjoy the experiment. Earlier, Downing had expressed this group's feelings well: "When smiling lawns and tasteful cottages begin to embellish a country, we know that order and culture are established."[19]

Consider the words of an original resident who described Llewellyn Park in its early days as full of "long-haired men and short-haired women."[20] Back in 1857, that observation would hardly have recommended the place to someone mindful of convention. It is a reminder of the distance we have come when we consider the suburb an icon of conformity.

Now read Frederick Law Olmsted, not on the subject of New York's Central Park or his other magnificent park systems, but writing about Riverside, Illinois, his first and most complete venture in laying out an entire community. (See Figure 6.5.) In 1869, Olmsted and his partner Calvert Vaux were retained to prepare what today would be called a large residential subdivision. It was located approximately nine miles east of Chicago's downtown, along a rail line from downtown to Quincy, Illinois. One of Olmsted's first decisions was to set aside some seven hundred of the sixteen hundred acres for parks and carriageways. Then, although there were no topographic impediments to extending the great grid of Chicago, he rejected that grid and instead laid out a curvilinear street pattern, as if carefully following an undulating terrain. The plan virtually mirrors the layout of Cambridge's Mount Auburn Cemetery, which is set on a hillside, and whose popularity earlier in the century led to calls for the creation of public parks, as Chapter 8 will describe. In his report to the Riverside Improvement Company that had engaged them, Olmsted and Vaux emphasized that the plan of a suburb should enrich not just its residents' private lives but their "harmonious association and co-operation" in a community. "The fact that the families dwelling within a suburb enjoy much in common, and all the more enjoy it because it is in common, the grand fact, in short, that they are christians, loving one another, and not Pagans, fearing one another, should be everywhere manifest in the completeness, and choiceness, and beauty of the means they possess of coming together, of being together, and especially of recreating and enjoying them together on common ground, and under common shades."[21] (See Figures 6.5 and 6.6.)

Olmsted went to the extreme of lowering the elevation of the streets by some two feet, so that from the living rooms of homes facing each other across those streets, the street itself would give way to the illusion of continuous and uninterrupted green lawn. The astonishing goal of removing boundaries between public and private realms, at least perceptually, across a community made up of hundreds of independent properties, is as radical an idea as any found among America's communitarian utopias.

Now let's stroll past the impressive gates into Westmoreland or Portland Place in St. Louis. The city is still struggling in the aftermath of urban renewal, but here we can experience a magical walling out of the world as if it were still 1888. (See Figure 6.7.) The original intention of these enclaves' wealthy residents, writes one historian, was "to exclude from their line of sight and smell all that was unpleasant in city living. The noise and smoke of industry; the swarming masses of the poor; the stifling heat of the treeless downtown streets: the risk of epidemic disease—all these could be avoided, or at least minimized, by distance and by enforced isolation."[22] These were not intended as an everyman utopia.

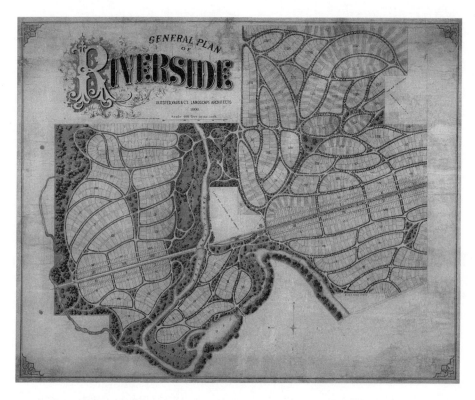

6.6   Plan of Riverside, Illinois. Compare to the plan of Mount Auburn Cemetery (see Figure 8.5).

St. Louis, located on bluffs just south of the confluence of the Missouri and Mississippi Rivers, and thus in command of continental river trade, grew from a population of fewer than five thousand in 1830 to a city of nearly six hundred thousand by 1900. It was destined to be the capital of America's heartland and, as its nickname claims, the "gateway to the West"—or at least it was until Chicago cast its lot with the railway rather than river transport as shaper of the future. As in burgeoning cities anywhere, St. Louis's growth attracted both rich industrialists and the supporting laboring classes. The former wished for a certain distance from the latter, and began to build a series of "private places." Between 1851 and the first decade of the twentieth century, more than fifty such private streets were laid out.

Many of these were developed under the direction of city surveyor and planner Julius Pitzman, who championed them as a means to control property values and uses in an era prior to municipal zoning. The goal was also, presum-

6.7   View of Westmorland Place, one of the Private Places of St. Louis, with a
neighboring Private Place at right.

ably, to protect the interests and gracious living standards of their inhabitants.
Many of these private places did not survive the tribulations of the twentieth
century, but some regained their status. As they did originally, they still represent
stability, land value, affluence, security, and control—the last being particularly
important for residents precisely because the city overall is so hard to control.
Yes, these were and remain gated enclaves, reserved for those few able to gain
admission. Yet, it is worth reminding critics of ordinary twentieth century suburban subdivisions that they were the means to break through the walls of exclusivity and grant access to the same conditions to people of more modest means.

Drive into Roland Park, within the city limits of Baltimore but removed
from the narrow row houses and largely treeless streets that characterize most of
the city's inner neighborhoods. It was developed as a residential enclave along a
streetcar line in the 1890s. A 1903 essay in *House & Garden* says that it "offers to
dwellers . . . the boon of detached houses without any sacrifice of proximity to
places of business and amusement."[23] The houses were not meant for just anyone. Among the deed restrictions imposed on owners was a minimum investment
in the construction cost of homes: $5,000 for homes lining Roland Avenue, the
main street, and $3,000 elsewhere. The typical investment was far more, reach-

6.8   A Roland Park street scene, the 1904 photograph labeled "the perfect street section."

ing $24,000 (over $600,000 in today's dollars) for houses boasting two or three bathrooms, a rather impressive hygienic achievement for the times.[24]

At the bottom of a 1904 photograph of Roland Park, someone has penciled in an annotation: "the perfect street section." (See Figure 6.8.) Indeed, as one peeks into this scene and sees the obvious care given to the design of the public streetscape and overall landscape, created under the direction of F. L. Olmsted, Jr., it is clear why the place would be called Roland *Park*. We can also see that the high initial cost of development was not only in the interests of class exclusivity (always present where there is insistence on minimum investments). The place was meant to be a park-like haven in contrast to the city, not an extension of it.

Now take the Long Island Rail Road's Main Line from Penn Station to Forest Hills Gardens, and you will reach the most complete, the most theatrically organized, and for many the most beautiful of all garden suburbs. From an elevated train platform, one descends to a plaza—Station Square—defined by a few shops and marked by an eight-story, campanile-like building, originally and even now an inn with rooms for rent. Walk under an arched pedestrian bridge connected to the campanile, and arrive (again, like Alice stepping through the looking glass) at a miniature central park surrounded by the most impressive of the residential structures. These are apartments, yet they are expressed as grand residences. (See Figures 6.9 and 6.10.) The rest of the "homes," ranging from single-family structures all the way to buildings with twelve separate units, are spread out along gently curvilinear streets beyond the central green. The sense of arrival in a very special place is orchestrated beautifully. The German Tudor architectural motif, courtesy of prominent architect Grosvenor Atterbury, lends a romantic European elegance and is carried forth throughout much of the town. An atmosphere of graceful living is further enhanced by the extensive and highly decorative streetscape elements—garden walls, fancy lighting, entry gates, hedges, nicely paved sidewalks, and a forest-like, continuous tree canopy— courtesy of Olmsted, Jr., once again, the planner and landscape architect, as he was for Roland Park.

A 1914 issue of *House Beautiful* quotes appreciative comments by residents. "It is a fairyland . . . it is all attractive," says one. Another adds: "It has a sense of mellowness, of repose and quiet, of sunshine and pleasure, which is contagious." And still another: "There is here a contented spirit which is catching. . . . The air is fragrant . . . it is as clean as a new pin."[25] In 1914, in the vicinity of the nation's largest city, neither clean air nor places of repose were easy to come by. The development was a venture of the Russell Sage Foundation, founded in 1907 for the "improvement of social and living conditions in the United States." It was, however, less a philanthropic project in itself than an attempt to use the financial means of the foundation to produce a better prototype for development, and to prove that substantial investment in architecture and landscape could be profitable. "We would like to set an example to the growing suburban districts of New York and other cities," wrote Sage Foundation vice president Robert Dee Forest, "of how the thing can be done tastefully and at the same time with due regard for profit."[26] Absorbing his father's lessons, Olmsted, Jr. added:

> Whereas the ordinary land-company will put upon the market only the same old standard article in the way of city lots that is already selling successfully in the vicinity, the Sage Foundation Homes Company is willing to risk something by introducing to some degree what may be regarded as novelties . . . which if successful will be copied by others and raise the general standard, but which are not sufficiently certain in their

6.9 Just inside the entrance into Forest Hills Gardens, with the train station in the background.

appeal to induce the average real estate man to try the experiment on his own account."[27]

It is a perspective on community-making still worth heeding. Not many followed the Sage Foundation strategy, but its success was quickly proven by rising real-estate values. The initial goal had been to provide a well-designed environment for middle-class New Yorkers—which was why so many of the dwelling units were in multi-family structures—but "the Gardens" soon become an enclave of the well-to-do.

The brilliant conception that is Forest Hills Gardens was never matched. In far less distinguished guises, of course, the suburb spread till it eventually became today's unromantic sprawl. It underwent a transformation from a special place at city's edge, tethered to the adjacent city's society and economic fortunes, to becoming ordinary. But for a period of time between its status as "a

6.10   Some of the multi-family housing in Forest Hills Gardens, but maintaining an iconography of domesticity, as if the individual units were just a part of a generous and graceful home.

utopia for the few" to its relegation to undistinguished commonplace, it was on its way to becoming a utopia for the many. Chapter 12 focuses further on that period of the suburb's legacy.

The Contemporary Case against Suburbia

To recognize why the suburb as a utopia for the many was inevitably a short-lived idea, it is useful to review the five main lines of critique against today's suburban landscape. Let's begin with aesthetics, one of the oldest critiques, if not always acknowledged as such. Recall the folk songs of the 1960s about "ticky-tacky" houses, and Ogden Nash's 1932 parody of a classic Joyce Kilmer poem: "I think I shall never see / A billboard lovely as a tree. / Perhaps, unless the billboards fall, / I'll never see a tree at all." While there is a trace of ecological concern in this doggerel, most critics assailed the physical environments produced by low-density settlement because they were untidy, generic, boring, and ugly. Some conjured up images of the human body sprawling across and disfiguring nature. It is no surprise that when the New Urbanists began to promote their suburban designs, one of the most effective strategies was simply to produce

6.11 A rendering of a new urbanist community, seeking to evoke characteristics of a traditional town, rather than that of a typical suburban subdivision.

images of prettier environments—recalling the charms but never the limitations of classic small towns.

Such Currier & Ives–like projections onto the future were somewhat ironic given that those old lithographs were known for portraying vernacular traditions that would never return. But they helped persuade some that the character of places vanished could be recreated to replace the visual chaos of the suburban landscape. (See Figure 6.11.) The theory that dressing up suburbs in town-like iconography can actually diminish sprawl remains, however, unproven.

A second argument against the suburb is sociological. As early as the 1950s, American writers such as journalist William H. Whyte and novelist John Keats portrayed suburban life as conformist, drab, and isolationist.[28] In the decades since, such arguments have expanded to suggest correlations between suburbanization and deepening social apathy and intolerance of neighbors of different classes, races, or political views. Concerns are voiced about alienated suburban youth, dependent on their parents to get anywhere; about the enslavement of parents, especially moms, to their chauffeur roles; and about the isolation of grandparents who can no longer drive themselves. Apprehension about the isolation of suburban stay-at-home moms has gradually shifted to worries about the difficulties of balancing child-rearing and careers across a dispersed landscape. Studies such as Robert Putnam's *Bowling Alone* also imply that lives spent in sprawled, disconnected America discourage group activities, although Putnam stops short of claiming a causal link between sprawl and a decline in civic engagement.[29]

The third argument against suburbia is that sprawl leads to boring lifestyles. It is a complaint we hear from dyed-in-the-wool urbanists, aging Baby Boomers, and current Millennials, many of them raised in the suburbs, who are pining for more convivial surroundings. Precisely what proportions of these cohorts feel this way is hard to establish, but various informal housing preference surveys, along with the recent rise in demand for downtown housing, provide considerable anecdotal evidence. A century ago, rural populations were lured to cities by economic opportunity. Today's young adults, less inclined to follow in the footsteps of their suburbia-pioneering parents, are drawn to the cultural and social stimulation, in addition to the career choices, of the city. Think of the sultry allure of New York in the popular television series *Sex and the City*, filmed from 1998 to 2004 and continuously airing in syndication since. By comparison, where is the action along perimeter highways once the day's work of inventing technologies or investing venture capital is done? Among many young and still active older Americans, the energy of the city has become intoxicating.

The fourth case against sprawl, more prevalent than many would admit, is self-protection—a desire to raise the drawbridge, often on the part of people who have just arrived at the castle themselves. Outwardly it is waged as a campaign, mostly in affluent communities, against the loss of open space and growing traffic congestion. Its underlying stance is less noble, constituting some variation of "don't harm my lifestyle by replicating the locational decisions

I made a few years earlier; your arrival will ruin my lovely neighborhood." *New York Times* columnist David Brooks, the author of *Bobos in Paradise,* notes this about exurban voters: "Even though they often just moved to these places, ex-urbanites are pretty shameless about trying to prevent more people from coming after them."[30]

This is understandable enough; no one wants their access to nature obstructed or commute to work lengthened. However, such a "not in my backyard" attitude only pushes development further out. The new developments simply "leapfrog" the areas resisting growth to further enlarge the area of sprawl.

The fifth critique is environmental and is the most compelling. This critique has slowly, too slowly for environmentalists, gained influence since the late 1960s and early 1970s—the era when Rachel Carson's *Silent Spring,* Ian McHarg's *Design With Nature,* the first Earth Day, and publications such as *The Limits to Growth* and *The Costs of Sprawl* helped arouse broader concern about human abuses of the environment.[31] Although worldwide environmental degradation has many causes, sprawl is certainly a major contributor. Few would claim that low-density development does not increase auto emissions, water use, pollution, trash, loss of species habitat, or energy consumption. To cite one example, most pollution of ground water, lakes, streams, and rivers in the United States is caused by runoff that collects various toxins on the high percentage of impervious surfaces, like roads and parking lots, in urbanized regions. The heating and cooling of freestanding homes, with their many exterior walls per structure, requires more energy than attached houses in denser development. Then there are those immaculate lawns that require vast quantities of water and chemicals to maintain. Finally, research into the relationship between public health and suburban lifestyles steadily accumulates. Auto emissions increase respiratory health problems; sedentary lifestyles contribute to obesity and associated diseases; toxins applied in lawn care damage water quality; and even mental health suffers (back to a former critique) from homogenous, unattractive—some would say "dispiriting and ugly"—suburban landscapes.[32]

In truth, most such conditions are created by increasing affluence and not by any particular pattern of settlement, though affluence and sprawl are certainly related. But environmentalists are among the fiercest critics of sprawl. Their concerns about the waste of land, resources, and attention spent negotiating dispersed patterns of settlement have done more to arouse opposition than any complaints about the lifestyles that suburbs allegedly promote. There is little doubt that demands for better environmental stewardship will only increase, influencing urbanization patterns considerably. The low-density subdivision will be seen less and less as a form of smart growth.

Nonetheless, a Paradise

Despite growing critiques and concerns about sprawl, and increasing fondness for city life among young and old, a majority of the American population continues to live in suburban environments. National surveys generally report that they do so contentedly. Because so many Americans are already there, rates of suburban growth, at least in North America, will not again approach those seen during the second half of the twentieth century. But the suburbs are not going to disappear and, indeed, more will be built, despite the recent spate of publications announcing the "End of the Suburb," and warning that "Sprawl Kills."[33] Indeed, in many parts of the urbanizing world a fascination with the suburban idea is just commencing.[34] As the impacts of the Great Recession have receded, and the Millennial generation heads into its family-making years, suburban developments have begun to rise again.

Focus for a moment on two photographs. (See Figures 6.12 and 6.13.) The first is a typical suburban view; particular foliage aside, it could be almost

6.12 An ordinary scene in suburban McLean, Virginia.

6.13   **A young family poses proudly in front of their first home.**

anywhere across suburban America. The second features a young family posing in front of a just-acquired first home in Westfield, New Jersey. It was carefully chosen to be within commuting distance by transit to the mom's job in New York City, and a short highway commute in the other direction to the dad's place of employment.

The two scenes are familiar and comforting. Does not the original appeal of the suburb remain embedded in these views? A pretty decent lifestyle during part of a family's life remains to be had in such places—environmental impacts, social isolation, and urban snobbery notwithstanding. The appeal of a house and yard will not dramatically diminish. It embodies too many attributes, especially for those simultaneously working and raising families, even if it is becoming a less universal ideal. Given the mounting costs of living in the cities experiencing renewed growth, affordability—one of the long-standing advantages of the suburb—will also remain a factor for younger families. Yes, the suburb remain a paradise for more than a few.

7.1 *American Progress*, John Gast, 1872. Lady progress, or "Divine Providence,"
leading settlers from St. Louis (upper right) to the promise of the West.

7

SEEDING SETTLEMENT: HOMESTEADS, LAND GRANTS, AND CAPITAL SEATS

And now the hour of twelve was at hand. . . .

I remember throwing my blankets out of the car window the instant the train stopped at the station. I remember tumbling after them through the self-same window. Then I joined the wild scramble for a town lot up the sloping hillside at a pace discounting any "go-as-you-please" race. There were several thousand people converging on the same plot of ground, each eager for a town lot which was to be acquired without cost and without price, each solely dependent on his own efforts. . . .

I found myself, without exactly knowing how, about midway between the government building and depot. It occurred to me that a street would probably run past the depot. . . . I proceeded at once to unstrap a small folding cot I brought with me, and, by standing it on end, it made a tolerable center pole for a tent. I then threw a couple of my blankets over the cot and staked them securely into the ground on either side. Thus I had a claim that was unjumpable because of substantial improvements, and I felt safe and breathed more freely until my brother arrived on the third train, with our tent and equipments.

HAMILTON S. WICKS, RECALLING THE GREAT OKLAHOMA LAND RUSH

7.2 Not a Hollywood reenactment, but a photograph of the actual stampede that began the Oklahoma Land Rush, on April 22, 1889.

Whether with a utopian or, more commonly, a speculator's fervor, little fueled the imagination of nineteenth-century Americans more than acquisition of an "unjumpable claim" on a piece of the west. The promise, as Richard Lingeman memorably puts it, was "rich, black, fertile land, hundreds of thousands of acres of it, unturned by the plough."[1] Not all were coming to farm. The "Boomer" in the above account, like everyone who tumbled out of the train with him, was rushing for a town lot. To be sure, there was not yet a town, but the prospect of owning and profiting from a lot there, especially where signs indicated a "government building" or "depot," might be located, seems to have been as intoxicating for some pioneers as a quarter section of land further out of town and away from the rail line.

7.3   **Guthrie, Oklahoma, taking shape just several days following the 1889 land rush.**

The pioneer settlement of the Oklahoma Territory began with an improbable land rush on April 22, 1889—four years prior to Frederick Jackson Turner's proclaiming the closing of the frontier, as he introduced his Frontier Hypothesis at a Chicago World's Fair symposium. For years, citizens had gazed ravenously toward what had long been designated Indian Territory. Tribes from across the Great Plains had been marshaled into the region, freeing up space for American settlement on former Indian lands. Pressure to release ever more territory for settlement was constant, so Congress agreed to open nearly two million acres under the authority of the Homestead Act. The General Land Office then surveyed the territory into 160-acre farm lots and towns of 320 acres, according to the continental survey. Fewer than twelve thousand homesteads would be available. But, as nearly five times that many hopefuls began to amass along the territory's perimeter before April 22, the border required the protection of the US Army. Gathering weeks in advance, they waited for that fateful day's noontime burst of ceremonial cannons and bugles to initiate the rush. (See Figures 7.2 and 7.3.)

Horace Greeley's famous urging to "Go west, young man, and grow up with the country," stands as a defining slogan of nineteenth-century America. The founder and editor of the *New York Tribune* believed that the American west could and should absorb the poor and underemployed from eastern urban areas, especially during economic downturns.[2] For others, there were grander imperatives for beating a path west. For William Gilpin, part-time politician, veteran of the Spanish-American War, author, indefatigable western propagandizer, and land speculator (in which capacity, by some accounts, he could be a scoundrel), the West represented "the untransacted destiny of the American people to subdue the continent." It was the duty of Americans, Gilpin wrote, "to rush over this vast field to the Pacific Ocean . . . to change darkness into light and confirm the destiny of the human race. . . . Divine task! Immortal mission![3]

This was the ideology of Manifest Destiny, a driving force behind the land rushes, responsible for routing native peoples from their ancestral lands, inscribed on the terrain by the transcontinental trails and rail lines, and promulgated in newspaper stories, advertisements, grainy photographs, ballads, dime novels, and monumental canvases and murals. A magnificent twenty-by-thirty-foot mural painted by Emanuel Leutze in 1861, *Westward the Course of Empire Takes Its Way*, still graces a wall on the US Capitol leading to the House of Representatives' chamber.

My favorite example of Manifest Destiny art is the 1872 John Gast painting *American Progress*. (See Figure 7.1) In it, Divine Providence personified as a young woman floats westward clutching a schoolbook to impart knowledge and laying a telegraph wire (to modern eyes appearing to carry a not yet wireless laptop). Light shines from the east, as if following Gilpin's instructions, as Providence leads settlers away from St. Louis on their journey westward and the natives cower ahead. Along with *American Progress*, consider the irresistible lure of a railroad poster offering cheap one-way travel to California from places east. (See Figure 7.4.) The instinct to decamp for open land and all that it promised was being culturally ingrained across much of the nineteenth century. That it was being exaggerated, even mythologized, can be seen by reviewing the census data between 1860 and 1900: for every pioneer heading west, there were dozens arriving in America's growing cities, whether drawn from farms, smaller towns, or abroad.

To be clear, I am not defending the vision of utopia represented by Manifest Destiny, or its corollary, American Exceptionalism. The doctrine entailed the brutal and often fatal expulsion of natives from their land. But nineteenth-

7.4 Railroad company poster encouraging migration to California, labeled as the "Cornucopia of the World," and promising "43,795,000 Acres of Government Lands Untaken."

century settlers were clearly driven in part by dreams, or promises, of a new and better life in the west.

In the first use of the phrase *manifest destiny*, in the summer of 1845, journalist John Louis O'Sullivan was defending the US annexation of Texas. By the end of the year, he used it again to argue for annexing the Oregon territory from the British. The words had a clear utopian feel. This was during the "Oregon Fever" days, when thousands of pioneers took the Oregon Trail to the fertile Willamette Valley—claiming, as O'Sullivan wrote, "the right of our manifest destiny to overspread and to possess the whole of the continent which Providence has given us for the development of the great experiment of liberty and federated self-government entrusted to us."[4]

A heroic task was somehow bestowed on Americans to promote, spread, and defend democracy across the continent. The origins of the idea date back to the nation's founders, who seemed to comprehend that civil order and cooperation among the colonies would depend on continuously enlarging access to natural resources rather arguing over those already at hand. That this would come at the expense of others was left unsaid. A noble phrase, *manifest destiny* was actually used in support of many ignoble endeavors, whether war with Mexico and the annexation of Texas, the extension of slavery to western states, the domination over Native American nations, the seizure of territory from rival nations, or the perpetuation of an imperialist stance. It was at heart a doctrine of conquest, not idealism.

Still, four phenomena emerging from the mindset of Manifest Destiny did have clear utopian aspects. First was the 1862 Homestead Act, the law enabling citizens to acquire sizable parcels of land at virtually no cost for the purpose of farming. Second was the use of federal land grants to railroad companies for the construction of the transcontinental lines. Third was the use of such grants to states, via the 1862 Morrill Act, to build public universities and broaden access to collegiate education. Fourth, was the somewhat curious policy of locating many state capitals away from major urban areas, an indicator not so much of agrarian influence, as is often argued, but of the preference of Americans for towns over large cities.

Before looking at these in detail, it is worth noting that granting land for social or economic purposes was not a new strategy for the age of Manifest Destiny. Its history extends back to the granting of "headrights," a medieval tradition that was adapted to colonial circumstances. To spur colonization while also ensuring sufficient labor for owners of farms and plantations, the English crown offered acreage, usually fifty acres, to any man who would not only cross the Atlantic but also cover the cost of transporting another man, and ideally several others. These were often the arrangements by which indentured servants arrived in America, having lacked the means to embark on their own. The sponsor was granted some number of acres for himself, plus the same for accompanying family members and any additional people they funded to come.[5] Initially, this also held true for transporting slaves. So an additional benefit of owning slaves in the British colonies during the seventeenth and eighteenth centuries was to be granted fifty acres of land for each one acquired and transported.[6]

A Homestead for All

Debates about the disposition of western lands began before the Revolution. By the fateful year of 1776, Adam Smith was observing in his *Wealth of Nations* that "plenty of good land, and the liberty to manage their own affairs their own way, seem to be the great cause of the prosperity of all new colonies."[7] Against the wishes of many Americans, however, the British crown had ordered a series of edicts, culminating with the Quebec Act of 1774, that land-control and distribution policies were no longer to be at the discretion of the individual colonies, as they had long been. This became an additional source of friction and resistance to British rule.

Despite Jefferson's advocacy, it took half a century of debate and the particular circumstances of the Civil War for Congress to adopt a Homestead Act. Positions were divided on the most equitable means of making land available to settlers in westward expansion. Should federal land be made available for free, or sold, being a valuable source of income for the federal government? Should it be made readily available to individuals, companies, or states? Did the government have a constitutional right to dispose of its land, or was it in the public domain? Among the tensions leading to the Civil War were the North's and South's quite different views regarding expansion. "Free soil" northerners insisted that all future states be designated free territories, meaning slave-free, as well, while southern voices vied for the extension of the plantation system and its dependence on slave labor. Earlier efforts at creating a Homestead Act were defeated by southern members of Congress, worried about increased northern political dominance resulting from the creation of additional slave-free states.

With southern votes absent in Congress as the Civil War raged, the votes in favor of free soil prevailed. President Lincoln signed the Homestead Act into Law in 1862, having promised prior to his inauguration, channeling Jefferson, that he was "in favor of settling the wild lands into small parcels so that every poor man may have a home." His predecessor, James Buchanan, had vetoed a version two years earlier, instead supporting the admission of Kansas into statehood as a slave-holding state, perhaps in an attempt to hold the Union together. The Homestead Act took effect on January 1, 1863, the same day as the Emancipation Proclamation.[8]

The 1862 Act supplanted an earlier Preemption Act that dealt with the problem of squatters on federal land. That act had enabled citizens—and they had to be citizens or at least petitioning to be naturalized—who had not borne arms against the nation and who were living on federal property, to purchase 160 acres (a quarter-section) for the low sum of $1.25 per acre. Otherwise, the land would be offered for sale to others—and there were always takers, particularly among the speculators. Indeed, speculators would often show up at land auctions to outbid squatters who had been saving a long time to purchase the land they occupied.[9] Under the Preemption Act, a portion of the sale price reverted to the state to help fund the building of roads, bridges, canals, and other public improvements. This led some state legislators to oppose the Homestead Act, anticipating that it would cut such funds.

Under the Homestead Act, citizens over twenty-one years of age who were heads of households, male or female, could claim up to 160 acres of federal land that had been surveyed and designated for settlement. To confirm ownership, they had to live on this land for five years and in that time improve it, usually by farming. After that, a full title to the land could be acquired for a mere ten dollars. Those who had the means could also exercise a "commutation clause" after only six months of residence. In that case, as under the Preemption Act, it would be possible to purchase the claim for a minimum of $1.25 per acre. Either option was a good deal for a pioneer inclined to become and remain a farmer, assuming the land was sufficiently arable, and sufficient in size and topography to sustain a farm. Such, of course, was not always the case.

There were many problems, not least with the Act's poor administration, that enabled abuses. There was no good way of confirming residency requirements. Bribes to officials on behalf of claimants were common. Countless dummy claims could not be investigated or prevented. Timber, mining, oil extracting, and trapping companies could falsely petition as individual citizens to assemble large landholdings or even gain rights to a water source at the expense of neighboring landholders equally dependent on the water. Families with children all petitioning for claims independently could also gain control over substantial territory. The limit of 160 acres was itself an occasional problem, as there was no assurance, given diverse geographic and climatic conditions, that a farm of that size could prove financially viable, especially as farming became more industrialized rather than family-run.

Historians continue to debate the ultimate merits of the homesteading policy. Some point to it as a path to upward mobility. As during colonial days, when only landholders had the privilege of voting, nineteenth-century landholders were held in higher esteem and considered more financially secure. By the time of the act's termination in 1935, somewhere between 245 million and 287 million acres of public land were granted or sold to homesteaders, with approximately 1.5 million individual homestead patents registered. That is impressive, especially considering those homesteaders' several generations of descendants, many of whom benefited from the land, as well. As sociologist Trina Williams Shanks has noted, the number of ultimate beneficiaries could be in the scores of millions.[10]

On the other hand, due to poor administration of the program and the rate of false claims by individuals or companies, the number of actual farms resulting from the Homestead Act might have been as low as four hundred thousand. More than a few of these, too, would gradually succumb to consolidation, mechanization, and the emergence of agri-business, or fail due to competition in international grain and produce markets. As Henry Nash Smith points out, the Homestead Act clashed with the arrival of the Industrial Revolution: it was impossible to sustain Jefferson's agrarian utopia in the "garden of the world" given the rise of land speculators and railroad barons.[11] Still, at the passage of the act, agriculture accounted for more than three-quarters of the nation's exports, the output of about two million farms. By the Great Depression, the number of farms would increase to six million. And while the rise of industry lowered the agricultural export percentage to 42 percent, it was still true that a quarter of the population lived on farms.[12]

Despite the decline in the number of farms and farmers since, and despite the role of speculators, railroad barons, and land companies in overspreading the garden of the world, traces of the settlers' old utopian dreams endure. Of course, this all was someone else's Eden first, Jefferson's agrarian republic having muscled out its prior inhabitants. But many farms on still-fertile land continue to exist, and large parts of America continue to exhibit the pattern of family-owned farmlands stretching beyond the horizon, occupying their quarter-section of the continental grid. (See Figure 1.1.) They are the legacy of a policy that made a vast continent available to citizens virtually for free.

Expanding the Privilege of a (Practical) College Education

A quite different tradition of public land grants emerged in the second half of the nineteenth century, not for the benefit of individuals but for the building of institutions. Indeed, the consequences of the Morrill Act of 1862 ramify to the present. Also known as the Land Grant College Act, it provided thirty thousand acres of federal land multiplied by the number of each state's Congressional delegation for the purpose of redirecting collegiate education "to promote the liberal and practical education of the industrial classes in the several pursuits and professions in life."[13] It was mandated that the proceeds from the sale of the granted lands should fund the establishment of universities in states that had not rebelled against the Union.

The need to educate the "industrial classes"—the equivalent, in today's terms, of the blue-collar or working classes—had been discussed for years, as it was recognized that economic progress required expertise and skills that traditional, classics-based instruction did not deliver. Today's equivalent would be the increased focus on STEM (science, technology, engineering, and mathematics) skills. The emphasis was on the establishment of agricultural colleges, but the maturing of the American engineering profession also owed much to the land-grant institutions. Some may not recall that Texas A&M University, born as the Agricultural and Mechanical College of Texas, was one of the Morrill Act institutions. The Reserve Officer Training Corps (ROTC) also had its roots in the act's stipulation that military training be included.

The aspirational goal of the Morrill Act was to provide technical training to many young Americans who otherwise would not have attended college, as the existing system mostly catered to the elite. Many early photos endure of the seventy land-grant institutions as they were being built, usually at the periphery of existing towns. Their first buildings seem like seedlings planted to grow new forms of community around them. (See Figure 7.5.)

Some saw a conflict between the Homestead and Morrill Acts. Whereas the former was dedicated to reducing land speculation by establishing an orderly process of land distribution to individuals, the latter seemed to encourage speculation. States, having been granted lands, had to sell them to support construction of their educational institutions, and therefore had an incentive to drive up the prices by offering them to speculators. A further problem was that northeastern states, which were more populated and had larger congressional delegations, were granted far more land than smaller and newer states were.[14] Nonetheless, could there be a more idealistic agenda, especially in the midst of a raging Civil War, than to provide advanced education at a national scale to the next generation of citizens?

7.5   **View of Cornell University, one of the Morrill Act institutions, "as pictured in its earliest days," 1880.**

Vermont Representative Justin Smith Morrill, for whom the Morrill Act is named, warrants additional credit. He argued that freed slaves ought to have access to the land grant institutions—and to homesteads, as well. His position was very clear: "Having emancipated a whole race, shall it be said that there our duty ends, leaving the race as cumberers of the ground, to live or to wilt and perish, as the case may be? They are members of the American family, and their advancement concerns us all. While swiftly forgetting all they ever knew as slaves, shall they have no opportunity to learn anything as freemen?"[15]

States "in a condition of rebellion" could not benefit from this legislation during the Civil War. And, indeed, Morrill's vision of education for the emancipated was resisted by southern states long following the war. It would take a second Morrill Act in 1890 to forbid any state receiving these funds from turning away capable students based on race—although they could establish separate institutions for people of color, Several of today's traditionally black colleges and universities resulted from this amendment to the original Morrill Act.

Land Grants to Railroads

As generous and important as the Morrill Act grants were, the greatest beneficiaries of federal generosity at the time were railroad companies. Coincident with the Homestead and Morrill Acts, the Pacific Railroad Act was also passed in 1862. That these three pieces of landmark legislation were passed during just a two-month period, in the midst of the Civil War, is remarkable. The Pacific Railroad Act supported the construction of transcontinental rail lines, clearly a national priority at mid-nineteenth century.[16] Beyond creating greater efficiency in transporting goods and products, the railroads cut travel time from New York to California from literally months to perhaps a week or so. It must have seemed no less a miracle than flying would seem in the early twentieth century.

Federal land had previously been available to states to study routes and subsidize rail enterprises, but now land and funds would go directly to private corporations. In addition to providing favorable long-term bonds for construction, a mind-boggling amount of land was granted. Over the two decades from 1850 to 1870, railroads received some 131 million acres of rights of way—about the same acreage as the states received from the Morrill Act. Yet, these lands were given to just a handful of companies, and initially to just two: the Union Pacific, which would build westward from Omaha, Nebraska; and the Central Pacific, which would lay track eastward from California. Famously, their efforts came together on May 10, 1869, at Promontory, Utah, where Leland Stanford, president of Southern Pacific and later founder (with his wife, Jane) of Stanford University, would drive the final spike.

In addition to ample rights of way along the track alignments, as many as ten more miles of public land was allocated to the railroad companies on either side of the alignment for each mile of grade, except through existing towns, topographic barriers, or lands where there were designated mining or water rights. By some estimates, this led to grants up to and even beyond 175 million acres. It also produced all kinds of confusion and exaggeration, especially in mapping.[17] Consider the poster printed in 1884 to publicize the Democratic platform and the map printed in 1883 of Nebraska. (See Figures 7.6 and 7.7.)

In the Nebraska map, that green snake includes the ten square miles to either side of the rail alignment. If this map was correct, then a huge portion of the state was the property of the Union Pacific Railroad Company. It is unclear, however, that the Union Pacific ever did control that much land; opponents of the railroad grants were known to use such maps and related statistics to question the wisdom of the grants. As lamented by the Democratic poster, they inevitably meant many potential homesteads lost. Even allowing for exaggeration, it is hard to understand why it was necessary to allocate so much land to the railroads. Much of it was not required for rail construction, and the rail companies were eventually able to sell it to individual pioneers and promoters of towns planned in proximity to rail stations. (See Figure 7.8.)

Historians still debate whether, or how much, the railroad companies profited from this largesse. Stephen Ambrose argues in *Nothing Like it in the World* that the total value of the land granted, even if all had been sold, represented a

HOW THE PUBLIC DOMAIN HAS BEEN SQUANDERED

Map showing the 139,403,026 acres of the people's land—equal to

871,268 FARMS OF 160 ACRES EACH

Worth at $2 an acre, $278,806,052,

GIVEN BY

Republican Congresses to Railroad Corporations

This is more land than is contained in New York, New Jersey,
Pennsylvania, Ohio, and Indiana.

We believe that the public lands ought, as far as possible, to be kept as homesteads for actual settlers; that all unearned lands heretofore improvidently granted to railroad corporations by the action of the Republican party should be restored to the public domain; and that no more grants of land shall be made to corporations, or be allowed to fall into the ownership of alien absentees.

DEMOCRATIC PLATFORM, 1884.

7.6   "How the Public Domain Has Been Squandered." A Democratic platform campaign poster from the 1884 presidential election critical of the scale of land grants to railroad companies.

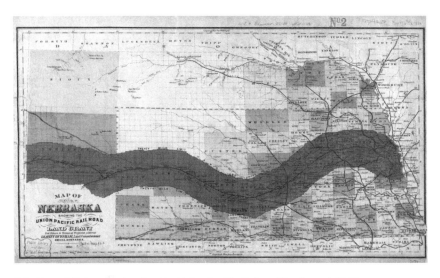

7.7   Map of Nebraska showing the Union Pacific Railroad land grant, 1883.

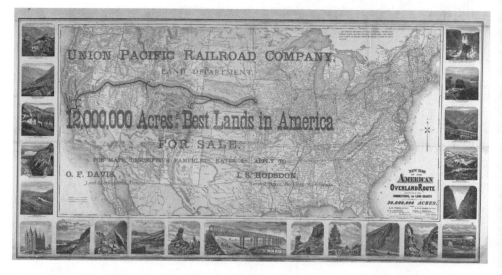

7.8   Union Pacific Company poster showing the alignment of the 12,000,000 acres of federal land grants for sale, and twenty-one scenes along the route.

fraction of the construction cost of the rail corridors.[18] What is not in debate is how dominant a force the railroad revolution was for America's nineteenth-century economy and settlement patterns.

Capital Seats

It may have all begun with the decision to move the nation's capital from Philadelphia, the second largest and the most cosmopolitan American city at the beginning of the nineteenth century, to a malarial swamp on the shores of the Potomac River (a place we will explore further in Chapter 11). Today, only seventeen of the fifty states' governments reside in their state's major population and economic center. The majority of state capitals are smaller places at some distance from the state's most prominent city. For example, the capital of Illinois is Springfield and not Chicago, the nation's third largest city. In Pennsylvania it is Harrisburg, which in 2017 had a population barely reaching forty-six thousand. Philadelphia, despite being among the oldest and largest cities in America, not to mention the home of Independence Hall and the Liberty Bell, wound up neither the nation's nor even its state's capital. Neither did New York City. Remarkably, and to the likely disbelief of visitors from capital cities abroad, only one of the nation's ten largest cities, Phoenix, is a state capital, though chances are that, at their present rates of growth, Austin and Atlanta will join the top ten soon.

There are a number of theories as to how this occurred, none entirely convincing. David Schuyler, in *The New Urban Landscape: The Redefinition of City Form in Nineteenth-Century America,* offers a common conclusion: "By artificially separating seats of government from the country's metropolitan areas, the revolutionary generation enshrined as cultural norms the agrarian ideas and the accompanying philosophical distrust of cities."[19] Those who are convinced of America's history of anti-urbanism would agree with Schuyler's supposition. However, it is not borne out by historic population statistics. In four of the original thirteen colonies—Georgia, Massachusetts, Rhode Island, and South Carolina—the state capital initially was and remains the largest city. In five others—Connecticut, New Hampshire, North Carolina, Vermont, and Virginia—the present capital was the most prominent city at the time of its designation, and it was only due to subsequent forces that other cities in those states prospered and grew larger. A tenth capital, Annapolis, while smaller than Baltimore thirty miles away, had already been established as the home of the Continental Congress in the 1780s, and so remained Maryland's seat of government upon statehood.

The two extreme examples from the original thirteen states, Harrisburg in Pennsylvania and Albany in New York, do support a Manifest Destiny perspective. Albany sat at the confluence of the Erie Canal and the Hudson River. Harrisburg was at the point of transition from river transport on the Susquehanna to an overland passage to the West. Both were thus seen as strategic locations, being central within their states, far enough inland to avoid harm from foreign aggression (another theory), and having ample access to the material resources of the state, and the spoils of the continent.

Other theories suggest the intent was to keep the functions of government away from undue influence from business and the carnal temptations of big cities. One can imagine state legislators debating such things, but there is little evidence that these were real factors. Far more important for capitals designated during the nineteenth century was centrality of location. Beyond symbolic importance, this reduced travel distances between capitals and many parts of their states and, consistent with the "overspreading the continent" ideology, positioned capitals to oversee their states' resources. Probably, it was also expected that the new capital designations would make what had been secondary cities more attractive to businesses and other investors, thus advancing the overspreading.

To return to Springfield, it is worth looking at the process by which it became the third capital of Illinois. First was Kaskaskia, an important eighteenth-century French colonial outpost well located on a peninsula of the Mississippi, but subject to frequent flooding. Second came Vandalia, founded in 1819 to serve as the state capital since Kaskaskia flooded so often, and because its own site was along the route of the National Road. This early federal highway, also known as the Cumberland Turnpike, was an answer to George Washington's failed dream of connecting the nation's capital to lands across the Allegheny Mountain Range by digging a canal between the Potomac and Ohio Rivers. That would have been the equivalent in this region to the Erie Canal up north, but the topography posed too many challenges. The National Road began to be constructed in 1811. Starting in Cumberland, Maryland, it extended some 620 miles to the area of Vandalia, and served thousands of settlers heading west. An economic depression in 1837, however, brought construction on the turnpike to a halt and Vandalia remained the terminus for a time.

The year 1837 also happened to be when Abraham Lincoln, a young attorney, chose to settle in Springfield. The town was seventy-six miles to the north of Vandalia, more centrally located within Illinois. As Lincoln gained local prominence, he and eight other tall colleagues in the Illinois General Assembly, collectively known as the Long Nine, led a successful campaign to designate his adopted home as the state's capital. The Long Nine's goal, achieved in 1839, was not likely based on their wanting to escape from the metropolitan distractions of tiny Vandalia.

Although much smaller than Chicago, Springfield has a current population of 115,000, making it impressive by comparison to state capitals such as Pierre, South Dakota (population 14,000), Frankfort, Kentucky (population 27,500), and Helena, Montana (population 30,000). Or consider Guthrie, the instant capital of the Oklahoma Territory, which during the first day of the Oklahoma Land Rush grew from zero to ten thousand, but has never exceeded twelve thousand in the century and a quarter since. (See Figure 7.3.) Oklahoma City, experiencing much faster growth and located absolutely at the center of the state, would replace Guthrie as Oklahoma's capital by 1910.

7.9   View of the Tennessee State Capitol commanding its hilltop site in Nashville, c. 1896.

Towns upon a Hill

It is a problem of language that the word *city* is generally applied, whether one is referring to Guthrie or New York. In the first half of the nineteenth century, most Americans had never even experienced one of the nation's biggest cities, and even fewer would have said they admired them. But towns were always appreciated, indeed were essential to the spread of settlement across America. There were instant towns such as Guthrie, Oklahoma, and the others that sprang to life in a matter of days around depots and stations of transcontinental lines. There were market towns to which the quarter-section homesteaders brought their products. There were towns set on hillsides whose august edifices could be seen for miles. (See Figure 7.9) And there were college towns that coalesced around the new institutions of higher learning funded by land grants. (See Figure 7.5.) Together, these towns, as historian Richard Wade understood, served as "the true spearheads of the American frontier."[20] It is an image of American settlement as enduring as that of the family homestead.

8.1 View of Central Park with the famed Dakota Apartments barely visible in the background, the city held back as Olmsted planned.

8

MAKING NATURE URBANE:
OLMSTED AND THE PARKS MOVEMENT

> Civilized men while they are gaining ground against certain acute
> forms of disease are growing more and more subject to other and
> more insidious enemies to their health and happiness and against these
> the remedy and preventive cannot be found in medicine or in athletic
> recreations but only in sunlight and such forms of gentle exercise as are
> calculated to equalize the circulation and relieve the brain . . .
>
> FREDERICK LAW OLMSTED, 1868

> He Saw Democracy in Dirt
>
> LIFE, 1972

THE SECOND OF THE EPIGRAPHS ABOVE was how *Life* magazine chose to headline its appreciation of Frederick Law Olmsted, on the 150th anniversary of his
birth. While not the first American to associate dirt with democracy, as prior
chapters attest, Olmsted was the renowned leader in the parks movement. He
advanced its romantic view of nature's virtues supported by emerging scientific
knowledge, and its commitment to fighting the Dickensian squalor of industrializing cities. The unprecedented scale and character of these cities, Olmsted
believed, demanded radical measures to guide their further growth. The way to
achieve a more humane city was, above all, to reintroduce nature into the heart
of the harsh, unhealthy metropolis.

Olmsted shared his belief in this imperative for public well-being with other social reformers of his generation, such as Andrew Jackson Downing, whose early advocacy stimulated the park movement. Downing's friend and earliest biographer, George William Curtis, put it this way: "The truth is, that if there be a Public Park, it is not of the greatest consequence whether Nobody (of the great family of Somebody) goes there or not. A Park is not for those who can go to the country, but for those who can not. . . . It is fresh air for those who can not go to the sea-side; and green leaves, and silence, and the singing of birds, for those who cannot fly to the mountains. It is a fountain of health for the whole city."[1] The harmful consequences of industrialization were plainly visible in the squalid living and working conditions of the new laboring classes. City dwellers needed access to nature's capacity to heal and restore.

Opposing tendencies were shaping American urbanization during the second half of the nineteenth century. Befitting the settlement of a New World initially anticipated as paradise regained, there lingered in the era of Olmsted a desire to build the city in the image of arcadia, holding to the possibility of maintaining a nature's nation. Progress and prosperity, however, seemed to advance only at the expense of that nature. As urbanization expanded, voraciously exploiting the natural environment, separate planning strategies evolved to recover some balance between nature and urbanization. It is no coincidence that Olmsted designed both parks and suburbs. Suburban estates, as explored in Chapter 6, were intended for families able to leave the blight of the city for healthier settings. Parks were intended to bring the same benefits of nature to those who did not have the option to move away.

In the city, Olmsted and his contemporaries were not interested in restoring lost bucolic scenery or perpetuating rural values. Bringing nature back to the city required rational planning and complex logistics. Their efforts were not acts of preservation, as a visitor today might infer as she enjoyed the pastoral qualities of a great urban park built during the period. An astonishing amount of construction was required to "preserve" those essential qualities of nature that the city was obliterating.

Olmsted and his partner Calvert Vaux, as well as Andrew Jackson Downing, Horace Cleveland, Robert Morris Copeland, George Kessler, and others of that remarkable first generation of landscape architects, acted as urban planners, applying social concern and emerging environmental insight on behalf of city

dwellers. Social reformers in action, Romantics in spirit, and utopians in ambition, they understood that the future of the nation did not lie in sentimentaliz-
ing small-town life. They saw, perhaps with some reluctance, that the nation's
progress required vast cities and ongoing modernization. Olmsted, the erstwhile
farmer, had experienced the backwardness of rural life and often referred to "a
strong drift townward" among his contemporaries. "Our country," he wrote, "has
entered upon a stage of progress in which its welfare is to depend on the convenience, safety, order and economy of life in great cities. It cannot prosper independently of them; cannot gain virtue, wisdom, comfort, except as they also
advance."[2] This was not the voice of an agrarian, or an unreconstructed Romantic.

Responding to the Strong Drift Townward

Between the Civil War and the First World War, many major American cities,
and cities aspiring to be great, undertook ambitious programs of park-building.
Olmsted scholar Albert Fein, who uses the modern label of *environmental planner* to describe Olmsted, argues that the urban park was America's foremost
contribution to nineteenth-century urban design, and suggests that the idea of
connecting parks into green networks in support of social planning was characteristically American.[3] When one stands in New York's Central Park, tours
Boston's Emerald Necklace, or looks over Kansas City from its Swope Park, that
assertion rings true. These are spectacular achievements. It is one thing to open
vast crown-held parks for public use following a social revolution, as European
cities did. It requires a different level of effort to allocate within rapidly growing
cities thousands of acres, and then design parks, parkways, and "pleasure
grounds" for the benefit of the public.

In these parks and park systems, nineteenth-century engineering was put in
service of an inspiring credo—that nature's virtues fortify human virtues—for a
great social experiment. Its hypotheses were, first, that generous green spaces
would enhance the life and health of the common citizen who, unlike the
wealthy industrialist or landed gentry, did not have access to the pleasures of the
countryside—those, that is, who lived most intimately with the city's unhealthi-
est conditions.[4] And second, that beyond pastoral beauty and cleaner air, nature's presence would provide a kind of democratic ether in which citizens
would shed cultural and class differences to become better and better socialized.

This was the movement's utopian conjecture. The urban park was intended to "civilize" the city by raising the civilizational standards of its inhabitants.

A less reverential view holds that it was a campaign by an elite class with self-serving interests—yes, with high-minded aspirations and commitment to social reform, but also driven by unease about the dangers of the growing labor and immigrant classes. According to this interpretation, the purpose of educating lower classes about morals, hygiene, and social decorum, and providing them with palliative settings, was to prevent the rise of a mob culture that might one day threaten those more privileged. In this Olmsted passage, for example, can be detected a hint of this: "We want a ground to which people may easily go after their day's work is done, and where they may stroll for an hour . . . . We want, especially, the greatest possible contrast with the restraining and confining conditions of the town, those conditions which compel us to walk circumspectly, watchfully, jealously, which compel us to look closely upon others without sympathy."[5]

In this view, the parks were a kind of distant American analog to the boulevards that Baron von Haussmann was concurrently cutting through Paris. Among the civic glories of today's Paris, Haussmann's boulevards were partially intended to improve hygiene and add open space, but also to help Napoleon III quell potential citizen unrest, the broad new boulevards facilitating the movement of troops to get to a protest or act of rebellion.

Olmsted's interests in social reform preceded and continued throughout his park-building career. Earlier, as a journalist, he established *The Nation,* a periodical known then and now for espousing social causes. Taking leave of his duties as the superintendent of Central Park during the Civil War, he headed the Sanitary Commission, the predecessor to the Red Cross. He was a founding member of the American Social Science Association, whose mission in part was to support the "responsibilities of the gifted and educated classes toward the weak, the witless and the ignorant."[6] That was a blunt way of expressing things but, according to Richard Foglesong in *Planning the Capitalist City,* it captured very well the ambitions of elite social reformers in the mid-to-late nineteenth century. Olmsted's social cohort sought a conservative sort of reform aiming to provide recuperative environments without unraveling prevailing social orders—a far cry from the radical socialism of Engels and Marx, who sought fundamental changes in the balance of social and economic power. These elites were not, however, cynical or lacking in compassion. They were also critical of their own class and genuinely sought to educate peers about the concerns and conditions of the working class.[7]

Historians will continue to debate whether altruism, class-defensiveness, or social engineering were primary motives behind the parks movement, but an underlying utopianism about the importance and possibility of social improvement cannot be denied.[8] Jane Addams, whom we will meet again in a subsequent chapter, expressed a common reformer's conscience in her 1910 autobiography. "My mind," she wrote as she recalled a childhood concern, "was busy, however, with the old question eternally suggested by the inequalities of the human lot."[9] So were the busy minds of the park builders.

The first great undertaking was New York's Central Park. It is hardly necessary to recall the history of advocacy, or the multiple political trials and tribulations behind the realization of the park, to appreciate the monumentality of the effort and of the result. Can we imagine Manhattan without it? Olmsted did. With remarkable clairvoyance he warned the park's commissioners:

> The time will come when New York will be built up, when all the grading and filling will be done, and when the picturesquely-varied, rocky formations of the Island will have been converted into foundations for rows of monotonous straight streets, and piles of erect, angular buildings. There will be no suggestion left of its present varied surface, with the single exception of the few acres contained in the Park. Then the priceless value of the present picturesque outlines of the ground will be more distinctly perceived, and its adaptability for its purpose more fully recognized. It therefore seems desirable to interfere with its easy undulating outlines, and picturesque, rocky scenery as little as possible, and, on the other hand, to endeavor rapidly, and by every legitimate means, to increase and judiciously develop these particularly individual and characteristic sources of landscape effects.[10]

A careless reading might conclude that Olmsted was calling for the preservation of an existing landscape, merely "to interfere . . . as little as possible." But focus on the second half of the sentence where he writes of the need "to endeavor rapidly, and by every legitimate means, to increase and judiciously develop" the natural landscape. Olmsted is telling the commissioners that it is necessary to construct, build up, even exaggerate, those priceless, picturesquely varied, rocky formations of the island that were being lost to urbanization. The

8.2   Tree-moving machine during the construction of Central Park.

design of Central Park was an invention of a landscape, a massive construction project requiring technological ingenuity and an enormous mobilization of brute human effort.

The enterprise took sixteen years, employing nearly four thousand laborers at the height of construction. It required more than one hundred miles of drainage pipes, the movement of massive quantities of earth, and by Olmsted's estimate the planting of some three hundred thousand trees and shrubs. An entire corps of engineers was needed to manage the drainage of swamps, the excavation and relocation of hundreds of tons of granite, the creation of various bodies of water and stabilization of their banks and bottoms, the tunneling of roads to mini-mize impact on the sylvan scenery, and the fertilization and reseeding of acres of depleted farmland to create meadows. Without tractors and earth-moving ma-chines, humans and horses were the means of conveyance. (See Figure 8.2.) The reason to move so much earth was to build up topography and natural features literally to remove the city from view for those in the park. In Olmsted's words, "we want depth of wood enough about it not only for comfort in hot weather, but to completely shut out the city from our landscapes."[11] (See Figure 8.1.)

8.3   **Aerial view of Prospect Park in Brooklyn.**

The interplay among civic aspirations, design ambitions, land assembly, and construction decisions must have been incredible, entailing constant arguments over spatial organization, species selection, logistical details, management headaches, and alternating moments of pride and despair. Contemporary accounts illuminate the wonder of what was being achieved. The park-building program, not just in New York, unfolded against rising optimism about America's urbanizing future. Momentum was sustained on the belief in the *necessity* of the effort, critical to the well-being of city dwellers as change continued without pause.

The Need for Nature's Presence

No matter how seminal the achievement of Central Park, or their equally majestic Prospect Park in Brooklyn, the creation of a single park was not sufficient for Olmsted and Vaux. (See Figure 8.3.) The need was to permeate the city with a network of open spaces at various scales, connected by green boulevards, creating the "lungs" and "arteries" of the urban body, to invoke Olmsted's biological metaphor. The opportunity to create such a network came to Olmsted only after his involvement with Central Park ended. Following a sojourn in California where he was confronted by the full grandeur of nature in the Yosemite Valley (the experience that would ultimately inspire him to help establish the

8.4 Mount Auburn Cemetery in Cambridge, Massachusetts: America's first rural
cemetery, dedicated in 1831. Still experienced as an arboretum as much as a
"sleeping place," the Greek root for cemetery, and one of the sources of inspiration
for the American Parks movement.

National Park Service), he found in Buffalo, and then in Boston, the chance
that had eluded him in New York.

The success of Central Park fueled desires in other cities to build comparable
environments. Among them was Buffalo—industrious, prosperous, and one of
the fastest-growing cities in the country. Commanding the intersection of the
Great Lakes and the Erie Canal, with an expansive web of rail lines, Buffalo was,
in fact, helping New York City to become the "capital of capitalism." In 1868,
local advocates for a park were having only modest success advancing their

ideas, so they invited Olmsted to visit, hoping to persuade the now-prominent firm of Olmsted and Vaux to advance their cause. A few years later, with similar expectations—and perhaps having heard news of Buffalo's progress—the recently formed Boston Park Commissioners invited Olmsted to Boston for consultations. There he would eventually establish his home and offices, tired of New York's politics and disappointments, and undertake an even more extensive park network: the city's beloved Emerald Necklace.[12]

Although Olmsted's work in Boston followed that in Buffalo, the Boston area had played an important precursor role for the entire park-building era. Earlier in the nineteenth century, Mount Auburn Cemetery in Cambridge, dedicated in 1831, ushered in an era of pastoral cemeteries. Soon to follow were the Greenwood Cemetery in Brooklyn, Spring Grove in Cincinnati, Laurel Hill in Philadelphia, Buffalo's Forest Lawn Cemetery, and more. Olmsted's mentor, Andrew Jackson Downing, had noted that the popularity of these extensive cemetery landscapes was due to their being, in fact, restorative gardens for the living. Not yet packed with family plots and tombstones, they appealed to peo-

8.5   A Google Earth aerial of Mount Auburn Cemetery. From this vantage point it might be mistaken for a suburban subdivision. And indeed the curvilinear layout would inspire Olmsted to organize suburban districts in a similar manner. See his plan for Riverside, Illinois, Figure 6.6.

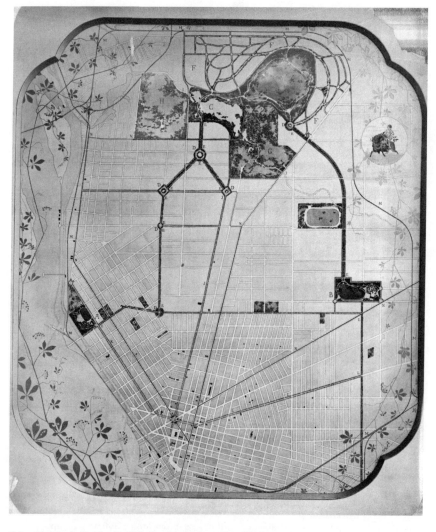

ple as places of respite from the city, whether or not they came to pay respects to the deceased. (See Figures 8.4 and 8.5.) Noticing families retreating to these cemeteries for picnics, Downing wrote in a campaigning mood: "does not this general interest, manifested in these cemeteries, prove that public gardens, established in a liberal and suitable manner, near our large cities, would be equally successful?"[13]

8.6   Olmsted plan for Buffalo's park system, New York.

Had Downing not died young—he drowned when a ship he was traveling on caught fire—he would perhaps be as renowned today as Olmsted as a father of the parks movement. He was a catalyst, campaigning endlessly during his short life to create city parks rather than leave people using cemeteries as surrogate recreational areas. He pushed in particular for a great park for New York, and demonstrated his own capacity to create such places with his 1851 design for the National Mall in Washington, DC. Indeed, it might be argued the Downing's work on the Mall, which preceded Central Park, first established the scenic, sanitary, and social goals that would characterize the urban park-building tradition to come. Unfortunately, his design was dismissed as not in keeping with L'Enfant's original vision and was replaced in 1903 by the McMillan Plan, produced by the Senate Park Commission, as described in Chapter 10.

Olmsted's admiration for Buffalo's Forest Lawn Cemetery and for its designer, Adolph Strauch, increased his interest in working in Buffalo. The impressive landscape of the burial park led Olmsted to locate what would become Buffalo's central park, today's Delaware Park, immediately adjacent to it. Ever entrepreneurial, Olmsted then seized on the possibility that New York never provided. Buffalo's original city plan, inspired by L'Enfant's design for Washington and laid out by Joseph Ellicott, the brother of L'Enfant's surveyor Andrew Ellicott, included several broad, diagonal streets. Olmsted convinced Buffalo's civic leaders to convert these to green parkways and have them connect the center of Buffalo to not one but three, and later other, substantial parks. To the city of Buffalo would go the honor of hosting Olmsted's first open space network, not merely a park. (See Figure 8.6.)

Olmsted also planned a large residential area immediately to the east of Delaware Park, called Parkside, modeled on Olmsted's and Vaux's first venture in suburban planning in Riverside, Illinois (described in Chapter 6). Today's ardent anti-sprawl activists might blame Olmsted for propagating the suburb. He was as concerned with improving the places of urban dwelling as with providing urban parks. In support of Parkside he wrote: "Let the citizen build up his stores and his warehouses as high and as close together as he pleases, but he doesn't want to live among them and there is no longer any need of his doing so. He can live in much better style and cheaper in a part of the city entirely given up to dwellings."[14]

Unlike Riverside, built miles from central Chicago, Parkside was part of the city and, as its name suggests, contiguous to Buffalo's major park, an ideal location. For Olmsted's generation it was easy to imagine citizens' lives benefiting from greater distance from the noxious and stressful places of labor and indus-

8.7   The Boston Fens, a portion of the city's Emerald Necklace, sinuously threading its way through the city.

try. Environments like Parkside were, indeed, an essential part of the kind of city Olmsted imagined.

In Boston, following his visit in 1875, Olmsted would grow bolder still. Over the course of the next two decades, he would direct the design of a network of parks and parkways emanating from the city's colonial-era Boston Common and its extension, the Public Garden. From them, it reaching outward to meander through and around city neighborhoods and bordering suburbs, and circled back to Boston's Harbor. It was an almost complete green necklace bedecked with individual parks—its jewels. Later overseen by his sons and disciples (notably, Charles Eliot, son of long-time Harvard University president Charles W. Eliot), it would grow into a broader regional system of public open spaces. An institution for regional governance of open space conservation would also be formed for this far larger necklace, the scale of which was not easily comprehensible as one system.[15] (See Figure 8.7.)

In and around Boston, Olmsted, nearing the end of the century and of his long, influential life, achieved the fullness of his vision for the future of the American city. The six components of his ideal urban park network were in evidence. There were public grounds adjacent to public buildings, exemplified by the relationship of the Boston Common to the Massachusetts State House. An array of small residential squares was distributed through neighborhoods, as in the city's South End. The city gained two large "rural" parks, Franklin Park and the Arnold Arboretum, the latter owned by Harvard. Extensive public reservations lay outside the city, after his disciples established the Trustees of Reservations and acquired some ten thousand acres of New England landscape. And last, there were the arteries—Commonwealth Avenue, the Jamaica Way, the Arborway—making beautiful, tree-lined connections between parks and neighborhoods. Not all of this resulted from Olmsted's vision. A number of these places existed before his arrival. Indeed, the Boston park commissioners determined the general outline of what became the Emerald Necklace before Olmsted started work. As an overall network, however, it certainly embodied his vision.

Ultimately, Boston's park network would not be the most extensive of the age. A larger one would unfold in the unlikely western boomtown of Kansas City, Missouri. Its development was directed by George E. Kessler, a former understudy in the New York offices of Olmsted and Vaux.[16]

The Civic Aspirations of an American Boomtown

In 2016, the US National Park Service added Kansas City's parks and boulevard system to its National Register of Historic Places. One could argue the agency was somewhat late in bestowing this honor on a truly remarkable set of environments.

Between 1890 and 1915, with a boomtown's typical brew of audacity, naivete, unabashed boosterism, and eye to real-estate profit, the city built the most elaborate park and boulevard system in the nation, if not the world at that time. Kansas City, Missouri had grown in population by about 140 percent in the single decade between 1880 and 1890, from roughly 56,000 to 133,000 people, so its leaders took the opportunity of the park planning to think simultaneously about how to pursue a host of other much-needed municipal improvements. The park plan served, in effect, as the town's overall development plan.[17]

The approach Kansas City took was unprecedented. Unlike Boston, it did not have two centuries of growth to improve upon. It did not have fragments of parks and green areas that could be threaded together to form a network. It had not grown up with a communitarian legacy of organizing around a town common. It did not have mature neighborhoods such as Boston's Back Bay, organized around a grand boulevard such as Commonwealth Avenue. What it did have was ambition, and in the manner of newly prospering towns everywhere, an inferiority complex toward cities like Chicago, St. Louis, and Boston, all further along in their evolution.

During its period of exponential growth in the 1880s, the city faced urgent needs for paved streets, sewage disposal, clean water, more and better homes, and expanded spaces for commerce and industry. There were dilapidated neighborhoods to repair, and steep ravines and bluffs to overcome. The group of civic leaders who were willing to step up to these challenges happened also to include several advocates for the kinds of parks and boulevards they had encountered in their travels to east coast cities and Europe. August Meyer, an industrialist, was appointed head of a newly formed park board—a role he would retain for many years. William Rockhill threw the full force of his newspaper, the *Kansas City Star,* behind a park-building campaign, helping to overcome taxpayers' initial resistance. Delbert Haff, an attorney, took on the task of creating the complex legal and fiscal framework that would underpin the construction of the system. George Kessler played the role of an Olmsted.[18]

By 1915, some $15 million of public expenditure (approximately $350 million in 2018 dollars) had been expended on Kessler's plan for parks and boulevards. Imagine a city today dedicating such resources within one decade to building parks. The result included nearly two thousand acres of parks, seven hundred acres of parkways, and ninety miles of boulevards and drives. At the time, London was the world's largest city, with a population nearly fifty times greater than Kansas City's, and that great city had inspired Olmsted's generation by opening

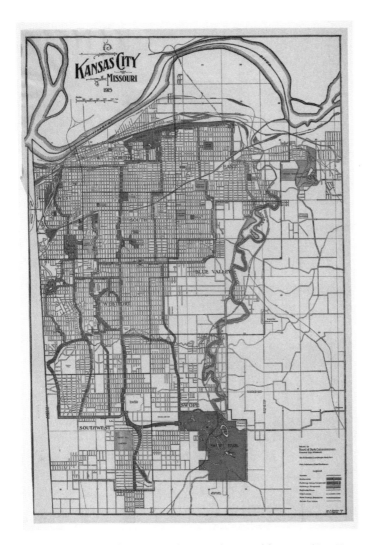

8.8 A 1915 map of Kansas City clearly describing the city's extensive park and boulevard system.

its extensive former royal grounds to public use. (See Figure 8.8.) But Kansas City could now boast more public open space.

In Kansas City, the motives for park building were much like those elsewhere: a mixture of civic altruism and elite-driven desires for social reform. But here, the expectations of the business and land-development communities were more pronounced. Park building had come to be recognized as a tool of economic development and real-estate speculation. Olmsted would have approved of how the parks served as a form of relief for the poor and laboring classes—but he might have had some misgivings about the boulevards in Kansas City,

8.9   Swope Park, Kansas City, in a 1909 photograph.

which were specifically intended to ensure neighborhood stability, maintain and raise the value of property, and guide the layout of the next wave of "proper" residential districts. Kessler presented plans for his parks and boulevards that he knew would necessitate the razing of slums and other undesirable areas, and open up areas up for redevelopment. The Kansas City effort was thus an early form of what by the mid-twentieth century would be called urban renewal.[19]

Building the park system in Kansas City became indistinguishable from planning the city more broadly. The construction of parks and boulevard spurred the improvement of municipal services, from sewerage to transportation corridors. It provided a stimulus for residential growth and the appreciation of property value. The boulevards provided a hierarchy over the generic street grid, and channels of growth. Tens of thousands of newly planted trees provided summer shade, better air, local beauty, and some of the restorative feel of nature back into the city. Park planning also provided impetus for earth-moving projects to overcome steep grades and other physical impediments to land development and city expansion. More generally, it gave the city new reason for civic pride. Leaders could point to these green places as symbols—evidence that Kansas City could stand up to comparison with competing cities.

Much of this is apparent in a remarkable 1915 photograph of Swope Park. Finely dressed citizens enjoy a Sunday's sojourn in their city's central park. The park's setting and size enables a temporary break from those daily frictions of city life. At the same time, it provides an overlook of their growing city, thoroughly modern and now newly graced with the beautiful and healing powers of nature. (See Figure 8.9.)

Look Forward a Century

Just as George Kessler was the Olmsted to the Kansas City park-building initiative, Horace W. S. Cleveland played that role for Minneapolis. To his city's park commissioners, he offered the advice to look ahead a hundred years.[20] He might simply have been acknowledging that great landscapes are not instantly produced; much growth is required for them to reach full glory. More likely, he meant to communicate something more profound.

On the streets of the late nineteenth-century American city, the pace of change was rapid, relentless, and nerve-racking. Whole blocks, entire neighborhoods seemed to appear overnight. Cities changed faster than their inhabitants, and the number of residents kept growing apace. It was important amid all this turbulence to find places of stability, as antidotes to the ephemeral qualities of an urban world being built—as it surely would be built and rebuilt again. The urban park, in addition to the curative powers it exerted, became America's answer to the medieval town square, an enduring place standing amid ceaseless change and bustle. This idea of nature's permanence echoed the mid-century Transcendentalists, who juxtaposed the indomitability of nature against the impermanence of our human presence on Earth.

Cleveland might have been postulating that the great parks of his generation, more than the town hall or the courthouse, would become the quintessential American civic monument. Though a product of human labor, the park would be a permanent outpost and manifestation of nature. The larger and more graceful it was, the more nature would be provided. It was to become the post-enlightenment analog to the European square, now a *green* public space of order and stability carved out of the grey, amorphous, cacophonous city. An endlessly modernizing society could not depend on its built form for endurance. Buildings and infrastructure become obsolete and give way to replacements. The park, embodying the immutability of nature, would remain, tempering chaos and providing stability for the otherwise transient city. That, Horace Cleveland may have been implying, was the ultimate contribution of the urban park movement, which the passing of a century would reveal.

Landscape Urbanism

A century later, a newly ambitious generation of landscape architects, seeking to emerge from the shadow of the architecture and planning professions, began to question the supposition that city building was the prerogative of those disciplines alone. Calling themselves "landscape urbanists" and "ecological urbanists," they proclaimed that urban planning needed to combine ecological awareness, dedication to the recovery of polluted ground, infrastructural engineering, and progressive social policy. It needed the special insights that landscape architects could offer about the environmental underpinnings of truly healthy human settlements. They asserted that, while urbanization in the twenty-first century might take many forms, an environmentalist's mindset—with its awareness of land and environmental constraints—should lead the way.[21]

One might suppose that such activist landscape architects, seeking to enlarge their sphere of influence, would consider Olmsted and his peers to be founding heroes of their profession. Were not Olmsted and colleagues practicing as landscape architects *and* urban planners, inventing both these disciplines with their work? Had they not advocated an early environmental perspective for urban design well prior to other professionals? Were they not planning for the long term, projecting how cities should grow into the future? Well, yes, but their sensibility—favoring naturalistic aesthetic effects—is largely out of fashion among progressive landscape architects. Their style is now considered too simplistic, as it casts nature and urbanism into binary opposition rather than intertwining them as contemporary ecological knowhow would advise us to do. At least that is a stated reservation. So while the present landscape urbanists concede influence from mid-twentieth century, environment-focused planners such as Ian McHarg, they do not often enough recall the seminal role of the original landscape urbanists. What they overlook is that the deployment of the picturesque or naturalistic style by Olmsted's generation was not merely a stylistic choice. We can discern this from a quick look at the intellectual origins of their movement.

The popularity of designed landscapes for the enjoyment of city dwellers originated with the Victorians, the result in England of a similar striving for social reform. Of course, the prevalence of country estates, hunting forests, royal parks, and similar properties that were long the domain of the elite, provided an easy solution for the growing demand for green spaces. As democratization unfolded, it was relatively easy to open these places to public use. Most reflected what had been a gradual shift in aesthetic preferences in the design of pleasure grounds and country estates. From the middle of the eighteenth century, landscape gardeners (as they were known) such as Capability Brown, and later Humphry Repton and Joseph Paxton (the designer of Birkenhead Park, much admired by Olmsted), had embraced the naturalistic style. This was a reaction, especially in England, against the overly geometric Baroque and Rococo styles that had been prevalent on the Continent. It was also congruent with the general flowering of English Romanticism and imagined Virgilian pastoral settings.

When the Duke of Marlborough called on his architect, John Vanbrugh, to modernize the grounds of his estate at Blenheim Palace, the architect supposedly offered terse advice: "You must send for a landscape painter."[22] Decades later, in the 1760s, the fourth Duke commissioned Capability Brown (whose work Olmsted much admired) to reconceive the grounds of Blenheim Estate. As the two plans show, by the end of the eighteenth century the grounds were fundamentally transformed, largely subsuming the axial composition of prior taste. (See Figures 8.10 and 8.11.) At Blenheim, and throughout England, a change in aesthetic sensibilities was being embraced. The prior prevalence of formal, geometric compositions made the new naturalistic look more appealing and fresh. The great Lord Byron himself would soon declare that "symmetry was not for solitude."[23]

For Olmsted's generation, however, the naturalistic approach had more of an ideological rather than an aesthetic underpinning. As in Central Park, the effort to make the landscape more naturalistic was believed necessary for the park to be experienced as a refuge from the surrounding city—producing, in Olmsted's words, "the greatest contrast with the restraining and confining conditions of the town." The parks had to look natural to serve their purpose of providing nature's healing affects. One hopes that the work and aesthetics of the present generation of "landscape urbanists" develops with comparably social-minded convictions.

Regardless of aesthetics, today's contributors to urban open space continue to broaden the role that parks, greenways, and public places play in serving city dwellers. In Boston, for example, a campaign on behalf of an Emerald

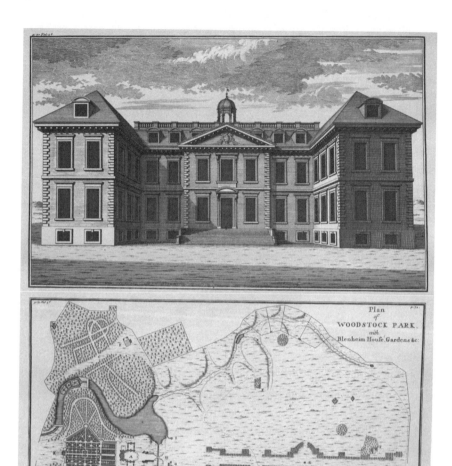

8.10   The grounds of Blenheim Estate, c. 1705, organized around a formal axis.

Network (not merely a necklace) is embarked on expanding the city's fabled park system to connect to areas less well served by open space, to improve public health and expand access to the recreational and commuting opportunities needed for thriving neighborhoods. New York City, where the parks movement achieved its first true monument, has recently witnessed an ambi-

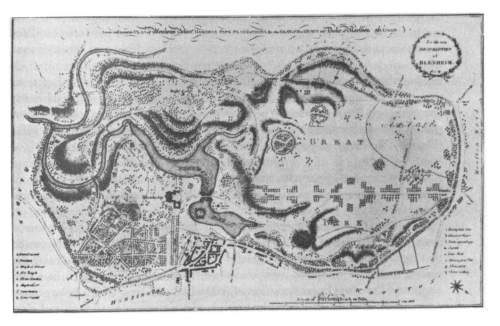

8.11   **The grounds of the Blenheim Estate, c. 1763.**

tious expansion and reinvestment in parks and park-like environments. Most famously, there is now the High Line, a landscape created along disused elevated tracks on the lower west side of Manhattan. But there have been other major projects such as the Brooklyn Bridge Parks, the Hunter's Point Parks in Queens, the Hills on Governors' Island, and the ongoing transformation of the Freshkills landfill on Staten Island into what will be one of the largest urban parks in America. Yet, a recent commentator offers a caution. Daring to observe that the High Line exists more for touristic pleasures and speculators in adjacent real estate than for locals, Aaron Betsky asks whether the social purpose of parks has become secondary. Are they now inadvertently abetting social injustice by being built in neighborhoods that are already desirable and prosperous, and thus serving as an accelerant for gentrification? [24] It is a reasonable warning and one that officials should be conscious of whenever and wherever new city parks are planned.

One way to temper such concern is to see a popular park on a sunny day—a place like Brooklyn Bridge Park, created on long abandoned piers by water's edge by a present-day Olmsted, Michael van Valkenburgh and his landscape

8.12   Away from the $15 cocktails at the DUMBO side of Brooklyn
Bridge Park, picnic tables attract a much more diverse crowd.

8.13   Overview of the Brooklyn Bridge parks with the recreational piers in the
foreground.

architecture firm. To see thousands of family picnickers, joggers, walkers, children, athletes, sun bathers, kayakers, and even waders testing the not-exactly-clean harbor waters—ordinary people who clearly have come from near and far—is to feel confidence in the work of current park builders, and to renew faith in the old belief in the recuperative role of urban parks. (See Figures 8.12 and 8.13.)

9.1   View of the Court of Honor at the Louisiana Purchase Centennial Exposition in St. Louis, 1904. Given their similarities, this photograph was mislabeled as a view of the *cour d'honneur* at the 1893 Columbian Exposition in Chicago, on a copy at Harvard's Loeb Library. The similarity was not accidental, rival St. Louis was determined to show off its own City Beautiful ambitions.

9

UTOPIANS AND REFORMERS IN A CAULDRON OF URBANIZATION

> At my feet lay a great city. Miles of broad streets, shaded by trees and
> lined with fine buildings, for the most part not in continuous blocks
> but set in larger or smaller enclosures, stretched in every direction.
> Every quarter contained large open squares filled with trees, among
> which statues glistened and fountains flashed in the late afternoon sun.
> Public buildings of a colossal size and an architectural grandeur
> unparalleled in my day raised their stately piles on every side. Surely
> I had never seen this city nor one comparable to it before.
>
> EDWARD BELLAMY, 1888

> There are now no cities in Altruria, in your meaning, but there are
> capitals . . . centers of all the arts which we consider the chief of our
> public affairs.
>
> WILLIAM DEAN HOWELLS, 1894

THE FINAL DECADES of the nineteenth century and the opening years of the twentieth have been variously labeled the Gilded Age, the Age of Enterprise, the Progressive Era, the Era of the City Beautiful, the American Renaissance, and, less positively, the Age of Excess.[1] The excess extended in two directions. For the rich, it was an excess of material goods, as they indulged in the conspicuous consumption that Thorstein Veblen made so famous in *The Theory of the Leisure*

Class. For the poor, living next door to the grand neighborhoods of the wealthy, it was a surplus of squalor. The harsh contrasts of the era spawned both radical utopians, who dreamed of a better world, and down-to-earth reformers, committed to street-level relief of social misery. Sometimes these people were one and the same. As they worked to redirect the energies of excess and enterprise to achieve broader social benefits, they saw the city as, in equal measure, a crisis to overcome and the hope of the future. While advocates of the City Beautiful pursued beautification and civic grandeur, seeking to create cities as impressive as any built by the venerable civilizations across the Atlantic, utopians and reformers focused on overcoming the despair found among the growing numbers of less fortunate urban dwellers.

By one historian's account, some 160 utopian narratives were published between the late 1870s and 1900, surely as astonishing a body of utopian literature as produced during any era.[2] These presented futures of civility, cooperation, equality, and health—conditions becoming scarcer by the day on the swelling and sweltering streets of late-nineteenth-century urban America. Other writers focused on political and managerial change as the path to improving urban conditions. Henry George, for example, first in *Progress and Poverty* and later in *The Menace of Privilege,* implored America to move away from private land ownership and embrace the principle of land as a shared social good. There was Henry Demarest Lloyd's steadfast campaign against industrial monopolies in *Wealth against Commonwealth* and other publications. Helen Campbell exposed the mistreatment of women in the sewing industries, and by extension all menial laborers, in her 1889 *Prisoners of Poverty.*[3] Many offered utopian economic and social ideas, but a few went further to imagine actual physical settings in which inequality would be unknown. We'll see this in the utopias of Edward Bellamy and William Dean Howells.

The historian Elisabeth Hansot captures the dual nature of the period in the title of her book *Perfection and Progress.*[4] Reformers sought steady if slow social progress, while utopians imagined a future miraculously free of all the afflictions of the present. Both saw many reasons for concern: turbulent economic times, unrest among the laboring classes, growing municipal corruption, worsening hygienic conditions amidst unseemly congestion, and throngs of immigrants with their own needs for employment, living accommodations, and social support. All these were consequences of a previously unimaginable and clearly unmanageable rate of urban growth. (See Figures 3.2, 9.4, and 11.1.) Responses differed ac-

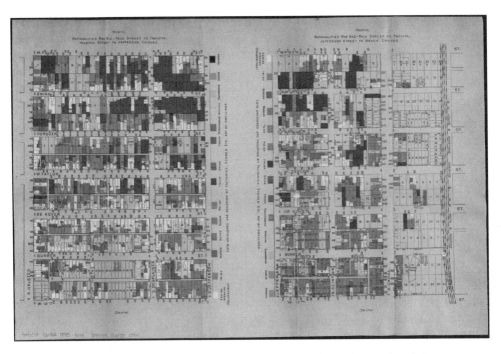

9.2 **Predigital-era data mining. Example of the kinds of information produced at Hull House to describe the diversity of immigrants living on several Chicago blocks: an effort to make visible social and demographic disparities and inequalities.**

cording to whether one wanted to advance change through the existing institutional framework, or design a more perfect future starting with a clean slate.

We in the twenty-first century marvel at the growth rates of cities in the still urbanizing world. In recent decades, China alone has seen some twenty to thirty million people migrate *every year* from rural to urban areas. On a worldwide basis, United Nations statistics suggest that upwards of sixty million people a year migrate to urban areas. A similar phenomenon was occurring in America 150 years ago, in the "furnace stage" of America's urbanization, as novelist Theodore Dreiser aptly called it. During the 1880s, Chicago more than doubled its population, as it had in each of the prior several decades, and it continued growing as fast as any city on earth, adding at least five hundred thousand people in each of the next three decades. New York City, already much larger, grew by at least a million people in the decades between 1880 and 1910, adding a staggering 1.8 million in the final decade of the nineteenth century. Other American cities were also growing exponentially. Out west, the population of Denver grew from fewer than 5,000 people in 1870 to nearly 110,000 by 1890. Los Angeles grew from around 11,000 in 1880 to 320,000 by 1910, and would exceed 1,200,000 by 1930. Local birthrates accounted for less than a quarter of this growth. Another 30 percent was migration from rural areas. The rest was immigration, as millions of new people arrived in the United States each year and most of them landed in cities, creating the added complexity of assimilating diverse peoples and cultures.[5]

The period was not distinguished by outpourings of affection for the city, except among a class of elites advocating for their City Beautiful. Most commentators agreed that cities were in trouble, but they disagreed intensely about the prospects for urban change. Some saw the emerging industrial city as a stew of chaotic forces that could only dehumanize life and overshadow the individual; others conceded that the present was intolerable, but saw in the forces of industrialization and laissez-faire capitalism an opportunity to achieve a new and positive urbanism. A dichotomous portrait emerged: the City of Hope and the City of Despair. Utopians and reformers were determined to reduce the despair and engender hope. And both camps would seek lessons from that amazing event briefly visited in previous chapters—the 1893 World's Columbian Exposition, Chicago's White City.

Lessons from the Fair

Most utopias are expressions of imagination conveyed in literary or pictorial form. The utopianism of Chicago's White City burst forth in three dimensions, and citizens were startled. Commemorating the four-hundredth anniversary of the European discovery of America, and obliging the Eastern Seaboard and indeed the world to acknowledge the rising economic and cultural heft of the Middle West, the fair greeted the future with exuberance. Gatekeepers recorded more than 27 million visitors during the six-month celebration, an astonishing number given that the country's entire population in 1890 was but slightly more than double that.[6] At a moment when the pace of urbanization threatened to overwhelm any traditional attributes of city life, the fair's displays of technology, commerce, striking architecture, and artistic sensibilities presented many reasons for hope. For those discouraged by the raw disorder of industrializing northeastern cities (southern cities being, for the most part, still mired in postbellum recession) the gleaming, efficient future projected by the fair was seductive.

The scale of the spectacle was astounding. For example, the steel and glass roof of the Manufactures and Liberal Arts Building, which had to cover forty-four acres of exhibition space, was the largest ever constructed. A diagram in the *American Architect and Building News* showed that it could shelter the Great Pyramid, Winchester Cathedral, and the US Capitol, with enough room left over to accommodate Madison Square Garden (which, for proud Manhattanites, surely rankled).[7] The fair presented numerous wonders beyond the spectacular exhibition halls and expansive public grounds. There were moving sidewalks, gurgling drinking fountains, sanitary facilities, swift garbage removal, and efficient crowd control. Electricity was at work everywhere, and there was even a monorail to transport visitors across the vast grounds. (It would take seventy-five years for another monorail to appear in the United States, and only thanks to Walt Disney). Technical ingenuity was around every corner, and the overall environment was awe-inspiring. Many considered it beautiful. Those flocking to the fair to pick up clues about the future of American life were rarely disappointed. They came away believing such wonders would come to pass—no less than if an ideal city had actually been realized.

An early proposal for the fair involved a single pyramidal structure of glass and steel some three thousand feet in diameter and seven hundred feet high. Its designer reasoned that Chicago could not compete in terms of architectural sophistication with the 1889 Paris fair (or the one in Vienna in 1873, or London's in 1851), but it could "outrival Paris in a truly American way" by building the biggest structure ever—"out-Eiffeling Eiffel by an eighth of a mile."[8] Cultural observers such as William Dean Howells, who would soon produce one of the more astonishing utopian sagas, hoped that this act of technical one-upmanship signified the end of America's cultural provincialism. The classical aesthetics of the fair suggested to Howells an even grander turning point. He perceived a new willingness to shift the national focus from material might to intellect and idealism; from competition to cooperation; from individual gain to social interest; and maybe even from self-enrichment to responsibility for the well-being of neighbors.[9]

Howells's hopes may have been naive, but he shared his optimistic spirit with most of the era's utopians, all of them eager to progress beyond industrial monopolization, cutthroat competitiveness, and gaping inequality. Howells saw the fair as the nearest approximation of his fictional Altruria, and predicted that future generations would "look back upon it, and recognize in it the first embodiment of the Altrurian idea among them, and will cherish it forever in their history, as the earliest achievement of a real civic life." The historian Henry Adams, struggling to chronicle a culture far more diverse than that of his illustrious ancestors, John and John Quincy Adams, similarly fell under the fair's spell, proclaiming it "the first expression of American thought as a unity."[10] The social critic Charles Eliot Norton remarked after his visit that the fair "forbids despair," and added that "I have never seen Americans from whom one could draw happier auguries for the future of America than some of the men I saw in Chicago."[11] Members of the country's many Bellamy Clubs, organized to advance Edward Bellamy's socialistic nationalism saw the fair's *cour d'honneur* as a preview of what the country would be like in the year 2000.

Bellamy's Boston in the Year 2000

Edward Bellamy's *Looking Backward: 2000–1887,* was the best known, most inspirational, and most read of the era's utopian novels. His tale of an egalitarian society arising from a just national economic monopoly, set in pastoral settings and replete with material comforts, caught the public's imagination. Why wouldn't it? The pastoral side of his utopia was a crucial part of its appeal. Indeed, utopians at the time frequently and hopefully imagined pastoral futures, partly to draw clear contrasts with the decidedly un-pastoral urban present, and partly to call forth Jeffersonian and Transcendentalist memories. Many were also inspired by the achievements of the great urban park builders, themselves social reformers. For a time, *Looking Backward* outsold even the Bible, which was far and away the most widely read and distributed book in America across the whole nineteenth century and much of the twentieth.

The story features a young, wealthy Bostonian, living in luxury but chagrined by the state of affairs for those less privileged. He falls into a 113-year long slumber and awakens to a Boston that has astonishingly transformed. A century removed from Bellamy's time, the inhabitants of the new Boston are peaceful, cooperative, well-educated, healthy, and happy citizens, who know nothing of crime, poverty, congestion, or competitive behavior. Freed entirely of the dirty factories and slums of the industrial era and the gritty realities of New York's and Chicago's mean streets, Bellamy's future Boston consists of "miles of broad streets, shaded by trees and lined with fine buildings," unsullied by soot or sewage. It is a lovely, infectious vision, its Edenic imagery precisely the opposite of how reformers saw the overworked, underpaid, unkempt crowds on actual city streets in 1887. Science and technology abound in this future, yet a familiar transcendental spirit prevails as Bellamy evokes a simpler New England past of public commons, gardens, and pastoral pleasures. The wealth of the community is channeled much less into ostentatious private goods and more into public infrastructure, arts institutions, and recreational amenities. "At home we have comfort," the narrator's host explains, "but the splendor of our life is, on its social side, that which we share with our fellows."[12]

Each Bostonian lives free of injustice and inequality and without the seductions of property, sharing equally in the economic output of society. There is no competition for resources, or unequal material accumulation, because abundance is shared. The most brilliant aspect of the story is that this transformation turns out to have had its beginnings in runaway capitalism—the very object of many reformers' wrath in Bellamy's time. The ultimate result of all those industries expanding and consolidating in the nineteenth century was that they congealed into one, vast monopoly, which was then taken over by and managed by the public, so that its profits and efficiencies could be distributed evenly to create a universal middle class. In Bellamy's future, "the industry and commerce of the country, ceasing to be conducted by a set of irresponsible corporations and syndicates of private persons at their caprice and for their profit, were entrusted to a single syndicate representing the people, to be conducted in the common interest for the common profit."[13]

It is a future in which banks, traders, and self-interested entrepreneurs have no place: "As soon as the nation became the sole producer of all sorts of commodities, there was no need of exchanges between individuals that they might get what they required. Everything was procurable from one source, and nothing could be procured anywhere else. A system of direct distribution from the national storehouses took the place of trade, and for this money was unnecessary."[14]

Is it any wonder that over 150 Bellamy Clubs formed to advance Bellamy's vision, not seeing it as a pipe dream at all? It was particularly reassuring for Americans that this socialist future seemed not to require the class struggle and revolution that Marx had predicted.

In the book's postscript, Bellamy claims that although the story takes the form of "a fanciful romance," his real intention was to produce "a forecast, in accordance with the principles of evolution, of the next stage in the industrial and social development of humanity." He is optimistic, moreover, that "the dawn of the new era is near at hand, and that the full day will swiftly follow."[15] This optimism is perhaps a reason that *Looking Backward* remains in print one hundred and thirty years later—a full twenty years, that is, after young Julian West, Bellamy's narrator, was to have awakened to a perfectly egalitarian future. One can imagine a version of *Looking Backward* being written today in protest against recent headlines, such as those proclaiming that America's twenty richest individuals hold as much wealth as much as the bottom 152 million, or the even more startling statistic that the eighty-five wealthiest in the world own as much as the 3.5 billion poorest.[16] Humanity still awaits Bellamy's utopia.

Calls to Conscience amidst Splendor

Recall that the era of Bellamy, Howells, Lloyd, and George was also referred to as the Gilded Age. Great fortunes were being made, and their many manifestations were deliberately made not just visible but unavoidable. Magnificent edifices and institutions were being erected, and not just in the form of fabulous mansions along New York's Fifth Avenue for industrialist "robber barons." The nation's growing wealth also appeared in splendid courthouses, post offices, train stations, libraries, state capitols, and civic plazas, The idea of *noblesse oblige*, the responsibility of the elite to contribute to the betterment of society, was in vogue around the time of the Chicago World's Fair. Many of the nation's cultural institutions owed their founding, expansion, and new buildings to philanthropic giving. Historian William Jordy captures the spirit of the times in a memorable description of Charles McKim, arguably the most prominent architect of the age: "In the cause of Art, and in the conviction that the highest calling of wealth was its civilizing effects on society, of which magnificent patronage of the arts was a cardinal aspect, [McKim] cajoled millions from his clients."[17]

Many were excited by the promise of a City Beautiful. Cultural pundits and growing numbers of civic organizations and municipal art societies were drawn to the idea of uplifting society by creating graceful cities filled with beauty. They saw aesthetic embellishment as a catalyst for investment, for boosting morale, and to instill patriotic pride.[18] The advocates of a City Beautiful tended to simplistically equate visual order with social felicity. Consider how Charles Mulford

Robinson, a City Beautiful polemicist, opened his *Modern Civic Art: Or, The City Made Beautiful:*

> There is a promise in the sky of a new day. The darkness rolls away, and the buildings that had been shadows stand forth distinctly in the gray air. The tall facades glow as the sun rises; their windows shine as topaz; their pennants of steam, tugging flutteringly from high chimneys, are changed to silvery plumes. Whatever was dingy, course, and ugly, is either transformed or hidden in shadow. The streets, bathed in the fresh morning light, fairly sparkle, their pavements from upper windows appearing smooth and clean. There seems to be a new city for the work of the new day. There is more than even the transformation that Nero boasted he had made in Rome, for night closed here on a city of brick, stone, and steel; but the morning finds it better than gold.[19]

A kindred spirit of Robinson, Lawrence Underwood, more succinctly proclaimed that "beautiful and clean cities attract desirable citizens, and real estate values increase. Clothes don't make the man, but they come pretty near making the city."[20]

Both statements are naive and elitist, though the matter of beautiful urban "clothing" is not entirely dismissible; it brings to mind the cities we love to visit as tourists, or how economic development officers and chambers of commerce present cities in their promotional literature.

What about all those "hidden in shadow" by the magnificent new buildings? Among the people working hard to make them more visible was Jacob Riis, a Danish immigrant working as a reporter on a police crime beat, carrying a heavy camera and a primitive strobe light. His book, *How the Other Half Lives*, was published in 1890 and it, too, is still in print.[21] The title was misleading, in a way, because in fact more than half of the urban citizenry was made up of the "wretched creatures" Riis made visible with his disturbing photographs. More worrisome still, the percentage was growing.

Not all were moved by Riis's photographs. Some thought they were more sensationalist than informative—an early version of what has been dubbed "ruin porn" in reference to modern images of blighted neighborhoods in places like Baltimore, Detroit, and St. Louis. There were even doubts about veracity, as close examination of some photos revealed they had been staged—a necessity,

9.3   One of Jacob Riis's startling photographs, though having to be
staged (notice the smile on the boy at left) given the limitations then
of photo illumination technology.

9.4   A typical urban street early in the twentieth century such as where Jacob Riis
would seek out the subjects of his photographs.

actually, given that camera and film technologies of the day required slow exposure in conditions of moderate light. Whether or not the photography was candid, the statistics Riis presented showed conditions to be woefully inadequate, as did evidence gathered by reform-minded journalists—the so-called muckrakers, Lloyd and Bellamy prominent among them—and municipal reform organizations such as tenement commissions. A survey of one New York block, for example, revealed that it had 39 structures containing 2,781 residents, but only 264 water closets and no baths. Among the rooms in these structures, at least 600 had inadequate airshafts, and another 440 had no ventilation at all.[22] Most of the occupants, who were of various ethnicities, were recent immigrants. Their living conditions had been chalked up to their "odd customs" or general lack of education or morals. Riis and other muckrakers were convinced that the poverty and social dysfunction of these neighborhoods was not due to their people's ethnicities but to their lack of opportunities. (See Figures 9.3 and 9.4.)

Concurrently, the pioneering social activist Jane Addams and her colleagues at Chicago's Hull House, and similar urban "settlement houses," were also asserting that poverty and other negative environmental circumstances produced social ills, not populations of certain races or ethnicities. Character defects were not a cause of poverty, they argued, but a consequence of it. Furthermore, if some people were living in poverty and inhumane conditions, this was the proper concern of the public and not just the individual sufferers. Ministering to the needs of the poor, the sick and impaired, the uneducated, and helpless women and children was not an act of pure altruism. "The good we secure for ourselves," Addams wrote, "is precarious and uncertain, is floating in mid-air, until it is secured for all of us and incorporated into our common life."[23]

Addams founded Hull House in 1889 with Ellen Gates Starr after reading about and then visiting the world's first "settlement house" on a visit to London. Not simply an institution for charity, Hull House began to offer a range of social, educational, cultural, and health-related programs, gradually growing into a complex of a dozen buildings visited by as many as two thousand people daily. The need was evident, and launched a movement. By 1920, nearly five hundred such institutions existed across urban America. Addams herself became a national institution. Her indefatigable personality led her to champion many causes, among them women's suffrage, child labor laws, worker safety, healthcare reform, pacifism, and immigration policy. Her campaigns helped to initiate the tradition of social work in America, and she even helped to found the

9.5   Jane Addams addressing a group of children at Hull House, 1930.

American Civil Liberties Union. In 1931, Addams was awarded a Nobel Peace Prize; she was the first American woman to receive the honor. (See Figure 9.5.)

Addams's autobiographical *Twenty Years at Hull House* was published in 1910 and depicts a selfless life. "If it is natural to feed the hungry and care for the sick," she writes, "it is certainly natural to give pleasure to the young, comfort to the aged, and to minister to the deep-seated craving for social intercourse that all men feel. Whoever does it is rewarded by something which, if not gratitude, is at least spontaneous and vital and lacks that irksome sense of obligation with which a substantial benefit is too often acknowledged."[24] If only all felt this way.

A few pages later, she recalls her earlier conviction that "the good must be extended to all of society before it can be held secure by any one person or any one class," then adds: "But we have not yet learned to add to that statement, that unless all and all classes contribute to a good, we cannot even be sure that it is worth having."[25]

The efforts of Addams, Riis, and fellow reformers at what might be called social stewardship did gradually lead to political and managerial reform. Urban America created institutions and regulations to at least improve physical conditions and the dignity of citizens. Sanitary commissions, sewerage boards, planning boards, and building and zoning commissions—along with fire-safety codes, sunlight and ventilation requirements, limits on workday hours, and other such health and safety provisions—were among the gifts of the Progressive Era. A professional urban planner would emerge, committed to considering the general welfare of urban citizens, regardless of class or ethnicity. Reformers also made advances in hygiene and sex education, age of consent legislation, the prohibition of prostitution, and other such issues of morality. But along with such advances there remained a sense that the selflessness emanating from a Jane Addams needed to be broadened, perhaps universalized. Let's then turn now to the utopia envisioned by William Dean Howells. As many other progressives despaired that inequality was becoming worse even as national economic growth expanded, he set out an alternative.

Altruria

Just as Thomas More did with his own imaginary community of Utopia, Howells located Altruria on a remote island, where a self-sufficient society lives cooperatively, rationally, and with full equally. Derived from the Latin *alter*, meaning "the other," Altruria was indeed, for Howells, the other America—the one that had not given up on its foundational ideals, especially about all people being created equal. This utopia was not set in a distant future like Bellamy's Boston— no, in Howells's story, visitors from Altruria travel to America to observe the gap between coveted American ideals and their actual realization in Altruria. Howells had set up a platform for judging America.

The visiting Altrurians wonder how the descendants of the drafters of the Declaration of Independence could live with such social stratification; exhibit so much selfishness, egoism, and brute competitiveness; and acquiesce to such inequality of opportunity. It's as if Alexander Hamilton's rush to an industrial America had trampled all over Jefferson's agrarian republic, without preserving the noblest ideals of either man—deplorable consequences now visible across urban America.

In *A Traveller from Altruria* (and the subsequent *Letters of an Altrurian Traveler*), published as a series of magazine pieces, Howells furiously condemns the city at his feet, then radically reinvents it. Mr. Aristides Homos, an emissary of the Altrurian Commonwealth, travels to America and describes a crisis point in distant Altrurian history that resembled the present America:

"We had, of course, a great many large cities under the old egoistic conditions, which increased and fattened upon the country, and fed their
cancerous life with fresh infusions of its blood. . . . We were very proud
of them, and vaunted them as proof of our unparalleled prosperity,
though really they never were anything but congeries of millionaires and
the wretched creatures who served them and supplied them. . . .

"Almost from the moment of the Evolution the competitive and monopolistic centers of population began to decline. In the clear light of
the new order it was seen that they were not fit dwelling-places for men,
either in the complicated and luxurious palaces where the rich fenced
themselves from their kind, or in the vast tenements, towering height
upon height . . . where the swarming poor festered in vice and sickness
and famine. . . . We let them fall to ruin as quickly as they would, and
their sites are still so pestilential, after the lapse of centuries, that travel-
lers are publicly guarded against them.[26]

The term "pestilential" may not have been accidental. It was the very word
Thomas Jefferson used a century earlier in advising Americans to avoid the
artificialities and social inequalities of Europe's urbanizing civilizations. The Altrurians had heeded such warnings. Their abandoned cities were given over to
"ravening beasts and poisonous reptiles" and served humans merely as a lesson.
In an ironic twist on historic preservation, the Altrurians maintain part of one
of the "less malarial" of their old cities "in the form of its prosperity" to be
"studied by antiquarians for the instruction, and by moralists for the admoni-
tion it affords."[27]

Where did the Altrurians choose to live once they had let their cities fall into
ruin? Homos describes the miraculous transformation:

There are now no cities in Altruria, in your meaning, but there are capitals, one for each of the Regions of our country, and one for the whole
commonwealth. These capitals are for the transaction of public affairs . . . [and as] the centers of all the arts, which we consider the chief
of our public affairs, they are oftenest frequented by poets, actors, painters, sculptors, musicians and architects. We regard all artists, who are in
a sort creators, as the human type which is likest the divine, and we try

to conform our whole industrial life to the artistic temperament. . . . In the capitals are the universities, theaters, galleries, museums, cathedrals, laboratories and conservatories, and the appliances of every art and science.[28]

For Howells as for the champions of the City Beautiful, the cities of the future were to be places free of the traumas that lurked immediately outside the World's Fair gates. What was remarkable about Howells's tale was how swiftly—in just a few pages—he eviscerates the city, at least the city around him, and then reinvents it as he wishes it to be. He condemns the reality of the industrial city, purging it of all of its shortcomings and failings. Yet in his utopia a special kind of city remains: it is the seat of the artist, the human type most like the divine. Howells is dismissive of all urban conceits, but remained attached, in his own life, to urban people and places, much in the way that Thomas Jefferson always loved Paris. Howells is unforgiving toward cities because they "drain the country of its life and force," yet is thrilled by their possibilities. It is revealing that he has Mr. Homos visit Chicago's Columbian Exposition—resplendent with classical architecture, clean, ordered and well managed—and write back to a friend in Altruria: "Of the effect, of the visible, tangible result, what better can I say, than that in its presence I felt myself again in Altruria? . . . I was at home once more, and my heart overflowed with patriotic rapture in this strange land, so remote from ours in everything, that at times Altruria really seems to me the dream which the Americans think it.[29]

The White City was an urbanism cleansed of all of industrial urbanism's faults and failings. It was not a city for "congeries of millionaires and the wretched creatures that served them and supplied them," but a "capital for the transaction of public affairs." Except the White City was just a temporary stage set, constructed of perishable materials, and Altruria, well, merely literature. What was needed was an opportunity to construct an actual place that might exhibit the qualities that seemed so appealing about the fair and about Howells's imagined America.

So it would be to America's capital that the era's utopians, reformers, park designers, and civic design advocates turned. Washington, a century into its existence, having grown slowly, but now with an expanding federal bureaucracy and a desire to compete on the international stage, was finally ready to fulfill its original, grandiloquent plan.

10.1   View from the base of the Washington Monument toward the
Lincoln Memorial, with the national World War II memorial in the foreground.

10

WASHINGTON: CITY OF MAGNIFICENT INTENTIONS

> It will be obvious that the plan should be drawn on such a scale as to
> leave room for that aggrandizement and embellishment which the
> increase of the wealth of the nation will permit it to pursue at any
> period however remote . . .
>
> PIERRE L'ENFANT TO GEORGE WASHINGTON, 1789

THE EPIGRAPH IS FROM a letter of solicitation. Major Pierre Charles L'Enfant, French expatriate, Revolutionary War veteran, friend to General Washington and designer of the general's military insignia, wanted a job. It was not yet clear what the job would entail. The official designation of a future capital along the Potomac River in the vicinity of Georgetown (named either for the King or for the two town founders named George, not the first president) was still months away. L'Enfant, however, was ready, already planning a monumental undertaking suitable not for a fledgling nation in its twelfth year of existence but for "any period however remote."

A century would surely have seemed remote to L'Enfant, President Washington, and Secretary of State Thomas Jefferson. How disappointed they would have been to learn that in 1891, an eminent author, James Bryce in *The American Commonwealth*, would declare that among the great countries of the world, the United States was the only one without a capital. In fairness, Bryce was referring to the distributed nature of political power in America, being himself an advocate of a stronger central government.[1] But it was nonetheless true that a century after its birth, the city of Washington was a physical disappointment, at best a work in progress. The "aggrandizement and embellishment" that L'Enfant had promised the president, and left room for in his plan, had hardly been achieved. The nation's capital required another moment of inspired utopian chutzpah, a full century after L'Enfant, to come into its own. And it would take much of a second century for Washington, DC, to finally become a bustling, dynamic, urban, and urbane environment instead of . . . well, just a capital.

For much of the nineteenth century, there was not much there apart from a few government edifices at considerable distance from each other, and broad streets heading off in undeveloped directions. The street alignments were defined not by buildings but by rows of poplar trees that Jefferson had ordered planted. Not located at a regional crossroads, the city had hardly any industry, no proper harbor, only a few cultural institutions, and little local banking or finance—let alone a stock exchange. It was considered a civic and economic backwater, and not just among Philadelphians, who continued to wonder why the capital had ever moved away from their city. London, Paris, and Berlin were capitals on multiple levels: centers of governance, yes, but also of commerce and culture, boasting substantial size, prestige, and economic clout. Their equivalent in America, even Philadelphians might have conceded, was New York. There are still people around the world who would be surprised to hear that it is not America's capital.

As Washington began to grow in the decades after the Civil War, as a result of the federal government's expansion and an influx of freed slaves and others either disenfranchised or empowered in the aftermath of the war, people began to be more bothered by the physical character of the place. Despairing of its mediocrity, disorder and emptiness, some members of Congress even agitated to move the capital elsewhere. Dissatisfaction spurred a variety of bold and sometimes naive ideas for improvement. Eventually one congressman was able to marshal support for a second grand plan for the city; he was James McMillan, a senator from Michigan who had earlier worked on the creation of Detroit's Belle Isle Park with Frederick Law Olmsted, Sr. To understand what the McMillan plan sought and achieved, however, we should first understand the origins and fate of its first great plan. Let's return to L'Enfant and the city's beginnings.

Planning for a National Capital

Between the Declaration of Independence in 1776 and the end of 1793, seven different places served as the nation's capital, if we count those temporarily designated by Congress such as Germantown, Pennsylvania, which stood in for Philadelphia when a Yellow Fever epidemic forced an evacuation. The others were Baltimore, Georgetown, Lancaster (Pennsylvania), New York, Philadelphia, and a site at the falls of the Delaware River. Finally, it was established by the Residence Act of 1790 that the capital would be sited on a ten-square-mile area designated as a federal district, distinct from the states, somewhere along an eighty-mile stretch of the Potomac River. The Act also required the appointment of a three-person commission to take charge of acquiring suitable land and to manage the planning. L'Enfant would clash repeatedly with these three as land acquisition, resale, and speculation played a more prominent role in the capital's early days than histories commonly acknowledge.

Among the reasons for the lengthy political indecision about a site was the dilemma of whether it should favor a northern or southern area of the thirteen states. Jefferson, key to a number of decisions regarding the capital, including its design, helped assure a southerly location by striking a deal with Treasury Secretary Alexander Hamilton. The latter pledged his support if southern legislators would back his plan for a national financial system and approach to resolving the states' Revolutionary War debts. Historians have speculated, too, that George Washington had always preferred a site along the Potomac. It was near his estate at Mount Vernon, where he might persuade his many friends among the nearby landowners to make land available, and perhaps even profit from the advancement of the plan.

Washington also promoted a loftier idea, arguing for construction of a canal long enough to connect the Potomac to the Ohio River, and ultimately to the Great Lakes, making transportation easy between the east coast and the interior of the country. Supportive of Jefferson's work on surveying the vast territories gained from the British, Washington wrote to him of the importance of opening up "all the communications, which nature has afforded, between the Atlantic States and the western territory."[2] Along with James Madison—his fellow Virginian, future president, and leading drafter and promoter of the Constitution and the Bill of Rights—Washington imagined the capital to occupy a continental cross-axis. It would stand roughly midway between north and south among the thirteen former colonies, with the Potomac River serving as its gateway to points west. Washington had been awarded substantial landholdings in the Ohio territories in recognition of his service to the nation, and earlier, for his service to the British during the French and Indian Wars. Gaining greater access to these may have been a factor in Washington's thinking. With his surveyor's background, Washington was as keen a land speculator as a military strategist. By the end of his life, he had acquired some thirty-two thousand acres of Ohio, and around twenty thousand acres across other parts of the new nation.[3]

Construction on Washington's canal began in the 1780s, and maneuvered around the first rapids of the Potomac just beyond today's Chain Bridge, but could not get past Cumberland, Maryland, given the challenge of cutting through the Appalachians. It would be the Erie Canal, begun in 1817 and completed in 1825, that would find a way through. By creating the first connection between the Atlantic Ocean and western waterways, it bestowed huge economic benefits on New York City and the Great Lakes region, favoring the industrialization and urbanization of the northern states.

Complex negotiations with Maryland and Virginia, the states that would have to cede land to create the new federal district, and with numerous landowners, resulted in a starting point for the capital involving two areas. One was along the northern bank of the Anacostia River, where a place called Carrollsburg existed mostly as a "paper town"—meaning it had been laid out by a landholder, but not developed. The other was just south of Georgetown at the mouth of Goose Creek (also called Tiber Creek, and eventually completely buried) near the present Ellipse park grounds, south of the White House. A portion of this area was platted for another barely inhabited town, called Hamburgh. Andrew Ellicott, a surveyor previously retained, was already busy surveying some of the extensive areas in between. Washington then did indeed commission L'Enfant. But to do what? We get a clue from Jefferson, who was helping Washington to oversee the commission responsible for the capital and who had been sketching his own plans. Jefferson wrote to L'Enfant:

> You are desired to proceed to Georgetown, where you will find Mr. Ellicot employed in making a survey and map of the Federal territory. The special object of asking your aid is to have drawings of the particular

grounds most likely to be approved for the site of the federal town and buildings. You will therefore be pleased to begin on the eastern branch, and proceed from thence upwards, laying down the hills, valleys, morasses, and waters between that, the Potomac, the Tyber, and the road leading from Georgetown to the eastern branch, and connecting the whole with certain fixed points of the map Mr. Ellicot is preparing. . . . I will beg the favor of you to mark to me your progress about twice a week, by letter.[4]

These instructions hardly offered a *carte blanche* to design an entire city and its buildings at a monumental scale, though L'Enfant was happy to interpret it that way. Jefferson's initial idea, characteristic of his strategic mind, was to start way south along the Anacostia so as to neutralize some of the land speculation happening closer to Georgetown, near which most people assumed the major public edifices would be sited. His interest in town layout was also at play: he drew a simple sketch showing a regular grid parallel to the Eastern Branch (the Anacostia River) so that the majority of the blocks would be square, and only a few facing the Potomac would be triangular. Those few along the Potomac would be reserved for government functions, while the majority would be "for persons in commerce."[5] Here Jefferson was signaling his political preference for limited central government, expressed in modest, non-monumental form. Despite his lifelong ambivalence about cities, he clearly recognized they were important to business. (See Figure 10.2.) The addition of the commercial element, however, would be achieved only much later in the capital's evolution. A subsequent sketch by Jefferson, again arguing for a confined geographical area for the capital, favored Goose Creek. Indeed, among the central debates about the capital's layout and design was how prominent the capital city should be; Federalists favored a stronger central government and thus a capital as a worthy representative of such, while Jefferson and fellow Republicans favored state rights and so argued for a modestly conceived home for a central government.[6] Few were imagining that the capital would need to extend all the way from Georgetown to the Anacostia.

The exception was L'Enfant, whose ambitions were grander, perhaps more in keeping with those of President Washington, for whom on September 9, 1891 the city would be named. He thought of Versailles, where grand boulevards radiated from the King's palace, and his goal was to equal if not exceed the splen-

10.2 A Thomas Jefferson sketch for a plan for the nation's Capital, suggesting a location at the confluence of the Potomac and Anacostia, labeled "creek." 1790.

dor of other great Baroque gardens designed by his near-contemporary André Le Nôtre. To the initial dismay of Jefferson, L'Enfant began to sketch over the entire area being surveyed by Andrew Ellicott. He did so, however, with Washington's blessing, as the president had gathered the landowners across that enormous area to accept a particular land purchase and retention scheme.

Heartened by Washington's support for a grand plan, L'Enfant asked Jefferson to send him maps of great cities, which Jefferson provided from his extensive library. L'Enfant surely pored over the plans of Paris, Karlsruhe, Bordeaux, and the Rome of Pope Sixtus V's transformations more than he studied

Philadelphia, just 130 miles away—even though, in Jefferson's opinion, the latter's grid plan was the better model. "They are none of them however," Jefferson wrote about the maps he had sent, "comparable to the old Babylon, revived in Philadelphia, and exemplified."[7]

The fact that Philadelphia was the operating capital, and that many there doubted the wisdom of forsaking it for Virginia, may have dampened L'Enfant's or Washington's enthusiasm for its grid-dominated plan. But Jefferson's conviction that the grid embodied democracy, or at least provided the possibility for a more egalitarian distribution of land, pressured L'Enfant, against his sensibilities, to incorporate a grid as an underlay for the grand diagonal vistas he preferred. The result was the famous street pattern that often confounds visitors trying to maintain their sense of orientation.

At one point L'Enfant wrote to Washington complaining about Jefferson's insistence on the grid, calling it "tiresome and insipid."[8] That rather imperious attitude would shortly cause L'Enfant to lose his dream commission. It would not be for a disrespectful comment, but for ongoing obstinacy and lack of diplomacy in dealing with the three commissioners and the major landowners—the neighbors, colleagues, and rivals of President Washington. As an example, he ordered the demolition of a home owned by a nephew of one of the three commissioners, because it projected by a few feet into a planned street.[9] Also undercutting L'Enfant's insistence on the precise alignment of each of his drawn streets was the fact that land sales were not as brisk as anticipated, delaying revenues the government was counting on to keep advancing the plan.

Still, before L'Enfant was relieved of his duties in February 1792—not quite a year after being retained—he produced a truly seminal plan. (See Figure 10.3.) Few initial visions for a city have had such impact on that city's evolution. Formal geometric audacity aside, L'Enfant's plan came with a remarkable array of specifics, in the form of many annotations to his 1791 reference plan. In addition to specifying the location of the "President's House," the "Federal House," and a "Grand Avenue" fully four hundred feet wide—the area of today's Mall—he located nearly two dozen public squares at the intersections of his diagonal boulevards—which he called "Lines or Avenues of direct communication." The squares were for various important civic functions, each to be dedicated to a current or future state of the union. In addition to siting an equestrian statue for his patron where the Washington Monument would later be built, he noted other locations for statuary and fountains for commemorative purpose. He specified the widths of many streets with great precision. He designated a

10.3   L'Enfant's plan for the capital as revised by Andrew Ellicott following
L'Enfant's dismissal.

prominent site for a national church, unaware or perhaps insensitive to the ideal
of religious freedom. Anticipating the needs of industry and public transportation, he proposed a canal, a "Grand Cascade," to run from the Potomac along
the northern edge of his Grand Avenue to the base of the hill on which the
Capitol Building would sit, then south to the Anacostia. In *Pastoral Cities,*
James L. Machor even suggests that L'Enfant's consideration of topography, orientation, the generous width of his boulevards, and what he called the "air of
natural openness" constituted an early form of environmentalist thinking.[10]
One would be hard pressed to find a more detailed prescription for a future city
being laid out on barely surveyed, undeveloped land after only a few months of
work.

    While L'Enfant was the visionary force behind the plan, his fame has some-
what obscured the contributions of two others. One was Andrew Ellicott, who
was surveying the area in preparation for L'Enfant's work, and to whom the task
of finalizing L'Enfant's ideas was entrusted after L'Enfant's dismissal. Ellicott

faithfully translated L'Enfant's sketches into the official plan, with only modest changes. Assisting Ellicott in the initial survey, and some say also in the final drafting of the plan, was Benjamin Banneker, a freed black man self-educated in astronomy and mathematics. Banneker was known for his popular "Benjamin Banneker's Almanac," published between 1792 and 1797, and as the "proof"— cited by Thomas Jefferson, no less—that members of the "Negro race" were not intellectually inferior to people of European descent.[11] Such proof, unfortunately, did not bring a prompt end to the curse of slavery, or even convince Jefferson himself to free his many slaves.

Whatever the extent of Ellicott's and Banneker's assistance, in the annals of nations or empires setting out to establish centers of governance it is hard to find a grander plan than that produced by Major L'Enfant—and this for an unlikely area of hills, forests, malarial marshes and a few plantations. One might even call it a bit pompous for what, after all, was a still a loosely affiliated and fiscally shaky (in fact, near bankrupt) set of newly liberated British colonies.

Brilliant plan notwithstanding, the city grew slowly, requiring neither exact adherence to L'Enfant's vision nor the resolution of compromises between the plan intent and the few pressures for growth that arose. For decades, the plan languished given the rather modest needs of the federal government, and the absence of much besides government to attract people or businesses. Many of the boulevards were surveyed and laid out, but remained largely free of the institutions that define them today. Jefferson's planting of poplar trees along some of these made them visible, at least. Important government edifices, such as the White House and the Capitol were erected, though the city suffered a major setback when the British set both buildings and much else in Washington ablaze during the War of 1812. Without the normal fabric of a developed city among them, they seemed placed too far apart. But the clever L'Enfant even had an answer for that: the delivery of material from the executive to the legislative branches deserved a certain formality, he argued, calling for a ceremonial procession through town by proper carriage.[12]

The earliest photographs of Washington, from the mid-nineteenth century, make it look like some sort of colossal undertaking that has been suspended in mid-realization, leaving visitors to their imaginations. (See Figure 10.4.) Irish poet Thomas Moore had carried away the same impression from his visit, much earlier, in 1804:

This embryo capital, where Fancy sees
Squares in morasses, obelisks in trees;
Which second-sighted seers, ev'n now, adorn
With shrines unbuilt, and heroes yet unborn,
Though naught but woods and Jefferson they see,
Where streets should run and sages ought to be.[13]

The impression of a primitive settlement in the woods was common to visitors. Having read rosy descriptions, a visitor in 1796 was surprised to be trekking through thick woods while being assured that he was already in the capital. He recalled: "After some time this indistinct way assumed more the appearance of a regular avenue, the trees having been cut down in a straight line. Although no habitation of any kind was visible . . . . I continued in this spacious avenue for half a mile, and then came out upon a large spot, cleared of wood, in the centre of which I saw two buildings on an extensive scale."[14]

Upon his visit in 1842, Charles Dickens called it skeptically a "City of Magnificent Intentions." A minister from Portugal referred to it as "The City of

10.4   Poplar trees planted to reinforce L'Enfant's boulevards with nary a building along them to be seen. c. 1861.

Magnificent Distances." "The palace in the wilderness" was another satirical pronouncement.[15] It would take the energies released around the time of the capital's centennial to achieve the magnificent intentions proposed by L'Enfant. By then an already powerful nation had few reservations about displaying its ideals at an imperial scale, and more resources to deploy in achieving such.

To appreciate the slow growth of the capital, let's compare it to the growth of Philadelphia, its predecessor as capital, and New York City, then beginning its journey to become the planet's capital of capitalism. As the federal government was moving to its carved-out district in 1800, the area's population was around eight thousand, the size of a modest town. Philadelphia, by contrast, had a population of forty-one thousand, while New York was a few citizens shy of eighty thousand, ten times the District's size. The arrival of the government quickly caused the new district's population to double. By 1850 it had reached almost fifty-two thousand, another threefold increase. Impressive, but Philadelphia was already at 121,000, and New York was nearing 700,000, future boroughs included. In 1900, at the centennial of the government's arrival, the population stood at 278,718, most of the growth having taken place since the Civil War. By then, Philadelphia had reached nearly 1.3 million and New York, already an international powerhouse, was a few thousand short of 3.5 million! Most Americans at the turn of the century were barely aware of Washington as a physical place, and had no particular reason to visit. Nor were they being lured there by the prospect of making their fortune, as they were to the industrializing cities. But this was about to change.

To understand one reason for the city's reawakening—or perhaps wakening—we must head again to Chicago, then growing as fast as any city on earth. Chicago's phenomenal growth is not, however, what takes our narrative there. Rather, we visit again the Columbian Exposition of 1893, taking care to reframe it this time in its role as herald of the City Beautiful Era. (See Figure 2.8.)

By contrast to its brief physical existence, the fair's hold on the American mind persisted long beyond its destruction. Memories imprinted by enchantment combined with an extensive photographic record (among the first of its kind) to substitute for its physical absence. The fair inspired a generation with the possibilities of civic grandeur all the more powerful because it exhibited a union of technological prowess of which America was justifiably proud, and with newly gained artistic sophistication. Many who encountered the fair were left simply in disbelief. "The time, surely, is the nineteenth century," wrote one visitor, "and the place the western metropolis of a crude new world. The whirl of the loom, the glare of the arc light, the rush of escaping steam, are on every hand; to all of these ear and eye are open, yet the mind refuses consent."[16]

Pundits began to ask why such order, grandeur, and beauty should be limited to a temporary event. After all, the fair's scale, arrangement, and form evoked a "L'Enfantian" ambition, even if Haussmann's transformation of Paris and the neoclassical grandeur of other European capitals had been foremost in the fair designers' minds. Why should such grandeur not be realized in permanent form? And why not in the nation's capital, which its founders had promised a century earlier would be grand, ordered, and beautiful? Besides, the federal government was beginning to grow almost as fast as the nation's industrializing cities. Facilities to house the growing bureaucracy were in short supply, despite construction having been completed in 1888 of what would remain the world's largest office building for many years—originally the State, War, and Navy Building, and now the Eisenhower Executive Office Building. When utopian ambition aligns with practical need, it can prove a potent combination.

The McMillan Commission and Its Plan

On December 12, 1900, the capital city celebrated its centennial. The specifics of the day's pomp and circumstance have been forgotten. An event that began a day later had more lasting impact. Many saw the capital at it approached its centennial as uncared for and unbeautiful, a place of dirt roads and open sewers unworthy of the nation's growing international standing and aspirations. Old photographs show various military barracks, storehouses, and other ill-suited structures placed alongside and within the area of today's Mall. Back in the 1870s, President Ulysses S. Grant, who scotched plans to move the capital altogether, had authorized the political boss Alexander R. Shepherd to undertake a program of modernization. Shepherd succeeded in improving some of the city's infrastructure, but also landed the city in bankruptcy. Progress stalled. During the 1880s, local and national journalists continued to lament the state of the city, helping to justify the creation in 1890 of Senator McMillan's Senate Committee on the District of Columbia. This committee examined and authorized several plans for improvement to the Mall, finding none of them to its general satisfaction.[17] The approaching centennial had, however, empowered the American Institute of Architects and its executive director, Glenn Brown, to take up the city's cause. Brown had been requesting a number of prominent architects to prepare aspirational plans to be shown at the Institute's annual convention, scheduled to begin in Washington on the very day following the centennial celebration.

Over the next few days, and to much fanfare, a series of imaginative designs were unveiled and discussed. Most favored the kinds of formal geometries and classical architectural expression then in keeping with the artistic sensibilities of the City Beautiful. Also speaking at the convention was Frederick Law Olmsted, Jr., who had previously advised Senator McMillan, a fan of Olmsted's father. Departing from the elder Olmsted's career-long view, his son advocated moving away from the naturalistic effects deployed by Andrew Jackson Downing in his 1851 design for the Mall, which had never been beloved. The son suggested an opposite approach, arguing that the Champs-Élysées in Paris should be the model for the Mall.[18] That suggestion would carry the day. With the spirit of Chicago's White City still much in the air, the refrain was quickly taken up that the nation's capital should be at least as majestic as that glorious fair! Cass Gilbert, a prominent Beaux Arts inspired architect, presented perhaps the most important plan. It was the most sophisticated in terms of its formal, White City–like geometries, and would influence the official design that would soon emerge. (See Figure 10.5.)

The architects' convention and their display of grand plans generated much discussion about how to address the city's shortcomings. By March 1901, at McMillan's urging, Congress passed a bill to form a Senate Park Commission, to actually proceed with a plan to enhance the capital.[19] Daniel Burnham, the mastermind of Chicago's fair, was immediately selected to chair the "experts" panel of the commission. He would later design Union Station when the decision was made to relocate it from its ill-advised, awkward Mall location. Also quickly appointed was Frederick Law Olmsted, Jr. Beyond advocating a formal design for the Mall, he was interested in the commission's broader mandate to fashion a district-wide park system, like one he had recently helped undertake in Boston, expanding the Emerald Necklace his father had designed to a metropolitan scale. Burnham then agreed to add his main design collaborator from the fair, Charles F. McKim, the most prominent architect of the time, whose firm would go on to remodel the White House, design New York's Pennsylvania Station, and create many other prominent public projects during the City Beautiful era. To fill out the artistic expertise of the commission, the preeminent sculptor August Saint-Gaudens was also appointed. These four set out to give the capital a stance worthy of the nation's nascent imperialistic ambitions, while

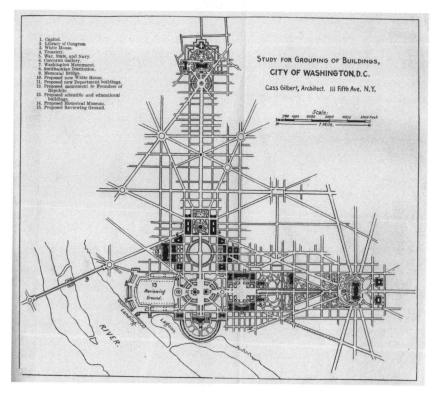

1. Capitol.
2. Library of Congress.
3. White House.
4. Treasury.
5. War, State, and Navy.
6. Corcoran Gallery.
7. Washington Monument.
8. Smithsonian Institution.
9. Memorial Bridge.
10. Proposed new White House.
11. Proposed new Department buildings.
12. Proposed monument to Founders of Republic.
13. Proposed scientific and educational buildings.
14. Proposed Historical Museum.
15. Proposed Reviewing Ground.

STUDY FOR GROUPING OF BUILDINGS,
CITY OF WASHINGTON, D.C.
Cass Gilbert, Architect. III Fifth Ave. N.Y.

10.5   Cass Gilbert's influential plan for the center of Washington; a further formalization and enlargement of L'Enfant's vision, including the suggestion to relocate the White House a mile to the north, and to terminate both White House and Capital axes with major monuments that became the sites of the Lincoln and Jefferson memorials.

enhancing L'Enfant's original vision. They produced a remarkable plan that has guided the Capital since, in the vicinity of the Mall even more so than the L'Enfant plan (though that may sound sacrilegious to the many local guardians of L'Enfant's vision).

A fifth individual, Charles Moore, deserves almost as much credit as the four designers. Though not an architect, Senator McMillan's design-minded assistant, had participated at the architects' convention, became secretary to the McMillan Commission, and no doubt was the principal author of their report. Moore was a tireless spokesman, chronicler, and cheerleader, as well as a later biographer of both Burnham and McKim. As the long-standing chairman of the Fine Arts Commission, created by Congress in 1910 to oversee the advancement of the McMillan Commission Plan, Moore committed a major portion of his life to advancing the plan, and the work of its famous designers.[20] With typical passion, he summarized the work of the commission as follows: "to prepare for the City of Washington such a plan as shall enable future development to proceed along the lines originally planned—namely, the treatment of the city as a work of civic art—and to develop the outlying parks as portions of a single well considered system. "[21]

While L'Enfant's web of diagonal streets and squares and the positioning of the White House and the Capitol still define the city, the experience of today's visitor to the Mall is shaped much more by the 1902 McMillan Commission Plan. The Federal Triangle of buildings lining Pennsylvania Avenue to accommodate the federal bureaucracy, the edging of the Mall by national museums and cultural institutions, the reflecting pool and Lincoln Memorial terminating the Mall at its western edge, the elongation of the axis southward from the White House where the Jefferson Memorial was eventually sited, the location and design of Union Station, the cluster of office buildings for the Senate and House of Representatives surrounding the Capitol Building—these are all inventions of the 1902 plan. While paying homage to L'Enfant's ideas, the commission further monumentalized the core of his plan. Finally, then, during the first decades of the twentieth century the long-promised "aggrandizement and embellishment" would become manifest. (See Figure 10.6.)

Curiously, the McMillan Commission Plan did not correct an omission in L'Enfant's original plan. L'Enfant had not provided a prominent location for the Judiciary, the third branch of government. As there were no precedents for such

10.6   One of the imposing renderings produced for the McMillan Commission in 1903, depicting an even more glorious, formal government center than L'Enfant had imagined.

an institution among European nations, and in those early years of the Republic it may have not been clear how prominent a role the judicial system would have in daily governance, L'Enfant's oversight might be forgiven. It is less understandable why the 1902 plan did not rectify the matter. From the middle of the nineteenth century, with cases such as *Dred Scott v. Sanford* that helped precipitate the Civil War, the relevance of the Supreme Court was hardly in question.[22] In the geometry set up by L'Enfant's plan, strengthened by the McMillan Commission, a fitting location for the Supreme Court might have been where the Lincoln Memorial was located, or perhaps the Jefferson Memorial, which the McMillan Commission had reserved as a site for a future memorial. Instead, the 1902 plan suggested that a building for the Court should be part of the cluster of structures that would frame the Capitol building. Historian John Reps expresses their oversight best: "To the extent that capital cities should in some way symbolize the form and style of government, the planners of 1902 failed to grasp one of their greatest opportunities, now lost forever."[23]

The improvement and elaboration of the area of the Mall was the commission's primary focus. The broader mandate, as the official name of the commission implies, to conceive a metropolitan park system, of which the Mall would serve as nucleus, would primarily fall to Olmsted, Jr. His work on the parks received less effort from his commission colleagues, received less publicity, and was presented with less graphic exuberance in the published plan. But the development of Rock Creek Park, the parks along the banks of the Potomac, and the initial conceptualization of the Fort Circle Trail were still major contributions of McMillan's Senate Park Commission, and largely due to Olmsted, Jr.

Becoming a City

Despite the capital's heroic planning tradition—with several further plans to preserve and enhance the L'Enfant and McMillan legacies undertaken during the twentieth century—not all of the District's areas prospered. While L'Enfant's plan stretched from the Potomac to the Anacostia Rivers, its geometric hierarchy clearly privileged the former. Similarly, the McMillan Commission, with its emphasis on completing the Mall, did little to address the environs of the capital's second river. One reason for this continuing geographic bias was the initial rationale for locating the nation's capital along the Potomac: its expected role in linking the ports along the Atlantic seaboard with Ohio and the greater Midwest. As with the nation overall, it was assumed that the city's destiny lay westward, rather than along the "Eastern Branch," as the mouth of the Anacostia was labeled on early maps.

The bias toward the Potomac remains in evidence. Northern Virginia across the Potomac from the monumental core has witnessed far greater urbanization than areas south of the Anacostia. The establishment of Arlington National Cemetery during the Civil War, on the estate of the family of Robert E. Lee's wife, great-granddaughter of Martha Washington, certainly helped. Other factors were the presence of the historic town of Alexandria founded back in 1695; the growth of Arlington, on land once part of the Federal District returned to Virginia in the 1840s; the location of the earliest airfields which became Washington National Airport (renamed in honor of President Reagan); and the decision to construct the Pentagon there during World War II.

Not that the banks of the Anacostia were particularly hospitable to settlement. Of course, neither were the Potomac's initially. Broad lowlands subject to tidal and seasonal flooding bound both rivers until they were reclaimed by the infilling of swamps and the construction of levees. But it was along the Anacostia that military installations such as the Navy Yard were deployed, and it was there that the bits of industry attracted to the capital were situated. As a result, along an increasingly polluted river, the area evolved into working-class neighborhoods and the center of local African-American life. For freed African Americans, Washington was especially attractive because the federal circuit court for the city permitted black residents to own property—a right denied them in many states. Soon after the Civil War, African Americans already made up half the city's population. Their future in Washington, however, came to resemble the future of black populations in other large American cities.

For much of the twentieth century, the nation's capital was, like many American cities, a place of dual identities, the proud symbol of a nation and the typically blighted city, marred by ghettos and sundered by highways, largely through poorer neighborhoods. Unlike the Potomac, toward which monumental Washington reached, the fate of the Anacostia districts—commonly absent from visitor maps of DC—was to be the capital's backyard; reserved for less civic enterprises like navy yards, and for less affluent neighbors. (See Figure 10.7.)

Even seminal plans require periodic reinterpretation. Plans at bold and modest scales continue to unfold for the capital city. While neither L'Enfant nor the McMillan Commission ultimately foresaw the Anacostia's potential to direct the city's, this is the present generation's challenge. Ongoing plans for Washington focus on the revitalization of Anacostia neighborhoods. In 1998, the Na-

10.7   In the proverbial shadow of the Capitol a derelict neighborhood, unfortunately quite common at mid-twentieth century.

tional Capital Planning Commission published its *Legacy Plan,* a sort of third grand plan for the capital, which highlighted growth potential along the Anacostia, South Capitol Street, and throughout the southeast quadrant of the District of Columbia. The District government followed with its own long-range framework plan for the Anacostia.[24] Washington's current planners, like those in other American cities, are intent on capturing some of the growth that Washington's suburbs have enjoyed for decades and channeling it back to the center, with the areas around the Anacostia providing the greatest opportunities to do so. (See Figure 10.8.)

Over the past half-century or so, Washington has evolved into a complex metro area. No longer simply a center of governance, it is now part of a combined statistical metropolitan area, as the US Census defines it, of over 8.5 million people. At metropolitan scale, it is finally larger than its once condescending predecessor as capital, Philadelphia. It is the hub of the fourth-largest urban region in the country, stretching from much of Northern Virginia to Baltimore, Maryland, beyond what even L'Enfant imagined for a future however remote. Washington is unquestionably now a real city—indeed, a world metropolis, now into its third century of magnificent intentions. (See Figure 10.9.)

Following a year-long search considering dozens of cities for its second headquarters location, Amazon initially announced a tie: it would split the much-hyped HQ2 across two locations. One was promised, as many had predicted, to

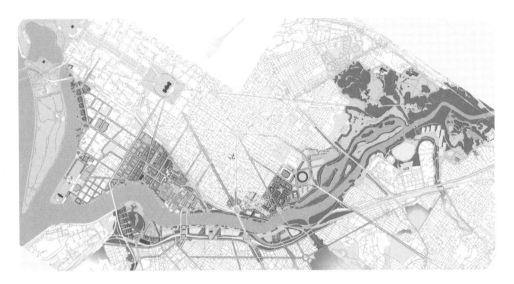

10.8   Plan for the areas of the city to either side of the Anacostia River, the result of a major Anacostia Waterfront Initiative plan to reinvest in the neighborhoods of southeast portions of the city, clean the river, and create a continuous set of public spaces along its banks.

10.9   Washington's commercial center at the end of its second century: finally as lively and bustling as any American downtown, actually more so than many.

metro New York, though soon retracted as local opposition surfaced. The other choice was a site in Arlington, Virginia, just across the Potomac from the capital. And thus one of the world's fastest growing corporations, led by a founder who in 2018 was the richest individual in the world, acknowledged the importance of being close to and growing along those magnificent intentions.

11.1 A downtown intersection in Chicago, 1909 (comfort to those despairing of current urban congestion?).

11

CHICAGO 1910: LOGISTICS UTOPIA

Laughing!
Laughing the stormy, husky, brawling laughter of Youth.

CARL SANDBURG, 1914

THERE ARE NOT MANY ACCOUNTS of the city of Chicago as Utopia, though Sandburg's famous poem "Chicago" comes close. In fact, there was much to dislike and even fear about this unruly cauldron of urbanization in the decades before and after the arrival of the twentieth century. This was, after all, the period of the utopians and reformers we encountered in Chapter 9, with their alternating moods of despair and hope about ongoing industrial urbanization.[1] The opening lines of the second stanza of Sandburg's poem acknowledge real problems.

> They tell me you are wicked and I believe them, for I have seen your
> painted women under the gas lamps luring the farm boys.
> And they tell me you are crooked and I answer: Yes, it is true I have seen
> the gunman kill and go free to kill again.
> And they tell me you are brutal and my reply is: On the faces of women
> and children I have seen the marks of wanton hunger.[2]

Commentary was often harsher: "Yes, Chicago. First in violence, deepest in dirt; loud, lawless, unlovely, ill-smelling, new; an overgrown gawk of a village, the 'tough' among cities. . . . Criminally wide open . . . commercially brazen . . . socially thoughtless and raw." That was Lincoln Steffens's conclusion in his 1904 *The Shame of the Cities*.[3] Or, recall the title of Upton Sinclair's 1906 novel, *The Jungle,* revealing the blood and gore of the stockyards, and condemning the exploitation of immigrant laborers and their inhumane work and living conditions.[4] Then there is socialist union leader and reformer Eugene V. Debs. In his 1908 essay "What's the Matter with Chicago?" he writes: "Everything that entered into the building of the town and the development of the city was . . . without the remotest concern for the health and comfort of human beings who were to live there, especially those who had to do all the labor and produce all the wealth."[5]

The environment was filthy, the streets a tangle of traffic despite the regular grid. Foul smoky air stung throat and eyes, with visibility often not much more than a block or two. Yes, there was much to dislike about Chicago. Still, that poignant line from Sandburg's poem—"Laughing the stormy, husky, brawling laughter of youth"—evokes something that turn-of-the-century Chicago shared with many a utopian imagination. There was the expectation there of endless possibilities and eternal youth.

Chicago's first century was the opposite of Washington's. No fancy plan was needed, just a simple street grid, extendable as needed across the prairie, and an unabashed faith in the future. The immediate setting was not promising. The marshy, mosquito-laden location was barely higher than the lethargic Chicago River and adjacent Lake Michigan. This created acres of mud that hindered development until several engineering breakthroughs rendered the area habitable. The place also stank well prior to the arrival of industrial waste. The area's native Indian name, "Chigague" meant (pick a favorite) "garlic," "stinky onion" or "skunk." The site did have an advantage, however: with a short portage between the Great Lakes and Chicago River and the Des Plaines and Illinois Rivers, it had access to the Mississippi.

Between 1830 and 1930, when the Great Depression curbed the city's phenomenal growth, Chicago rose from a remote, insignificant hamlet to a metropolis just short of 3.4 million. Change was the constant, exemplified by the composition of its population. It was an immigrant's paradise, harshness and exploitation aside. In 1910, more than a third of Chicagoans were foreign-born, another 40 percent had at least one foreign-born parent. During the decades between the Civil War and the First World War it was said that Chicago was in a constant fever. The waves arriving weekly were enveloped by that fever, by this utopia of opportunity. Mark Twain remarked: "She is always a novelty; for she is never the Chicago you saw when you passed through the last time."[6]

The laughter heard by Carl Sandburg may have been in anticipation of Chicago surpassing New York in size and influence, having experienced exponential growth for the prior seventy years. One could argue that Chicago was the Capital of Capitalism—the ultimate setting for making, trading, buying, and selling—before Manhattan acquired that moniker later in the twentieth century.[7] Never shy about hyping their city's greatness, local boosters brought new meaning to Chicago's nickname of the "Windy City." When New York journalists called it that, they were not referring to the harsh winds descending from Lake Michigan.

Despite the city's inhospitable local terrain, its geographic location would prove favorable. Chicago would make itself the fulcrum for much of the economic activity of nineteenth-century America. As William Cronon explains in *Nature's Metropolis,* the city's success was proof of the symbiotic relationship between city and country; their economies intertwined as never before imagined.[8] Chicago's position at the center of a continental spider's web of communication, trade, and manufacturing made it exceptional. Memories of what it meant to be the nexus of a booming industrial economy might be fading but the city's pregnant modernity is worth recalling. I will focus on a dozen aspects of it here.

Capital of logistics. This was where stuff arrived, was processed and transformed—wood to lumber, hogs and steers to meat, iron to steel, coal to fuel—and then consumed or distributed. Chicagoan's ambitions were not to become a repository of culture and advance time-honored urban traditions. The city was instead a facilitator, an organizer—its purpose, in J. B. Jackson's insightful phrase, "to organize space for the expediting of a process."[9] Access to the heartland's seemingly infinite natural resources predisposed citizens to believe in an ever more prosperous future and not to worry about the means of getting there. The place was hurtling at breakneck speed toward a vision of fortune, but at the expense of the immediate well-being of its citizens. Nonetheless, they believed or were willing to gamble that they would come out ahead in that bountiful future.

The place was a marvel of logistics a century prior to the magic of today's online commerce. Pine would arrive from the forests of Michigan and Wisconsin; iron and copper ore from the Upper Peninsula; furs from most directions;

wheat, corn, and hogs from the agricultural mecca that was and remains the Midwest; cattle from the open ranges of Texas and western territories. It was all processed and packaged, then distributed via the Mississippi to the south, the Great Lakes to the east, and, once the trains arrived, pretty much to everywhere else. Coal arrived in vast quantities, too, from nearby mines in Illinois and Indiana—the key to powering the whole enterprise. Efforts to perfect the means of receiving and sending were constant, and of critical importance. In 1850, Chicago had no train lines. A decade later, more than a hundred trains a day were arriving and leaving on ten trunk lines. Soon after the Civil War, from which the city emerged unscathed thanks to its distance from the fields of battle, more ships cruised daily into Chicago than into America's six busiest coastal ports—never mind that the city was a thousand miles from an ocean! One history of the city begins with a chapter named "Prairie Seaport," highlighting that geographic anomaly.[10] Arrivals found the place overwhelming and incomprehensible but also intoxicating, the fever being contagious.

With its networked rail yards and stockyards, its opportunistic marketing of the by-products of slaughtered animals (including fertilizer, lard, leather, glue, and oil), its pioneering use of refrigerated railcars, its manufacture and distribution of farm machinery, and its invention of the mail-order catalog business, Chicago worked every angle of the handling, commodification, and sale of nature's yield as consumable products. Constantly honing, optimizing, and perfecting, the city was a model of modernity at the opening of the twentieth century.

The value of mobility. In 1910, Chicago was, as it had been for the prior half century, the hub of the national transportation system. The scope of its interlocked networks of railways and waterways gave it enormous economic power. The space devoted to railroad operations was astonishing. (See Figure 11.2.) In addition to conveying the lion's share of the nation's freight, thirteen hundred passenger trains transported some 175,000 people daily to and through Chicago. For local purpose, an elevated transit loop was constructed—the "Loop" that still defines the city's center—while expansion of the region's overall transit network enabled an ever-wider horizontal spread.

Having shifted over the decades from horse-drawn cars to reliance on cable cars, and then larger and faster steam-powered vehicles, the city's transport system was by 1910 on the verge of becoming consolidated into a thousand-mile network that would soon provide some 600 million annual rides. That much of

11.2   A 1930s aerial showing the extent of railroad infrastructure serving Chicago.

this survived the transition to the age of the automobile marked a contrast with transit systems elsewhere. (Most dramatically, Los Angeles's extensive streetcar system built by private interests crumbled quickly when the advent of buses, cheaper to operate and easier to maintain, made its economics untenable.)[11] Chicago's formidable rail enterprises no doubt enabled the system to be sustained. Myriad commentators of the time describe a place in constant motion.

The vertical extension of the grid.   Chicago's role as container, processor, and transfer point required a colossal assembly of depots, docks, stockyards, grain elevators, warehouses, and managerial spaces that would eventually require the city not just to spread horizontally but to rise up. The city extended its two-dimensional street grid skyward, giving it volumetric expression. (See Figure 11.3.) New York might have soon erected buildings much taller and with more conspicuous marketing and aesthetic ambitions, creating "cathedrals to commerce," as some would call them. But the skyscraper, the twentieth century's most

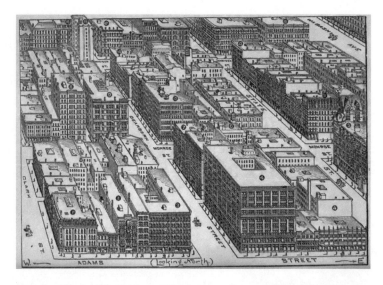

11.3 Downtown Chicago in an 1893 drawing: the vertical extension of the grid to form the first city of skyscrapers.

conspicuous urban icon, was first built in Chicago, and that remains a source of local pride.

Chicago's skyscrapers were practical in origin, responding more directly to need than to any tendency toward ostentation. They capitalized on brand-new technologies, such as the use of caissons to lay foundations in muddy soil, steel frame construction to free perimeter walls from bearing weight, and elevators powered first by steam and then by electricity. These and other inventions enabled greater height and larger window openings. By 1895, when only a few cities saw any need at all for electrical elevators, Chicago already had three thousand.[12] Its rows of commodious blocks sprouting directly from the regular street grid produced the canonical image of a commercial downtown that remains with us today.

Suburban spread. As it was growing upward, Chicago was spreading outward. Its tradition of suburbanization is as old as that of any American city, ample rail transit and a lack of geographical impediments across the prairie making it possible. The Great Fire of Chicago, which destroyed more than three square miles of the city in 1871, played a major role in accelerating this spread (and also prodding the city's upward growth). By leaving one hundred thousand people homeless, it forced the immediate construction of housing, which was much easier to accomplish away from the burned districts. Homebuilders headed to the periphery in part because, as the city imposed far stricter building codes, the higher costs of noncombustible building materials made it harder for projects to be profitable. Large-scale commercial structures were still feasible, but homes would need to be built on cheaper land to stay at prices people could afford. After the fire, few still lived at the city's center.

Chicago grew through annexation, as well, as adjacent communities chose to join the city and gain access to municipal services. In 1889, for example, several outlying areas voted to do this. In one banner day, Chicago grew by 125 square miles and nearly a quarter of a million citizens.[13] The characteristic silhouette of the American urban skyline, featuring a vertical downtown and horizontal, far-flung neighborhoods, was rapidly taking shape. And with it, the tradition of separate locations for work and home life was becoming established.

Precursor to Detroit. While Henry Ford was an employee of the Edison Illuminating Company and still fiddling with a "Quadricycle"—two decades prior to the introduction of his vaunted assembly line—another kind of highly efficient production line was already in operation in Chicago. Precisely engineered in the 1840s, its purpose was not to assemble machines but to disassemble hogs and cattle. These ruthlessly efficient slaughterhouses were organizational and technical marvels. Starting with the Civil War and the Union Army's immense demand for beef and pork, and extending through the 1920s, the Chicago yards processed more meat than anywhere else on earth. Consolidated into the Union Stock Yard and Transit Company following the Civil War, the yards grew exponentially. By 1910, the place where Upton Sinclair heard "the hog-squeal of the universe" had spread across five hundred acres, was crisscrossed by more than 140 miles of railroad tracks, employed some thirty thousand people, and slaughtered more than fourteen million animals per year. A surrounding rough-and-tumble neighborhood of tenements and meager services for the largely immigrant labor force completed this vast "Porktown," making it a city within the city.[14] Gory and dehumanizing, the Chicago stockyards were also one of the world's industrial wonders. (See Figures 11.4 and 11.5.)

An engineered metropolis. Chicago could have adopted "Necessity being the Mother of Invention" as its motto. Consider, for example, the Chicago River. The south fork of the river was the primary recipient of stockyard waste and the city's sewage. It turned into a rancid open sewer, a major health hazard that

11.4   A 1941 photograph giving a sense of the vast scale of the famous Union stockyards in Chicago.

caused frequent outbreaks of cholera, dysentery, and typhoid fever. Worse, it threatened to contaminate Lake Michigan, source of the whole city's drinking water. By the late 1880s, Chicagoans had had enough. The state legislature passed the Sanitary District Enabling Act of 1889, funding the implementation of an old and "crazy" idea: reversing the flow of the river. Engineers finally completed the massive project in 1900, causing the river to drain southward away

11.5   The work conditions in the Stockyards were unsanitary, dangerous, and unregulated: excruciatingly long hours for adults and children as young as three to five!

from Lake Michigan and, as local wise guys put it, to fertilize the shores of the Illinois and Mississippi Rivers, along with rival St. Louis, too.[15]

This was the boldest but not the only infrastructural transformation to overcome topographic troubles. Three decades earlier, engineers built a brick tunnel under the lake bed two miles offshore, then floated a huge octagonal box, fifty feet in diameter, across the water and sunk it to connect with the tunnel and create a clean water intake. A decade earlier still, Chicago City Council members decided to beat the incessant seasonal flooding by raising the streets. Over the course of the next two decades, buildings small and large were literally jacked up to new elevations as high as ten feet above natural grade, drains were laid, and streets were refinished atop massive introductions of new soil.[16] It's worth reintroducing the name of George Pullman here; prior to becoming a railroad magnate, he made his first fortune perfecting mechanisms to raise buildings.[17] (See Figure 11.6.) Looking to the future, an updated version of the process might be in store for many coastal cities of the world. But, back to Chicago in the nineteenth century, the city had earlier still constructed plank roads to enable movement above the constant mud. And in 1848, just eleven years after the city's incorporation, the Illinois and Michigan Canal had been opened, enabling the first oceangoing vessels to arrive via the Great Lakes. Hundreds of thousands more ships would follow.

Delivered to you. Today's marvel of shopping from home was available to settlers across the United States, compliments of Chicago, a full century prior to Amazon. During a visit to Chicago in 1862, Henry Ward Beecher wrote: "The place has no adaptations for a fine city. . . . It would seem to be merchant's beau

Over Nebraska: citizens' homesteads contained by the grid of the Continental Surveys, remaining evidence of Jefferson's agrarian republic.

By mid-twentieth century Jefferson's promise of 160-acre homesteads had become eighth-of-an-acre suburban lots.

Jefferson's homestead, Monticello, with the Mullbery Row gardens at right, managed by scores of slaves.

Detail of the colonnade that defines the great lawn at the University of Virginia.

(left) *Kindred Spirits*, Asher B. Durand, 1848. Depicts the painter Thomas Cole and journalist/poet William Cullen Bryant (of "Go West" fame) enjoying a Catskills scene.
(right) Places of awe remain: A family enjoying a Grand Canyon overlook.

George Inness, *The Lackawanna Valley*, 1855.

Thomas Cole, *The Course of Empire: The Savage State*, 1836.

Thomas Cole, *The Course of Empire: The Arcadian or Pastoral State*, 1836.

Thomas Cole, *The Course of Empire: The Consummation of Empire,* 1836.

Thomas Cole, *The Course of Empire: Destruction*, 1836.

Thomas Cole, *The Course of Empire: Desolation,* 1836.

Across the Continent. "Westward the Course of Empire Takes Its Way," Frances Flora Bond, 1868. Manifest Destiny art: The train facilitating the spread of civilization, while the Native Americans are left in its smoke. An unintended interpretation would be of civilization polluting the wilderness, the train leading passengers away from this town to despoil a territory further away.

The Town Common in Westport, New York, exhibiting the charm that stirs the small-town ideal.

The Town of Seaside, Florida, the design of which helped initiate and give momentum to the New Urbanism movement.

Aerial view of the center of Celebration, Florida, founded by the Disney Companies in the 1990s and named "New Town of the Year" by the Urban Land Institute in 2001.

View of the main commercial street in Celebration, Florida, named Celebration Avenue because a Main Street already existed in Osceola County, of which Celebration is part.

The Ponemah Mills in
Taftville, Connecticut, view
of a classic New England
mill town.

The "Spheres," an amenity for employees and an emerging local landmark at the recently completed Amazon corporate headquarters in downtown Seattle.

A suburban corporate haven characteristic of the second half of the twentieth century.

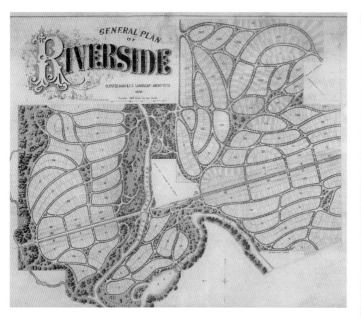

Plan of Riverside, Illinois. Compare to the plan of Mount Auburn Cemetery.

American Progress, John Gast, 1872. Lady progress, or "Divine Providence," leading settlers from St. Louis (upper right) to the promise of the West.

Union Pacific Company poster showing the alignment of the 12,000,000 acres of federal land grants for sale, and twenty-one scenes along the route.

Railroad company poster encouraging migration to California, labeled as the "Cornucopia of the World," and promising "43,795,000 Acres of Government Lands Untaken."

View of Central Park with the famed Dakota Apartments barely visible in the background, the city held back as Olmsted planned.

Aerial view of Prospect Park in Brooklyn.

Mount Auburn Cemetery in Cambridge, Massachusetts: America's first rural cemetery, dedicated in 1831. Still experienced as an arboretum as much as a "sleeping place," the Greek root for cemetery, and one of the sources of inspiration for the American Parks movement.

Away from the $15 cocktails at the DUMBO side of Brooklyn Bridge Park, picnic tables attract a much more diverse crowd.

One of the imposing renderings produced for the McMillan Commission in 1903, depicting an even more glorious, formal government center than L'Enfant had imagined.

View from the base of the Washington Monument toward the Lincoln Memorial, with the National World War II Memorial in the foreground.

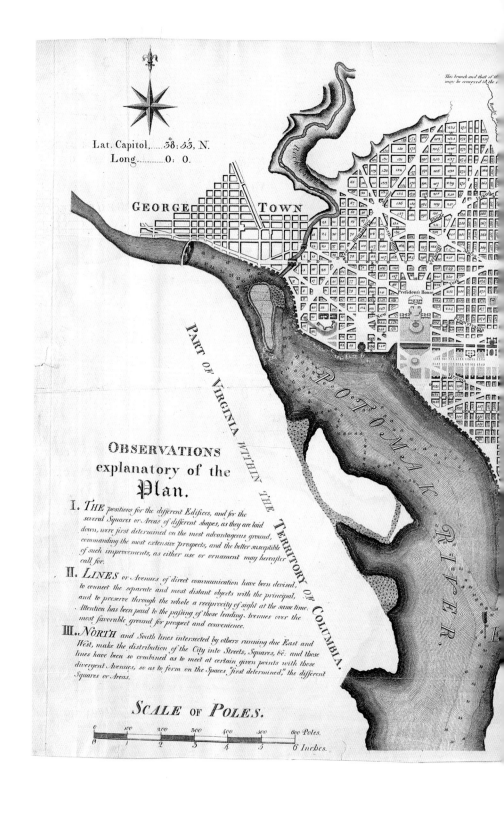

Lat. Capitol,......38:53, N.
Long..........0: 0.

GEORGE TOWN

This branch and that of th
may be conveyed to the

PART OF VIRGINIA WITHIN THE TERRITORY OF COLUMBIA.

President's House

POTOMAK RIVER

OBSERVATIONS
explanatory of the
Plan.

I. THE positions for the different Edifices, and for the
several Squares or Areas of different shapes, as they are laid
down, were first determined on the most advantageous ground,
commanding the most extensive prospects, and the better susceptible
of such improvements, as either use or ornament may hereafter
call for.

II. LINES or Avenues of direct communication have been devised,
to connect the separate and most distant objects with the principal,
and to preserve through the whole a reciprocity of sight at the same time.
Attention has been paid to the passing of these leading Avenues over the
most favorable ground for prospect and convenience.

III. NORTH and South lines intersected by others running due East and
West, make the distribution of the City into Streets, Squares, &c. and these
lines have been so combined as to meet at certain given points with those
divergent Avenues, so as to form on the Spaces "first determined," the different
Squares or Areas.

SCALE OF POLES.

0   100   200   300   400   500   600 Poles.
0   1   2   3   4   5   6 Inches.

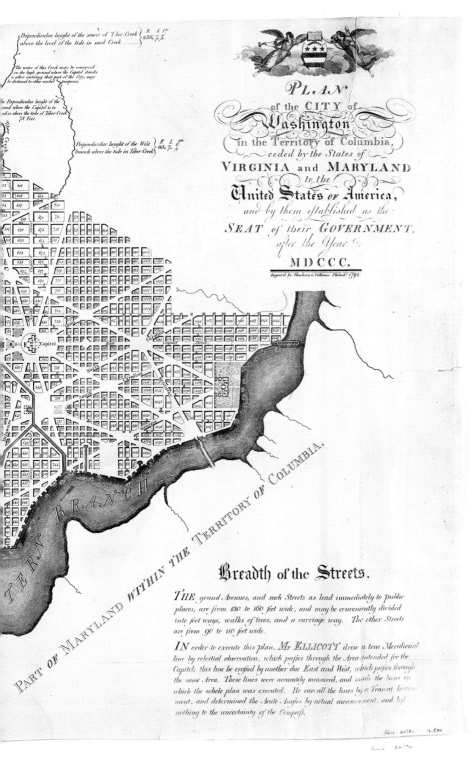

L'Enfant's plan for the capital as revised by Andrew Ellicott following L'Enfant's dismissal.

Plan for the areas of the city to either side of the Anacostia River, the result of a major Anacostia Waterfront Initiative plan to reinvest in the neighborhoods of southeast portions of the city, clean the river, and create a continuous set of public spaces along its banks.

Insight for a new millennium from a 2001 cartoon in the *Pittsburgh Gazette.*

Map of the proposed park system for the city from the 1909 Plan of Chicago.

Crossing the Frank-Gehry designed pedestrian bridge from the lakefront to Millennium Park and the downtown.

An audacious 1977 advertisement inferring that the family car might be more than a means of conveyance, and perhaps as important as the home in the background where mom stands.

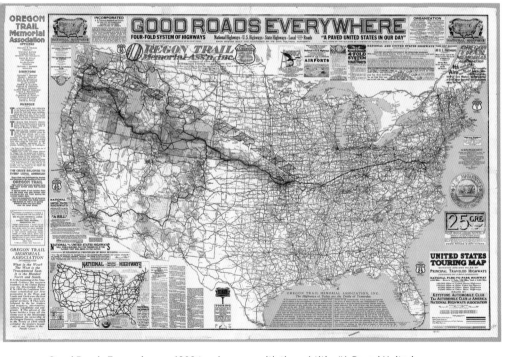

Good Roads Everywhere, a 1929 touring map with the subtitle: "A Paved United States in Our Day."

A 1960s commune on wheels.

Hancock Shaker Village historical site: the third of nineteen such villages established between 1783 and 1836.

By 1981 James Rouse, the creator of Columbia, had concluded that old cities could be fun, too. Here he is holding Boston's Faneuil Hall, having achieved much acclaim for restoring the adjacent (and long empty) Quincy Markets into the first "festival market place." He would replicate this in a number of other cities, helping revitalize downtown shopping around renovated historic districts.

Suitable arrival at the famous sign that welcomes you to fabulous Las Vegas.

Rendering of the enormous underground service center to which cars and trucks were restricted so as not to interfere with the pedestrian experience above.

One of the many remarkable renderings produced at Walt Disney's direction by the company's "imagineers" to describe his future EPCOT.

View of CityCenter, Las Vegas.

Tourists making the best of a flooded Piazza San Marco in Venice.

A California entrepreneur consummating deals on his laptop from his home and office overlooking the Pacific Ocean.

The American dream heading out further into the Mojave desert, in a particularly unsustainable way.

Chicago's majestic lakefront with Millennium Park in the foreground. Only a portion of Grant Park, envisioned in the 1909 Plan of Chicago, as the centerpiece of the downtown. During the August 2018 weekend when this photo was taken, as the annual Lollapalooza music festival was taking place in Grant Park, elsewhere in the city eleven people were murdered and seventy more were wounded. A disheartening reminder of America's dual urban circumstances.

11.7   Advertisement for the 1909 Sears, Roebuck and Company catalog, the nineteenth-century equivalent of Amazon online.

securely packed, to any part of the country. No doubt we shall soon have the exhilaration of reading advertisements of these town-makers, to the effect that orders for the smallest villages will be thankfully received; county towns made to order; a metropolis furnished with punctuality and dispatch . . ."[19]

His claim of buildings for sale was only a slight exaggeration. In addition to supplying clothing, furniture, appliances, and equipment, it was possible for the mail-order firms to deliver parts of homes by train. While primitive balloon-frame construction, the key to this effort, dates back to Colonial times, Chicago's carpenters are identified with its refinement, and certainly with the expansion of its use. To meet demand, Chicago carpenters began to build sections of walls entirely with nails, without the complex mortise and tenon joints of traditional post-and-beam construction, for easier assembly elsewhere. The mail-order companies were thus able to illustrate complete houses in their catalogs, ready to be shipped in ready-made sections for easy assembly on site. All of this was no less a miracle to a nineteenth-century citizen than today's ability to order a product on one's cell phone and have it arrive in a day or two—or tomorrow's ability to order up design files and have building projects accomplished by 3-D printers.

A buyers and sellers' exchange. By the middle of the nineteenth century, Chicago was the nexus of an increasingly networked world. As Cronon describes, Americans had access to goods from all over:

> The Iowa farm family who raised corn for cattle purchased from Wyoming and who lived in a farmhouse made of Wisconsin pine clothed themselves with Mississippi cotton that Massachusetts factory workers had woven into fabric, worked their fields with a plow manufactured in Illinois from steel produced in Pennsylvania, and ended their Sunday meal by drinking Venezuelan coffee after enjoying an apple pie made on an Ohio stove from the fruit of a backyard orchard mixed with sugar from Cuba and cinnamon from Ceylon.[20]

Maintaining and expanding such networks required sophisticated financial systems. The Chicago Board of Trade, established in 1848, is the oldest commodity trading exchange in the western world. While Dutch tulip growers in the seventeenth century and rice merchants in eighteenth-century Japan had earlier pioneered market-based ways to price forward-looking transactions, the Chicago Board of Trade first listed standardized "futures contracts." Initially designed for corn, wheat, and soybeans, they soon expanded to other commodities. Having a formal mechanism by which two parties could arrange for an asset to change hands at an agreed-upon price at a specified future date was a great facilitator of economic activity. From finding ways to add value to commodities, as in prefabricated home construction, to devising more efficient financial processes, Chicago was constantly streamlining the flow of goods from raw materials suppliers to manufacturers to merchants to consumers, and allowing their interactions to become more complex. At the same time, given the growing challenges of managing large-scale commercial and industrial enterprises, the gulf between management and labor was widening, and class distinctions were becoming more and more apparent on city streets and between neighborhoods.

A city of gardens. In the city's infancy in the 1830s, with Windy City bluster already in evidence, Chicago's leaders adopted the Latin phrase Urbs in Horto as its motto—"City in a Garden." Very few gardens were then present amidst the mud and stinky onions, and installing them on the featureless terrain would not be an easy task, but park lands were soon set aside and "pleasure grounds" began to be built. As both Olmsted and Horace Cleveland complained when invited to plan parks decades later, pretty much any park-like feature had to be artificially constructed.[21] A citizen-inspired movement to create a parks and boulevard system began in the 1850s, about as early as anywhere else in the country; even in New York City, the design competition for Central Park did not take place until 1857.

Around this time, Dr. John Henry Rauch—following in the footsteps of another doctor, James Bigelow, who created Mount Auburn Cemetery in Cambridge, Massachusetts—was able to facilitate the allocation of some sixty acres of cemetery grounds to establish what became Lincoln Park.[22] His main aim was to improve citywide sanitation. By the early 1870s, three separate park commissions were busily planning large, open spaces. The Lincoln Park commissioners began to expand that park by initiating what would become Lake Shore Drive. West Park's commission started work on what became Humboldt, Garfield, and Douglas Parks. And the commissioners for South Park hired both Horace Cleveland and Frederick Law Olmsted, whose plans for an entire park system would, decades later, yield Washington and Jackson Parks. Jackson Park's grounds served in the interim as the site of the great 1893 Fair.[23] Following Chicago's 1889 annexations of several peripheral districts, more places—to this day called "forest preserves"—were set aside in some of them. And this was just the beginning. (See Figure 11.9.)

A people's lakefront. Among the most distinctive qualities of the city, virtually unmatched, are some twenty-five miles of continuous parks and public areas along Lake Michigan. (See Figure 11.8.) The struggle to keep this space in the public realm has had a long and substantial history. Lois Wille begins her history of the lakefront by pointing to a map from 1836 (a year before the city's incorporation) drawn up for the purpose of selling lots to pay for a shipping canal. Clearly indicated on it is the provision of a broad strip of "Public Ground" set aside as "A Common to remain forever Open, Clear, & free of any buildings,

11.8 View northward along Lake Michigan and its continuous public edge, photo from the observatory of the former John Hancock Center, then the world's second tallest building.

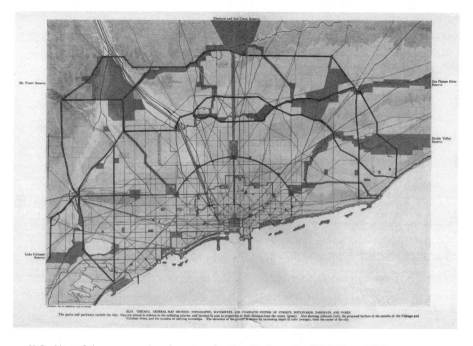

11.9 Map of the proposed park system for the city from the 1909 Plan of Chicago.

or Other Obstructions Whatever." As Wille writes, the area was "dedicated to pleasure and beauty, not to commerce and industry."[24] Daniel Burnham would spend years after the 1893 Fair persuading others that the fairgrounds, slated to become a permanent park (as originally designed by Olmsted) could be linked to the downtown nine miles away via a lakefront promenade. His Plan of Chicago, adopted by the city in 1909, insisted: "The Lake front by right belongs to the people. . . . Not a foot of its shores should be appropriated by individuals to the exclusion of the people. . . . It should be made so alluring that it will become the fixed habit of the people to seek its restful presence at every opportunity."[25] (See Figure 11.8.)

This was virtually unheard of in 1909, when urban waterfronts were almost all maritime work areas with adjacent industrial sites. Burnham's plan focused substantially on park and lakefront planning, perhaps reflecting the influence of Olmsted, Sr., during the days of the fair, and Olmsted, Jr., from their McMillan Commission interactions in Washington. It also called for relocating rail yards away from the lakefront—an instruction that proved unworkable and was later amended to adding landfill, east of and sometimes over the tracks to establish the lake's public edge. Later, hundreds of other cities worldwide would reject the idea of having rail yards and factories at water's edge, and start converting their waterfronts to "front yards." Chicago was decades ahead of them.

An audacious master plan to guide the future. Two of the *Plan of Chicago's* six areas of focus were parks and open space, and its improvements to the lakefront were arguably the most vital to the city's later evolution. The organization of this lavishly illustrated plan, printed in book form, is brilliant. It begins by recalling the splendor of the World's Fair, acknowledging the influence of Haussmann's Paris, and displaying a portfolio of Burnham's planning experience in other cites since the fair. It dedicates a substantial chapter to "The Chicago Park System." Toward the end, it summarizes the six main courses of action to which the city should commit: improvement of the lakefront; a system of perimeter highways; consolidation of railway terminals; acquisition of an "outer park system and of parkway circuits"; a systematic arrangement of streets (which would feature, no doubt inspired by Burnham's experience in Washington, DC, the addition of diagonal boulevards); and the development of "centers of intellectual life and of civic administration."[26]

The last two attracted considerable attention, in the forms of both awe and derision, due to the splendor (or pomposity) of the book's illustrations. These are extravagant renderings of impossibly monumental buildings and boulevards in Beaux-Arts style. But Burnham assures readers that the plan's intent is to "direct the development of the city towards an end that must seem ideal, but is practical."[27] He cleverly places the burden on readers, writing that the Plan's realization will depend "entirely on the strength of the public sentiment in its favor."[28] Then, over the next several pages, Burnham lists the city's biggest infrastructural, technical, business, and cultural achievements across the prior decades, to suggest that, by comparison, nothing in his plan could be so hard to achieve. He then concludes: "Thus do the dreams of to-day become the commonplaces of tomorrow; and what we now deem fanciful will become mere matter-of-fact to the man of the future."[29]

Burnham mused about this plan for a decade and a half between 1893 and the plan's completion in 1908. His various forays to plan other cities, both domestic and international, including the nation's capital, were all fodder for Chicago's plan. Many have critiqued the grandiloquent, imperial scale of Burnham's vision, and especially the absence of any emphasis on housing and housing reform, a desperate need in a city whose working-class neighborhoods were bursting and barely habitable. Burnham's less-than-satisfactory rationale was that the plan was about enhancing the public realm, whereas the production of housing was the responsibility of private investment. No less than Harvard president Charles Eliot, whose son became a collaborator with Frederick Law Olmsted, Jr. on the regional open space system around Boston, seemed to support this focus on the public realm, finding in the plan "democratic enlightened collectivism coming in to repair the damage caused by exaggerated democratic indi-vidualism."[30]

In a recent book about the Burnham Plan, Carl Smith points out that only ten of its 142 images showed existing conditions.[31] Burnham was not presenting the existing city to its citizens. He was illustrating a glorious future in the spirit of the city's unabashed optimism. Hardly any of it seemed doable, despite Burnham's insistence on its practicality. Completed in 1908 and officially accepted by city officials in 1909, its implementation was left to a Windy City–sized commission of 328 members. In the two decades leading up to the Great Depression, Chicagoans approved over eighty plan-related bond issues—and the plan has remained a civic blueprint for Chicago ever since. It called for miles of continuous parks along the lakefront and the construction of Lake Shore Drive; the anchoring of the city on the grand, green, harbor-front stage that became Grant Park (see Figure 19.1); the construction of several multilevel streets (Michigan Avenue and Wacker Drive) to separate service from daily traffic; the partial reorganization of rail terminals away from the lakefront; and the integration of forests gained by annexations into the city's park system. All this was achieved—and a measure was devised to keep the plan in the public's focus.

Pathway to Burnham's civic utopia. A companion document to the official plan itself, *Wacker's Manual*, served as a public school textbook and was required reading for the city's eighth graders through the 1930s. What better way to sustain the dream than instilling it in future generations? The manual's very first sentence lays out the aspiration and what it will take to achieve it: "Chicago is destined to become the center of the modern world, if the opportunities in her reach are intelligently realized, and if the city can receive a sufficient supply of trained and enlightened citizens."

Many might view *Wacker's Manual* as propaganda, indoctrinating the children of the city's middle and lower classes with the agenda of the city's elite. But the book's broader curricular purpose was to introduce young people to civics, a subject that could use much more attention today, as well. Each chapter concluded with a set of questions to test comprehension. For example, the chapter "Creating a Park System for Chicago" ended by asking students to "state the only way for Chicago to increase and maintain the vigor of her people." The answer could be found on the previous page:

> The only way to this, and the best way to do this, is to bear constantly
> in mind the necessity and wisdom of always and actively working in be-
> half of the park projects contained in the Plan of Chicago.[32]

Pretty clear! In the "Municipal Economy" chapter, the final question asked: "How can we make Chicago a truly great, convenient, healthful, and beautiful city?" The bright student would zero in on this passage for the response:

> Here is a chance, though, for us to be both pioneers and scientists—
> leaders and workers in the new and fascinating science of city building
> on a plan sure to result in tremendous economy to millions of people
> and tremendous fame for Chicago and for the men and women who

share in the work of making Chicago a truly great, convenient, healthful and beautiful city by encouraging and developing the "Plan of Chicago." [33]

The *Wacker's Manual* was the brainchild of Walter D. Moody, the managing director of the Chicago Plan Commission and its most effective booster after Burnham's untimely death in 1912. Moody considered the decision to incorporate the textbook into the public school's eighth-grade curriculum critical. He believed students at that age were old enough to comprehend the material while still being impressionable. For many of that era, the eighth grade would be the end of their formal education. Thus, among their last lessons would be the importance of city planning. If one overlooks the heavy emphasis on this particular effort, introducing young people to the discipline of urban planning and encouraging them to think about the importance of parks and public spaces, traffic and transportation, sewerage and infrastructure—all the factors

11.10   Crossing the Frank-Gehry designed pedestrian bridge from the lakefront to Millennial Park and the downtown. Enthusiasm for their city common among Chicagoans of all ages.

that enable people to live in cities comfortably and enjoyably—seems wise. A comparable effort, if less biased, could be an important means of inspiring students in today's urban public schools.

City of the Century

One historian dubbed Chicago the City of the Century, but to which century was he referring? Donald Miller's history of nineteenth-century Chicago hedges its answer, since by 1910 the city was already offering a complete preview of twentieth-century urbanization. Miller reminds us how visitors to Chicago then believed they were witnessing the forces that would shape the coming century.[34] Take, for example, the wonder expressed by an Englishman named Walter Marshall, who concluded during his nine-month visit to America that the city, "so young, so flourishing, possessing such vast interests, such grand resources . . . has a future before it such as no other city in the world can anticipate."[35] Today, a handful of rapidly transforming cities in various parts of the world, such as Shanghai, Seoul, or Dubai, induce similar jaw-dropping effects on visitors. Will any of their plans and planners rise to the level of what was achieved on the shore of Lake Michigan a century ago? It remains to be seen who will become Chicago's heir, as the preeminent laboratory for urbanization in the twenty-first century. (See Figure 11.10.)

12.1 An audacious 1977 advertisement inferring that the family car might be more than a means of conveyance, perhaps as important as the home in the background where mom stands.

12

AUTOPIA: THE DRIVE TO DISPERSE

> Sprawl is bad aesthetics; it is bad economics. Five acres are being made to do
> the work of one, and do it very poorly. This is bad for the farmers, it is bad for
> communities, it is bad for industry, it is bad for utilities, it is bad for the
> railroads, it is bad for the recreation groups, it is bad even for the developers.
>
> And it is unnecessary.
>
> WILLIAM H. WHYTE, 1958

> It's opener there in the wide open air.
>
> DR. SEUSS, 1990

FOR MUCH OF THE TWENTIETH CENTURY, the sunny sentiments of Dr. Seuss's
Oh, The Places You'll Go! would have inspired more Americans than the earnest
condemnation of suburbia by William "Holly" Whyte. Whyte's concern may
have been prescient, but Dr. Seuss's optimism is more appealing.

Whyte's critique was published in the same year as *The Insolent Chariots* by
John Keats. I refer to the American cultural provocateur, not the English
Romantic poet—although his focus is on a romance of sorts. "Once upon a
time," Keats writes, "the American met the automobile and fell in love. Unfortunately, this led him into matrimony, and so he did not live happily ever after."
Keats goes on to proclaim—and, mind you, this is 1958—that the "American's
marriage to the automobile is now at an end, and it is only a matter of minutes
to the final pistol shot."[1] Sixty years later, the trigger has yet to be pulled,

largely because Americans haven't wanted to just read about wide-open air. They want to get out with their families and enjoy it. And those insolent chariots have proved a very convenient means for doing so, never mind Keats's clever commentary.

A year earlier, Keats had published *The Crack in the Picture Window,* an equally satirical account of suburban life starring a Mr. and Mrs. Drone. Sounding much like Whyte would a year later, Keats writes: "even while you read this, whole square miles of identical boxes are spreading like gangrene . . . developments conceived in error, nurtured by greed, corroding everything they touch."[2] Some surely enjoyed such wit—Manhattanites no doubt smirked at Keats's and Whyte's skewering of the 'burbs—but the majority of Americans were happily anticipating their next retreats to open air in all their insolent chariots.

A variant of the word *utopia* in ancient Greek is *eutopia,* meaning "good place." As previous chapters have shown, the desire to find or build good places has been a constant spur to American progress. (See Figures 12.2 and 12.9.) It has sent waves of people spreading out across a continent, first arduously by foot and wagon train, then more easily by train, and later by car, truck, and airplane. In his history of the Brooklyn Bridge, symbol of America's late-nineteenth-century engineering prowess, Alan Trachtenberg suggests it has not been the homestead or the garden "but the road . . . that has expressed the essential way of American life."[3] Much earlier, de Tocqueville wrote of our "restless temper," and Walt Whitman began his "Song of the Open Road" with that sense of restlessness:

> Afoot and light-hearted I take to the open road,
> Healthy, free, the world before me,
> The long brown path before me leading wherever I choose.[4]

It is hard not to hear the echo in Dr. Seuss:

> You have brains in your head.
> You have feet in your shoes.
> You can steer yourself
> Any direction you choose.[5]

12.2 Canonical 1861 photo of wagon trains heading out west.

Around the middle of the twentieth century, more began to steer themselves out to the suburbs. Once regarded as a refuge for the few who could afford it, the suburb became a desired haven for the many. The marriage was actually between the car and a form of settlement. Like the suburban home itself, the car became a symbol of self-worth and arrival, and a virtual necessity for the new way of life. For a pre-twentieth-century mind, the idea that there might be an affordable, comfortable, incredibly fast, and private means of transport would have been as utopian a notion as any. Yet such an invention conquered society within a matter of decades after the advent of the internal combustible engine. And what a ride it has been!

In his *Geography of Nowhere,* James Kunstler, vehement critic of the car-dependent suburban lifestyle, pauses to empathize with early customers of the automobile: "It must have been exciting and lovely to live in Los Angeles in 1932, to motor freely out Wilshire Boulevard under that as-yet unsmoggy sky and see those bare brown Hollywood hills looming above the bright new stucco buildings on Sunset. . . . It must have seemed like heaven on earth."[6]

Kunstler quickly dismisses that fool's paradise and reverts to a reproving tone. But, even though America in 1932 was in the grip of the Great Depression, the experience he evokes *was* heavenly for many, and it would be for many more in the following decades. This was the era heralded early in the twentieth century as the "automobility age."

Everywhere, Not Nowhere

Whitman's open road, where he could "inhale great draughts of space," and the invention of the machine that allowed so many to follow, take us directly to Frank Lloyd Wright's extraordinary vision, Broadacre City. The specifics of this utopia—which Wright considered merely pragmatic—are less compelling than its complete commitment to a decentralized future. Wright repositioned the suburb from a realm parallel to the city, a place to retreat following an arduous city workday, to a full replacement for the traditional city. Never at a loss for grandiose proclamations, Wright expressed his conviction about the obsolescence of the traditional city in various ways:

> I believe that the city as we know it today, is to die. We are witnessing the acceleration that precedes dissolution.[7]

> The success of verticality is but temporary . . . because the citizen of the future preferring his horizontality—the gift of his motor car, and telephonic or telegraphic inventions—will turn and reject verticality . . . . He will gradually abandon the city.[8]

> He has the means—his car—and his horizon widens as he goes. . . .

> So the city is going where and as he goes, and he will be gone where he may enjoy all that the centralized city ever really gave him plus the security, freedom and beauty of the ground that will be his.[9]

Broadacre was to be everywhere across America: where "every man, woman, and child may put foot on their own acre and every unborn child finds his acre waiting for him when he is born."[10] It was to be a universe of one-acre farms tethered to ample roadways along which service stations doubled as commercial centers. (See Figure 12.3.) Note that he imagined this future decades prior to today's ubiquitous roadside gas stations with convenience marts attached.

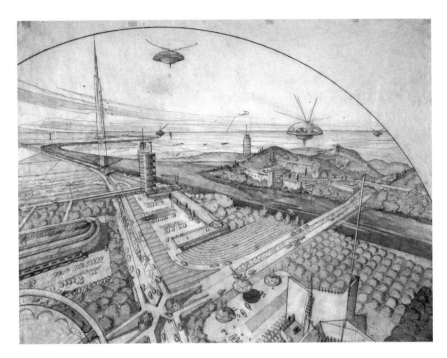

12.3   Frank Lloyd Wright's Broadacre sketch entitled *The Living City.*

Consistently, Wright preached this vision of a city-less world; he did so in
several book-length publications and numerous lectures and articles from 1932
to 1958, a year before his death at ninety-two. The idea depended on a con-
founding polemic advocating minimal government, a new, decentralized system
of credit provision, a combination of social cooperation and unfettered individualism, and, at the base of it all, a new focus on the nuclear family—idealized as it may have been in Wright's view. In 1935, prior to embarking on a
national and European tour, Wright exhibited a model of a mile-square section
of Broadacre at Rockefeller Center, an epicenter of the very kind of metropolis
Wright said would soon be obsolete. By 1943, even with the world at war,
Wright amazingly managed to organize a citizens' petition urging President
Roosevelt to move the nation toward a Broadacre future. Sixty-four prominent
Americans, including Albert Einstein, John Dewey, Archibald MacLeish, and
Nelson Rockefeller, signed the petition.[11] It is not clear that the president re-
sponded, but he may have felt no need to. The nation seemed to be headed in
the direction of Broadacre already. (See Figure 12.4.)

12.4   A landscape not markedly different than Wright's Broadacres: to either side of a major road various commercial enterprises with low density residential areas beyond.

There have been many unsympathetic responses to Wright's Broadacre. It has been dismissed as a sort of romantic Luddite's pining for the world of Whitman, Emerson, and Jefferson. Historian Robert Fishman quips that Wright, with his faith that new technologies would allow people to disperse to the countryside, seemed to believe "Edison and Ford would resurrect Jefferson."[12] Some, however, admire Wright as a seer who understood that the arrival of the car, universal electricity, and the telephone would have fundamental impacts on settlement patterns. Planner Jonathan Barnett, for example, nodding to today's reverence for Marshall McLuhan—the man behind "the medium is the message," and the terms "global village" and "mechanical bride"—points out that, when McLuhan was still an undergraduate English major in Manitoba, Wright was already predicting how modern communication technologies would revolutionize life by enabling decentralization.[13]

Centrifugal Attractions

Decentralization was an important theme for reformers between the 1870s and
the 1930s even though, or perhaps because, cities were rapidly concentrating
capital, labor, and population. Many with utopian leanings saw Wright's call for
low-density living as a necessary response to this deeply problematic concentration. The idea of spreading out, of course, had historic precedents. It was rooted
in Jefferson's agrarian republic and had been amplified by Americans' Manifest
Destiny to "overspread the continent." Calls for decentralization continued to
attract new voices and rationales. During the 1930s, a complex array of perspectives came together to support the cause of decentralization, as the Great
Depression was blamed in part on the monopolistic concentration of capital in
large cities, and technologies that could reverse that concentration were now at
hand. Wright was the decentralists' illustrator. "Whereas Marx and Engels
wanted to eliminate what they called the 'idiocy of country life' by revising the
differentiation between town and country," Martin Meyerson observes, "Wright
aimed at eliminating what he regarded as the idiocy of city life."[14]

Adding to this complex brew of ideas were diverse streams of thought inherited by Wright and his supporters from the nineteenth century. In literature, the
Transcendentalists had seeded a suspicion of modernization and urbanization,
and utopian novelists like Edward Bellamy and William Dean Howells had
posed thought experiments about the future to provoke greater disgust with urban squalor. Social reformers, meanwhile, beginning with Charles Fourier and
Robert Owen, had introduced models for establishing communities in new and
healthier locations, while activists like Jane Addams, Edward Ross, and Jacob
Riis had exposed just how badly the burgeoning cities were failing their residents. Wright interpreted Henry George's *Progress and Poverty*, the popular and
influential reformist treatise published half a century earlier, as a plea for decentralization. While George was mainly concerned with economic inequality and
argued that the land and its resources should be public goods, not allowed to be
sold into private hands, he had also spelled out what his vision would mean for
cities: "The destruction of speculative land values would tend to diffuse population where it is too dense, and to concentrate it where it is too sparse; to substitute for the tenement house, houses surrounded by gardens, and to fully settle
agricultural districts before people are driven from neighborhoods to look for

land." The result he predicted was certainly what decentralists sought: "the people of the city would thus get more of the pure air and sunshine of the country and the people of the country more of the economics and social life of the city."[15]

Wright's generation also included tax reformers and critics of corporate monopolization such as Charles Beard, Thorstein Veblen, and John Maynard Keynes; Depression-battling staffers in Roosevelt's Resettlement Administration; and return-to-the-land proponents including Ralph Borsodi and Baker Brownell. They were surrounded by those sylvan suburban estates that had been gaining popularity since the mid-nineteenth century, enabling citizens to escape from urban misery to greener, more hospitable landscapes. And they had the inspiration of the great Olmstedian parks, which tried to mitigate the problems of overcrowding and pollution that came with centralization—and, in their own way, made an argument for decentralization. If people needed more nature and less city, perhaps it would be best to leave the city altogether.

Historical thinkers had also introduced more eccentric ideas to the public debate that, from surprisingly early in the nineteenth century, suggested that new technologies could be the key to utopian living conditions. One notable exponent of this view was John Adolphus Etzler, who back in 1833 laid out his plan to harness the energies of wind, water, and sun to produce a superabundant utopia he called "The Paradise within the Reach of All Men, without -Labor, by Powers of Nature and Machinery."[16] A full century prior to Frank Lloyd Wright, Etzler applauded technological progress, hardly seeing it, as the Romantics did, as a force that would estrange humanity from nature. In Wright's own generation, similar futurist ideas entered the mainstream through the work of H. G. Wells. In 1902, Wells wrote of the tension between the centrifugal forces causing people to disperse from the city's core and the centripetal forces pulling them in. He predicted that the "centrifugal attractions"—the passion for nature, charm of gardening, craving for a stand-alone cottage, and "wholesome isolation" only possible away from crowded centers—would always endure, while the opposing centripetal ones—desires to be near good shopping districts, schools, and doctors, and many people's "love of the crowd"—would exert far less force as mobility and communication technologies made all of those accessible from further away.[17] Wright's Broadacre was more than a mere tributary of such ideas, but whether we consider it an architect's naive dream or

12.5   A member of the Pioneer Automobile Party in a Toledo car at the rim of the Grand Canyon, February 5, 1902, thirteen years prior to Ford's first assembly line.

a preview of the suburbanization that was yet to come, it owed a great deal to the previous century's yearnings for decentralization.

Henry Ford played a particular role in Wright's, and by extension the decentralist, dream—not only because he produced the most potent agents of dispersal, but because of his short-lived attempt in the 1920s to bring the "miracle of Detroit" to the rural South. The federal government had begun construction of a hydroelectric dam on the Tennessee River in Muscle Shoals, Alabama, in the midst of the First World War, but when that war ended and industrial production needs dropped, it chose not to open it. Ford offered to lease the dam, as well as two factories the government had also built for munitions production, envisioning that the dam's energy could power an entire decentralized region of small factories, farms, and homes. Wright was intrigued by Ford's utopian plans for a "75-Mile City"—really, a large rural area with industrial infrastructure spread evenly across it. One of its attractive ideas was that, aside from their industrial labors, workers and their families would be able to engage in subsistence farming on their sizable lots. Perhaps, then, they could then be compensated more modestly than urban workers. It was a brilliant and idealistic concept, even if it would also have further enriched the man who proposed it. Congressional resistance to the privatization of the dam (and other bids inspired by Ford's perhaps too-modest offer) complicated the negotiations, and Ford ultimately gave up on the scheme. To the disappointment of many, no one else followed through with any competing plan. But eventually, Franklin Delano Roosevelt saw the potential in Ford's vision and created the Tennessee Valley Authority.[18] Ford was left to continue to produce his insolent chariots back in Detroit. Still, his admirer Wright enjoyed elaborating on Ford's idea, agreeing that society now had "the means to take all the real advantages of the centralization known as the big city into the regional field we call the countryside." Why not, in other words, let the automobile take the city to the country?[19] (See Figure 12.5.)

Anticipating a Horseless (and Mud-Free) Age

The idea of a mechanical carriage was initially most attractive in agricultural areas. For citizens of still relatively compact cities, it was relatively easy to get around on foot or with horses and streetcars.[20] Farmers looked forward to mechanized wheels and better roads to overcome the burdens of seasonal mud, and to transport products faster to markets over broader territory. City dwellers, if initially less enthusiastic, nonetheless looked forward to curbing a public health crisis caused by the existing mode of transport. Around the turn of the century in New York City alone, horses deposited several million pounds of manure and tens of thousands of gallons of urine every day. We think of the automobile as a major emitter of pollution, but around 1900, the motorcar promised a cleaner, calmer, and more orderly urban environment. As naive as this seems from our own perspective, an 1899 *Scientific American* story predicted that "the improvement in city conditions by the general adaption of the motor-car can hardly be overestimated. Streets clean, dustless, and odorless, with light rubber tired vehicles moving swiftly and noiselessly over their smooth expanse, would eliminate a greater part of the nervousness, distractions, and strain of modern metropolitan life."[21]

A decade prior to the unveiling of Ford's Model T, a journal called *The Horseless Age* was already being published, and the US Patent Office was inundated with over five hundred applications for patents pertaining to motor vehicle de-

12.6   Cover of *The Horseless Age*, 1903: four years prior to Henry Ford announcing his intention to create "a motorcar for the great multitude."

sign.[22] (See Figure 12.6.) A national campaign, the good roads movement, was gaining strength, led by bicycle enthusiasts demanding that better surfaces be funded by the public.[23] With cycling today on the rise, and many calling it more efficient and far healthier than commuting by car, a bit of history is worth recalling: those enthusiastic "wheelmen" actually accelerated the automobile's arrival. Once the argument for better roads was accepted, the car was quickly recognized as the superior vehicle to take on them. Meanwhile, echoing Ford and anticipating Wright, automotive-oriented news stories were predicting how easy it would be "to dwell within city limits, as well as bringing the country nearer."[24]

By 1910, nearly half a million vehicles were on America's roads (a tiny fraction of the twenty-one million horses in use for transportation). The number of vehicles would increase dramatically each year over the next three-quarters of a century. By 1930, Frank Lloyd Wright could ruminate about a fully decentralized

12.7   A private transit line built to support the selling of home lots of a subdivision somewhere around Los Angeles County, 1885.

America because there were already twenty-two million vehicles on American roads, one for every 5.3 people.[25]

Horizontal spread was by then well on the way, prompting Wright to make better plans for it. His Chicago had been sprawling as rapidly as any city in the decades since the catastrophe of its 1871 fire. In fact, its growth was of the nature of Dr. Jekyll and Mr. Hyde: it featured both skyscrapers and far-flung horizontal residential districts, equally responding to the fire's devastation. As we saw in Chapter 11, the city had mandated noncombustible building materials at the town's center, thus forcing any construction using less expensive wood—the usual material for housing—to the periphery. Los Angeles in the meantime had been spreading outward as a consequence of its vast network of electric railways, eleven hundred miles in all, mostly built by real-estate developers eager to get buyers to their far-flung subdivisions. (See Figure 12.7.) Once the developers' lots were sold, however, they became less interested in maintaining their transit lines, forcing buyers of those lots to seek other means of getting about.[26]

Angelinos were thus eager early consumers of automobiles, dependent on roads converted from abandoned streetcar lines. In the hottest of regions, Phoenix, Arizona, was also spreading horizontally, in part following the system of irrigation canals built to bring water from the Salt River to farmlands. Early twentieth-century Chicago, Los Angeles, and Phoenix—all cities known to Wright from his travels—helped to inspire his Broadacre vision as the Automobility Age progressed.

Autopia

By 1955, as Keats and Whyte were preparing to publish their critiques, America was a country of 165 million people owning 128 million cars—one insolent chariot for every 1.3 people. Unlike Keats and Whyte, European architects and planners—like Ludwig Hilberseimer, one of Walter Gropius's many Bauhaus disciples—were impressed by the contrast between America's dynamic modernism and what they saw in war-torn Europe. In 1955, Hilberseimer would write that "the real cause of our woe is the failure of the city to keep pace with technological development. The city built for an ancient pedestrian age has failed to adapt itself to the requirements of the motor age."[27] (See Figure I.6.) In the same year, California's Disneyland opened with a children's car ride called *Autopia*, which remains an attraction at several Disney parks. Leave it to Disney to be more in touch with long-term cultural trends than mid-century urban pundits.[28] As recently as 1980 (just before Japan and Germany overtook Detroit's car manufacturing dominance), the automotive industry and everything that it necessitates accounted for about one out of six American jobs.[29] As of this writing there are (and Keats would surely recoil at the statistic) more than 265 million insolent chariots in America, one for every 1.2 people. When Sigfried Giedion, one of the most influential chroniclers of modern architecture, observed that "the space-time feeling of our period can seldom be felt so keenly as when driving," he was sensing not only the scale of a New York parkway but also what an integral part of the city the car had become. [30]

The British architecture critic Reyner Banham appropriated the term *Autopia* to describe the fourth "ecology" in his popular *Los Angeles: The Architecture of Four Ecologies*. He was amazed by LA's system of freeways, at least as he experienced them in 1970, and considered them one of the most tangible places in what was for him an otherwise formless city.[31] He saw the entry ramps to those highways as thresholds akin to a driveway or a front door, enabling Angelinos to enter a special realm, often for hours, a realm alternating between Eden and purgatory. Banham may not have been familiar with Joan Didion's 1970 novel *Play it as it Lays,* but it would have boosted his confidence in his intuition that LA's highways were more than mere conveyer belts. Maria, the novel's protagonist, struggling to find relief from constant depression, seeks solace on those highways:

> Again and again she returned to an intricate stretch just south of the interchange where successful passage from the Hollywood onto the Harbor required a diagonal move across four lanes of traffic. On the afternoon she finally did it without once braking or once losing the beat on the radio she was exhilarated, and that night slept dreamlessly.[32]

A full-spread magazine advertisement from the same period, for a 1977 Buick LeSabre, promises even greater intimacy with one's car. Dad sits in the capacious Buick in the driveway of a lovely suburban home with his admiring wife and three kids looking on. The ad's headline reads: "There's no place like Buick." (See Figure 12.1.) And thus a machine perfected to get you to better places has itself had the status of place bestowed upon it. A 1995 Nissan ad took its messaging to a different level, claiming that the Infiniti in it is "not a car. It's an aphrodisiac."[33] A pretty good history of twentieth-century America and its various preoccupations might be assembled entirely from automobile industry advertising.

Autopia or Asphalt Nation?

At a 1953 confirmation hearing, President Eisenhower's nominee for Secretary of Defense, Charles E. Wilson, president of General Motors, was asked by one Senator whether he could make a decision in the interests of America even if it were extremely adverse to GM. He said he could but added it was hard to conceive of one: "For years I thought what was good for our country was good for General Motors, and vice versa. The difference did not exist."[34] His answer was immediately misquoted and to this day is recalled as an arrogant "what's good for General Motors is good for America." That is a bit unfair but at the same time understandable. If the head of the world's largest corporation had really said that, representing the world's dominant economy in the aftermath of World War II, most people would have said he was only stating the obvious.

The upward mobility of the postwar era was in full advance in no small measure due to the car. Around the same time, William Levitt was moving on from completing his first suburban Levittown in New York to building a second and larger one in Pennsylvania.[35] Competitors were emulating his success elsewhere. The GI Bill, in combination with the low-cost mortgage provisions of the earlier Federal Housing Administration (FHA) and Veterans Administration (VA), were enabling millions of veterans and their families to reach their American Dream.[36] If that dream took them to one of Mr. Levitt's inexpensive developments, it was available for little or no money down, and a monthly mortgage bill of just thirty to fifty dollars. Projects to expand roads and utilities were expanding everywhere, supported by funding programs created in the Depression era, and by the even older Bureau of Public Roads dating to 1916, during the Wilson administration. The National Interstate and Defense Highways Act of 1956, the most ambitious public works project in the nation's history, was simultaneously committing to provide 90 percent federal funding to build forty-one thousand miles of highways across America over a decade or two, a commitment that would be met. (See Figure 12.8.)

For citizens faced with decaying urban neighborhoods, the traumas of urban renewal, public policies supporting home ownership, and brewing civil rights

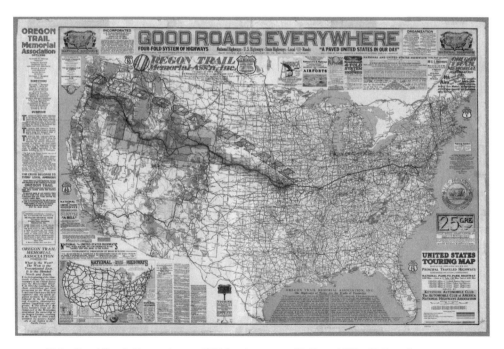

12.8   Good Roads Everywhere, a 1929 touring map with the subtitle: "A Paved United States in Our Day."

unrest, the lure of a leafy escape to well-equipped new homes with inexpensive mortgages was irresistible. Why would GM's president not feel secure in his belief? Another four decades would go by before Congress, in 1991, passed the Intermodal Surface Transportation Act, which declared that, to improve transportation for the future, the country needed more than just roads and cars—and more importantly, that only more wide-ranging plans would be eligible to receive federal funding.

The first public doubts regarding the dominion of the "automobility age" had come earlier, however, beginning with the oil crisis in 1973, the result of an oil embargo on the United States by the Organization of Petroleum Exporting Countries (OPEC). A second shock came in 1979, caused by a decrease in worldwide oil production following the revolution in Iran. Other consequences of the car's dominance were also becoming harder to ignore. Environmental concerns were emerging—notably as smog choked LA's autopia. The sheer extent of residential suburbanization also dragged commerce and businesses out of cities, causing city-style congestion and other inconveniences in the suburbs themselves. The acceleration of "white flight" following the 1960s civil rights protests did more to hollow out industrial-era cities—even (and especially) in Detroit, the birthplace of Autopia. Prolonged disinvestment in city centers came to be understood as a consequence of the ease with which people decamped to the suburbs in their insolent chariots, becoming increasingly oblivious to the plight of the "inner city." Even as Reyner Banham was marveling at LA's freeway system, a 1973 editorial in the *Baltimore Sun,* months prior to the oil embargo, addressed the sorry state of the nation's highways. It argued that "the highway has passed the point of merely linking towns and cities, until now it functions mainly to channel congestion and pollution back and forth from cities to suburbs. . . . To continue to ram roads into our cities without making a major effort to develop parallel systems is to assure our strangulation."[37] (See Figure 12.9.)

In the years since that prescient article, a number of American cities have embarked on new projects to expand and diversify their transportation infrastructure, among them some surprises, such as Dallas and Phoenix. Momentum for further expansion is gaining, even if funding is grossly insufficient. But while the American love affair with the car has waned somewhat, the marriage continues—and ardor for a similar romance is growing in parts of the world currently undergoing rapid modernization. A milestone was reached in 2015 as annual worldwide sales of cars first exceeded eighty million. Despite a diminution in

12.9 Famous 1952 photograph from *Life* magazine of a newly built residential area entitled *Moving Day*. The title also referring to the fact that at mid-twentieth century, Americans were moving approximately every four to six years.

affection, especially among the younger generation of Americans, we are not nearly done with the car culture.

The Uber phenomenon, the driverless cars in development, and the more distant prospect of hydrogen-fueled vehicles (all of them surely just steps along the way to hovering shoes and drone conveyance) promise a future of easier, more convenient, and cleaner personal mobility yet. It is easy to relate to the expectations for the motorcar in 1900. That does not, however, bode well for an immediate reduction in travel, or for the number of daily or weekly trips a person may wish to take. It may take some other development—like Amazon and Wal-Mart delivering more to our doors—to ultimately alter the fact that greater capacity and convenience has always increased amounts of travel.

It may seem hard to believe that millions of visitors were once enthralled by Futurama, an exhibit that General Motors choreographed at the World's Fair in 1939, and again at the 1965 New York World's Fair, with charming "magic motorways." The 1939 fair's overall theme of "Democracity," offering a preview of a pollution-free city dispersed over thousands of square miles, and relying on the convenience of those magic motorways, seems simpleminded today. Nor are we likely to be entranced by the "Motopia" promoted by the British planner Geoffrey Jellicoe in 1961, perhaps with tongue in cheek. But we have not yet shed Autopia. Keats's insolent chariot, the dominant force in shaping—or, as many would say, misshaping—the twentieth-century city remains a formidable force early in the twenty-first century. This is not least because the innumerable miles of low-density development built over the past century cannot all be abandoned. We remain dependent on the continued convenience of personal mobility.

Assigning the Costs of Autopia

In *Sprawl: A Compact History,* his well-reasoned shot across the bow of the anti-sprawl movement, Robert Bruegmann reminds us that for much of American history—really, from Jefferson's time on—decentralization was considered progressive, a social good, and a measure of citizens' economic advancement. It was the opposite of the major environmental and social problem many consider it to be today.[38] While it may be hard to dismiss Bruegmann's views from a historical perspective, many have called his championing of low-density urbanization irresponsible. Some consider it heresy to suggest that many Americans actually prefer low-density environments, or to imply that suburbanization was not primarily the result of misguided public policy, corporate marketing (especially from the auto industry), and land developers' eagerness to subdivide that additional one hundred greenfield acres. Many are skeptical that the instinct to spread out in the face of congestion and urban stress may be as human as the desire to congregate in cities in search of economic opportunity or social propinquity. They are reluctant to admit that a lowering of urban densities tends to follow innovations in mobility and increases in economic means, or to consider that, as some anthropologists theorize, humanity might be biologically wired to thrive in and be attracted to small social groups and natural settings, rather than immense and crowded congregations of people. Bruegmann intimates, as others have, that the enormous and dense nineteenth-century industrial city—the city that provoked Charles Dickens's ire—was an aberrant form of human settlement, rather than the ultimate destiny of humankind.

While all this is debatable, a growing number of critics of dispersal respond with a tough question about costs and benefits. While low-density settlement is appealing to many, whether real estate moguls or individual homeowners, who enjoy the lifestyle or profit from it, it is hardly an efficient use of land or of the world's finite resources. And the cumulative burdens of pervasive urban sprawl on the natural environment cannot be ignored simply because it is popular. There is that not insignificant problem of multiplication. It is one thing if several thousand Englishman plant themselves on the outskirts of sixteenth-century London—an example of old sprawl from Bruegmann's book. It is quite a different matter if all three hundred million Americans or, in the near future, a billion affluence-gaining Chinese, choose to sprawl.

Putting one's love or disdain for cars aside, what must be brought to the fore in the debate over low-density urbanization is this: the benefits of sprawl—notably, the acquisition of more space at a lower cost and the promise of eventual appreciation—still tend to accrue to Americans individually, while sprawl's costs—the need for additional infrastructure, greater energy generation, and pollution mitigation—tend to be borne by society overall. Understanding this imbalance is essential, and finding ways to distribute the costs and benefits more fairly remain a real challenge. Can political will be summoned for measures to shift some of the costs of dispersion onto the sprawlers—ideas like impact fees, user assessments, regional tax-sharing, gasoline taxes, highway tolls, streamlined permitting and upzoning in already developed areas, ceilings on mortgage deductions, surcharges on second homes, and open-space and amenity assessments? There is little evidence of such will, but there is hope that growing awareness of the environmental impacts of sprawl will slowly lead to change. Yes, continuing to find additional arguments against sprawl is useful, but the campaign to create a more diverse, rewarding, and environmentally sound urban future will ultimately depend on whether America finds better ways to rein in short-term self-interest to achieve long-term social value.

13.1   Photo used for the cover of *What the Trees Said: Life on a New Age Farm*,
1971, a memoir about the first year of an experimental community.

13

COMMUNITARIAN JOURNEYS

> One morning I wakened with a strange, new joy in my soul. It came to me at that moment with indescribable poignancy, the thought of walking barefoot in cool, fresh plow furrows as I had once done when a boy. So vividly the memory came. . . . I thought of sitting in quiet thickets in old fence corners, the wood behind me rising still, cool, mysterious, and the fields in front stretching away in illimitable pleasantness. I thought of the good smell of cows at milking—you do not know, if you do not know!—I thought of the sights and sounds, the heat and sweat of the hay fields. . . . I thought of a certain brook I knew when a boy that flowed among alders and wild parsnips, where I waded with a three-foot rod for trout. I thought of all these things as a man thinks of his first love.
>
> DAVID GRAYSON, 1906

THE PASSAGE IS FROM A MAGAZINE PIECE titled "Adventures in Contentment." David Grayson was the pen name of Ray Stannard Baker, an accomplished journalist, historian, and Pulitzer Prize–winning author of a multivolume biography of President Woodrow Wilson. Baker also wrote about inequality and the nation's racial divide. He served as a war correspondent in Europe and as Wilson's press secretary at the Paris Peace Conference at the end World War I. One imagines Baker, educated and worldly, as a consummate urbanite. Yet, as "Adventures in Contentment" reveals, he was happiest with his feet dug down into the soil. Under his pen name, Baker let his alter ego express a dream harbored by many Americans.

The desire to head out and get one's feet into soil would guide many others. "Well, I think we ought to move the news service to a farm," announced Marshall Bloom, the cofounder of the 1960s radical Liberation News Service, a conduit in a time before social media among five hundred underground newspapers. He wanted to move to "a place where people can begin to think clearly, a place to get all of those city poisons out of their systems." The farming commune he helped establish in Montague, Massachusetts, in 1968 was one of the more successful of many founded in that period. Indeed, it was the subject in its first year of Stephen Diamond's bestselling *What the Trees Said: Life on a New Age Farm,* which remains in print to this day.[1] Bloom was a leader of the 1960s counterculture movement, and his hopes for the commune were clear: to establish a new grounding "where chaos stops at our border and Nature's order and unity may begin."[2] The farm he imagined did manage to survive, presumably free of city poisons, until 2002. Sadly, his personal chaos followed him across the commune's borders and he wasn't able to shake it; he committed suicide within a year of the farm's beginning. Setting out for utopia does not always lead to contentment.

Rural settings, or the lure of "Nature's order," have long beckoned Americans away from "unnatural surroundings"—a euphemism for unruly city life that recalls Adam Smith's conclusion that "unnaturalness and dependence" are the city dweller's burden. The image of the independent, self-reliant citizen—removed to a rural landscape, a pastoral domain, or like Daniel Boone to a nearby frontier—recurs in American history. Even in a culture that celebrates individualism, there are parallel searches for fulfillment in the company of others. As at Montague in 1968, the ideal has been to withdraw from the world as one finds it, to a context that one has a hand in creating with like-minded individuals to be better. Such collective removals have occurred in multiple waves—beginning soon after Columbus sailed, as many wondered how a newly discovered world might enable spiritual rebirth. (See Figure 13.2.)

From the moment of its discovery, many saw the New World as a haven for those in the Old World who were persecuted, disenfranchised, or shunned, and for those whose vision of either a heavenly or secular Eden required land for the creation of a new community. The Dutch Mennonites in Delaware, the Puritans who settled New England, the Quakers who colonized Pennsylvania, and

13.2   Hancock Shaker Village historical site: the third of nineteen such villages established between 1783 and 1836.

the Catholics of Maryland were among the early arrivals seeking to escape persecution and create nurturing kingdoms. They, along with the Huguenots, the Shakers, the Moravians, and the Amish, are but the remembered few of many groups who came in search of religious freedom. Others came to set up paradises more secular, unburdened by particular spiritual teachings and unharnessed as a society from the shackles of feudalism, oligarchy, or, later, capitalism. These communitarian ventures, often assumed to be at the margins of American history, form a powerful counterpoint to the more common projection of the self-reliant, individualist American.

At the risk of understating the variety and extent of such communitarian experimentation, five major waves can be identified. First, there were those resolute religious groups seeking freedom from intolerance and persecution. From the early seventeenth well into the nineteenth century, they came determined to build an earthly paradise in this new world. Some remained sequestered amongst their own, while most gradually assimilated into the mainstream. Second, early in the nineteenth century, nascent forms of socialism begat numerous secular communitarian utopias, for people concerned about the negative effects of modernization and industrialization on matters such labor, equity, and social well-being. Third, toward the end of the nineteenth century, there was a similar reaction to the inhumane conditions being produced by the industrial city, now much more complex. This was an outpouring of literary utopias. Few of those imagined utopias led to the establishment of actual communities, but they inspired many progressive reforms in existing communities. We can also thank them for the emergence of new professions, among them urban planning, aimed at better managing urbanization. Fourth, the Great Depression, blamed partially on the economic monopolization that seemed endemic to large cities, unleashed a new back-to-the-land movement, abetted by federal policies encouraging rural development and urban decentralization. And fifth, during the tumultuous 1960s, young idealists formed upward of two thousand communes, rejecting the materialism and conspicuous consumption of mainstream America, and the imperialistic forays that led to war in remote parts of the world.

Common to all of these has been a desire to "head for the woods," at least metaphorically, and exchange a complex environment for a simpler one, with hopes of creating a more controlled and soul-enriching existence. A few urban communes were established, particularly during the 1960s, but the majority of what Robert S. Fogerty has termed "journeying" involved removal to places more remote, where a retooling of a portion of society could be more easily undertaken and hopefully maintained. Let's look at each of these five waves in turn.

Building Zion

Most of the religious groups that crossed the ocean and set off into the wilderness aimed to forge ideal communities—their special Zions, which they hoped would endure and expand. But in most cases the founding idealism proved hard to sustain and very few left substantial physical traces.[3] Today, some have become tourist curiosities. We might, for example, enjoy visiting a restored Shaker Village (with nary a Shaker about) or relish owning a Shaker reproduction chair. Or we might head in search of remnants of the "Zoarites," German Separatists who founded Zoar, Ohio, in 1817, naming their village for the place to which the biblical Lot fled from Sodom with his family. We might similarly visit New Harmony, Indiana, the setting of two successive utopian enterprises, now with an impressive modern interpretive center that helps explain how the communities came about and why they did not last. Weekending in a charming New England village, especially at leaf-turning season, is a particular delight, whether or not we recall the place's origin as a covenanted community of colonists escaping religious intolerance, but also intolerant of others. Perhaps our children have been amused, while visiting Plymouth Plantation, by the playacting of staff pretending it is still 1624.

These are the vestiges of temporal utopias. While there are towns named Zion in twenty-three states, most contain little evidence of the founders' original intentions. The ethos binding the founding group together rarely lasted more than a few generations and, even when the communities were young, their styles of building were rarely very distinctive. After all, enrichment of spirit was the overriding goal, not the building of iconic places. There were, however, two religious traditions that did produce avid town builders, and the towns they designed are important to understanding idealized forms of American settlement.

As we saw in Chapter 4, the covenanted villages of the New England Puritans, as physically enhanced by subsequent generations, came to form an ideal of small-town life that was emulated by settlers as the country expanded west. "All the me in me is in a little Missouri Village, half-way around the world," Mark Twain would pine while traveling, and he was hardly alone in his sentiments.[4] Village life on the New England model still summons agreement with David Grayson's lament about city life in another installment of "Adventures in Contentment": "Oh, my friend, say what you please, argue how you like, this crowding together of men and women in unnatural surroundings, this haste to be rich in material things, this attempt to enjoy without production, this removal from first-hand life, is irrational, and the end of it is ruin."[5]

Adherents of one of the youngest of the religious societies, the Church of Jesus Christ of the Latter-Day Saints, would prove to be even more prolific town-builders than the Puritans. A small group of followers gathered by Joseph Smith in 1830 grew in just half a century to over 140,000 members strong, spread across several hundred new communities from Canada to Mexico. Mormon doctrine establishes a case for the building of a holy city. While Jerusalem is the Bible's sacred capital, it speaks on several occasions of a second holy city called Zion. The Mormons foresaw a Zion located in the western hemisphere that would serve as their Jerusalem: "And it shall be called the New Jerusalem, a land

of peace, a city of refuge, a place of safety for the Saints of the Most High God,"
state the Mormon doctrine and covenants. "And the glory of the Lord shall be
there, and the terror of the Lord shall be there, insomuch that the wicked will
not come unto it, and it shall be called Zion."[6]

In an 1833 letter to his followers, Joseph Smith included A "Plat of the City of
Zion." It is a remarkable treatise on urban design, containing a number of similarities to Ebenezer Howard's famous Garden City conception, though it precedes Howard by sixty-five years. The plan for Mormon "garden cities," as they
were called, like Howard's *Garden City*, contained elements that would become
common to twentieth-century garden-city-inspired planning. For example, it
prescribed an optimum town size, recommended specific land uses and density
measures, supported common ownership of land, favored a synthesis of rural
and urban qualities, and required permanent agricultural zones between cities.
But this grid also carried additional significance: it was God's mandate.

As the Mormons migrated west under the leadership of Brigham Young, they
adapted the Plat of Zion, also heeding the description of Jerusalem in the New
Testament Book of Revelation: "the city lieth foursquare." Fortuitously, this lent
itself nicely to the grid of the continental surveys. Square-mile towns were
planned to accommodate fifteen thousand to twenty thousand people, with all
streets at right angles. But a unique platting system called for blocks of houses
to alternate between having their houses positioned north-to-south and east-to-
west, forming a kind of checkerboard of houses all facing their neighbor's gardens. Joseph Smith attributed this design to divine revelation, but he might also
have been familiar with Thomas Jefferson's writings on cities. "Take, for
instance, the chequer board for a plan," Jefferson writes to one correspondent.
"Let the black squares only be building squares, and the white ones be left open,
in turf and trees. Every square of houses will be surrounded by four open
squares, and every house will front an open square. The atmosphere of such a
town would be like that of the country, insusceptible of the miasmata which
produce yellow fever."[7]

For the Mormons, the checkerboard pattern appealed to their doctrine of
"consecration and stewardship."[8] Overall unity of purpose was most important, and it was vital that life be connected to the land. Thus, a beautiful idea
emerged that every house should overlook a field or neighbor's garden, rather
than the front of a neighbor's house. Kinship with each other and with the land
would be the Mormons' measure of harmony. (See Figure 13.3.)

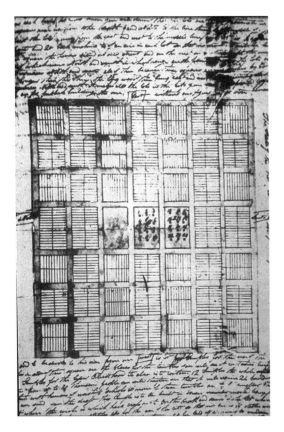

13.3   Joseph Smith's Plat of Zion: detailed instructions on how to lay out a Mormon town based on a revelation from God.

Seeking Harmony

Many others set out across America in searches for harmony. By the time of the Mormon migration westward, groups with a bewildering variety of names—Fourierists, Harmonists, Impressionists, Millennialists, Separatists—already existed, and must have influenced Joseph Smith's disciple Brigham Young. Nascent forms of socialism propelled many utopian journeys.[9] (See Figure 13.4.) In 1803, for instance, self-proclaimed profit George Rapp brought a following of German Separatists to western Pennsylvania, where they established a farming community and called the place *Harmony*. A few years later, in 1814, as followers and farming ambitions increased, they acquired thirty thousand acres of richer agricultural land in Indiana, and gathered in a place they called *New Harmony*. But just a decade later, most chose to return to Pennsylvania to be nearer to

13.4 Members of the Kaweah Colony, a utopian socialist community founded in 1886 amidst the giant Sequoia groves in the Sierra Nevada Mountains. Disbanded by 1892 partially due to the creation of Sequoia National Park.

profitable markets, as their activities had expanded to include industrial work such as the production of silk. (A few Rappists, as they were called, did venture further west). Those back east named the third town they founded *Economy*, intentionally or inadvertently reflecting the evolution of the group from Millennialist to more capitalist ambitions. Similar transitions were not uncommon as the lures and benefits of material prosperity loosened spiritual or communitarian ties.

The entrepreneurial Harmonists found another utopian to whom they would sell the town of New Harmony. Robert Owen, a British textile manufacturer, had published *A New Vision of Society* in 1813, calling for the establishment of future industrial towns as more humane settings in which a new labor class could prosper in work and life. He concluded that America would be more amenable than Britain to his rather monastic enclaves featuring some twelve hundred people engaging in both traditional agricultural and new manufacturing endeavors. Only a few years after he had purchased New Harmony in whole

13.5   An imagined Philanstery depicting Charles Fourier's utopian vision.

from the Harmonists, the enterprise succumbed to organizational chaos and a failed struggle for self-sufficiency. Owen never got the chance to construct his much-publicized rendering of a quadrangular campus, which was to form the heart of New Harmony. (See Figure 13.5) His influence, however, endured among socialists inspired by the dream of a new kind of laborer-citizen thriving in communal settings.[10]

Another pied piper, Charles Fourier of France, inspired other American socialists to build what he called *Phalansteries,* large edifices for communal living. These were organized around the eccentric idea that all of human life was governed by twelve common passions. Each Phalanstery was a huge, symmetrical structure housing a standard hierarchy of social units. Seven people constituted a "Group," five Groups formed a "Series," and all the Series together—since each was based on a different occupation—comprised a *Phalanx* of something less than two thousand people. Fourier believed that a rational system of human organization built around shared passions would create a society at once more productive and more altruistic—at least, one supposes, toward others in the Phalanstery. He argued that industrialization could satisfy human needs more fully and equitably only if it was tied to such a system of communal living.[11]

Fourier's theories attracted many enthusiastic supporters, among them Americans Albert Brisbane and Horace Greeley (of "Go West" fame). Brisbane advocated Fourierism in publications such as his 1840 *Social Destiny of Man* and a journal called *The Phalanx*.[12] Greeley popularized the ideas in the pages of his *New-Yorker* and *New York Tribune* publications. Even Brook Farm, an admired Transcendentalist farming community near Boston associated with such notables as Ralph Waldo Emerson, Margaret Fuller, and Nathaniel Hawthorne, declared itself a Fourierist community.[13] Work on several dozen other Philansteries got underway in the 1840s. Still, even the longest-lasting of them, the North American Phalanx in New Jersey, disbanded after just twelve years, providing further evidence of how fleeting most utopian efforts are.

Anticipating Altruria

The rapid growth of northern cities in the decades following the Civil War shifted the focus of American socialists. Instead of advocating that people withdraw from mainstream society, head west, or join Phalansteries, which only a few were realistically able to do, they focused on alleviating the plight of those living and working in those miserable industrializing cities. Recall from Chapter 9 the outpouring of utopian literature during the last decades of the nineteenth century, and the rise of urban social activism.

The literary utopias of Edward Bellamy, William Dean Howells, and their peers were not about escaping from growing cities. On the contrary, they were about harnessing the might of urban industry and capital markets to more socially-minded values, such as equality, shared prosperity, and dignity. This was a purer utopianism that predicted—or hoped—that, despite evidence to the contrary, the very drivers of economic and social inequality would somehow reverse course and lead to reform. In Howells's Altruria, or Bellamy's future Boston, the benefits of a giant, publicly-owned industrial monopoly enabled citizens to enjoy lives of plenty, without social stratifications or competition, and with ego subordinated to altruism and selflessness. Historians characterize the era as one of progressive reforms, and many reforms were indeed enacted. The prevailing utopian instinct was truly optimistic, positing a socialist future without the need for revolutionary upheaval.

Unfortunately, Altruria never materialized. Instead, urban growth and robber-baron monopolization continued, eventually helping to plunge the nation into the Great Depression. In response, the familiar instinct to withdraw to the land resurfaced.

Reconnecting with the Land

The Depression-fighting policies of the Roosevelt Administration did not aim to revive communitarian socialism but only to promote decentralization. (See Figure I.3.) As the effects of the Depression intensified, President Roosevelt began to argue that there was "a necessary limit to the continuance of the migration from the country to the city." More than that, he said, "I look, in fact, for a swing of the pendulum in the other direction. All things point that way."[14] Perhaps it was not true that all things did, but the programs launched by many of Roosevelt's famous one hundred "alphabet agencies" helped push them that way. The Agricultural Adjustment Administration, the Rural Electrification Administration, the Subsistence Homestead Division, the Tennessee Valley Authority, the Works Progress Administration, and the Resettlement Administration were just some of the new bureaucracies working to spread out resources, jobs, and housing. They laid the foundation for the massive suburbanization that would take place in the postwar period, but their short-term goal was to help people weather economic catastrophe by fostering greater self-sufficiency.

Supportive of federal policies favoring decentralization, rural idealists took up their efforts again in the spirit of Fourier and Albert Brisbane. A largely self-taught economist, Ralph Borsodi, was able to persuade many readers with his advocacy of a return to farming, which he saw as the path to more contented and less dependent life. By the middle of the 1930s, a majority of Americans lived in urban areas, but Borsodi argued that it would be better if more lived self-sufficiently on new forms of homesteads.[15] At the height of the Depression, in 1933, the unemployment rate reached 24.9 percent. To many of these displaced workers, homeless and despairing, Borsodi offered hope. Evoking Jefferson, he revived the narrative of a life well spent close to the land, the sort of "adventure in contentment" that David Grayson had pined for. He echoed William Jennings Bryan's insistence that rural life would never perish ("destroy our farms, and the grass will grow in the streets of every city in the country"). Southern agrarians, too, rallied to this old narrative, having never entirely abandoned it, and now expressed it with a kind of "told you so" defiance, continuing the antipathy to northern urbanization (even as the disenfranchised among them kept streaming into northern cities in search of better lives).

Borsodi set out to demonstrate self-sufficiency by running several small homesteads with his family. The accounts he published about their challenges and triumphs were filled with humor and written in simple, reassuring prose:

> A comfortable home in which [one finds] labor and play, with trees
> and grass and flowers and skies and stars; a small garden; a few fruit
> trees; a workshop with its tools, and three big dogs to keep the sales-
> men out. . . . Living in the country has been called "the simple life."
> This is not true. It's much more complex than city life. City life is the
> one that's simple. You get a job and earn money and you go to a store
> and buy what you want and can afford. The decentralist life in the
> country, on the other hand, is something else again. When you design
> your own things and make plans about what you're going to produce
> and really live in a self-sufficient manner, you've got to learn . . . all
> sorts of crafts and activities that people in the city know nothing
> about.[16]

It is unclear how many Americans actually followed Borsodi to a farming life. Certainly, far more would move to suburbs than rural homesteads. But the policies of the New Deal broadened enthusiasm for decentralization, and at the same time for the modernization of much of rural America with water, electricity, and road infrastructure.

Borsodi lived until 1977, so he was able to witness the communal utopias of the 1960s. The young men and women of that era who also sought that more complicated life of the country must have pleased him. In a 1974 interview with *Mother Earth News,* he reaffirmed where he thought Americans should head: "Man is a gregarious animal. He's not supposed to live in isolation. He should actually live in a community, but a community does not necessarily have to be a city. There's all the evidence in the world that the building of cities is one of the worst mistakes that mankind has ever made: For both physical and mental health we've got to be close to Mother Earth."[17]

Aside from this fierce condemnation of cities, Borsodi's ideas speak to today's environment-minded citizens who, like him, support local food production, the conservation of resources and energy, and various cooperative endeavors on behalf of the planet. He was the hero to the heroes of the 1960s back-to-the-land movement, such as Scott and Helen Nearing, whose Good Life Center in rural Maine was a mecca for many hoping to drop out of mainstream America, and even live off the grid.[18]

Dropping Out

The young idealists of the 1960s shared with their Eden-seeking predecessors a desire to leave behind a culture that was unresponsive to their values and preferred lifestyles. They all wanted to start anew. Reacting against the suburban conformity of the 1950s and the values of what President Eisenhower called the "military-industrial complex," most shared Borsodi's and the Nearings' belief that regeneration would come about by living closer to Mother Earth. The famous Joni Mitchell lyrics expressed their feelings well:

Don't it always seems to go
That you don't know what you've got
Till it's gone
They paved paradise
And put up a parking lot [19]

They thus headed for environs less paved. During the tumultuous 1960s, "dropping out"—the signature expression of the times—seemed a sensible course of action to all kinds of Americans. Historian Dolores Hayden, immersed at the time in the study of American utopias, and herself sharing their youthful communitarian affinities, acknowledged this diversity in her dissertation: "They describe themselves as Jesus freaks and atheists, revolutionaries and apolitical types, hip and straight, puritan and promiscuous, feminist and male chauvinist, urban and rural, technologically primitive and sophisticated."[20] They were also mystics, anarchists, pacifists, profits of dubious revelations, and cultists, too, with apocalyptic visions headed for tragic consequences. There were curious builders, too, such as Paolo Soleri, who spent more than half a century constructing Arcosanti in the Arizona desert, turning it into a must-see for anyone wanting to view a utopia under actual construction. Soleri died in 2013, but Arcosanti lives on as a devoted group of residents continue to build, however slowly, relying on income from the sale of locally produced bronze "windbells."[21] Anyone trying to dismiss the era's widespread utopian inclinations as some aberrant outburst of youthful exuberance or "Marxist gobbledygook," as some have done, seriously misunderstands the history of the nation.

13.6   A 1960s commune on wheels.

13.7   Emblematic scene of the 1960s idealists' desire to find individual fulfillment while part of a small community.

The phenomenon of dropping out in the 1960s revived interest in older communitarian traditions. This is how an 1870 publication, *History of American Socialisms,* came to be rediscovered and turned into a primer of sorts for the '60s utopians. Its author, John Humphrey Noyes, was the founder of the Oneida Community, one of the more exotic experiments in congregate living. In it, he summarizes the communitarian impulse of his era: "The revivalists had for their great idea the regeneration of the soul. The great idea of the Socialists was the regeneration of society, which is the soul's environment. These ideas belong together, and are the complements of each other."[22]

Regenerating the soul, and with it society, was a message that appealed to many during the 1960s and, indeed, has resonated across American history. From the earliest European arrivals escaping oppression, the American communitarian DNA has been made up of these intertwining utopian strands: first, the desire to find individual fulfillment while part of a small community, and second, a resolve to remake community so that individual enrichment could be promoted. (See Figures 13.6 and 13.7.) Both inclinations are still in play, and there will surely be future waves of remaking and journeying, perhaps in response to climate change, biological crisis, or artificial intelligence, or perhaps driven by some yet unanticipated situation begging for radical social action by the idealists among us.

14.1 Some 40 riverfront blocks in downtown St. Louis demolished in preparation for the Jefferson National Expansion Memorial. 1942 photo.

14

MISGUIDED RENEWAL: THE URBAN CLEARANCE DECADES

> The Congress hereby declares that the general welfare and security
> of the Nation and the health and living standards of its people require
> housing production and related community development sufficient to
> remedy the serious housing shortage, the elimination of substandard
> and other inadequate housing through the clearance of slums and
> blighted areas, and the realization as soon as feasible of the goal of a
> decent home and a suitable living environment for every American
> family.
>
> FEDERAL HOUSING ACT, 1949

WITH THIS NOBLE PREAMBLE, the Housing Act of 1949 committed the federal government to substantial fiscal support to the nation's cities. An important part of President Truman's "Fair Deal" agenda, the act included the impressive goal of building 810,000 units of public housing and thus marked the beginning of the era of urban renewal. As we will see, however, its aspirations and ambitions were far from sufficient to ensure that a fair deal in housing would be extended to all Americans.

To anyone unfamiliar with the period, the term *urban renewal* might sound unambiguously positive. Why would it not be a good idea to keep renewing neighborhoods and, for that matter, entire cities? Instead, the era proved deeply tumultuous and traumatizing. (See Figure 14.12.) More than half a century later, memories conjure up few images of renewal but many of neighborhood demolition—hardly a fair deal, especially for the urban poor who were most affected. Jane Jacobs referred to urban renewal as the "sacking of cities."[1] The phrase itself has been struck from the planner's vocabulary. If a planner began a community meeting today by promoting urban renewal, the meeting would end abruptly.

So why, in a book about utopian aspirations, include a chapter about such a notorious period? The answer is that the era emerged from another long-standing American ideal, misguided though it might be. It is the ideal of new beginnings: the notion that starting over rather than improving what exists will yield a brighter future.

American Progress

Consider again a painter's evidence. The theme of John Gast's 1872 painting *American Progress* is Manifest Destiny. In it, as we saw in Chapter 3, Lady Progress ushers civilization to the West. (See Figure 3.1.) But behind Lady Progress? Well, that would be St. Louis being left behind for the lures of California or Colorado. "Go west, young man," was the nineteenth-century analog of urban renewal. Why would someone wrestle with difficult circumstances at home when, as Frederick Jackson Turner put it in 1893, "with a slight effort he might reach a land wherein to become a co-worker in the building of free cities."[2] Turner's "frontier thesis" was simple: if social or economic conditions became stifling, or impeded freedom, any American could pick up and head off to seek fortune elsewhere. There was a "gate of escape." Notice the emphasis on escape rather than repair. Turner was articulating a predisposition among Americans to improve their lot by moving away. In a sense, this was only in keeping with long tradition, starting with the colonists escaping the Old World's deficiencies.[3]

To go west was to be freed from the limits imposed by existing cities. Turner, however, largely ignored a parallel narrative: the dramatic growth of those very cities. While nineteenth-century westward migration was a safety valve for some, it did not depopulate prospering eastern cities. On the contrary, the opportunities presented by industrial-era urbanization were an irresistible lure for rural populations no longer enchanted or sustained by farming or small-town life, and for waves of immigrants seeking to better their lives in America. The cities boomed.

But at mid-twentieth century, as suburbanizing "pioneers" left the equivalents of St. Louis, there were few people taking their place. Population growth in older cities leveled off, as opportunities for better lives seemed to be found only at their outskirts. Turner's safety valve had become the expanding suburb, and those *Edge Cities*—a term coined by Joel Gareau and explained by his book of that name—began to supplant the centers of cities. Gareau understood the persistence of Turner's ideal of withdrawal. The subtitle of his book is *Life on the New Frontier.*[4] And if those inner cities as they emptied could be thought of as yet another frontier, well, there was a certain logic to starting there anew by clearing and rebuilding.

Consider the perspective of one of President Franklin Roosevelt's key economic advisors during the Great Depression: "Go just outside the city centers of population, pick up cheap land, build a whole community and entice people into them. Then go back into the cities and tear down whole slums and make parks of them."[5] Rexford G. Tugwell was describing what he hoped to achieve as the head of one of Roosevelt's Depression-fighting programs, the ominously named (to today's ears) Resettlement Administration. Its actual mandates were rural resettlement, rehabilitation of exhausted farmlands, and suburbanization, including the construction of twenty-five new greenbelt towns (a mandate that was never fulfilled). But Tugwell saw the potential to solve a city problem at the same time. While his statement preceded urban renewal legislation by more than a decade, it was a premonition.

Concerns about substandard urban housing and concentrations of poverty had grown with the progressive reform movements during the final decades of the prior century. But these produced regulations rather than more affordable housing, and some argued that the regulations themselves—for fire protection, ventilation, and reduced densities—were, while individually sensible, collectively raising the cost of housing. During the 1930s, several newly formed agencies, among them the Federal Housing Administration, the Home Owners Loan Corporation, and the Federal Deposit Insurance Corporation, were working to improve the situation. With hundreds of banks failing, financing of construction was limited, as was the availability of mortgages. The Federal Housing Administration set out to dramatically reorganize lending policies. The goal was to revive home ownership through innovations such as long-term, low-interest, tax-deductible mortgages, which continue to benefit homebuyers today. The government also hoped to revive the moribund construction industry, but with loan restrictions that favored development on the outskirts of cities, since it was believed that urban slums would have to be cleared before inner cities could attract investment.

As an example, consider St. Louis—yes, the place in the background of *American Progress*. Using the same basic approach Tugwell advised, it proceeded during the 1930s to demolish forty blocks of warehouses, shops, and homes along its Mississippi riverbank. (See Figure 14.1.) They were some of the city's oldest buildings, and the aim was, indeed, to replace them with a large park. With President Roosevelt's support, the cleared land would be turned into a public space commemorating Jefferson's Louisiana Purchase, the Lewis and Clark Expedition, and westward expansion. The resulting national park was initially named the Jefferson National Expansion Memorial but often referred to as the Gateway to the West. Its official name change in 2018 to Gateway Arch National Park honors the magnificent stainless-steel catenary arch, 630 feet high, that stands at its center. At the Museum of Westward Expansion beneath the Arch, Turner's frontier thesis is not prominently featured, but in a way the entire undertaking is a monument to new beginnings. This certainly would not be the last time that an American city, or even the last time that St. Louis itself, would resort to wholesale demolition in the name of "renewal."[6] (See Figure 14.7.)

The intent of federal urban renewal programs was not to build parks. It was to provide financial resources for cities to address their deteriorating physical condition and inadequate supply of decent urban housing. During the nearly two decades that included the Depression and the war years, minimal investment in cities occurred. Postwar municipal leaders were more worried about increasing their cities' tax bases by becoming more attractive to business interests than they were about providing better housing for their ill-housed residents. The "clearance of slums" was the part of the Housing Act's preamble that was embraced with urgency, not the reference to "a decent home and a suitable living environment for every American family." Slum clearance became a mid-twentieth-century substitute for the free-soil mania of the nineteenth century, at least for prescient urban investors.

A decent home would not be easily available to African Americans in particular. As Congress passed the 1949 Housing Act, it rejected a half-hearted effort to include an integration amendment and thus perpetuated local housing authorities' habit of designing separate projects for blacks and whites. (See Figure 14.2.) Lending policies were overtly discriminatory well into the 1960s (and, indeed, even though it is against the law, discrimination distorts lending to this day). In *The Color of Law*, Richard Rothstein provides voluminous data and meticulously researched and disheartening examples of racist decision-making across all levels of government, and by banks and builders. Even if William Levitt had wished to enable African American families to purchase homes in his Levittowns, Rothstein shows how that would have been blocked. The federal government would have declined to subsidize such development, and banks would have refused credit.[7] Not that many African Americans would have qualified for Federal Housing Administration or Veterans Administration loans, anyway. Mid-century notions about good neighborhoods did not yet allow for racial integration. And while integration might be discreetly avoided in publicly supported projects, private housing estates often were quite explicit in their restrictive covenants. A typical clause of the time specifies that "no part of said premises shall be used for [anything] other than a dwelling for people of the Caucasian Race."[8]

14.2   Despite the pleasant scene, two kids pointing as if to a brighter future, most public housing was unavailable to African Americans prior to civil rights legislation in the 1960s.

Urban Blight

There was an obsession with slums during much of the twentieth century, not unrelated to who seemed to occupy them. (See Figure 14.3.) After Senator John F. Kennedy, campaigning for the presidency in 1960, hosted a conference on the state of urban America, his office issued a press release with alarming news: "More Americans live in slums than on farms."[9] Both for those worried about the continuing decline of rural America and for those concerned with the state of urban America, this was lamentable. A prominent architect, Eliel Saarinen, used a common metaphor to offer an equally common prescription: "Now, slums are cancer in the urban body, and it is a well-known fact how cancer must be cured. If the cause of this blight is not removed in time, the disease will inevitably spread itself, for palliative remedies are no good in the long run. . . . The planner must first of all open adequate arteries so that both the city and the population can spread themselves toward the country—towards air, light, and nature."[10] Those who would spread out to air, light, and nature would be white Americans, while those left behind to be displaced would find ever fewer housing choices.

The continuing spread of what came to be called urban decay was a mystery to mainstream Americans and a source of shame for civic boosters. They had celebrated the rise of the modern city with its technological advances, improvements to sanitation and transit, and promise of civic beauty. Social reformers had responded to the kinds of ills documented in Jacob Riis's chilling photos, making regulatory gains and creating the new profession of urban planning. How could it be that unhealthy, unsightly, barely habitable areas of cities continued to spread? Even as hundreds of thousands of affordable homes for the growing middle classes were built in the suburbs, the "slum problem" back in cities attracted ever greater scrutiny.

As slum clearance efforts got underway, and given deliberate disinvestment in neighborhoods designated for clearance, the stock of inexpensive housing within cities kept diminishing. The future seemed to lie in expanding suburbs, except that this future was not available to all those who needed decent housing. In the forms of restricted access to credit, the redlining of neighborhoods by cities and lending institutions, and ethnic and religious considerations in mortgage applications, racism plainly impeded the federally stated goal that every American family should have a decent home and suitable living environment.

14.3 Somehow most images of those mid-century slums featured a particular color of American resident.

Growing calls for highway building, as the automobile lobby constantly demanded better roads, intersected handily with slum-battling initiatives. (See Figure 12.8.) The new world of the automobile required that cities, and not just their peripheries, be crisscrossed with modern expressways. To help achieve this, a powerful Public Roads Administration was established in 1939. Improved roads accelerated the rate of car ownership, which created even more demand for more and better roads—a mutually reinforcing cycle that continued throughout the twentieth century and hasn't yet fully waned. (See Figure 14.4.)

The impact on older cities was nearly catastrophic as federally funded highway construction presented a double temptation for city leaders. They loved the idea of reducing congestion (rarely achieved for long) with new wide roads, but the side effect—the demolition of many dilapidated and unsightly "slums"—was equally welcome. (See Figure 14.5.) Bill McKibben notes that such a dynamic was recognized and satirized early, as in Russell Baker's 1963 essay about

NATIONAL GEOGRAPHIC
AUGUST 1962

Yesterday . . .
the Old Boston Post Road

First Boston-to-New York highway was the Boston Post Road, now U.S. Route 1. Post riders began carrying the mail over this route in 1673. Regular stagecoach service was inaugurated in the late 1700's.

Today..a fabulous network of superhighways

Today, the great turnpikes and thruways of the six New England states beckon the traveler, promise you more time to enjoy your favorite haunts, less time getting there and back. And there's more of the same to come — much more. Boston alone is slated for three new expressways in addition to the present four.
    Come see for yourself, and if there's any way we can help make your trip more enjoyable, just call on us. We've been building and growing with New England for 178 years — and if we don't know all the answers, we know where to get them!

The FIRST
NATIONAL BANK *of*
BOSTON
MEMBER F.D.I.C.

OLD COLONY
TRUST COMPANY

14.4 Great optimism in a 1962 *National
Geographic* ad for the First National Bank
about the arrival and the promise of still
more superhighways.

"The Great Paver" pouring concrete and asphalt over homes, shops, and parks with a simple mandate: "The world must move cars."[11]

Many great pavers contributed to building Autopia. A 1969 National Commission on Urban Problems estimated that 330,000 urban housing units had fallen to highway construction since 1956, the official start of President Eisenhower's Interstate Highway program.[12] Another 425,000 households, totaling perhaps 1,200,000 people, were displaced by urban renewal programs. The Federal Bulldozer, to borrow the title of a 1964 book, was hard at work. With African Americans constituting 60 percent of those forced to find new homes, "negro removal" was becoming a slogan. Making matters worse, of the 810,000 housing units promised by the 1949 Housing Act, only some 350,000 were constructed by the time the programs were halted, and many of these were unavailable to those displaced.[13] This combined attack on the "inner city" (a term which came to signify that place where the wrong people lived) by urban renewers and great pavers left deep scars—geographic, demographic, and emotional.

What today seems so insensitive—no, thickheaded and embittering—was, in the era of slum clearance, the way that many people thought and spoke. A 1941 Federal Housing Administration handbook distributed to cities for "dealing with slums and blighted urban areas," began in this way: "If a fire were to wipe out a large number of city blocks, any citizen at once would recognize the need for rebuilding. Physical signs of deterioration seem to be ignored by these same citizens, even though the signs indicate that forces more destructive than a conflagration are continually and insidiously eating away the vitality of large areas."[14]

Even more colorful language was common: "Amid the piles of rotten garbage, tumbledown porches and junk-filled back yards, the human spirit seems to wither away. This malignancy of urban flesh was considered incurable—even unavoidable—for generations."[15] Incurable, that is, until powerful administrators of highway building and urban renewal programs, such as New York's legendary Robert Moses, took charge. Moses, seeing himself as a latter-day Baron

14.5 Newspaper headlines portrayed local excitement about the coming of an elevated highway through downtown Boston. Compare to Figure I.7, approximately the same view after the demolition of this highway and its replacement in a tunnel.

von Haussmann and wielding more authority over his domain then the Baron had over Paris, could be particularly blunt at community meetings. "When you operate in an overbuilt metropolis, you have to hack your way with a meat ax. I'm just going to keep right on building. You do the best you can to stop it."[16]

With the specter of "malignancies" and "forces more destructive than a conflagration," a meat ax analogy might not seem so outrageous, except to those about to be axed. According to Robert Caro, Moses's unforgiving biographer, the sixteen expressways that Moses helped build—six through densely settled areas—required the relocation of over 250,000 people. While Moses also oversaw the construction of nearly 150,000 apartments, these were, again, not for the citizens of color being displaced.[17] Caro does acknowledge that Moses was responsible for hundreds of playgrounds, baseball diamonds, new and refurbished parks, great public beaches, and other major public works. For much of his career, his success was associated with the modernization of New York. The recovery from the Depression and America's triumph in World War II created a generational confidence in public enterprise, and Moses was seen as the deliverer of public benefit. As his slightly more charitable critic, Marshall Berman, puts it, Moses presented the agencies that he led as "the moving spirits of modernity."[18] To oppose his highways and renewal efforts was simply to impede progress, to deny the spirit of the age.

To some extent, this was a shared cultural belief early in the age of urban renewal and urban highway building. Modernization required tough actions and sacrifices to replace the dilapidated old with a better new. The imagined ends justified the means. "Necessary surgery" is what one historian of modernism, Siegfried Gideon, calls it, agreeing with that patron saint of modernity Walter Gropius. In a lecture in Chicago, a city that would undertake some of the largest and ultimately some of the most destructive urban renewal projects, Gropius offered this advice: "We have to go the whole hog: it is obvious that piecemeal plans, partial reforms, and appeasing concessions are but retarding factors on the way to a tightly coordinated, overall pattern of planning which would promote a healthy twentieth-century community life."[19] (See Figure I.6.)

Such grand proclamations were common, but not precise about whose health should be of primary concern. The 1949 Act promised a decent home for all but, in practice, the funds it made available were often used for other purposes. A municipality could determine that an area was deteriorating, designate it as a renewal area, and petition the federal government to fund the cost of preparing the area for redevelopment. Then, after using those funds to acquire and demolish the area, it could make it available to private developers, whose interests might not be to build housing. Local officials often used urban renewal designations to advance downtown redevelopment in general, sometimes geared toward stemming white flight and changing racial demographics. During the 1950s, the city of New York lost some 750,000 white, middle-class citizens to its suburbs, while Manhattan alone gained some 650,000 African American and Puerto Rican residents. Without ever articulating the goal out loud, officials often hoped that urban renewal programs could reattract some of those who were leaving.

Few visitors to one of the world's premier cultural centers, Lincoln Center for the Performing Arts, realize that some seven thousand residents, most of them black or Hispanic, were displaced to create this modern home for the New York City Opera, New York Philharmonic, New York City Ballet, and Metropolitan Opera. The old San Juan Hill neighborhood, possibly called that in memory of an all-black cavalry unit that fought in the Spanish-American War's Battle of San Juan Hill, had as early as 1940 been deemed "the worst slum section in the City of New York" by the City's Housing Authority.[20] It would take years for New York's political and cultural leaders, including Robert Moses and John D. Rockefeller III, to transform the area, but in the 1950s an urban renewal area was designated and clearance began. In 1962, Lincoln Center opened to considerable acclaim. Millions of patrons since have enjoyed these remarkable venues made possible by the Housing Act of 1949. (See Figure 14.6.) It was not the only such metamorphosis.

14.6   Aerial of the Lincoln Center complex in New York City, replacing some 7,000 residents.

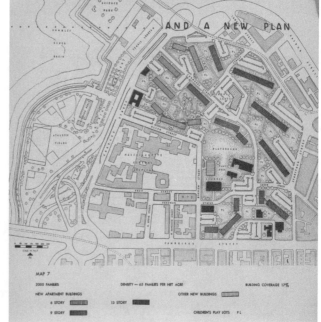

14.7   An Obsolete Neighborhood and a New Plan. Diagrams from a 1950 city document outlying the benefits of demolishing Boston's West End.

Renewing Boston

For nearly a half-century, between World War I and into the 1960s, the old city of Boston hibernated, losing its old industrial and mercantile economic base and nearly a third of its population. People regarded it as a city without a future, describing it more than once as a "hopeless backwater." Even a newly elected mayor, John Collins, spoke in 1960 of a "malaise of the spirit" and how ashamed people were of the state of their city. Shame, along with unacceptable economic stagnation, instigated what many first considered a hopeless effort at large-scale redevelopment. Propelled by the generosity of the urban renewal programs, a near-desperate period of demolition and reconstruction ensued. As in New York under Moses's spell, Boston citizens initially placed faith in bold public initiatives. Edward Logue emerged as Boston's counterpart to Moses. He, too, rarely minced words and, like Moses, favored a line often attributed to another wielder of axes, Joseph Stalin: "You can't make an omelet without breaking eggs."[21]

By the early 1960s, the Boston eggs to be broken included ten neighborhoods which together encompassed a huge portion of the city, and there were six more neighborhoods under study for inclusion. It was simple and enticing for local officials: every part of the city designated as an urban renewal area meant that much more funding from Washington. As elsewhere, until later amendments to the Housing Act made the replacement of housing mandatory, Boston's leaders used urban federal funding for broad economic development goals, relegating housing for the poor to a secondary concern. Demolition of older neighborhoods invariably led to reductions, not increases, in the local supply of affordable housing.

The 1950 *General Plan for Boston* set the tone. On one full spread, it features before-and-after plans with the caption "An Obsolete Neighborhood . . . And a New Plan."[22] (See Figure 14.7.) The "obsolete" is an existing working-class neighborhood made up largely of European immigrants, and the "new" is literally a clean-slate reconceptualization. Modernization was not to come from updating or adapting, much less preserving the old, but from complete teardown and replacement with new block patterns and new architectural forms. Clearly, Boston's old architecture and historic neighborhoods were just impediments to progress—at best, reminders of work yet to be done.

The *General Plan* may have been inspired by the audacity of modernism-imbued planners like Martin Wagner, a young disciple of Walter Gropius. In 1947, he had published the ultimate reconstruction plan, proposing to clear the entire Shawmut Peninsula on which Boston was established in favor of a continuous megastructure following the alignment of a highway.[23] (See Figure 14.8.) Selected remnants of the old city—a few historic monuments—would be retained as pavilions in a vast park that would cover the peninsula, echoing Tugwell's dream. A 1964 photo of downtown shows how perilously close to Wagner's vision Boston came. With much of the center already demolished, planners were confident that only a step this radical would produce economic and social revival. (See Figure 14.9.)

The "omelet" made from demolishing the West End was Charles River Park (note the enticing word *park*). Approximately 1,600 luxury apartments, mostly in high-rise towers, unaffordable to those displaced, replaced some 2,300 lower-rent apartments and a few homes. A pair of large signs placed at the edge of the new Charles River Park, at a point where a parkway connects to a highway out of the city, made the pitch for convenience: "If you lived here . . . You'd be home by now." The sign is still there, and famous to those of a certain age as a reminder of an earnest, if naive, hope of the times—that replacing "slums" in the middle of the city might stem the flow of citizens decamping for the suburbs or the Sun Belt. Ultimately, the bulldozing of the West End became a national symbol of the socially damaging aspects of urban renewal, and the personal tragedy suffered by families from what others defined as progress.[24]

Boston received an array of urban renewal treatments. A state transportation plan funded the construction of an elevated highway, over which Wagner hoped to build his future Boston. The highway would displace several thousand homes and businesses. (See Figure 14.5.) It was supposed to ease traffic to Boston's enfeebled business district but, like most highways, it led businesses out of town even more quickly. At the expense of sixty more acres of demolition, another 1960s endeavor produced a modern acropolis for government. A seedy neighborhood called Scollay Square was self-consciously renamed Government Center and rebuilt to herald the reemergence of the "Cradle of Liberty" as a vital modern city.[25] The heart of Government Center became a vast ten-acre plaza and a monolithic city hall. The subject of an international design competition

14.8   For a 1944 competition, seeking the best planning ideas for renewing Boston, this submission proposed demolishing the entire city center, and constructing a giant megastructure over the proposed highway. The author was Martin Wagner, also responsible for Figure I.6.

14.9   Central Boston in 1964, the result of two adjacent urban renewal demolition projects: the future Government Center (replacing Scolley Square) and Charles River Park (replacing the West End). Giving places new names was part of the renewal.

held in 1962, both plaza and hall were widely acclaimed upon completion. As an example of the strand of mid-century modern architecture called "New Brutalism," the new city hall was thought to convey a newly confident Boston emerging from its lengthy decline. The utopianism of the Modern movement, with its disregard for what came before, had invaded historic Boston.

Though initially proud of the achievements of renewal, Bostonians never grew to love their austere city hall or the barren plaza in which it sat. With bulldozers heading to other neighborhoods, anger grew among those removed from their homes. By the late 1960s and into the 1970s, neighborhood activists, preservation groups, and advocacy planners began to get the upper hand, organizing to save other areas designated for renewal. (See Figure 14.12.) This included rescuing the historic Back Bay, returning it gradually to its status as among the most valued and wealthy of Boston's neighborhoods. Subsequently, in a rejection of urban renewal's radical approach, planners started appreciating traditional urban patterns, valuing history, respecting local activism, and seeking citizen input more—to the point that the symbolism of Government Center came to be reassessed. As the surrounding downtown district slowly renewed itself, relying on a mixture of commercial, cultural, and residential investment, Government Center's indifference to history and functional isolation came to represent the shortcomings of mid-century, top-down planning. Like the citizens of other places undergoing rapid change, Bostonians—planners and politicians included—came to believe that renewal should be an ongoing and measured process, rather than an epochal event.[26]

And the Promised Public Housing?

Some public housing was constructed under the aegis of urban renewal, though it continues to be debated how many net new units were produced with the demolished ones taken into account. There is also controversy about the forms of the housing, which seemed at times to constitute experimentation on the poor. Noble intentions were no doubt behind these new housing designs. Why not let the poor benefit from the most progressive mid-century ideas about architecture and site planning? Members of architecture's modern movement, echoing its European visionaries, argued passionately and persuasively for better social housing. (See Figure I.6.) Reacting to the intolerable conditions endured by the ill-housed urban underclasses, the modernists projected forms of housing that emphasized space, sunlight, proper ventilation, sanitation, and plentiful greenery—all salutary elements.

What were produced, however, were undifferentiated rows of mid-rise towers bereft of most services, isolated from existing neighborhoods and sited on large, awkward, and unkempt lawns. Children wanting to play with friends were left to a choice between unsupervised ground levels and bleak upper-level corridors, and there were no eyes on the street. In fact, there were few streets. This was hardly the most thought-through response to the needs of the poor. The designs were especially unsuited to those families of modest economic and educational backgrounds who were migrating from nonurban areas. Soon, having an address in such places was like wearing a scarlet letter—perhaps a *P*, as in "I am Poor." Unlike the homes in which the proper middle classes lived, the blocks of uniform apartment towers were where poor people and disadvantaged minorities lived, surrounded by crime, litter, and all kinds of asocial behavior. Could one have better isolated—while still focusing a spotlight—on those less able to house themselves? It took some time for the unsuitability of such planning to become evident. Along the way, much blame was heaped on the inhabitants themselves for the dysfunctionality of such places, while the average American's view of public housing took a further turn for the worse.

Two infamous examples were Pruitt-Igoe in St. Louis and the Robert Taylor Homes in Chicago, both now demolished. Erected between 1955 and 1956, Pruitt-Igoe's thirty-three identical high-rises consisted of 2,870 units. Vacancy rates would reach 65 percent a decade later, and keep increasing. Every building in the complex was spectacularly imploded in the early 1970s, and four decades later, the site remains empty. (See Figure 14.10.) Chicago's Robert Taylor Homes were built adjacent to a major highway, and consisted of twenty-eight buildings offering nearly 4,500 units. These sixteen-story towers stretched for two miles and accommodated up to twenty-seven thousand people. As at Pruitt-Igoe, a toxic mix developed of poor management, lack of upkeep, few nearby services, gangs, drugs, and abandonment. They were all demolished by 2007.[27] With little appreciation of the irony, the Feds were clearing slums again—but this was several decades after urban renewal began, and these were the slums that urban renewal had created.

14.10 The iconic images representing all that went awry during the urban renewal era: demolition of the Pruitt-Igoe housing complex in St. Louis less than 20 years after being built and lauded as a renewal effort.

Besieged by criticism (and possibly chastened), the Department of Housing and Urban Development (HUD) finally embraced a different tactic for subsidized housing. Its 1990s HOPE VI program funded some renovation of urban renewal projects, but favored brand new mixed-income, mixed-use projects that were smaller and less isolated. HUD engaged developers to build and manage such mixed housing, some providing a home ownership option, the agency having concluded that the private sector was better suited to create, maintain, and supervise home construction. The new insight was to "domesticate" public housing in scale and appearance. Partial credit for this must be given to the New Urbanists. While arguing against the conventional suburb, they began to illustrate denser, multifamily housing alternatives wrapped in traditional residential iconography. This influenced HUD officials, and an idea emerged to build ordinary-looking housing for the poor. Hope VI housing will never make the pages of avant-garde architecture periodicals; it is conventional in appearance. Precisely because of this conventionality, however, it has had the effect of somewhat destigmatizing subsidized housing—or "the projects," as they were often called. It has made public housing invisible. (See Figure 14.11.)

The Hope VI Program cannot be called an outright success. Among its failings is that it, too, produced an overall reduction in the number of subsidized units, as fewer replacement homes were developed than were demolished. However, the idea to deinstitutionalize public housing, at least in appearance, and to mix it with market housing was a step toward separating the word "housing" from some of its pejorative connotations.

Housing versus Houses

A pejorative association with the word *housing* has not been a minor problem. Language reflects but also creates a culture's beliefs. Home, as represented by a house and yard, has been among the most cherished symbols of the American Dream. The concept of "housing," meanwhile—especially as evoked by such terms as *public housing, multi-family housing, social housing,* and even more generally, *urban housing*—has been harder for mainstream Americans to embrace. The fact that we commonly refer to apartments in multifamily housing as *units* hardly helps. Occupying a unit of housing surely sounds like something less than living in a home with grace dwelling in it.

14.11   A federally subsidized Hope VI Project in Boston. In the foreground affordable housing looking no different than conventional housing. The tower behind, which many might associate with public housing, is in this example the market or "luxury" housing.

All people want to be comfortably and affordably housed. It is a national belief that this is attainable, or ought to be attainable, through hard work and perseverance. A reward for earning a good living is the opportunity to move up from housing into a house that one would call home. The idea of a home carries positive associations. A homeowner enjoys social status, family well-being, economic stability, independence, and a sense of personal pride. Homeowners experience a form of grace, as nineteenth century ministers preached. Never mind that a single unit in one of those thousand-foot-tall Manhattan towers can be worth more than an entire suburban subdivision. For the majority of Americans, the ideas of prosperity and good living remain yoked to the idea of a home, meaning a house in a good neighborhood of similarly well-kept houses.

Politicians, poets, and pulpit orators have long reinforced this idea, as prior chapters have explored. Around the conclusion of the First World War, with a rise of international socialism, there emerged a sense that preventing the spread of Soviet-style collectivism required reaffirming American values. A realtors trade association asserted that "socialism and communism do not take root in the ranks of those who have their feet firmly embedded in the soil of America through homeownership." The Department of Labor initiated an "Own Your Home" drive.[28] This was followed by numerous federal campaigns and policies to help inculcate Americans' belief in the social and economic value of home ownership.[29]

It is worth emphasizing, again, that the initial motivations for public housing programs early in the twentieth century were not to serve those who could not afford proper housing, but to increase the supply of adequate housing for those who could afford it but faced shortages. Thus, it is not surprising that Americans rarely campaign for public housing or for policies to assist those economically unequipped to house themselves well. For some Americans, lamenting the insufficiency of public housing is tantamount to admitting that the ideal of a house in a good neighborhood may not be within the reach of all. Better to hold on to the dream and its idealized form. Americans have not yet fully accepted that cities are built of *housing*. The history of public policy has only tightened this association of housing—as opposed to *homes*—with the lower tiers of society.

Renewing Urban Renewal

In hindsight, it seems to some that the proponents of urban renewal—whether federal administrators, city officials, or planners—must have actually disliked cities. Speculations along these lines are not hard to find. Back in 1965, William Whyte wrote that "the rebuilding under way and in prospect is being designed by people who don't like cities. They do not merely dislike the noise and the dirt and the congestion. They dislike the city's variety and concentration, its tension, its hustle and bustle. The new redevelopment projects will be physically in the city, but in spirit they deny it."[30] At mid-twentieth century there was a palpable pulling-away from older cites as the new suburban landscape exerted its cultural appeal. In 1972, a Gallup poll asked Americans: "If you could live anywhere in the United States that you wanted to, would you prefer a city, suburban area, small town, or farm?" Just 13 percent chose the city—a precipitous drop from the 22 percent who had given that answer in 1966.[31]

14.12   Poster in opposition to an impending act of "renewal" in a Boston neighborhood.

It is no surprise that signs such as "To Hell With Urban Renewal" gradually began to be displayed in neighborhoods slated for renewal. (See Figure 14.12.) Even so, despite the well-documented failures, it is important to recall that the era of urban renewal represented the federal government's only substantial and sustained intervention in cities. In a contrarian spirit, one can argue that the era witnessed the first embers of the kind of interest and investment that many cities are experiencing today. This is not to defend the erasure of neighborhoods, the racism, the absence of citizen participation, the transfer of property to well-healed developers, and the use of radical forms of housing that characterized the period. But it was, after all, a huge slug of dollars specifically earmarked for urban areas, misspent though much of it was on demolition and highways.

An unfortunate additional consequence of the era has been the federal government's disinclination (perhaps in part to memories of failure) to craft any further major urban investment programs. There are still plenty of "blighted" areas in need of care and rehabilitation. An inadequate supply of affordable housing remains, as do rapidly growing economic disparities. There are mobility needs that the funding of urban transit could serve. Federal timidity about investing in cities today is as unhelpful as the faulty programs of that earlier era were. Much has been learned since the mid-twentieth century about cities and their care. It is time, without forgetting or excusing the past, to use public dollars to initiate a different national urban renewal, determined to improve, enhance, and build upon—rather than replace—our cities.

15.1   Walt Disney pointing to his planned EPCOT in 1966.

15

WALT DISNEY'S EPCOT AND THE NEW TOWN MOVEMENT

Not a reading man but has a draft of a new Community in his
waistcoat pocket.

RALPH WALDO EMERSON, 1840

And the need is not just for curing the old ills of old cities. We think
the need is for starting from scratch on virgin land and building a
special kind of new community.

WALT DISNEY, 1967

LIKELY UNAWARE of Emerson's quip a century earlier about the outbreak of socialist communitarian experiments, Walt Disney announced in the mid-1960s
that he, too, had a draft of a new town—an ambitious "experimental prototype
community of tomorrow." This was the phrase, and project, that would become
EPCOT.[1] Expectations rose, just as they would several decades later when
the Walt Disney Company announced its intention to build Celebration, Florida (as discussed in Chapter 4).

During the 1960s, enthusiasm for building cities from scratch was much in
the air. Ambitious town founders were hard at work, most of them wealthy
businesspeople with ideas different from those that drove experimentation in
Emerson's day. The Irvine Company, for example, was well along in adapting
the holdings of the old Irvine Ranch into the model town of Irvine in southern
California. Real estate entrepreneur Robert E. Simon, having exchanged ownership of New York's Carnegie Hall for some 6,700 acres of farmland outside

Washington, DC, was busy laying out Reston, Virginia. Shopping center developer James Rouse was creating Columbia, Maryland. Oil industry investor George P. Mitchell, keeping an eye on the successes and setbacks of Rouse and Simon, would soon take advantage of a new federal funding program and embark on The Woodlands, near Houston, Texas.

It was a decade when Americans were becoming increasingly concerned about the well-being of the nation's cities, with various pundits predicting inexorable decline. Americans felt insecure in the face of growing urban poverty, civil unrest, and crime, and frustrated about increasing traffic congestion, too. They were unsatisfied with urban renewal efforts and the consequences they were producing. Civil rights disturbances were escalating despite, or because of, the passage of the Civil Rights Act of 1964. Opposition to the war in Vietnam was gathering momentum, as there seemed to be no end in sight for America's entanglement. Families continued to flee to the suburbs, but planners, opinion leaders, and some citizens began to raise concerns about consuming so much land for low-density development. Some objections were expressed in song. Malvina Reynolds's 1962 hit "Little Boxes," subsequently recorded by Pete Seeger and more than two dozen artists since, melodiously mocks middle-class conformists living in tract homes that are "all made out of ticky-tacky" and "all look just the same." The fledgling environmental movement did its part, too, to turn *sprawl* into a pejorative term for the suburb.

Hope arose that building whole new towns from scratch might be an alternative to making marginal adjustments to unlovely and unloved city neighborhoods and soulless, peripheral subdivisions. It was the kind of enthusiasm that afflicts Americans periodically: the promise of a humane town rather than a harsh big city; the hope of enjoying the best of both urban and rural life; the conviction that a better tomorrow can result from starting over with a better design. Identified by the media as visionaries, Disney, Simon, Mitchell, Rouse, and others were seen as agents for the restoration of community. They were full of entrepreneurial zeal, usually had deep pockets, and were committed to using comprehensive planning and design to improve both city and suburban life.

Walt publicly unveiled his EPCOT idea in 1966. A year earlier, as plans for an ambitious "Disney World" to be built in Florida were being announced, Congress under President Johnson's War on Poverty and Great Society agendas, was revamping federal housing and urban development policies. A new agency, the US Department of Housing and Urban Development (HUD), was created to manage these. By 1970, growing enthusiasm for new towns led to passage of the Urban Growth and New Community Development Act, making federal support available to build them. The part of the act focused on new communities, Title VII, directed HUD to make bond guarantees up to $50 million available to private entities capable of developing new towns. To get such funding from HUD's New Community Development Corporation, a proposed program had to show that it would "provide an alternative to disorderly urban growth . . . make substantial provision for housing within the means of persons of low and moderate income and that such housing will constitute an appropriate proportion of the community's housing supply," and "make significant use of advances in design and technology."[2]

Initial optimism ran high. A 1971 article in *Fortune* magazine began: "The new-town movement is about to come of age in America. Powerful forces—public and private, natural and directed—are converting into a thrust toward large, planned communities all over the US. The decade of the Seventies will see scores if not hundreds of such new developments spring up, transforming not just the physical landscape, inside and outside of cities, but the human affairs of millions of Americans as well."[3]

Title VII was billed as an updating of the earlier Model Cities Program, but in fact was the beginning of its end. Established in 1966, the Model Cities Program had intended to revitalize poor and minority urban neighborhoods, but it was proving to be ineffective. Title VII again favored development *away* from existing cities, in the same way that the 1930s Resettlement Administration had favored greenbelt towns. History was repeating itself. While more than two hundred initiatives were announced, only slightly more than a dozen were deemed eligible for federal financial support. Most did not get very far. Developers experienced difficulties in meeting land sales projections, citing various problems such as uncooperative local governments, economic inflation, and recession. Many soon faced default on their HUD agreements. The entire federal program would be scrapped within a decade. The Woodlands in Texas, which took advantage of Title VII support, did come to fruition largely thanks to additional private investment.[4] Columbia, Irvine, and Reston (the last after some early setbacks) grew, prospered, received enormous media attention, and were seen as exemplars of the new town movement, but were largely private enterprises, not Title VII projects. We'll return to these and The Woodlands—but first, let's look at Walt Disney's unabashed, optimistic venture.

Accident-Free, Noise-Free, Pollution-Free

It would surely be the first "accident-free, noise-free, pollution-free city center in America." That is how New York's Robert Moses described the promise of his friend Walt Disney's venture.[5] But the EPCOT theme park that millions of tourists enjoy annually, symbolized by its "Spaceship Earth" geodesic sphere, is not quite what Walt Disney imagined. He had not intended a mere amusement park for visitors, but an entire city, "a city of tomorrow," where "the pedestrian would be king." It was characteristic of a particular strand of American utopian aspirations, conceived as a place of perpetual technological sophistication, yet where traditional values associated with family and community could forever be maintained.

Disney envisioned a community of some twenty thousand residents living in a showcase of technology and industrial ingenuity, continuously experimenting in planning, building design, management, and governance. If engineers in the planned industrial park came up with an innovation in, say, the design of refrigerators or air conditioning, every household in EPCOT could test the result and benefit from the progress. Given Walt Disney's legendary tenacity, it would have been fascinating to witness how far his vision might have advanced. Sadly, Disney died in December of 1966, less than a year after the unveiling of his idea. Planning continued, but Walt's brother Roy, who assumed greater leadership over the company, may have lacked Walt's zeal for the more experimental, utopian aspects of the endeavor. When urged by a Disney designer to follow through on Walt's plans, Roy's alleged answer was "Walt is dead."[6] In fairness, Roy worked hard to push forward many of what he considered the more attainable aspects of his brother's vision in the five years he had before his own death, shortly after the Walt Disney World Resort officially opened in October 1971. The theme park called EPCOT Center opened a decade later, in 1982, minus its envisioned city center, progressive industrial park, and residents. It remains a popular Disney World destination, whose exhibits in some respects still recall Walt's more ambitious city-making ideas. And certainly, it is very low on accidents, noise, and pollution, as Robert Moses predicted.

A captivating twenty-five-minute film produced by the "Imagineers" at Walt Disney Productions contains the best articulation by Walt Disney himself of his vision.[7] Following a narrator's short salute to Disneyland and Walt Disney Productions, he appears. In a reassuring, fatherly manner, as if announcing a family outing, he describes the company's acquisition of 27,400 acres—forty-three square miles—of central Florida. Disney outlines the overall plan, stressing, as multiple pioneers had done, this abundance of land as the key. Here he would achieve all that could not be done at Disneyland, which had been surrounded by the unregulated commercial chaos of suburbia that Walt found so unruly. He had learned a lesson about protecting borders. The land on which Disney World would be built, he proudly announced, was twice the size of the island of Manhattan. (This was impressive, even if it was dwarfed by the Irvine Ranch's ninety-three thousand acres, of which about 60 percent was reserved for wilderness conservation and recreational use.)[8]

Disney World would, of course, contain an amusement park, in itself five times bigger than California's Disneyland, but there was much more to the plan. A "Vacation Land" would provide hotel and resort accommodations, not possible in the more compact and crowded Disneyland. An industrial park of approximately a thousand acres would be established to develop innovative technologies. An "airport of the future" would enable quicker travel to and from Disney World. At the central arrival complex, visitors would then board a rapid transit system to traverse the twelve-mile length of Disney World and reach all its attractions. As if all this were not sufficiently ambitious, Walt, standing in front of a plan twice his height, points to another feature: "But the most exciting, by far the most important part of our Florida project—in fact, the heart of everything we'll be doing in Disney World—will be our experimental prototype city of tomorrow." Amazingly, in this second Disneyland—now a "world"—the park that would eventually be known as the Magic Kingdom would be only a secondary attraction! Foremost in Disney's mind were his civic-minded ambitions. Before yielding to an invisible narrator to describe the EPCOT plan in detail, Walt makes the following comments about his purpose:

> I don't believe there is a challenge anywhere in the world that's more important to people everywhere than finding solutions to the problems of our cities . . . .
>
> And the need is not just for curing the old ills of old cities. We think the need is for starting from scratch on virgin land and building a special kind of new community. . . .
>
> It will never cease to be a living blueprint of the future, where people actually live a life they can't find anyplace else in the world.

15.2 One of the many remarkable renderings produced at Walt Disney's direction by the company's "imagineers" to describe his future EPCOT.

The idea of a living blueprint for the future unlike anything else in the world was certainly compelling. Three decades later, the Chairman of the Walt Disney Company, Michael Eisner, would invoke Walt's EPCOT dream and some of his words as he introduced the town of Celebration in the inaugural issue of the *Celebration Chronicle.*[9]

What, then, were the components of this future city, a city that was meant to be "always in a state of becoming"? In truth, each of the components was rather conventional. A thirty-story hotel with a convention center at its base would mark the center of the large, radial plan, its bold structure serving as a kind of modern-day campanile or skyline feature. (See Figure 15.2.) A weather-protected zone of themed shops, restaurants, and entertainment amenities, essentially a covered shopping center, would surround the hotel and convention complex. Apartment buildings providing a modicum of density, perhaps suitable for more modest wage earners, would surround and complete the town center. Not emphasized in the promotional film was that the residents of EPCOT might be employees of the Disney Company. This was to be a place not for retirees, but for productive citizens. One might consider the venture one of the last attempts to build a company town, extending that paternalistic tradition from Lowell, Massachusetts, by way of Gary, Indiana, examined in Chapter 5.

A park zone surrounding the town center was to form a recreational green belt, beyond which petal-shaped, single-family home subdivisions fanned out

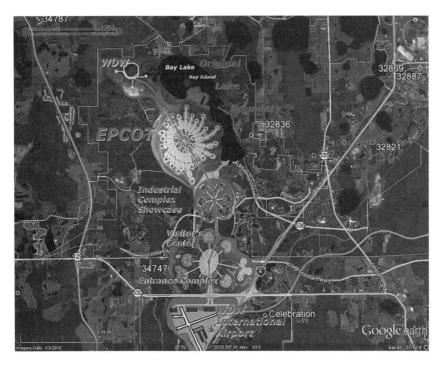

15.3 Conceptual plan for Disney World, where EPCOT was going to be the star attraction. Note the progression: the airport leading to the "Entrance Complex" and "Visitor's Center," then through the "Industrial Complex Showcase" to EPCOT, and finally to the Magic Kingdom amusement park, shown quite modest in size by comparison to the featured EPCOT.

to complete the outermost circle. The industrial park dedicated to perpetual innovation was to be a separate, radially-organized area connected by the monorail. (See Figure 15.3.)

For all of its utopian promise, the genius of the plan was that it all seemed doable, being composed of familiar urban prototypes: a somewhat vertical "downtown," an enclosed shopping center, some residential density in the form of apartment blocks, a green belt, low-density single-family home neighborhoods, and a separate office and industrial park requiring a short commute. The entertainment zone, the theme park, would exist as still a separate area. It was, overall, an agglomeration of elements commonly found in modern metropolitan areas, but fused into a system deliberately designed and managed by a single authority. The renderings evoked the kind of futuristic world the popular cartoon series *The Jet-*

15.4   Rendering of the enormous underground service center to which cars and trucks were restricted so as not to interfere with the pedestrian experience above.

sons was presenting on Saturday-morning television. But perhaps it had more in common (apart from its size) with a medieval ducal village.

The enticing illustrations and diagrams accompanying the narration also harked back to other precedents: to begin with, the World Fairs. Disney had visited several, and the company had produced exhibits for the New York World's Fair; this was the 1964–1965 event where the "Progress City" embedded in General Electric's "Progressland" was one of the most popular attractions. Disney might even have picked up the phrase "city of tomorrow" at the 1939 World's Fair, also held in New York. He was fascinated with the pioneering work of the Austrian American architect Victor Gruen, whose enclosed shopping centers were starting to win suburban retail developers' attention. The tradition of Garden City planning, promulgated by various American planners since the 1930s, and the basis for the British new towns built around London after the Second World War, was another inspiration. And most recently, Disney had been a keen student of Columbia and Reston as they began to take shape.

One innovation that appealed to him was the partial banishing of the automobile. The solution could be a vast underground system enabling cars to arrive, park, and buzz about under the city center without disrupting the world above. Still another underground layer could accommodate trucks and service functions. (See Figure 15.4.) Such measures would allow the entire fifty-acre town center to be free of cars, just as the Magic Kingdom would be. The mono-rail and people-mover system, more extensive than anything achieved at Disneyland, would shuttle people anywhere beyond a comfortable walking dis-tance. In the car-crazed America of the 1960s this was a truly radical idea. Walt Disney was as much of a pioneer in advocating pedestrianism in urban design as Jane Jacobs—and achieved more of it—albeit for a different purpose than Jacobs had in mind.

Another consideration in Disney's planning of EPCOT was equally unusual: consider that millions of tourists were expected to visit it as part of their Disney World experience. Thus, its twenty thousand lucky residents and employees had to be seen as living to some extent on a stage. They were inadvertent performers living out a model contemporary lifestyle—and one that was neither tradition-ally urban nor typically suburban. As Walt put it, it was a lifestyle unavailable anywhere else. Keeping cynicism at bay, we can assume a hope on his part that the experience would embolden many visitors to rethink their own living and work environments back home. Like the tourists returning from European vacations, smitten by historic city centers, they would question why their own cities did not possess similar charms. Walt Disney's EPCOT, intended to be-come a true "Progress City," did not ultimately live up to the dream he had for it. Yet it probably inspired other innovations in community planning, in towns that opted for less dramatic forms and did not expect to have theme parks as economic anchors and tourist attractions.

Progress Cities

Columbia, Irvine, Reston, and The Woodlands—all of which won accolades in their formative years and faced criticism in later years for not being even more innovative—were ambitious, complex endeavors with admirable inten-tions and progressive planning ideas. James Rouse hired panels of sociologists to help him understand what sort of environments might best foster sociabil-ity. In Reston, Robert Simon placed faith in striking modern design that found fewer initial takers but a loyal coterie of modern architecture fans. (See Figure 15.5.)

A second reason for Reston's slow start was Simon's insistence that Reston would be an open, integrated community, one of the first in Virginia's history. Prior to the Civil Rights Act of 1964, racial segregation was the norm. Simon

15.5   View from a balcony overlooking Reston's Lake Anne and the townhomes surrounding it.

later recalled that perhaps fifty banks turned down his requests for construction loans for Reston, in part due to the untested idea of a real estate venture blind to race.[10] (See Figure 15.6.)

While Rouse sought sociologists and daring planners, the Irvine Company's Raymond Watson, who served on Disney's board for decades, was an early advocate of market research about consumers' preferences. At The Woodlands in Houston, the most progressive environmental considerations of the times, in part courtesy of Ian McHarg's pioneering *Design with Nature,* were incorporated into the original planning.[11] To varying degrees, these new towns conserved high percentages of land for open space, protected natural systems, embraced then-accepted notions of environmental stewardship, attempted to limit ad hoc development at their borders, and sought to minimize peripheral sprawl. Each incorporated a mixture of uses, at least in the areas of their "villages" and "town centers." They attempted to balance housing with the provision of nearby job opportunities, provided for some transit (mainly buses), and accommodated higher densities than typical suburban development did. Each was aiming for those neighborly qualities that planners associated with clustered, village-scale neighborhoods.

15.6 A statue of Robert E. Simon greets residents at the original town center. There are often admirers sitting with arms around his shoulders having their picture taken.

Did these towns, all intended to counter the ills of suburban sprawl, provide a substantial solution to sprawl? Ultimately, no, because their very attractiveness attracted other suburban development to their borders. Few were able to pursue Disney's strategy of acquiring enough land to control peripheries; a Google Earth search generally reveals buildup all around them. Perhaps because of this, James Rouse later became a fan and promoter of older cities. Beginning with the Faneuil Hall Marketplace repurposing Boston's historic Quincy Market, he spent the final decades of his life helping to support preservation efforts with revitalized downtown shopping districts. (See Figure 15.7.)

It became hard to argue that these new town developments were not just more sophisticated forms of suburbanization, and that became a complaint. What critics, especially the ardent urbanists, overlook is that their planners were not trying to replicate the physical characteristics of downtown Boston or New York. During the 1960s and 1970s, and for many constituencies today, that would not have produced many home sales. The founders and planners of these towns were aiming for something else. They were seeking that long-desired middle ground between town and country.

15.7   By 1981 James Rouse, the creator of Columbia, had concluded that old cities could be fun, too. Here he is holding Boston's Faneuil Hall, having achieved much acclaim for restoring the adjacent (and long empty) Quincy Markets into the first "festival market place." He would replicate this in a number of other cities, helping revitalize downtown shopping around renovated historic districts.

"All the Advantages of the Country with Most of the Conveniences of the City"

The above claim was part of an 1823 advertisement for the "Lots on Brooklyn Heights" on offer from Hezekiah Beers Pierrepont.[12] The language chosen by that suburban developer of a residential subdivision seems prescient when considered alongside newspaper advertisements a century and a half later in Baltimore and Washington, DC. Here is one placed by the Rouse Corporation on behalf of the town of Columbia in 1967:

> Where can you live today with swimming pools, golf courses, riding stables, tennis clubs, acres of green meadows, woods, lakes, streams forever preserved in their natural beauty, where the symphony concert is just a few minutes from your door, where you can swim while you see the snow fall, where you can canter over miles of equestrian trails before breakfast, where you can work as butcher, baker, candlestick maker, lawyer or industrial chef, where a speedy little mini-bus whisks you almost anywhere to any place else in a city for only a dime, where you can rent,

buy or build an apartment, townhouse, home or country place, where a great city's excitement is beginning to happen in the middle of historic estate country, where you can walk your hound in the woods or hunt pheasant, quail or duck in a game preserve, where you can stroll downtown to go sailing, where tomorrow your children will be educated in the nearest schools, junior college or university, where you can get a pastrami on pumpernickel at two in the morning from the delicatessen, where shops, theatres, restaurants will bring you to the best the world has to offer, and where you will live like you earned $5,000 a year more than you do.[13]

A more earnest summary of the appeal of the middle landscape ideal is hard to find, and it neatly encapsulates the overall aspirations of the new town movement. The new towns of the 1960s, those few that were built, came closest—considerably closer than Disney's imagined EPCOT—to that long-standing American dream of finding a better place to live. They did offer settings well positioned between the blessings of nature and the buzz of urban civilization and able to partake of both, more or less concurrently.

The new towns were attempting to fulfill Emerson's century-old wish to combine rural strength and religion with city facility and polish. They were refashioning the ideal of small-town life and, by supporting resident associations and community programming, summoning faint memories of communitarianism. They aimed for Ebenezer Howard's "third magnet"—combining the attractions of Town and Country—a synthesis never quite achieved in the various Garden City experiments themselves. (See Figure 6.2.) They were determined to provide those "City Homes on Country Lanes" that Americans seem to pine for (a modern kitchen within a colonial exterior, as Andrés Duany, the leader of the New Urbanism, likes to say).[14] They were aiming at the heart of a mid-twentieth-century suburban dream, permitting proximity (and easy access) to the best of town and country. Each new town, whether Columbia, Maryland, in the 1960s, or a place like Las Colinas, Texas, in the 1990s—the latter being promoted as located in the "countryside" between Dallas and Fort Worth—has been peddled as an improved middle ground, an alternative to overgrown cities on the one hand and to homogenous suburbs on the other. Paradoxically, most have only hastened the suburbanization of existing city centers, as downtown shopping malls and densities began to emulate the perceived success of the new towns. (See Figure 15.8.)

As this is being written, Columbia has swelled to more than one hundred thousand residents, and includes a diverse range of retail, commercial, and business establishments. It remains unincorporated, governed by the Columbia Association with representation from each of its "villages." Reston, having survived early financial troubles and ownership changes, is growing rapidly. It has acquired a large, mixed-use center that serves the sprawling Dulles Office and Technology Corridor; and has recently been linked to Washington, DC, Tyson's Corner, and Dulles Airport by a new Metro line. (See Figure 15.9.) Its population is not expected to stop at the current sixty thousand. Irvine became an actual municipality, has a population of 260,000, and is home to nearly two dozen international corporate headquarters and various high-tech companies. More impressively, it boasts seven colleges and universities. The Woodlands, currently owned by the Howard Hughes Corporation, exceeds one hundred thousand residents and keeps growing, along with the overall Houston metro area, and now features large corporate campuses.

Over time, each town has become more diverse demographically, as well. Columbia is 25 percent African American. Irvine's population is 45 percent Asian. Reston and The Woodlands both have Hispanic populations of about 10 percent, though The Woodlands remains 85 percent white. Each of the four still describes itself as a collection of villages—forty-six of them in the case of Irvine—and each is regularly ranked as a top-ten "most livable" American city. These are successful and desirable environments.

But no consensus has formed around their experience among urban activists new or old. Way back in 1968, William Whyte, an indefatigable critic of sprawl—some claim he introduced the term *sprawl* to condemn suburbia—dismissed the new towns:

> But these are not to be cities as we know them. . . . As a community, the self-contained new town is a contradiction in terms. You cannot isolate the successful elements of a city and package them in tidy communities somewhere else. And if you could do it, would you be able to have only the good and none of the bad? The goal is so silly it seems profound.[15]

It is a conclusion one would expect of a lifelong resident of Manhattan. These were not meant "to be cities as we know them." Whether Whyte liked it or not, they were manifestations of what legions of Americans, ordinary and utopian-minded, sought. The majority of Americans reside in environments that presume to blend the qualities of town and country. Of course, the risk of seeking a

15.8 A portion of the Irvine Ranch, now an actual municipality with a population exceeding 200,000.

15.9 Looking quite downtown-like in this night view, the recently developed new Reston "downtown."

middle landscape is the spoiling of both town and country—which many would argue that modern development, including these new towns, has achieved. Somewhat in the way that the nineteenth-century industrial city came perilously close to choking on its own energy and enterprise, the ever-spreading suburban realm may go too far in displacing all else. As the traditional boundaries between cities and rural areas have given way to Wright's imaginary Broadacres, or Jean Gottman's quite real Megalopolis, not everyone cheers the loss of those boundaries. The rekindling of interest in the centers of older cities suggests that more Americans are recognizing the limits to the middle-landscape ideal.

16.1 Suitable arrival at the famous sign that welcomes you to fabulous Las Vegas.

16

FABULOUS AND COMMONPLACE: SEEKING PARADISE IN LAS VEGAS

Las Vegas: The New All-American City

Time (cover story), 1994

With the phallic grandeur of Bob Stupak's wet dream casino fantasy, the Stratosphere Tower, situated midway between the heart of Las Vegas Boulevard casino development to the south, and the newly renovated Freemont Street Experience at its northern base, the Strip opens up like a woman's legs straddling the spectacle.

Kathryn Hausbeck, 2002

The reason you should go to Las Vegas is because, for only the second time, the second time ever, they have rebuilt Sodom and Gomorrah. It's back!! And you have the opportunity to see it before it turns to salt.

Lewis Black, 2010

LAS VEGAS INVITES HYPERBOLE, tons of it, about itself and by extension about American culture broadly. Its formidable marketing engines promote in grandiloquent terms a city of opulence, excess, and indulgence. The rhetoric focuses on the "Fabulous Strip," the jaw-dropping four-and-a-half-mile-long boulevard lined with hotels and casinos, once but a narrow road leading out of an insignificant town. But surrounding the Strip is an important metropolitan area exceeding two million people and growing, even if it still comes as a surprise to some Americans that there are people who actually live in Las Vegas. The city spreads out in a familiar pattern of single-family subdivisions, sprawling strip centers (of the shopping kind), and isolated office and industrial parks. It's pretty much like the rest of metro America, except that its climate is so unconducive to human comfort. It also shares poverty, crime, racial and immigrant tensions, and others of urban America's less laudable characteristics.

It is the exaggerated bifurcation between the fantastical tourist areas and the miles of ordinary perimeter that makes Las Vegas worthy of study. Two worlds coexist, intertwined yet mostly oblivious to each other, each aiming for a different middle-class ideal. One offers temporary escape from daily existence via entertainment, the other a mainstream path for those seeking access to the American dream.

First is the lure and lore of the Strip, of spectacle, amusements, pleasure—the prospect of "self-indulgence and sanctioned deviance," as one historian of the city puts it. It may seem odd that a historian would be chronicling a place that he himself describes as "a city without any claim to a past, one that purposefully markets the destruction of its history."[1] But this is hyperbole, too, as a growing curiosity about the city's history has led to dozens of websites dedicated to old Vegas photographs, and sentiment-arousing attractions such as the Neon Museum and the Mob Museum.[2] The theme of perpetual newness is often sounded, especially by the always-boasting Las Vegas Convention and Visitors Authority, and the builders of the latest spectacle. Announcing the next new thing is vital, lest boredom set in with the usual Elvis impersonators, gondolas and volcanos, and dancing fountains at the Bellagio—practically the size of Lake Como itself. The newest things, as of this writing, are two big-league sports franchises, approved after years of opposition from those concerned about mixing sports and gambling. The Vegas Golden Knights arrived in time for the National Hockey League's 2017–2018 season—and made it to the Stanley Cup finals in their first year. And the relocation of the Raiders, a National Football League franchise, from Oakland, California, will have them playing in Vegas by 2020. They make Las Vegas seem more like a true American city, not some aberrant form of urbanism.

Away from the Strip, there is extensive evidence of an ongoing, comforting American Dream. It's the dream D. J. Waldie alludes to in the opening lines of his poetic *Holy Land: A Suburban Memoir:* "I live where a majority of Americans live: a tract house on a block of other tract houses in a neighborhood of even more. . . . My parents bought this house in 1946, less than a year after the war ended, and they felt extraordinarily lucky."[3]

Lucky and grateful: Waldie was writing about a part of Los Angeles County, not Las Vegas, but the passage beautifully evokes the satisfaction that families of modest means feel on acquiring their first home. It can seem like a miracle. For hundreds of thousands, such a miracle has defined life in Las Vegas away from the Strip. Decades of low taxes, inexpensive land, abundant low-skilled but well-paying jobs, and a still-intact unionized labor system (earning the place a reputation in some quarters as the "last Detroit") have facilitated the twin miracles of home ownership and relative financial stability.[4] The increasing difficulty of reaching middle-class status was (until the recent recession) considered a problem elsewhere, not in Vegas.

In Vegas one finds two middle-class ideals. There's the modern-day El Dorado—the mythical city of gold made accessible—which for decades has made a "luxury" vacation available at middle-class cost. And adjacent to it is a holdover of the mid-twentieth-century suburban dream: the belief in property as the basis of well-being, where a homestead—not a Jeffersonian spread of 160 acres, but a modest plot for an ordinary family—could be available to virtually all. A 2010 magazine article labeled Las Vegas an "American Paradox," because, as the writer found, "Vegas is unlike any other American city, and yet Vegas is America."[5] Maybe the very dualities of Vegas are what make it, as the earlier *Time* cover story declared it, the All-American City.

A Brief History of a City Pretending Not to Have One

Before all the present fabulousness—before neon signs, roadside architecture, the Rat Pack, showgirls and the Mob, before quickie divorces, wedding chapels, and gambling, before the Hoover Dam, before the construction of a minor depot along a rail line linking Southern California and Salt Lake City, and before a series of boom-and-bust mines—before all of that, there were meadows (*vegas*) with a welcoming desert spring running through them. It appeared along a trail through the harsh Mojave known as *jornado de muerta*, the journey of death. (See Figure 16.2.) Those daring the trail would not have bet on the success of a substantial town sprouting right there. And for quite a while, one didn't.

Even those intrepid town-builders the Mormons, whom we met in Chapter 13, abandoned an effort at a missionary settlement in 1857 after only two years,

16.2 The Mojave, among the harshest desert environments on the
North American continent, an unlikely setting for a large city.

unwelcomed by the local Paiute tribe. By 1930, when the population of Los Angeles exceeded 1.2 million, a mere 5,200 people made up the entirety of Las
Vegas County. But that would soon change. It is noteworthy that, as Chicago
holds the distinction of being the nation's largest city founded after 1800, Las
Vegas is the largest and most notable American city founded during the twentieth century. The place was proclaimed a city in 1905 and incorporated in 1911,
following an auction that partitioned Helen Stewart's old farm and its invaluable
water rights into town lots.[6]

Among the unlikely circumstances spurring the growth of Las Vegas were the
Great Depression and the Second World War. In 1931, in the midst of the Depression, three events forever changed what was just a forgettable railroad junc-
tion. First, in its struggle to find additional sources of revenue, the state of
Nevada decided to permit gambling, Second, it changed the law around divorces
so that they could be granted to petitioners after a mere six weeks of residency.
Third, construction began on one of the great public works projects of the era,
the Hoover Dam—ultimately a source of water, but first the source of many construction workers and their families who required shelter and services. Another
wave of change came with the Second World War, which further stimulated
growth, especially as the theatre of war shifted to Asia. This isolated western out-

post proved attractive for military training and operations, centered on what became Nellis Air Force Base, among the largest fighter air force bases in the world.

Given the presence of so many men, most of them young—construction workers, military personnel, gamblers, and divorce seekers staying at dude ranches (the primitive incarnations of today's resorts)—is it surprising that enterprises would begin to crop up to facilitate those sinful indulgences and "victimless crimes" of drinking, gambling, and paying for sex? Or that the area would then attract various unsavory characters to finance, construct, and manage such operations? The tradition of locals of dubious character goes back to the city's earliest days—starting with none other than Nevada Senator William Clark (as in Clark County), who bought the Stewart farm and had it platted into town lots. It was said of Clark that "if you took away the whiskers and the scandal, there would be nothing left of him."[7]

The postwar period witnessed the first great wave of fabulous venues built and owned by outsized personalities, such as the legendary Flamingo and its legendary mobster owner, Bugsy Siegel—now fondly memorialized at both the Neon and the Mob Museums. (See Figure 16.3.) The 1950s also brought nuclear testing nearby, with lounges and living rooms providing fine viewing. Mushroom-cloud parties were scheduled at some of the casinos, providing impressive sunsets, and fallout radiation, too, before awareness of the consequences mandated underground testing in the 1960s. (See Figure 16.4.)

To complement "gaming," the friendly local term for gambling, developers added entertainment and shopping, and slowly the inevitable transition from mob to corporate rule occurred. By the mid-1980s and through the 1990s, as gambling was legalized in other states, the pressure to expand the tourist base led to rapid expansion in the variety and quality of entertainment, dining, and shopping, and in creature comforts available at the ever-grander casino hotels, now called resorts.

Maybe, promoters speculated, Vegas could even be family-friendly. For a period leading to the turn of the millennium, a campaign ensued to shift the Vegas brand "from vice to nice." Symbols of that hope included the establishment of a permanent Cirque du Soleil in town, shows featuring pirate-ship battles, a children's museum, and the M&M's candy emporium right on the Strip. (See Figure 16.5.) The makeover did not entirely take hold. It did not deter those seedy-looking people on the sidewalk from handing out small cards not appropriate for viewing by kids or the moms at their side, with directions to old-time Las Vegas attractions. (See Figure 16.6.)

16.3 (left)   The first and most infamous of the mid-twentieth-century casinos due to its ownership by the Mob. When it opened in 1946 it was billed as the "West's Greatest Resort Hotel." It went through a series of ownerships and transformations following the murder of Bugsy Siegel, with the last parts of the original structure demolished in 1993, by which time a much larger Flamingo Las Vegas complex was in place, as it remains.

16.4 (right)   A Mushroom headdress, perhaps at one of the casino's atomic parties, celebrating the nearby bomb testing.

Soon the promotion strategy shifted again, building on perhaps the most brilliant slogan in the annals of the tourist industry: "What Happens in Vegas Stays in Vegas." Moms might choose to accompany dads, given the increasing sophistication of shopping, dining, and entertainment, but kids were best left home. So the hyperbole, never in remission, chugged anew, generally vacillating between amazement and repudiation. *Las Vegas Babylon,* a book focusing on the latter, begins: "Las Vegas is America's version of ancient Babylon, a mixture of eye-catching architecture and sensual excess, where the desires and foolhardiness of its visitors and residents are played out in full, sometimes tragically. . . . Vegas is like Satan, looking on and smiling as people make their thoughtless, selfish choices that may destroy themselves and others."[8]

That may be true for some, but the forty million or so visitors who arrive each year—for an average of 110,000 per day—are hardly in search of tragedy or Satan.[9] They are in search of a momentary paradise.

16.5 (left)   Entrance to the M&M World emporium on the Strip.

16.6 (right)   Handing out directions to entertainments no longer offered along the Strip itself, but amply available nearby.

Paradise, Nevada

As one flies into Las Vegas, one actually lands in Paradise. An obscure but un-canny fact is that McCarran International Airport and most of the Fabulous Strip are not actually in the City of Las Vegas but in an unincorporated town called Paradise. The name was bestowed, perhaps ironically, early in the twenti-eth century on a local area with a high water table, rare for the desert region.

Landing in a paradise is the promise of that famous sign that greets visitors: *Welcome to Fabulous Las Vegas.* (See Figure 16.1.) It is the promise of possibilities unavailable in daily life. Never mind the titillating suggestions of self-indul-gence, sanctioned deviance, winnings at roulette tables, or the casting off of inhibition, Las Vegas is fundamentally a weekend's or precious vacation week's respite—not rest, mind you, as at the beach, but release from routine, life's pres-sures, and lingering disappointments. The unwritten Vegas slogan might well be "what happens at home or work stays there."

Tourist bureaus and downtown chambers of commerce around the world try to send a similar message, that theirs is the place to set aside for a few days the rigors of daily life. As cities seek to brand themselves in their own distinct way to attract cor-porate and visitor dollars, many keep a keen eye on what might be next for Las Vegas. Its ability to transform continually, while maintaining a broadly recognized brand, is increasingly viewed as a brilliant achievement in the context of global competition. Contrary to many assessments, in the city of the half-scale Eiffel Tower, the indoor Venetian canal, and the hollow Sphinx, an authenticity prevails. The art and culture critic David Hickey, who lived and taught in Las Vegas for a number of years, expressed a reasonable preference "for the real fakery of Las Vegas over the fake reality of Santa Fe—for the genuine rhinestone over the imitation pearl."[10]

All-American City

Prior to the Great Recession of 2007–2009, which severely if temporarily dented the local real estate market and optimism about perpetual growth, observers were convinced that metropolitan Las Vegas had supplanted Los Angeles as the preeminent laboratory for emerging patterns of American urbanism (not necessarily in the most positive ways). One reason was that, between the 1980s and the recession, without entirely shedding its mid-twentieth-century reputation as Sin City, Las Vegas, or rather Clark County overall, was growing more rapidly than any other American metro area. The growth was not exclusively the result of the Strip. While good jobs in tourism and construction were certainly magnets, the area was also becoming a center for back-office and logistics operations, a popular destination for national conventions (given the lure of the Strip) and a mecca for retirees. An affordable cost of living, especially by comparison to adjacent California, which many were leaving, was a key factor. Independent of the Strip, a conventional middle-class suburban region flourished.

The 1990s saw national media beginning to retell the story of Las Vegas as an all-American city. Some pundits, however, liked to point out that this wasn't because of change on the city's part. The shift was on the other side: the sins associated with Las Vegas had gone national. Earlier commentary, typified by Tom Wolfe's highbrow fascination and revulsion, or the drug-fueled outrage of a Hunter S. Thompson, was being replaced by less judgmental assessments in, for example, the *New York Times*. In a lengthy 1991 feature, the city beyond the Strip was portrayed as a domestic haven. It was "a Las Vegas of backyard barbecues, slow-pitch softball games and sidewalks full of kids on Rollerblades."[11] Given the city's hundred-degree days, evenings, and even nights, this was perhaps an exaggeration, but a reconsideration of Las Vegas as a wholesome, even ideal, place to live was underway. It was being repositioned in relationship to Southern California's problems of growth.

The *Times* article devoted considerable space to the growth woes of Los Angeles, pointing out that, while the Southern California lifestyle had long been the envy of the rest of the country, or at least had been portrayed as such, its image had been frayed "between the drive-by shootings, the air no one can breathe and houses few can afford." To such a dispiriting list the reporter could have added the barely tolerable traffic, the immigration concerns, the racial unrest, the drought worries, the utility grid inadequacies, and more. A decade or so later, many of these problems would arrive in Las Vegas. If the article were written today, probably it would be critical of Las Vegas for replicating rather than altering the pattern of urbanization that challenged Los Angeles. Instead, an admiration emerged for how it was becoming like its neighbor to the west: "in every direction, California-style planned subdivisions are being built as fast as the supply of Spanish roofing tiles can be replenished."[12] The *Times* anointed Las Vegas as the New California.

Several years and multiple stories about the New California later, when *Time* magazine made Las Vegas its cover story, its use of the label "All-American" could be interpreted somewhat ironically.[13] Las Vegas was now an All-American city because it shared the problems of all American cites, some to an exaggerated degree. *Time* pointed out that Las Vegas was a profligate user of water that required piping from afar. Air conditioning was virtually a life-or-death matter. Having an automobile, and one with functioning air conditioning, was absolutely essential to getting around. Air polluted by traffic and construction dust trapped by the surrounding mountains hung over the valley as if the infamous LA smog had relocated there along with Californians. Harsh "interactions" between white police and African Americans and other minorities were underreported precursors of today's Black Lives Matter movement. The generally more affluent and growing retiree community resisted increased public expenditures on services it did not use, like schools, while the simultaneously growing but poorer populations, often minorities, needed more investment in schools, libraries, playgrounds, and other services by more supportive municipal and county governments.

Such liabilities, like the vices available but removed from public view in the fancy resorts, play no role in the lavish brochures marketing surrounding subdivisions. Gaze at the photograph of families attending the Summerlin Sounds summer concerts, and life in Summerlin, the nation's largest private residential development, looks just fine. (See Figure 16.7.) And folks are moving to the region again, albeit in fewer numbers than prior to the recession, and now sometimes drawn by the prospect of catching a deal on a home lost to foreclosure

16.7 Summerlin Sounds summer concerts in the Las Vegas master-planned community of Summerlin, one of the nation's largest private residential developments.

during the recession. Mythologizing the good life to be had in Las Vegas may not be the same as hyping the fabulous Strip, but it runs in a parallel direction.

City Theming

In a cluster of dazzling buildings totaling just shy of eighteen million square feet, about the amount of office space in Atlanta's entire downtown, a project called CityCenter continued to be built through the Great Recession. (See Figure 16.8.) According to its developers—this being larger-than-life Las Vegas—the complex of commercial and residential towers, casinos, and hotels was the largest private construction project in American history. It was somewhat reminiscent of Nelson Rockefeller in the 1930s, who was determined to continue building Rockefeller Center throughout the Great Depression. In CityCenter's case, it would require the financial wherewithal of Dubai World to help it avoid foreclosure as the economy tanked. The Emirate of Dubai, heir in many ways to Las Vegas (though forbidding gambling and certain other vices, as Muslim culture dictates), was willing to invest in order to learn.

CityCenter is the most recent extravagance along the Strip, and among its fascinating ambitions was the desire to add big-city design sophistication to the place. The classic themed casinos—from the very first of them, Caesars Palace,

16.8   View of CityCenter, Las Vegas.

to the New York-New York Hotel and Casino—have a kitschy, cartoonish quality. The skyline of New York on the latter property appears from most vantage
points like a giant cardboard cutout. (See Figure 16.9.) The stage-set or avatar
quality of these edifices, however, is part of their mystique. One is undeniably
in Vegas, but enjoys the illusion of being teleported (Star Trek–style) to New
York City or Rome or Paris or Venice.

CityCenter, however, aims to be urban and real. Its components include a shopping center, convention hall, casino, three hotels, and two residential towers, each
designed by a world-renowned architect, all connected by a privately run monorail
and commonly owned by MGM Resorts International. A slick promotional video
extols the density, the architectural excellence, and the place-evoking sophistication of the complex, while of course praising its overall environmental stewardship.[14] The distinguished architecture critic Paul Goldberger seems less impressed:
"You can glide over the project on a monorail, but there is no pleasant place to
walk, except inside the buildings. . . . Its planners have crammed more square footage than anyone else has managed in Las Vegas and that may make it seem like an
antidote to sprawl. But it still isn't much of a center or much of a city."[15]

Getting back onto the crowded sidewalks of the Strip remains a more urban
experience, and the actual city, with all of its imperfections and the hopes of its
residents, lies beyond.

16.9   The New York, New York casino and hotel complex in Las Vegas.

Fabulous and Commonplace and Likely on Borrowed Time

Michael Sorkin's condemnation of Las Vegas was that it was "an incredible advertisement for the selfishness of capital."[16] Acerbic, yes, but it captures City-Center's pretensions, and to an extent applies to the entire metro area. For convenience, one speaks of Las Vegas as one place, but there are at least the two of this chapter: the fabulous and the ordinary. In the age of climate change, the future of neither is assured. The fact that Death Valley, one of the hottest places on earth, lies only a hundred miles away should raise anxiety. It is a very thirsty metropolis, and past reliance on its wealth to gain water at the expense of regional neighbors may not be easy to sustain in the future. (See Figure 16.10.)

The growing inequalities being experienced across America will continue to have their particular local focus in the tug of war between the civic stinginess of wealthier retirees and the basic civic needs of younger immigrants and minorities. The frequency of demolitions, a common and celebrated occurrence in the '80s and '90s as old resorts and hotels gave way to new, may diminish given the extraordinary level of capital—and embedded energy—invested in the current behemoth resorts. If fewer fabulous transformations occur, the city's ticket to perpetual success—its capacity for change to keep ahead of a Dubai, Macau, or a future competitor—will be challenged.

In 1911, the year of the city's incorporation, Herbert Croly published *The Promise of American Life*, a book that has been described as a manifesto of Progressive beliefs. "All the conditions of American life," he claims in it, "have tended to encourage an easy, generous, and irresponsible optimism."[17] Croly probably could not have imagined those conditions producing Las Vegas—and yet, the city does represent an irrepressible faith in the future. That is what makes it characteristically American, despite its many peculiarities. Those utopian inclinations—to start fresh, yet again, to overcome or ignore limits, to idolize the new, to disperse innocently if recklessly across the land, to depend on technology to overcome environmental shortcomings—all of them live on in Las Vegas. At least, they do today, but how much further into the twenty-first century they will remains unclear.

16.10   The American dream heading out further into the Mojave
desert, in a particularly unsustainable way.

17.1   One of the sturdier levees built following hurricane Katrina.

17

NEW ORLEANS AND ATTACHMENT TO PLACE

> You will observe that the land . . . is of peculiar formation. Throughout
> nearly the whole country, the bank of a river is the lowest spot; here,
> on the contrary, it is the highest.
>
> FATHER VIVIER, 1750

> One day this city, rapidly increasing as it is in wealth and consequence,
> will be swept into the Gulf of Mexico, if the Mississippi happen to
> rise unusually high at the annual inundation, and at the same time the
> south-east wind raise the sea . . .
>
> JAMES EDWARD ALEXANDER, 1833

> Everyone who loves New Orleans learns to love it with its flaws.
>
> TOM PIAZZA, 2005

THE CRESCENT CITY, its moniker referring to the large bend in the Mississippi
around which the original settlement was founded, maintains a remarkable
hold on many, including both residents and admirers around the world. It is
our Venice and it, too, is sinking. Had the existential philosopher Albert Camus
been a local, his essay *Myth of Sisyphus* might have been set in New Orleans.
Camus ends his story with a conclusion about Sisyphus that seems to fit the
residents of the Crescent City: "The struggle itself toward the heights is enough
to fill a man's heart. One must imagine Sisyphus to be happy."[1]

What may be considered utopian about New Orleans, or merely quixotic, is
that for three centuries its citizens have harbored the idea that their city can

17.2   New Orleans under water in late August 2005.

resist nature. They have insisted on remaining, even thriving, in a setting noto-
riously poorly suited for human settlement. It is a place steadfast and proud of
its mixture of cultures, which gives off an Afro-Caribbean vibe. At least since
the birth of jazz, the place has been known for its art and music, its distinctive
physical grace acquired over generations, and its famously relaxed pace of life—
the inspiration for another nickname, *The Big Easy*. Life in New Orleans marks
a real contrast with the harried life of the Big Apple and other fast-paced cities.

Despite taking a battering from more than thirty hurricanes and about a
hundred notable floods—and probably also because of these—the place has fostered fierce loyalty among its inhabitants. There is pride in the perseverance required to sustain existence there, always in the process of surviving one storm
and preparing for the next. The preparations usually involve another round of
expensive public engineering to mitigate nature's periodic fury. An observer
wryly referred to the city as "practiced in the art of recovery and forgetting."[2]
Following each effort at recovery and forgetting, however, it seems that a more
fragile and more flood-susceptible city emerges.

There was little reason to conjure utopian thoughts at the end of August 2005, as Hurricane Katrina caused severe damage along hundreds of miles of the Gulf Coast and flooded 80 percent of the City of New Orleans—a nearly lethal blow from which the city has yet to fully recover. (See Figure 17.2.) For days and weeks, people around the world watched in horror as the devastation and misery unfolded in a city where those remaining were mainly poor and African American. Local, state, and federal officials were unprepared—indeed, appeared hapless and, some would say, indifferent—in response to the crisis. More than eighteen hundred people lost their lives to the hurricane, hundreds in New Orleans alone; bodies floated in the terribly slow-receding floodwaters. It seemed to take forever for authorities to reestablish a semblance of civic order and, fifteen years later, it is still not fully restored. In the wake of the disaster, the city's population fell by almost half. Often forgotten amidst what seemed like unprecedented destruction was that New Orleans had faced similar crises during its three-hundred-year history. A quick lesson in that history will be useful here to establish just how precarious the city's environmental fortunes have been, and remain.

A Perpetual Standoff with Nature

French explorers, eager to gain control of continental trade for the French Crown, founded the city in 1717. It was no less strategic a spot than the confluence of the Mississippi River fourth-largest watershed in the world and avenue to the interior of the American continent, and the Gulf of Mexico, southern gateway to the oceanic trade corridors of the planet. While the Port of New Orleans has yielded its historic prominence to others, it remains important to continental and international trade, still processing millions of tons of cargo every year, providing space for fifty thousand annual visits by inland shipping barges, and welcoming more than a million annual cruise ship visitors. At one of the commercial docks close to the cruise ship terminal, newly arrived visitors, perhaps hoping to catch an early glimpse of Bourbon Street, may instead witness large freighters being loaded with thousands of crates of frozen chickens, midway on their journey from a midwest farm to an international destination. Among its other roles, New Orleans remains the nation's number one exporter of poultry.

Advised by local natives, the French explorers decided to set down roots at a great bend in the river, near a bayou (Bayou St. John) connecting the Mississippi to Lake Pontchartrain. It was a point where a naturally formed levee maintained a bit of high ground. The original port was established there, near the site of to-day's Jackson Square. With that, a long, difficult, and in some accounts fool-hardy confrontation began between the settlement and its setting. To the extent the effort was justified, it was because of the promise of strategic geographical control and entrepreneurial opportunity. Historian Pierce Lewis sums up New Orleans as an inevitable city built on an impossible site.[3] (See Figure 17.3.)

Within three years, the town washed away. Undaunted, the French tried again, determined to prevail by constructing an earthen levee to protect against the mighty river's seasonal fluctuations. These are not trivial fluctuations. While an average of 600,000 cubic feet of water per second flow past the city, sixty inches of annual rainfall are added to the water-laden climate. Despite the new levee, an inundation followed two years later, in 1724. The water overflowed again in 1735, and then in 1770, 1775, 1782, 1785, 1791, 1796, 1797, 1799, and 1801, two years prior to Jefferson's purchase of the Louisiana Territory. Weary perhaps of the battle with nature, the French relinquished the strategic promise of the location to Jefferson's America.

Nature was no kinder to the city's new owners. Consider this list of years, each featuring an inundation: 1809, 1811, 1813, 1815, 1816, 1817, 1823, 1824, 1826, 1828, 1832, 1836, 1840, 1843, 1844, 1847, 1849, 1850, 1851, 1854, 1858, 1859, 1862, 1865, 1867, 1868, 1871, 1874, 1875, 1876, 1881, 1882, 1883, 1884, 1886, 1890, 1892, 1893, 1897, 1903, 1907, 1912, 1913, 1916, 1922, and 1927.[4] Here a pause seems warranted, not only to let the predicament sink in (pardoning the pun) but be-cause the 1927 flood had a size and significance of special note, to which we will shortly return. One can continue listing storm events right up to the present.

The scale of the challenge becomes apparent when we recall how much work went into flood-proofing the city after Hurricane Katrina, and how vulnerable it nonetheless remains. Prior to Katrina, the city and the Army Corps of Engi-neers who manage flood protection were too complacent. The worst prior hur-ricanes had been Camille in 1969 and Georges in 1998. Georges caused misery throughout the Caribbean and Gulf, but had shifted direction just short of New Orleans to make landfall at Biloxi, ninety miles to the east. It produced substan-tial local flooding and, prior to shifting its course, called for a massive evacua-tion of the city, the largest prior to Katrina. The Superdome was used as a shel-ter of last resort, just as it would be, infamously, seven years later. But that near-miss did not prompt any substantial work on the levees, and no substantial hardening of them took place in the years leading to Katrina—one reason why the Corps became a target of local anger in 2005.

17.3 The Mississippi River delta and the water-filled world that constitutes Southern Louisiana.

It was different after Katrina. Complacency was impossible, especially given how much worse the disaster could have been. The hurricane struck as a Category 3 storm, but it had been a deadlier Category 4 and Category 5 storm over open waters a day or two earlier. It also veered somewhat to the east of the city, sparing New Orleans the even more catastrophic blow it would have sustained had the eye of the storm passed directly over it. The nation has since invested about $20 billion on sturdier levees and newer pumps in the effort to make the city more resilient than it was in 2005. The investment has made the city more secure. But how secure? Consider the brutal hurricane season of 2017.

Twelve years after Katrina, the late summer of 2017 witnessed four devastating tropical storms. Hurricane Harvey virtually drowned Houston under fifty-one inches of rain over a five-day period. Hurricane Irma, maintaining unprecedented wind speeds of up to 187 mph for several days, battered several Caribbean islands before damaging areas of Florida. These two were closely followed by Jose, which ravaged more of the Caribbean, and then Maria, incapacitating the entire island of Puerto Rico for months, taking some three thousand lives, and leaving destruction that will affect the island for years. National headlines naturally focused on the epicenters of these monumental tragedies. But a number of reports kept New Orleans in mind. The city had recovered 75 percent of its pre-Katrina population, including new residents who came to help rebuild and then chose to stay, perhaps assuming that the chastened and reengineered city was now safe. But here's a sample of headlines just prior to and during Hurricane Harvey:

> It Was Like a Mini-Katrina: Shaken New Orleans Overwhelmed by
> Saturday's Sudden Flooding – *The Advocate*, August 6, 2017
>
> It Wasn't Even a Hurricane, But Heavy Rains Flooded New Orleans as
> Pumps Faltered – *The Washington Post*, August 9, 2017
>
> New Orleans Under Water: 12 years after Katrina, Officials Can't Get
> It Right . . . The city has seen rain almost every day since April—but
> pumps continue to malfunction as water board administrators offer
> wrong information – *The Guardian*, August 15, 2017
>
> Amid Pump Failures, New Orleans Readies for Possible Harvey
> Flooding – CNN report August 26, 2017.

And these were headlines during a season when the hurricanes spinning ashore were far from New Orleans.

Perhaps the rebuilt levees will withstand the force of the next Katrina, Harvey, Irene, Jose, or Maria, but they are unlikely to eliminate the sort of problems evident in 2017. Indeed, a *Boston Globe* story summarized things well: "New Orleans today is a fortress city, equipped with the best environmental protection it has ever had—probably the strongest, in fact, that any US city has ever had. Yet, even the system's creators have conceded it might not be strong enough."[5] The underlying problem is not underinvestment or that old cliché of official incompetence. It is the location of the city.

As Father Vivier observed back in 1750, the setting is quite unusual. In most cities, land tends to be higher than adjacent bodies of water. But here, the city spreads from the raised banks of the Mississippi onto lower ground. Visualize the topography of New Orleans as an ordinary saucer with a raised perimeter edge. That is what centuries of levee building have produced, some now rising thirty feet—ten times higher than the originals the French built centuries ago. When several inches of heavy rain fall, hardly an uncommon local occurrence, this urban-scaled saucer begins to fill, taxing the elaborate system of pumps built to channel water away. Now consider that the land between the Missis-sippi on one side of the city and Lake Pontchartrain on the other was once an alluvial cypress swamp. Historically, its sediments were replenished by seasonal deposits from the Mississippi, but the levees have long blocked these from flow-ing in. The combination of no seasonal deposits and decades of work to drain the swamps to expand areas for settlement (and reduce the scourge of mosquito-borne diseases) has caused the base of this saucer to steadily subside. The land on which most people in New Orleans live continues to sink. The place is gradu-ally, inevitably, turning from a saucer into a deeper bowl, but without a handy lid to use in times of storms. Imagine the pumping systems that will be required to drain the city from future storms induced by global warming. (See Figure 17.4.)

This is not to press for abandoning New Orleans, any more than there are serious thoughts of giving up on Venice and letting it sink into the Adriatic Sea after centuries. (See Figure 17.5.) Passionless logic might suggest otherwise, and there have been voices supportive of abandonment.[6] But across history, a very human instinct kicks in after disaster to recapture what was taken away. Consider the Polish cities destroyed during World War II and rebuilt as soon as possible to look just as before, or the reaction after London's devastating seven-teenth-century fire. In its aftermath, six innovative plans for redesign were drawn up, but none was followed. This was despite the fact that Christopher Wren's plan was sufficiently visionary to influence subsequent city planning around the world, including L'Enfant's plan for Washington, DC. (Wren also

17.4   A portion of the enlarged pumps constructed following Katrina.

17.5   Tourists making the best of a flooded Piazza San Marco in Venice.

introduced a new style to the city with his buildings). Thus, when some people suggested it was not wise to rebuild the Lower Ninth Ward, situated at the bottom of the bowl, submerged by Katrina, and surely susceptible to future inundations, protests about insensitivity to the Ward's residents quickly squelched the idea.[7]

Demographics of a Flood-Prone Place

Storms do not discriminate against particular categories of people, and nor do floods, but people with means can usually avoid the most flood-prone areas. This truism reflects an uncomfortable local history.[8] The French Quarter, the home of old and wealthy New Orleans society and the main attraction for multitudes of tourists, occupies that elevated sandbar on which the city was founded. It suffered relatively little during Katrina. By contrast, the mostly poor and black residents of the Lower Ninth Ward suffered horribly. From the city's beginning, the poorest populations, mostly nonwhite, have tended to inhabit the most vulnerable ground. Compounding their vulnerability is the fact that poor families have less means to leave once a mandatory evacuation is called. Finally, the pace at which help arrives often seems to disadvantage those who need help the most. Over the days and weeks following Katrina, the trauma borne by the least prepared, most of them African Americans, was painfully exposed.

17.6   Sage advice, sadly, in a post-Katrina cartoon.

The world witnessed both the near-destruction of a city and rescue efforts that seemed to lack a sense of urgency. Richard Campanella, chronicler of the city's geography, wrote of scenes one would more readily associate with Haiti or Bangladesh. It was the "shocking spectacle of a modern First World society coming apart at the seams."[9] In an essay entitled "Katrina and Social Justice," Bettina Aptheker spreads the blame across the whole nation: "In the flood waters of Hurricane Katrina everything about the social, economic, and racial injustice of American society floated to the surface."[10] A Katrina-inspired cartoon was more blunt. (See Figure 17.6.) The same would be said a decade later of the level of urgency perceived in federal recovery efforts in Puerto Rico.

Among those suffering the aftermath of Katrina, difficult memories were surely awakened in parents and grandparents. Older residents would have grown up with stories about the spring of 1927, a season of disaster from their childhood. Fifteen inches of rain fell in New Orleans in less than one day that April, but that was not city leaders' main worry. Following an unusually rainy period the prior summer and fall along the Mississippi, the river was surging south that spring, ultimately flooding twenty-seven thousand square miles of America. Through parts of Tennessee, the river reached the unimaginable width of sixty miles. At a national scale, it remains the most destructive river flood in American history.

Before this deluge was to reach New Orleans, then the largest and most prosperous city in the South, the Governor of Louisiana agreed to dynamite a section of levees some thirty miles upstream. St. Bernard Parish, east of the city, rural, poor, and largely black, was to be the sacrificial lamb, the planned destination for diverted waters. Though carried out, the explosions turned out to be unnecessary, as the swollen river had breached several levees even further upstream. These natural levee breechings, aided by the dynamite downstream, allowed the river to flow past New Orleans below flood level, leaving people in New Orleans to enjoy summer as if the deluge just to the north had not occurred. However, the dynamite's long-term impact was the conviction—deeply ingrained to this day—that it was used to protect wealthier, and whiter, areas in the path of the flood. The 1927 flood ultimately displaced three-quarters of a million people along the Mississippi. Among them were more than three hundred thousand African Americans, many stranded in poorly managed relief camps for days—some forced at gunpoint to help white women and children into boats before being allowed to take their own refuge.[11] A recent documentary, *The Great Flood,* which uses archival film and music characteristic of the period of black migration northward (which accelerated after the flood), powerfully portrays those intolerable conditions. Its scenes are eerily analogous to some footage from 2005.[12] (See Figure 17.7.)

Attachments to Place in the Era of Climate Change

Climate change, as it determines the fate of New Orleans and other coastal cities around the world, will severely test our attachments to place. Camus's depiction of life's absurdities remains pertinent to New Orleans, Houston, the coast of the Carolinas as experienced in 2018, and innumerable other flood-prone places.[13] Finding utopian traces among low-lying urban environments around the world will become increasingly difficult. In New Orleans, the utopianism emerges from those existential attributes assigned by Camus to Sisyphus: a sense of purpose found in devotion to a place, dedication to the arduous task of perseverance, and happiness, or at least contentment, attained as a consequence of that perseverance.

Houston has recovered from Hurricane Harvey, and the towns along the coast of the Carolinas are moving on after Florence, just as New Orleans (barely) survived Katrina. These places are functioning again, but it seems inevitable that they will suffer again. Residents will fiercely protect and rebuild their weather-prone domains as long as possible. New Orleans will not be abandoned. Nor will Houston or Venice. Tourists will continue to flood into Venice, though

17.7 A scene reminiscent of Katrina, stranded citizens waiting to be rescued, but this is a photo of the 1927 flood.

very few people would now choose to make Venice their home. Continued engineering and environmental manipulation—sturdier levees, coastal barriers, restoration of wetlands and barrier reefs, and more—will be demanded and deployed. Still, as waters rise, it seems wise not to add more hostages to fortune, and to resist building new versions of Venice or New Orleans. Sisyphus has enough weight to push already.

Sisyphus's burden aside, climate change does present an existential crisis, as the circumstance of New Orleans suggest. On a global scale, the poor and least responsible for carbon release will suffer earliest and ultimately most devastatingly—while those who contribute more to the problem, enjoying their more affluent lifestyles, will face consequences slowly. Yet, to avoid ultimate catastrophe, those better off must soon acquire compassion for the already suffering and recognize their own responsibility to assure that the yet unborn may be able to inherit and thrive on a habitable planet. Two timely books with disquieting titles— *The Uninhabitable Earth* and *Losing Earth*—call for such responsibility to be acquired soon, while acknowledging that such has never yet been required of humanity.[14]

Engaging the full implications of climate change is beyond the scope of this book, but a current dilemma related to attachment to place is illustrative. For centuries, urban waterfronts served primarily as industrial and transport yards, but as those uses have waned, people have discovered life's delights at waterfront settings. Large-scale redevelopment and investment proceeds just as these now alluring urban "front yards" become vulnerable to climate change.

17.8   The human pull to water's edge: By 2018 "King tides" and winter storm surges overlapping this recently created promenade in Boston were no longer a rare occurrence.

To visit a city at water's edge is to immediately feel the power of place made possible by inhabiting a special portion of the earth. (See Figure 17.8.) It is hard to imagine Sydney's Opera House, Bilbao's Guggenheim, or even Cleveland's Rock and Roll Hall of Fame not alongside its city's body of water. The London Eye, London's majestic Ferris wheel, actually sits *in* the Thames. Much of contemporary Chicago's identity and self-image—not to mention wealth—is surely to be found along its spectacular lakefront facade stretching nearly thirty miles along Lake Michigan. Where else but along their portion of the mighty Mississippi would the citizens of St. Louis construct their monumental Gateway to the West? Urbanization will surely continue at water's edge. It will have to, however, radically adapt its form. Requirements to raise buildings' ground-floor levels, and to relocate mechanical equipment to rooftops, will not be sufficient.

Urban planners today often deploy the word *resilience* with intent to protect places that are likely to suffer or have already suffered from rising waters. But we will need more than determination to bounce back following a storm surge. We will need to exercise more forethought and respect for how water wishes to flow. Hard though it might be to acknowledge, the builders of our various coastal cities have historically not shown such respect. Could a utopian call to action from the nation's origin be of use? In *Common Sense,* Thomas Paine follows up his words about America's power to begin the world again with a proclamation that "a situation, similar to the present, hath not happened since the days of Noah until now."[15] With storms of biblical proportion more common—others will have occurred between my writing these words and your reading them—the new "days of Noah" are upon us. So let's use our power less on behalf of levee building, and more on day-lighting streams, protecting marshes, restoring coastal wetlands, minimizing further urban intrusion unto water-rich territory, and beginning strategic retreats from water-edge conditions. In other words, let's not do what is shown in the image below. (See Figure 17.9.) Perseverance is a valuable quality only if dedicated to a wise cause.

If we believe in the idea of *smart cities* (the subject of Chapter 18), a current utopian-minded concept and a term as much in vogue as *resilience* and *sustainability*, then the thought expressed by a historian we met in Chapter 16 should lose its relevance: "For as long as it exists, Las Vegas will be a testament to the ability of humans to transform a difficult natural setting into a comfortable one."[16] That may be true, but pushing hazardous forces of nature aside and hoping they won't return with a vengeance hardly reflects the kind of wisdom we require on the road to a smarter (if always short of utopian) urban future.

17.9   New homes on a low-lying area in Galveston, Texas. Neither memories of the flood that devastated Galveston in 1904 nor concern about impending sea level rise apparently hindering development.

18.1 The IBM operations center for the city of Rio de Janeiro, making the city "smarter."

18

E-TOPIA: SMART CITIES FOR THE CREATIVE CLASS

> Congestion, global warming, declining health—all can simply be
> computed away behind the scenes. Sensors, software, digital networks,
> and remote controls will automate the things we now operate
> manually. Where there is now waste, there will be efficiency. Where
> there is volatility and risk, there will be prediction and early warnings.
> Where there is crime and insecurity, there will be watchful eyes.
>
> ANTHONY M. TOWNSEND, 2013

CONFIDENT ABOUT A FUTURE perfected by technological advance, like the literary utopians a century earlier, a chorus of digital-age proselytizers heralds tomorrow's utopia: the *smart city*. The term has gradually superseded *smart growth*, a phrase that had been popularized earlier by environmental activists and other critics of sprawl. Smart cities—which presumably also support smart growth—are to come about through the integration of advances in information technology, communications, sensors, video, the "internet of things," and artificial intelligence. The theory is that compiling and analyzing vast amounts of data will allow all the physical and social systems that make cities run to be optimized. Dramatic improvements will result in the management of traffic, the power grid, water, waste disposal, education, health care, law enforcement, and the myriad details of daily activities and governance. The utopian conjecture is that any inefficiencies in these systems can "simply be computed away." It is an alluring, optimistic idea, promulgated by sanguine techies, by progressive media, and by corporations such as IBM, Cisco, and Google, ever ready to sell cities, and the rest of us, smarter software.[1]

The idea is finding its way to universities. In 2018, MIT's School of Architecture and Planning established a new undergraduate major called *Urban Science*. According to *MIT News,* "the goal of the program is to train undergraduates in the theory and practice of computer science, urban planning and policy-making including ethics and justice, statistics, data science, geospatial analysis, visualization, robotics, and machine learning." All of this knowledge to be applied "with a humanistic attitude."[2] Academic studies, among them Michael Batty's *The New Science of Cities*, address a growing belief that data analytics and urban planning are destined for greater interaction.[3] Years earlier, William J. Mitchell, as dean of MIT's School of Architecture and Planning, anticipated this as the coming of "E-topia" in a book of the same name.

Mitchell was hypothesizing in 1999 that, as digital technologies evolved, people would spend less time accumulating material possessions and more on gaining wisdom and improving their well-being through the flow of information. They would depend less on geography and more on virtual connectivity. We would all learn how to manage and consume fewer resources.[4] Mitchell's new world remains but a twinkle in an E-topian's eye. The acquisition of material possessions has hardly been reduced—indeed, the internet has led to new forms of spontaneous, one-click consumption. We are only at the beginning of limiting use of finite resources. And, unexpectedly for early predictors, the pull of place has increased as the entanglement of physical place with terabytes of data continues. Half a millennium after Thomas More conflated the Greek syllables *eu* (good) and *ou* (no) to signify that his Utopia was a good place nowhere, we are talking about a virtual world of data assembled "in the cloud" as a mechanism for perfecting the physical world.

During the final decades of the twentieth century, few were initially betting that cities would benefit from the coming of a digital age. Given remaining angst about the state of America's older cities, with their troubled cores and expanding suburbs, it seemed likely that mobile phones, the home computer, and the internet would further accelerate metropolitan dispersion. Why would people subject themselves to congested, polluted, unsafe cities when a connectivity revolution would allow them to link up from anywhere? Perhaps even more than the car, the internet would confirm decentralists' decades-old predictions about the obsolescence of the traditional city form—Frank Lloyd Wright's "ev-

18.2   A California entrepreneur consummating deals on his laptop from his home and office overlooking the Pacific Ocean.

erywhere and nowhere" cities indeed! (See Figure 18.2.) Yet something quite different has occurred. In the age of ubiquitous computing, American anxieties about cities seem somewhat to have waned.

Discovering Urbanity

As a new millennium began, America witnessed an urban revival the extent of which continues to be debated. Memories of mid-twentieth-century urban decay faded. Various city centers became focal points for considerable private investment. They witnessed expansions of their cultural and sports facilities, convention spaces, and entertainment complexes. The most attractive cities also saw—reversing decades of outmigration to suburbs—job growth and increased demand for housing. The *Boston Globe* reported on the new cachet of a city zip code. An advertisement for a fancy condominium project in Miami featured a chic woman in a shimmering, alligator-print dress. Under the headline of "I live in the *Everglades*," its copy celebrates "the triumphant return of an endangered species, the urban dweller." Yes, urban living and access to the Everglades. (See Figure 18.3.)

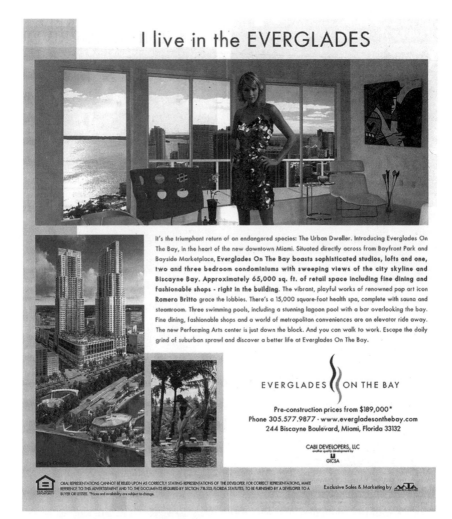

I live in the EVERGLADES

It's the triumphant return of an endangered species: The Urban Dweller. Introducing Everglades On The Bay, in the heart of the new downtown Miami. Situated directly across from Bayfront Park and Bayside Marketplace, **Everglades On The Bay** boasts **sophisticated studios, lofts and one, two and three bedroom condominiums with sweeping views of the city skyline and Biscayne Bay. Approximately 65,000 sq. ft. of retail space including fine dining and fashionable shops - right in the building.** The vibrant, playful works of renowned pop art icon Romero Britto grace the lobbies. There's a 15,000 square-foot health spa, complete with sauna and steamroom. Three swimming pools, including a stunning lagoon pool with a bar overlooking the bay. Fine dining, fashionable shops and a world of metropolitan conveniences are an elevator ride away. The new Performing Arts center is just down the block. And you can walk to work. Escape the daily grind of suburban sprawl and discover a better life at Everglades On The Bay.

EVERGLADES (ON THE BAY

Pre-construction prices from $189,000*
Phone 305.577.9877 · www.evergladesonthebay.com
244 Biscayne Boulevard, Miami, Florida 33132

CABI DEVELOPERS, LLC
another quality development by
U
GICSA

ORAL REPRESENTATIONS CANNOT BE RELIED UPON AS CORRECTLY STATING REPRESENTATIONS OF THE DEVELOPER. FOR CORRECT REPRESENTATIONS, MAKE REFERENCE TO THIS ADVERTISEMENT AND TO THE DOCUMENTS REQUIRED BY SECTION 718.503, FLORIDA STATUTES, TO BE FURNISHED BY A DEVELOPER TO A BUYER OR LESSEE. *Prices and availability are subject to change.   Exclusive Sales & Marketing by

18.3   An advertisement for an apartment complex in Miami, identifying "the triumphant return of an endangered species, The Urban Dweller."

This must still amaze older Americans whose image of the city, and especially the so-called inner city, has been shaped by heavy use of terms like *crisis, demise, pathology, blight, alienation,* and *disinvestment.* For at least half a century, America's mature cities were treated like problematic and often scary patients, at best relegated to "rust belt" status. Today, the cultural buzz sends an opposite message. Cities have become cool, sexy, and "good for you," as a Bill Griffith "Zippy" comic declared them back in 2001.[5] (See Figure 18.4.)

This is particularly noticeable in the choices being made by two large citizen cohorts about where to live. First are those who have finished their educations but have yet to start families. Though diverse in economic and ethnic background, Millennials (following in the footsteps of previous young-adult cohorts the Yuppies, Generation X, and Generation Z) are collectively seen as upwardly mobile and interested in nontraditional careers. In caricature, they gravitate to urban neighborhoods where they expect to meet like-minded colleagues and life partners, and make fortunes marketing creative apps—while enjoying overpriced coffee, artisanal products, and yoga classes, among other self-enriching urban enthusiasms.[6] City officials, landlords, and restaurateurs cannot seem to get enough of them, since these Yuccies (young urban creatives) do not, at least initially, draw on municipal services like schools much, but do consume generously. The second group consists of aging Baby Boomers, empty nesters (sometimes called Ruppies, for retired urban people) who no longer need to maintain generous suburban homes, and who want, while they are physically and financially able, to enjoy city attractions.[7]

City boosters may exaggerate how large this shift truly is, but growing appreciation for urban lifestyles within these two cohorts, which constitute a sizable majority of all households, is a long-term trend, not a short-term fad. Longer lifespans are a significant cause. As life expectancy extends to eighty, ninety, or even one hundred years, the percentage of any individual's life dedicated to child-rearing and family nurturing diminishes. Those years of family building happen to be when the virtues of suburban living are most appealing. During a prolonged earlier period of education and career exploration there is less interest in a family nest, a house and yard removed from the din of the city. For many of this "staying young longer" cohort, a preference for living closer to municipal services, social life, and professional opportunities makes darned good sense.

18.4 **Insight for a new millennium from a 2001 cartoon in the *Pittsburgh Gazette*.**

Once children are grown and gone, today's and tomorrow's empty nesters will have decades of active living ahead of them. Liberated from family responsibilities, looking forward to less lawn management, taxiing kids, and commuting—perhaps eager to embark on second careers, to reactivate delayed cultural interests, or to live near city-based adult children—a portion of this cohort will find living closer to urban centers appealing (among the exceptions being those wishing to live along golfing resort fairways.)

Such distinct phases across longer lives have reduced the dominance of that demographic mainstay—the household made up of a married couple with a school-aged child or two (and likely a pet). Early in the twentieth century, that description would have fit more than half of all households. It now represents less than 25 percent, and by some accounts less than a fifth of all households.[8] A considerable portion of the remaining 75 to 80 percent is not in search of a quarter-acre lot off a cul-de-sac, at commuting distance from jobs and social propinquity.[9]

What appeals to both young and old, for whom suburban experience has become commonplace and dull, is the spectacle of cities in all their diversity. A walk about town, an appreciation for something called "pedestrian urbanism," has gained favor as a welcome turn away from constant auto-dependence. A recent business mantra has it that innovation is advanced by interdisciplinary collaboration. To be among like-minded entrepreneurs and innovators therefore requires setting up shop in mixed-use districts near cultural amenities, not along suburban commercial strips. Where else but in cities, many have come to believe, will smart data in the hands of smart citizens lead to economic progress, cultural enlightenment, wiser environmental stewardship, and social justice, too?

The promise of smarter cities brings to mind an Aristotelian thought: "The city comes into existence, originating in the bare needs of life, and continuing in existence for the sake of a good life."[10] That's a welcome idea, but does it suggest the promise of a good life in smarter cities for more than a small elite? Can managing data also be the answer to overcoming a growing divide between those who have and those who lack proper access to economic opportunities?

A theory has emerged that the future of cities—in particular, the most desirable cities—depends on the arrival and cultivation of the *creative class*. Richard Florida pronounced this in *The Rise of the Creative Class* back in 2002. Many soon absorbed it as gospel, and made Florida an urban pied piper.[11] Florida's insight emerged from research on cities such as San Francisco, where he found relatively high percentages of artists and designers, foodies and celebrity chefs, tech wizards, app inventors, venture capitalists, pundits (such as himself), and gay people. This led him to conclude that future urban economies would depend on just such creative residents, usually with an additional stimulus provided by the residents' general youthfulness and progressive politics. Well, that may be lovely and exhilarating, but these creative types hardly comprise a majority of any urban population.

Nevertheless, the idea caught the imagination of mayors, economic development officers, the media, builders of upscale housing, and proselytizing urbanists. It happens not to be a new idea, or nearly as useful as proponents came to believe. Indeed, in subsequent publications, Florida has retreated somewhat from his early certainty. A recent book, *The New Urban Crisis*, appends a long subtitle warning of what happens when cities focus too much on serving narrow constituencies: *How Our Cities Are Increasing Inequality, Deepening Segregation, and Failing the Middle Class—and What We Can Do About it.*[12] So much emphasis on cultivating creative classes may have contributed to these consequences, making the work of "what we can do about it" much harder and less certain.

The Risks of a Too Particular Idea about Cities

The partial return to the city, from places formerly seen as more conducive to the good life, has spiked the cost of living in cities, for both newcomers and residents who hung in there during less attractive times. This is not such a "smart" development—in fact, it is at odds with the long tradition of cities, historically homes to people of modest means seeking upward economic and social mobility, just as such people are still the major constituency driving urbanization in the modernizing world. Maintaining access for many by maintaining affordability must become a priority for the engineers of smart cities. Escalation in the cost of land assembly and housing construction, coupled with growing disparities in earning power between the upper tiers and the majority of Americans, will mean that fewer Americans, young or old, will be able to respond to the new attractions of the city. A disquieting catchphrase makes the rounds among arrivals confronted by high housing costs: "drive till you qualify." Every mile you go from the heart of the city, in other words, makes it more likely you can afford a mortgage. To the extent that this is true of a given city, its long-term ability to support citizens in a socially just way is in jeopardy.[13]

In *Purging the Poorest*, Lawrence Vale, a housing historian, describes how efforts across three phases of federal housing policies between the 1930s and 1990s were "not just about clearing sites, but about clearing sights—a cleaning out of things that should not be seen."[14] As we saw in Chapter 14, the desire to enhance the image of the city often took precedence over providing for those ill-housed, despite the stated purpose of federal housing polices. Perhaps we have not yet traveled far enough from that unabashed City Beautiful argument about how beautiful and clean cities attract desirable, and now creative, citizens.

From the mid-nineteenth century onward, municipal officials, intellectuals, and planners sought, understandably, to impose order upon the disorderly processes of urbanization. That turned to eliminating its undesirable conditions. Howells's Altruria and Bellamy's Boston in the year 2000 were, indeed, antecedents to Richard Florida's city of the creative class, but they were literature, not policy. Other canonical portrayals of the future of cities early in the twentieth century also cleansed the city of undesirable characteristics: Tony Garnier's *Cité Industrielle* presented the city as efficient as a machine, but empty of pollution; Le Corbusier's *Ville radieuse* showed the city decongested, green, and radiant; Ebenezer Howard's garden cities were similarly green, healthful, and carefully zoned to keep incompatible activities apart. We might add the ambitions of the urban renewal decades, with their aims to clear the city of slums to make way for finer development. Lastly (though surely this borders on sacrilege), one could mention Jane Jacobs's mid-century Greenwich Village, which—if presented as a universal model, as some of her followers have presented it—treats the city as far less complex, and more particular, than any great city actually is.

This raises a profound question. Cities have long been domains of the creative and the entrepreneurial, and of ruling classes, too, and they shall continue to be so. But with the temptation to purge cities of whatever and whomever seems undesirable—un-slumming and beautifying them—can they still accommodate all who seek to better their lives in them? The myriad urban poor must, indeed, be creative and enterprising to survive, but that is not the image conveyed by the phrase "creative class." If we associate urban success with a particular category of citizens, we risk removing the right to the city for many.

The "right to the city," asserted in the 1960s by the Marxist philosopher Henri Lefebvre, has been much debated and variously interpreted, but warrants another look.[15] Present-day Boston offers a cautionary tale. Over the past fifteen years, Boston has seen its population increase by around seventy-five thousand people, or around 15 percent, with the rate of growth accelerating during the past half-decade. That may not be impressive by comparison to a Shanghai or Lagos, or even sunbelt powers like Houston and Phoenix, but it is a significant reversal from a 30 percent decline in population between 1950 and 1990, when some 240,000 Bostonians left for the suburbs or the sunbelt. Who are the newcomers? There is an assumption that the vast majority of these are those well-educated, ambitious, creative professionals, and empty-nesters cashing in their suburban paradise. In truth, more of the newcomers to Boston have been immigrants, with the Dominican Republic, China, and Haiti providing the largest shares of them.[16]

Not all city seekers, it turns out, happen to be budding entrepreneurs seeking to unite with their creative brethren in the next "innovation cluster." But, just like ambitious young professionals and prosperous empty nesters, these newcomers are in search of opportunity, community associations, and good dwelling places. The arrival of these diverse groups—and, oh yes, the international "one percenters" seeking safe havens for investment—has created enormous pressure on local real estate, making Boston one of the nation's most expensive places to live. Thousands of units of housing are being built, but few are affordable to the majority of old residents and new arrivals.

Other American cities are witnessing a similar paradox of prosperity and rising inequality as they regain some of the population lost during the suburban diaspora. Philadelphia, while still half a million people down from its mid-twentieth century peak, has gained around 5 percent since 2000. Our nation's capital has witnessed impressive population growth since the millennium, though it may again surprise people that the ratio of arriving Millennials to all newcomers has been decreasing for several years.[17] So-called rustbelt cities such as Pittsburgh have stabilized their populations and local economies, too, while New York City, always an exception, has gained about half a million people since 2000. Considerable pressure on living costs is felt in all these and many other cities. At the end of 2018, the *New York Times* headlined an article "Happy New Year! May Your City Never Become San Francisco, New York or Seattle (Or Portland, Denver, Boston, Dallas, Houston or Los Angeles)." Underneath that goofy title was a serious look at what by then was a real problem: could the costs of urban revival and prosperity for some outweigh the benefits to most?[18]

Yes, there remain places like St. Louis, Baltimore, and Detroit. Each has shed population for decades, but pockets of renewal are evident, attracting a trickle of newcomers and local hopes for broader recovery. These cities may well be testing grounds for the durability of the current enthusiasm for city reinvestment. If they fail—if Detroit, for example, stays to its present course of a severe bifurcation between pockets of wealth and broad rings of remaining poor—then large cities may not remain the traditional path to the "American Dream."

It was during the Great Depression, a period of little optimism, that a historian little remembered today, James Truslow Adams, coined the term "American Dream." He could not have foreseen its evolution into a cliché, a term most often either lampooned or applied cynically—as in the branding of one developer's giant shopping and amusement park complexes in New Jersey and Florida as "American Dream malls."[19] Adams meant to signify the quest to fulfill one's individual potential: "a dream of social order in which each man and each woman shall be able to attain to the fullest stature of which they are innately capable, and be recognized by others for what they are, regardless of the fortuitous circumstances of birth or position."[20]

Remaining accessible to people regardless of their circumstances is not where most of our newly thriving cities, whether Boston, Washington, DC, San Francisco, or that marvel Brooklyn, seem headed. Once merely the shadow of Manhattan's skyscrapers, Brooklyn was in the past century a place that housed citizens striving toward the middle class. It was home for the humble. Today it is a haven for hipsters. It is a pleasure to observe ambitious young professionals, seniors with means, "makers" and entrepreneurs, and tourists from near and afar all enjoying conviviality and thriving neighborhoods, as construction cranes remain at work producing more for their habitation and enjoyment. Somehow the less prosperous portions of Brooklyn, and they do still exist, have become less visible.

Joel Kotkin has called today's recovering urban centers, our E-topias, "adult Disneylands." Inside their gates, he says, the wishes of average citizens—better homes, good schools and neighborhoods, access to better jobs—come second to maintaining the "entertainment machine."[21] That may be too harsh a critique of places such as the new Brooklyn which do offer a quality of life that many enjoy. But America may be heading toward a too-narrow a view of what a successful city is. Jacob Riis's "other half" remains, if not in quite the squalid conditions that his 1890s photographs depict. Instead of illuminating the plight of the poor, which is what Riis set out to do with his camera, we seem to be nudging them away from the camera and the fun. As only a cartoon can, Tom Toles's

18.5 The message in this 1998 cartoon by Tom Toles, remains relevant now with regard to gentrification as well as race.

1998 gentrification cartoon titled *The Plan* exposes a trend that subsequent census data confirms. (See Figure 18.5.)

Portland, Oregon, is experiencing this dilemma. Its much-hailed solution to combat sprawl with a "growth boundary" that severely restricts new peripheral development has had the effect of causing housing costs within the boundary to soar. One consequence has been the loss of 10 to 12 percent of its historically small African American population over the past decade. And it is not alone: Chicago and Washington, DC, both traditional hubs of black American life, have been witnessing declining black populations.[22] Many of our recently dubbed "successful" cities are losing minorities and others whose incomes are not keeping pace with rising costs of urban living. As displacement continues, or accelerates, so does the issue of access for newcomers wishing to become part of new urban successes.

Countering the sizable literature boasting of America's urban revival, publications with more anxious titles are also appearing. One is *How to Kill a City:*

Gentrification, Inequality, and the Fight for the Neighborhood, in which Peter Moskowitz chronicles the effects of gentrification in four cities: New Orleans, Detroit, San Francisco, and New York. "Gentrification in much of Detroit," he writes, "seems to have skipped the beginning phase with the artsy folks, the laid-back coffee shops, and the activists and instead jumped straight from broke dystopian metropolis to yuppified playground."[23] But while that is true for a tiny fraction of Detroit's 113 square miles, which once accommodated nearly two million people, much of the rest of the city remains in a near-dystopian state. The city grew by 1.1 million people just in the decades between 1910 and 1930, as the miracle of the assembly line brought immigrants and rural southerners (many of them minorities) to its well-paying factory jobs. Then it shed 1.1 million during the second half of the twentieth century, the result of a perfect storm for abandonment. The retrenchment of the automobile industry coincided with a suburban diaspora both in residents and jobs, racial tensions leading to white flight, and municipal mismanagement—with the result being a depleted tax base insufficient to maintain basic city services. As of 2017, Detroit's population has fallen below seven hundred thousand people. Today, many locals anticipate (and pray) that the 2020 census will reveal a population gain—which, if it materializes, will be the first in seven decades.

Reestablishing Access

Back in the middle of the twentieth century, good housing was made available to average-earning Americans with the assistance of four public subsidies, though these were not explicitly referred to as subsidies, or so understood by the millions who benefited from them. (And by the way, prior to civil rights legislation, minorities did not benefit from them). Now well recognized as subsidies, these programs were: 1) the Federal Housing Administration's creation of low-cost, long-term mortgages that were government secured; 2) the generous mortgage-interest deduction allowed on personal taxes, an accident of the first tax code allowing all interest to be deducted; 3) the building of the interstate highway system; and 4) the expansion of utilities and services—water, sewage and power—necessary for urbanization beyond existing city limits. These and related policies, such as the liberal rezoning of farmland for development, opened up huge territories for inexpensive construction of housing before, during, and since Mr. Levitt began building his Levittowns. Combined with inex-

18.6   The kind of newspaper headline, in a 1953 Levittown, Pennsylvania publication, that is not often seen today.

pensive cars and cheap gas, these affordability-enablers allowed suburbia to metastasize, and were key to the near-miraculous expansion of America's middle class in the mid-twentieth century.

Now that urban vitality and amusements, more than green acres, are of interest to more Americans, could equivalent subsidies be devised? With policy interventions aimed at increasing affordability, could we alleviate what economist Joseph Stiglitz calls today's "inequality of opportunity"?[24] Where are today's Levitts, working to make homes accessible to any wage earner? (See Figure 18.6.) The challenge is enormous. What the prior century's city exodus relied upon was inexpensive land—for everyone an acre, in Frank Lloyd Wright's famous pitch, with most happily settling for a quarter-acre. By the year 2000, two-thirds of American households occupied affordable homes on such quarter-acres. But rising demand for a finite supply of urban acres will, of course, drive up costs as buyers compete for those acres. Overcoming this problem, not least by making more Americans comfortable with greater urban densities, may be among the hardest challenge for E-topia. But it is a precondition to delivering on the promise of cities that are truly smart—which is to say, also just.

19.1 Chicago's majestic lakefront with Millennial Park in the foreground. Only a portion of Grant Park, envisioned in the 1909 Plan of Chicago, as the centerpiece of the downtown. During the August 2018 weekend when this photo was taken, as the annual Lollapalooza music festival was taking place in Grant Park, elsewhere in the city eleven people were murdered and seventy more wounded. A disheartening reminder of America's dual urban circumstances.

19

POSTSCRIPT: HEADING TO THAT BETTER PLACE

> Whatever was the beginning of this world, the end will be glorious and
> paradisiacal, beyond what our imagination can now conceive.
>
> JOSEPH PRIESTLEY, 1768

TODAY'S PROMOTERS OF THE SMART CITY e-topia may be channeling Joseph
Priestley, the eighteenth-century theologian, scientist (he was a discoverer of
oxygen) political theorist, Enlightenment philosopher, and all-around optimist.
Optimism has indeed been at the heart of every utopian effort noted in these
chapters. And David Riesman, among America's leading intellectuals at mid-
twentieth century, wished it could be even more so. He called for, if not irresponsible optimism, a return to an earlier time in America's history when, as he
put it, "the country itself seemed to be a functioning utopia to peoples elsewhere."[1] Back then, the expectation of a brighter future—heading to that better
place—had seemed to imbue American life.

In the 1947 *Yale Law Review* essay that he later expanded into *The Lonely
Crowd: A Study of the Changing American Character*, Riesman lamented the decline of nineteenth-century optimism and aspiration. He saw growing conformity and consumerism among America's middle classes, especially as they
melded into suburbia. He worried that American culture had shifted to become
"outer-directed" rather than "inner-directed." Americans, he felt, were defining
themselves not by ideals or family values, but relative to how others lived, how
others viewed politics, and their neighbors' material accumulations. For him,

this was evidence of complacency and diminished cultural potential. He argued that a turn to aspirational—he used the word "utopian"—thinking was an essential response for the time.[2]

Not many took up Riesman's challenge as America's "outer-directed" middle classes enjoyed their upward mobility in a consumer's paradise following America's World War II triumph. As Lizabeth Cohen shows in *A Consumer's Republic: The Politics of Mass Consumption*, postwar politics assumed the "citizen consumer" would be the enabler of continued national economic growth, and so encouraged more and more consumption.[3] The rebellious 1960s produced ample criticism, temporary withdrawals from mainstream culture, and hard-fought gains in civil rights, but not much optimism as an unwinnable war swirled far away. During the 1970s and 1980s (Ronald Reagan's celebration of America as "a city on a hill" aside), an unrelenting focus on private consumption and corporate profits, to the exclusion of public welfare, put the economy on a path to growing inequality. As the digital age dawned, utopian thinking seemed old-fashioned or irrelevant except as applied to expectations of wondrous technological breakthroughs. But even as these wonders arrive, the benefits of e-topia remain elusive for many, as wealth accumulates to the upper one percent—and even worse, to the upper one-tenth of a percent—of households.

Commenting on the recent reinvestments in and modest population returns to some American cities, activist Ashley Dawson issues this stern challenge: "The good city cannot be a version of today's city, newly embellished with green trimmings like bus lanes and ribbon parks in front of high-end condos. The good city will only heal the wounds of calamitous environmental degradation if it is rebuilt to overcome today's yawning economic and social inequalities."[4] It is a call to arms no angrier than Rene Dubos's half a century earlier, as he began *So Human an Animal* with a blistering indictment: "Environmental ugliness and the rape of nature can be forgiven when they result from poverty, but not when they occur in the midst of plenty and indeed are produced by wealth."[5]

Greater concentration of wealth hasn't produced greater environmental care, but has derailed that once-fundamental American belief in an ever-growing middle class, made up of enterprising individuals sharing paths to prosperity. The possibility of this derailment was not unforeseen. As early as the 1830s, de Tocqueville was warning readers of the rise of a "manufacturing aristocracy" (today's term would be a corporate elite) and predicting that if, in the future, an oppressive upper class has established itself in America, "it will have been by that door that they entered."[6] John Adams expressed a similar worry about the potential that resources might be concentrated into too few hands. Anticipating Louis Brandeis's oft-quoted "curse of bigness," he warned Jefferson that, "as long as property exists, it will accumulate in individuals and families. . . . The snow ball will grow as it rolls."[7]

That snowball has, indeed, grown. Politics favoring an economic aristocracy have caused many to believe their votes and voices no longer count. Majorities coming out in support of ideas for more progressive taxation, universal health care, action on climate change, tighter gun control, and minimum wage hikes do not lead to policy changes. Bold statements of priorities such as the Green New Deal, calling for urgent action on climate change, inequality, health care, and aging national infrastructure, are met with derision and strident rejections of "socialism." John Ellis, historian of the early Republic, believes that today's economic inequality undermines democracy. But his historian's conviction is that "the study of history is an ongoing conversation between past and present from which we all have much to learn."[8] He therefore plumbs the egalitarian intentions of the Founders, as reflected in their phrase "We the People." In the same spirit, I would revisit America's oldest cultural inclination toward utopian visions. What themes can we find in them to keep today's governing from benefiting only the few? Four come to mind.

Sharing access to abundance. Many of America's leaders have embraced plans that were never fully achieved or achievable, from Jefferson's hope for an egalitarian distribution of land and Henry George's arguments against land speculation, to Herbert Hoover's promise of "a chicken in every pot and two cars in every garage," Roosevelt's New Deal, and Johnson's later Great Society. An underlying expectation of shared access, whether to land, mobility, or poultry, long persisted. But such expectations are difficult to maintain in, say, Detroit, with its extreme bifurcation between a modestly recovering downtown and the pervasive poverty surrounding it, made unmistakable by upwards of ninety thousand abandoned properties. Our nation needs a renewed dedication to providing universal access to a decent standard of living—a fair chance of having a life in good health in a desirable setting.

When Americans were predominantly of European ancestry it seemed easier for them to champion such a future; the anxieties and resistance presently mounting may be about having to accommodate many others from many other parts of the world. Cultural critic Frederic Jameson argues provocatively that this resistance is precisely what needs to be overcome. The analogy he draws is to disparate recruits finding themselves in common barracks and somehow emerging as a coherent unit. "Being thrown together with people utterly unlike you, from wholly different and incompatible backgrounds, classes, ethnicities, and even sexes," he hypothesizes—and respectfully accepting "the inescapable elbow-rubbing with people with whom you have nothing in common and would normally avoid"—is the only route to the true democracy that is "normally concealed by the various class shelters, the professions, or the family itself."[9] This somehow echoes James Truslow Adams's hope of all being able to fulfill their potential "regardless of the fortuitous circumstances of birth or position."

Minimizing inequality. Egalitarianism suggests both sharing resources and minimizing differences in social standing. The Founders had both in mind, even if they were not thinking of women, slaves, or Native Americans. Recently, journalist Bill Moyers expanded on Brandeis's famous warning about the difficulties of maintaining democracy when wealth accumulates in the hands of a few. Conceding the inevitability that the rich would acquire more goods and services than their fellow Americans, Moyers insists that "they should not be able to buy more democracy." Yet he sees them increasingly doing just that. Using a metaphor more dire than John Adams's growing snowball, he calls this "a despicable blot on American politics that is now spreading like a giant oil spill."[10] As the motto from the great seal of the United States, *E Pluribus Unum*, fades from public discourse, movements such as Black Lives Matter urge us to recall its intent. As do the words of Langston Hughes :

> Let America be America again.
> . . . .
> Let America be the dream the dreamers dreamed—
> . . . .
> O, let my land be a land where Liberty
> Is crowned with no false patriotic wreath,
> But opportunity is real, and life is free,
> Equality is in the air we breathe.
> . . . .
> *Say, who are you that mumbles in the dark?*
> . . . .

I am the poor white, fooled and pushed apart,
I am the Negro bearing slavery's scars,
I am the red man driven from the land,
I am the immigrant clutching the hope I seek—

. . . .

O, yes, I say it plain, America never was America to me,
And yet I swear this oath—America will be![11]

To reverse the spread of inequality will require more than better data-managed cities. It will require new thinking about political priorities. For example: Would wealth and income inequality be so extreme today if we as a nation had not spent upwards of six trillion dollars on wars since September 11, 2001? Just as William Dean Howells had his Altrurians abandon their unjust cities for egalitarian capitals, Americans will need to commit to remaking America as a place "where Liberty / Is crowned with no false patriotic wreath, / But opportunity is real, and life is free."

Stewardship of the environment. Let's rekindle the dream of a nature's nation. Without resorting to a collective retreat to cabins at the edge of Walden Pond, much less naively assuming that the earth's resources are unlimited, we can commit to determined environmental care. Science makes clear that if environmental abuse continues to outpace the earth's restorative response, catastrophe will ensue. As early as 1864, George Perkins Marsh was forewarning in his *Man and Nature* that human interactions with nature have reciprocal consequences, yet it has taken a century and a half for the implications to be widely acknowledged.[12] As we come to recognize the limits to the planet's carrying capacity, and admit that climate change demands arduous measures of us, an old saying seems to hold more wisdom: "Treat the earth well: it was not given to you by your parents, it was loaned to you by your children."

We are reminded often that we are becoming an urban species, but it is more important to embrace the role of environmental stewards. Celebrating an annual Earth Day while awaiting biotechnology and geoengineering breakthroughs is insufficient. There must be greater sharing of services and less enchantment with the cornucopia of goods to be consumed. Why not tax luxuries and channel the proceeds to environmental repair? Why not further monetize recyclable waste?[13] There must be greater reliance on renewable resources, and more active efforts to reduce consumption, minimize waste, rely on more efficient forms of mobility, and make do with less space at work and home. Consider the dwelling featured in a recent *New York Times* article—a home measuring one hundred thousand square feet, complete with four outdoor and three indoor pools, on the market for $500 million.[14] Or the more modest example of excess represented by a house "addition" left unfinished by the Great Recession. (See Figure 19.2.) Such undertakings deserve no social applause.

Responsibility to a common good. Taking the idea of American individualism to the point of what Myra Jehlen, in *American Incarnation*, calls defining oneself in "a dichotomy with society" is rarely helpful to one's community.[15] Several strands of the anti-urbanism discussed in Chapter 3 originate in a reluctance to assume responsibility for common purpose. Still, any poll about preferred places to live reveals a desire among Americans for community, however defined. The communitarian experiments across American history, the tradition of the annual town meeting and home rule, and the sentiments attached to small-town life all reveal an inherent appreciation for shared experience. All are remaining evidence of de Tocqueville's identification of a "spirit of association." But in a sad irony, today's ubiquitous digital interactions, whether in social networking or e-commerce, have resulted in social isolation and diminution of face-to-face association. Under these conditions, common purpose further splinters. It seems important to broaden the idea of common purpose—beyond one's favorite social network, cul-de-sac, gated subdivision, immediate neighborhood— and not only in the aftermath of some moment of crisis, or in the afterglow of a city's professional sports triumph.

Unworthy Utopias

It might be best if the tendency to decamp—to go West, young man—continued to wane. It carries with it a tendency to privilege individual gain over common good. The perpetual quest for a new start accelerates the building of redundant infrastructure, impinges further on virgin land and ecological systems, abets additional social and economic segregation, and devalues places left behind. Perhaps we should not be surprised that citizens of the "Motor City," famous for enhancing personal mobility, would be quick to take flight at times of either opportunity or anxiety. It is well past time that we should be shedding

19.2   An "addition" at left to the older Levittown-type home on the right, left
unfinished as the Great Recession advanced.

our remaining affection for the Frontier Hypothesis and Manifest Destiny. The
return of interest in America's older cities thus holds considerable promise, despite current imbalances in affordability and access.

Equally, that dream of a middle landscape, an alluring place between city
and country, imperfectly manifested across America's suburban peripheries,
should continue to lose luster. While the decade of the Great Recession saw
suburban growth slow, prompting predictions about the decline of the suburb,
recent statistics show suburban development picking up again. At the end of
2017, the US Commerce Department reported that the number of housing
starts—primarily in single-family homes—had returned to prerecession levels.[16]
This is partially due to the Millennial generation's aging into its family-rearing
years, when homes and yards gain appeal. It is also driven in part by the increasing cost of living in cities, where the supply of housing production has not met
demand. One hopes that the vast middle landscapes of sprawl have exposed the
limits of a middle landscape ideal, shifting desire for the more genuine qualities
found in rural, small town, or urban contexts, rather than in bland in-betweens.

Finally, the instinct to sanitize the city is of dubious value, threatening to sap
the vitality emblematic of great urban areas. Valuing and enabling diversity al-
lows it to persist. An infrastructural image comes to mind. Serving Dallas is an
incredibly complicated highway interchange known locally, if not lovingly, as

the "mixmaster." Like the classic kitchen appliance, it is a contraption that pulls many streams together into a tight, dynamic space. For downtown Dallas it creates a terrible tangle of looping traffic, but the metaphor suits cities wonderfully. The various promoters of distilled and sanitized urban scenes make a mistake when they gear their cities, consciously or inadvertently, to pull in only certain categories of citizens—the creative classes, say. They fail to appreciate that cities thrive on their intertwining, looping, overlapping mixmaster energies. America's urban revival will broaden only when this is recognized again.

These last few pages only reiterate what many identify as current concerns. But it is worth issuing a David Riesman-like reminder that the aspiration to pursue ideals has been in the DNA of centuries of arrivals to the New World. That fundamental idealism need not be abandoned, but it should now be refocused. As more of us (all across the globe) congregate in urban regions, that near-utopian goal in the preamble of the Constitution—to form a more perfect union—should compel us to aim for more perfect cities, where citizens inevitably need to live in union.

Like Riesman, Oscar Wilde understood the importance of utopian imagining. "A map of the world that does not include Utopia is not worth even glancing at," he wrote, "for it leaves out the one country at which Humanity is always landing." And no sooner does Humanity attain that desired ideal than it "looks out, and seeing a better country, sets sail." Thus, Wilde added, "progress is the realization of utopias."[17]

For half a millennium, the American instinct has been to build newer cities on more distant hills. Now that so much of Humanity has landed in cities, a different utopian predisposition must take hold. Rather than continue to set sail, we must now finally resolve to stay, and improve.

NOTES

Preface

1   Gordon S. Wood, *The Radicalism of the American Revolution* (New York: Knopf, 1991), 229.

2   Leo Marx, *The Machine in the Garden: Technology and the Pastoral Ideal in America* (New York: Oxford University Press, 1964), 3.

3   John Egerton, *Visions of Utopia: Nashoba, Rugby, Ruskin, and the "New Communities" in Tennessee's Past* (Knoxville: University of Tennessee Press, 1977), 87.

4   Lewis Mumford, *The Story of Utopias* (1922) (Middleton, DE: Shape Bookstore, 2016), 9.

5   Anne Mackin, *Americans and Their Land: The House Built on Abundance* (Ann Arbor: University of Michigan Press, 2006), 7.

6   Isaiah Berlin, *The Proper Study of Mankind: An Anthology of Essays,* ed. Henry Hardy and Roger Hausheer (New York: Random House, 1998), 12.

7   Alissa Quart, *Squeezed: Why Our Families Can't Afford America* (New York: Ecco / Harper Collins, 2018).

8   For a range of perspectives, see Jack P. Greene, *Pursuits of Happiness: The Social Development of Early Modern British Colonies and the Formation of American Culture* (Chapel Hill: University of North Carolina Press, 1988). Christopher Sale, *The Conquest of Paradise: Christopher Columbus and the Columbian Legacy* (New York: Penguin, 1990); Sharon Zukin, *Landscapes of Power: From Detroit to Disney World* (Berkeley: University of California Press, 1991); and Howard Zinn, *A People's History of the United States* (New York: Harper Collins, 1980).

9   The quote continues: "Utopias are like holy spirits which give the breath of life to matter." Rene Dubos, *Dreams of Reason: Science and Utopias* (New York: Columbia University Press, 1961), 50.

10 Paul Tillich, "Critique and Justification of Utopia," in Frank E. Manuel, *Utopias and Utopian Thought* (Boston: Houghton Mifflin, 1965), 296.

11 Jean Baudrillard, *America* (London: Verso, 1988), 76. See especially the chapter "Utopia Achieved," in which Baudrillard expounds on the idea of America "escaping from history," achieving a pure modernity. Paine's statement is from the appendix to *Common Sense,* first published on January 10, 1776.

12 John R. Stilgoe, *What is Landscape?* (Cambridge, MA: MIT Press, 2015).

Introduction

Dolores Hayden, *Seven American Utopias: The Architecture of Communitarian Socialism* (Cambridge, MA: The MIT Press, 1976), 3.

1 Charles Sanford, among others, has suggested that the Edenic myth was among the most important organizing forces in American culture. Charles L. Sanford, *The Quest for Paradise: Europe and the American Moral Imagination* (Urbana: University of Illinois Press, 1961), 6.

2 Allen Ray Billington, *Land of Savagery, Land of Promise: The European Image of the American Frontier* (New York: W. W. Norton, 1981). Billington relies in part on Edmundo O'Gorman's thesis that the New World needed to be "invented" as much as discovered. Prior to Columbus's voyage, the world as God banqueted it to humanity consisted of three continents, Europe, Africa, and Asia. If a fourth continent existed, "outside of the Island of the Earth," then it had to be paradise. Edmundo O'Gorman, *The Invention of America: An Inquiry into the Historical Nature of the New World and the Meaning of America* (Bloomington: Indiana University Press, 1961).

3 Mircea Eliade, *Paradise and Utopia: Mythical Geography and Eschatology in The Quest: History and Meaning in Religion* (Chicago: University of Chicago Press, 1969), 264.

4 Michael Kammen, *People of Paradox: An Inquiry Concerning the Origins of American Civilization* (New York: Vintage Books, 1973), 9.

5 Nearly a century of European exploration of the New England coast preceded the arrival of the Pilgrims and, of course, settlements of Native Americans had long existed. Ironically, a devastating epidemic, long assumed to be smallpox (though recent doubts have surfaced), wiped out about 90 percent of the Patuxet Nation a year prior to the arrival of the Pilgrims. See William Cronon, *Changes on the Land: Indians, Colonists, and the Ecology of New England* (New York: Hill and Wang, 1983).

6 Christopher Tunnard, *The City of Man: A New Approach to the Recovery of Beauty in American Cities,* 2nd ed. (New York: Charles Scribner's Sons, 1970), 11.

7 Francis J. Grund, *The Americans in Their Moral, Social, and Political Relations* (London: Pierson Longman, 1837), 263–264.

8   Jean Paul Sartre, "American Cities," *Literary and Philosophical Essays* (London: Hutchinson Publishing Company, 1955). Reprinted in Alan Trachtenberg, *The City: American Experience* (Oxford: Oxford University Press, 1971), 197–205.

9   Joseph J. Ellis, *American Sphinx: The Character of Thomas Jefferson* (New York: Albert A. Knopf, 1997), 22.

10   "Country Calls: Where Americans Say They Would Live If Money or Circumstances Were Not an Issue," *USA Today,* August 27, 2002.

11   *Founding Gardeners* focuses on the passions of Jefferson, Washington, Adams, Madison, and others of the founders for agriculture as the basis of the new nation's productivity, along with fascination with botany, horticulture, and the sheer joys of gardening. Andrea Wulf, *Founding Gardeners: The Revolutionary Generation, Nature, and the Shaping of the American Nation* (New York: Alfred A. Knopf, 2011).

12   Henry Ford, *Ford's Ideals: Being a Selection of "Mr. Ford's Page" in The Dearborn Independent* (Dearborn, MI, Dearborn Publishing, 1922), 425.

13   Mimi Kirk, "The Seductive Power of a Suburban Utopia," CityLab website, March 16, 2018, https://www.citylab.com/design/2018/03/the-seductive-power-of-a-suburban -utopia/555329/.

14   While African American neighborhoods were disproportionately in the path of the renewal bulldozer, they were not exclusively so. See, for example, Herbert Gans, *The Urban Villagers: Group and Class in the Life of Italian-Americans,* updated and expanded ed. (1962; New York: Free Press, 1982). It chronicles the destruction of a Boston neighborhood of first- and second-generation European immigrants, briefly described in Chapter 14.

1 Jefferson's Blueprint for an Egalitarian Republic

Frederick Jackson Turner, *The Frontier in American History* (New York: H. Holt, & Company, 1920), 253.

Le Corbusier, *The City of Tomorrow and Its Planning* (1929; New York: Dover Publications Paperbacks 1987), 11.

1   Thomas Jefferson to James Madison, October 28, 1785, The Founders' Constitution Web Edition, ed. Philip B. Kurland and Ralph Lerner, Chap. 15, Document 32, http://press -pubs.uchicago.edu/founders/documents/v1ch15s32.html.

2   Quoted in William B. Scott, *In Pursuit of Happiness: American Conceptions of Property from the Seventeenth to the Twentieth Century* (Bloomington: Indiana University Press, 1977), 41. Adams was, however, concerned about the accumulation of wealth as a consequence of land assembly.

3   Garry Wills, *Inventing America: Jefferson's Declaration of Independence* (Garden City, NY: Doubleday, 1978), 240–258. Wills goes through a number of speculations as to why property,

so important to Jefferson and other founders, disappeared from his final draft. As an example, the Virginia Constitution adopted just a month earlier states: "That all men are by nature equally free and independent and have certain inherent rights . . . namely the enjoyment of life, liberty, with the means of acquiring and possessing property."

4 Psalm 115, Verse 16, as phrased by the King James Bible.

5 Thomas Jefferson, *Notes on the State of Virginia* (1787), ed. William Peden (Chapel Hill: University of North Carolina Press, 1955), 164.

6 A. Whitney Griswold, "The Agrarian Democracy of Thomas Jefferson," *American Political Science Review* 40, no. 4 (1946): 657–681, 668.

7 George W. Geib, "The Land Ordinance of 1785: A Bicentennial Review," *Indiana Magazine of History* 81, no. 1 (1985): 1–13; William C. Pattison, "Beginnings of the American Rectangular Land Survey System, 1784–1800," Research Paper no. 50, Department of Geography, University of Chicago, 1957; Edward T. Price, *Dividing the Land: Early American Beginnings of Our Private Property Mosaic* (Chicago: University of Chicago Press, 1995).

8 Joseph Rykwert, *The Idea of a Town: The Anthropology of Urban Form in Rome, Italy and the Ancient World* (Princeton, NJ: Princeton University Press, 1976), 202.

9 Frederick Law Olmsted, *Landscape into Cityscape: Frederick Law Olmsted's Plans for a Greater New York City,* ed. Albert Fein (Ithaca, NY: Cornell University Press, 1968; New York: Van Nostrand Reinhold, 1981), 64.

10 Anne Mackin, *Americans and Their Land: The House Built on Abundance* (Ann Arbor: University of Michigan Press, 2006), 33.

11 Griswold, *The Agrarian Democracy,* 662.

12 Walt Whitman, "Wicked Architecture," *Life Illustrated,* 1856; Emory Holloway, ed., *Walt Whitman, Complete Poetry & Selected Prose & Letters* (London: Nonesuch Press, 1938), 607.

13 Adelaide Wilson, *Historic and Picturesque Savannah* (Boston: Boston Photogravure Company, 1880), 193.

14 Quoted in Mills Lane, *Savannah Revisited: A Pictorial History* (Savannah, GA: Beehive Press, 1969), 23.

15 The idea of a middle landscape and the older notion of the "ethic of the middle link" are explored in A. O. Lovejoy, *The Great Chain of Being* (Cambridge, MA: Harvard University Press, 1942); Leo Marx, *The Machine in the Garden: Technology and the Pastoral Ideal in America* (New York: Oxford University Press, 1964); James L. Machor, *Pastoral Cities: Urban Ideals and the Symbolic Landscape of America* (Madison: University of Wisconsin Press, 1987); Peter Rowe, *Making a Middle Landscape* (Cambridge, MA: MIT Press, 1991); Charles L. Sanford, *The Quest for Paradise* (Urbana: University of Illinois Press, 1961); David Schuyler, *The New Urban Landscape: The Redefinition of City Form in Nineteenth-Century America* (Baltimore, MD: Johns Hopkins University Press, 1986).

16 Quoted in Marx, *Machine in the Garden,* 105, 73.

17 L. P. Wilkinson, *The Georgics of Virgil: A Critical Survey* (Cambridge: Cambridge University Press, 1969), 302.

18 Adam Smith's *An Inquiry into the Nature and Causes of the Wealth of Nations* was first published in London in 1776, the same year as Jefferson's "Declaration of Independence." A number of the phrases in it could as easily have come from Jefferson, such as "to cultivate the ground was the original destination of man." Smith, *Wealth of Nations* (London: W. Strahan, 1776), Book III, Chap. 1, 462.

19 Henry Nash Smith, *Virgin Land: The American West as Symbol and Myth* (Cambridge, MA: Harvard University Press, 1970), 126.

20 Ralph Waldo Emerson to Thomas Carlyle, 1840. Ralph Waldo Emerson, *The Heart of Emerson's Journals,* ed. Bliss Perry (1926; Boston: Houghton Mifflin, 1937), 208.

21 J. Hector St. John de Crèvecoeur, *Letters from an American Farmer,* ed. with intro. and notes by Susan Manning (1785; New York: Oxford University Press, 1997). Not one for understatements, he also wrote: "We have no princes for whom we toil, starve, and bleed: we are the most perfect society now existing in the world." Quoted in H. N. Smith, *Virgin Land,* 127.

22 Turner, *Frontier in American History.*

23 By 1816 Jefferson was writing: "we must now place the manufacturer by the side of the agriculturist." John P. Foley, ed., *The Jefferson Cyclopedia: A Comprehensive Collection of the Views of Thomas Jefferson* (London: Funk & Wagnalls, 1900), 533.

24 Thomas Jefferson, letter to G. K. van Hogendorp (a Dutch statesman) October 13, 1785, National Archives Founders Online, https://founders.archives.gov/documents/Jefferson/01-08-02-0497.

25 Annette Gordon-Reed and Peter S. Onuf, *"Most Blessed of the Patriarchs": Thomas Jefferson and the Empire of the Imagination* (New York: Liveright, 2016), 89–81.

26 The quote is as recollected by a contemporary chronicler of Washington society. Margaret Bayard Smith, *A Winter in Washington; Or, Memoirs of the Seymour Family* (New York: Bliss and White, 1824), Vol. 2, 261.

27 Walter Creese, *The Crowning of the American Landscape: Eight Great Spaces and Their Buildings* (Princeton, NJ: Princeton University Press, 1985), 9–42. As Creese aptly put it, "He wanted the farmer present, but he did not want the agrarian log cabin or flimsy wooden shack," 9.

28 Joseph J. Ellis, *American Sphinx: The Character of Thomas Jefferson* (New York: Albert A. Knopf, 1997). Ellis devotes substantial effort to understanding Jefferson's contradictory relationship to slavery. Also Conor Cruise O'Brien, "Thomas Jefferson: Radical and Racist," *Atlantic Monthly,* October 1996, 53–74.

29 O'Brien, "Thomas Jefferson," 106.

30 Mackin, *Americans and Their Land,* 121.

2 A Nature's Nation in the Garden of the World

Thomas Cole, "Essay on American Scenery," in *The Native Landscape Reader,* ed. Robert E. Grese (Amherst: University of Massachusetts Press, 2011), 27.

Bill McKibben, *The End of Nature* (1989; New York: Random House, 2005), xxiii.

1 William B. Scott, *In Pursuit of Happiness: American Conceptions of Property from the Seventeenth to the Twentieth Century* (Bloomington: Indiana University Press, 1977); Daniel M. Friedenberg, *Life, Liberty and the Pursuit of Land: The Plunder of Early America* (Buffalo, NY: Prometheus Books, 1992).

2 Ernest Callenbach, *Ecotopia: The Notebooks and Reports of William Weston,* 40th Anniversary Epistle Edition (1975; Berkeley, CA: Banyon Tree Books, 2014), 47. Rachel Carson, *Silent Spring* (New York: Fawcett World Library, 1962), 19. Carson was protesting the indiscriminate use of toxins such as DDT. The manuscript was first published in the *New Yorker* and, predictably, was much criticized by the chemical industries. It became an international best seller and is considered among the seminal points of departure of the modern environmental movement.

3 Perry Miller, *Errand into the Wilderness* (Cambridge, MA: Harvard University Press, 1956), 207.

4 Carl L. Becker, *The Heavenly City of the Eighteenth Century Philosophers* (1932; Clinton, MA: Colonial Press, 1974), 51.

5 Miller, *Errand,* 207. See also Isaiah Berlin, *The Roots of Romanticism* (Princeton, NJ: Princeton University Press, 1999).

6 Henry David Thoreau, "Sounds," in *Walden; or, Life in the Woods* (1854; Boston: Houghton-Mifflin, 1893), 181.

7 Thoreau, "Sounds." For Bill McKibben, the modern analogy is the chain saw. He writes of how it disturbs the silence of his Vermont. Bill McKibben, ed. *American Earth: Environmental Writing since Thoreau* (New York: Library of America, 2008), 718.

8 Henry James, *The American* (New York: Scribner's and Sons, 1907), 45.

9 e e cummings, "Voices to Voices, Lip to Lip," in *Complete Poems Volume One 1913-1935* (London: MacGibbon & Kee, 1968), 264.

10 Thomas Cole, "Essays on American Scenery," *The American Monthly Magazine* 1 (January 1836); repr. in *The American Landscape: A Critical Anthology of Prose and Poetry,* comp. John Conron (New York: Oxford University Press, 1973), 578.

11   Montgomery Schuyler, "Last Words About the Fair," *Architectural Record* 3 (January–March 1894), 271–301; repr. in *American Architecture and Other Writings: The Writings of Montgomery Schuyler,* ed. William H. Jordy and R. Coe (Cambridge, MA: Harvard University Press, 1961), 572.

12   Alex Krieger, "Civic Lessons of an Ephemeral Monument," *Harvard Architecture Review IV: Monumentality and the City* (Cambridge, MA: MIT Press, 1984), 149–165.

13   Frederick Law Olmsted, "A Report upon the Landscape Architecture of the Columbian Exposition to the American Institute of Architects," *American Architect and Building News* 41 (September 1893), 151–152.

14   The "ethic of the middle link" and the "cult of the noble savage" (both essentially sentimental extensions of natural law theory) held that the best human condition was a middle position between rational and animal being, intellect and instinct, mind and spirit. European social theorists frequently perceived the New World as having the potential to become an actual embodiment of such balances. See Leo Marx, *The Machine in the Garden: Technology and the Pastoral Ideal in America* (New York: Oxford University Press, 1964).

15   Hamlin Garland, *A Son of the Middle Border* (New York: Macmillan, 1914), 458–461. A good account of Garland, the novelist, and his family's visit to the Chicago Fair is found in Frederick Turner, *Spirit of Place: The Making of American Literary Landscape* (San Francisco: Sierra Club Books, 1990), 3–19.

16   Ralph Adams Cram, *My Life in Architecture* (Boston: Little Brown, 1936), 340.

17   Hjalman H. Boyesen, "A New World Fable," *The Cosmopolitan* 16, no. 2 (December 1893), 183.

18   Cram, *My Life in Architecture,* 35.

19   Henry David Thoreau, journal entry, 1857, in *The Writings of Henry David Thoreau: Journal, Vol. 10,* ed. Bradford Torrey (Boston: Houghton Mifflin, 1906), 80.

20   Ralph Waldo Emerson, "Farming," in *Society and Solitude* (1870; London: J. M. Dent, 1912), 72.

21   Neil Harris, *The Artist in American Society: The Formative Years 1790–1860* (1966; Chicago: University of Chicago Press, 1982), 174.

22   Thomas Cole, "Essay on American Scenery" *American Monthly Magazine* 1 (January 1836), https://www.csun.edu/~ta3584/Cole.htm.

23   William Cronon, *Nature's Metropolis: Chicago and the Great West* (New York: W. W. Norton, 1991).

24   A good introduction to John Muir is Terry Gifford, *John Muir: His Life and Letters and Other Writings* (London: Seattle Mountaineers, 1996). For more on Benton MacKaye, see Larry Anderson, *Benton MacKaye: Conservationist, Planner, and Creator of the Appalachian*

Trail (Baltimore: Johns Hopkins University Press, 2002). For the first New York Regional Plan see David A. Johnson, *Planning the Great Metropolis: The 1929 Regional Plan and Its Environs* (London: Taylor and Francis, 1995). Bill McKibben's environmental anthology concludes with an excellent chronology of the American environmental movement; *American Earth*, 977–1003. A fine overview of the literature of environmental studies is Lawrence Buell, *Writing for an Endangered World: Literature, Culture, and Environment in the U.S. and Beyond* (Cambridge, MA: Harvard University Press, 2001).

25 Aldo Leopold, *A Sand County Almanac* (1949), repr. McKibben, *American Earth*, 277.

26 Henry George, Jr., *Progress and Poverty: An Inquiry into the Cause of Industrial Depressions and of Increase of Want with Increase of Wealth* (New York: E. P. Dutton, 1879).

27 Alan R. Nettles, "Standing for Environmentalists: Sierra Club v. Morton," *Urban Law Annual* 6 (1973): 379–386.

28 Carson, *Silent Spring*, 244.

29 George Perkins Marsh, *Man and Nature: Or, Physical Geography as Modified by Human Action* (1864; ed. David Lowenthal, Cambridge, MA: Harvard University Press, 1965; repr. Seattle: University of Washington Press, 2003), 3.

30 Marsh, *Man and Nature*, 5. Prior to Marsh, Alexis de Tocqueville observed that Americans "do not see the marvelous forests surrounding them until they begin to fall beneath the axe," marching "through wildernesses, drying up marshes, diverting rivers, peopling the wilds, and subduing nature." Alexis de Tocqueville, *Democracy in America*, ed. J. P. Mayer and Max Lerner, trans. George Lawrence (1835, 1840; New York: Harper and Row, 1966), 485.

3 Interpreting America's Anti-Urban Bias

Josiah Strong, *The Challenge of the City* (New York: American Baptist Home Mission Society, 1907), 61.

Lewis Mumford, "Regions—to Live In," *Survey* 54 (1925), 151–152.

Simon and Garfunkel, "El Condor Pasa," recorded November 1968, Track 2 on *Bridge over Troubled Water* (New York: Columbia, 1970).

Barbara Kingsolver, *Small Wonder* (New York: HarperCollins, 2002), 38.

1 Donald Culross Peattie, *The Road of a Naturalist* (London: Readers Union / Robert Hale, 1948), 101.

2 Quoted in Walter Isaacson, *Leonardo da Vinci* (New York: Simon and Schuster, 2017), 25. The sentence ends a Leonardo fable in which a rock on a hillside, looking down on a city, rolls down to join in the fun but, amid the tumult, regrets its decision.

3 Irving Lewis Allen, ed., *New Town and the Suburban Dream: Ideology and Utopia in Planning and Development* (London: Kennikat Press, 1977), 23.

4 Charles Dickens, *Barnaby Rudge: A Tale of the Riots of 'Eighty and Hard Times: For These Times* (London: Chapman and Hall, 1858), 223.

5 Thomas Jefferson, "Query 19: The Present State of Manufactures, Commerce, Interior and Exterior Trade," in *Notes on the State of Virginia,* ed. William Peden (Chapel Hill: University of North Carolina Press, 1954), quoted in A. Whitney Griswold, "The Agrarian Democracy of Thomas Jefferson," *American Political Science Review* 40, no. 4 (1946): 657–681, 668.

6 Roger G. Kennedy, *Mr. Jefferson's Lost Cause: Land, Farmers, Slaves and the Louisiana Purchase* (New York: Oxford University Press, 2003), 53.

7 *The Writings of Thomas Jefferson,* ed. Andrew A. Lipscomb and Albert Ellery Bergh (Washington, DC: Thomas Jefferson Memorial Association, 1903), 75.

8 Henry David Thoreau, "Sounds," in *Walden; or, Life in the Woods* (1854; Boston: Houghton Mifflin, 1893), 181.

9 Josiah Strong, *Our Country: Its Possible Future and Its Present Crisis,* ed. Jurgen Herbst (1888; Cambridge, MA: Harvard University Press, 1963), 172.

10 Interpretations of the Bible have been a frequent source of anti-urban thought. Millennialism and "end of times" predictions, dating back to the colonial arrival of religious groups, anticipated a return to paradise.

11 Steve Johnson, *The Ghost Map: The Story of London's Most Terrifying Epidemic and How It Changed Science, Cities, and the Modern World* (New York: Riverhead Books, 2006), 90.

12 From Bryan's "Cross of Gold" speech. Quoted in Louis W. Koenig, *A Political Biography of William Jennings Bryan* (New York: G. P. Putnam's Sons, 1971), 197.

13 Henry James, *The American* (New York: Scribner's, 1907), 45.

14 Louis H. Sullivan, *Kindergarten Chats and Other Writings* (1918; New York: George Wittenborn, 1979), 112.

15 Andrew Nelson Lytle, "The Hind Tit," in *I'll Take My Stand: The South and the Agrarian Tradition* (1930; Baton Rouge: Louisiana State University Press, 1977), 203.

16 Louis D. Rubin, Jr., "Introduction," in *I'll Take My Stand,* xxx.

17 Gloria L. Cronin and Ben Siegel, eds., *Conversations with Robert Penn Warren* (Jackson:: University Press of Mississippi, 2005), 20.

18 Morton White and Lucia White, *The Intellectual versus the City* (Cambridge, MA: Harvard University Press, 1962), 11.

19 Stephen Diamond, *What the Trees Said: Life on a New Age Farm* (New York: Dell, 1971), 69.

20 Benton MacKaye, *The New Exploration: A Philosophy of Regional Planning* (New York: Harcourt, Brace, 1928), 24.

21 David Schuyler, *The New Urban Landscape: The Redefinition of City Form in Nineteenth-Century America* (Baltimore: Johns Hopkins University Press, 1986), 25.

22 Roger A. Salerno, "Imagining the Urban Poor: Poverty and the Fear of Cities," in *Fleeing the City: Studies in the Culture and Politics of Antiurbanism,* ed. Michael J. Thompson, 139–160 (New York: Palgrave Macmillan, 2009).

23 Steven Conn, *Americans against the City: Anti-Urbanism in the Twentieth Century* (Oxford: Oxford University Press, 2014).

24 Quoted in James L. Machor, *Pastoral Cities: Urban Ideals and the Symbolic Landscape of America* (Madison: University of Wisconsin Press, 1987), 3.

25 Lewis Mumford, "Utopia, the City and the Machine," in *Utopias and Utopian Thought,* ed. Frank E. Manuel (Boston: Houghton Mifflin, 1965), 3.

26 Michel Cowan, *City of the West: Emerson, America, and Urban Metaphor* (New Haven, CT: Yale University Press, 1967), 30–31.

4 The Small Town as an Ideal

Ross Rymer, "Back to the Future: Disney Reinvents the Company Town," *Harper's Magazine,* 293, no. 1757, October 1996, 65–78.

Richard L. Lingeman, *Small Town America: A Narrative History, 1620 to the Present* (New York: Houghton Mifflin, 1980), 481. A wealth of such literature exists, divided equally between sentimental and condescending views of small-town life.

1 Eduardo Porter, "Abandoned America," *New York Times,* December 16, 2018, Ideas, 1. See also Richard C. Longworth, *Caught in the Middle: America's Heartland in the Age of Globalism* (New York: Bloomsbury, 2008). For a different point of view, see Catherine Tumber, *Small, Gritty, and Green: The Promise of America's Smaller Industrial Cities in a Low-Carbon World* (Cambridge, MA: MIT Press, 2012). Tumber challenges this "metropolitan bias" and makes a case for the renewed relevance of the smaller industrial city.

2 William Bradford, *Of Plimouth Plantation,* Book 1, chapter XI. Cited in Bill McKibben, ed., *American Earth: Environmental Writing since Thoreau* (New York: Library of America, 2008), 978; and in Jedediah Purdy, *After Nature: A Politics of the Anthropocene* (Cambridge, MA: Harvard University Press, 2015), 51.

3 Lingeman, *Small Town America,* 29.

4 Alan Emmett, *So Fine a Prospect: Historic New England Gardens* (Hanover, NH: University Press of New England, 1996), 43.

5 Emily Talen, ed., *Charter of the New Urbanism,* 2nd ed. (New York: McGraw Hill, 2013). The preamble was originally prepared in 1991 as the Ahwahnee Principles at a conference held at the Ahwahnee Hotel in Yosemite National Park. The conference was organized by a nonprofit California Government Commission interested in smarter land-use guidelines. Participants included Peter Calthorpe, Michael Corbett, Andrés Duany, Elizabeth Moule, Elizabeth Plater-Zyberk, Stefanos Polyzoides, and Daniel Solomon. These people became the leaders of the Congress for the New Urbanism that was formally established in 1993. Judy Corbett and Michael Corbett were additional early activists, with Judy playing an important role in writing, editing, and disseminating the Ahwahnee Principles.

6 Victor Dover and John Massengale, *Street Design: The Secret to Great Cities and Towns* (Hoboken, NJ: Wiley, 2014). Dover and Massengale describe how to wrest the design of streets away from engineers concerned only with moving cars.

7 Michael Pollan, "Town Building Is No Mickey Mouse Matter," *New York Times Magazine,* December 14, 1997, 56–63, 76, 80–81, 88.

8 Rymer, "Back to the Future."

9 "It's a Small Town, After All: Celebration, Florida," *Economist,* November 25, 1995, 27–28.

10 Douglas Frantz and Catherine Collins, *Celebration, U.S.A.: Living in Disney's Brave New Town* (New York: Henry Holt, 1999), 35.

11 Andrew Ross, *The Celebration Chronicles: Life, Liberty, and the Pursuit of Property Value in Disney's New Town* (New York: Ballentine Books, 1999), 318.

12 "Disney Is Selling a Town to Reflect the Past," *New York Times,* January 16, 2004. A decade later roof leaks and mold exposed faulty construction; "There Is Little Celebration in the Town Disney Built," *Wall Street Journal,* November 16, 2016.

13 Lewis Mumford, *Sticks and Stones: A Study in American Architecture and Civilization,* 2nd rev. ed. (1924; New York: Dover, 1955), 9.

14 Thorstein Veblen, "The Country Town," *The Freeman,* July 11, 1923, 417–420, quoted in Sidney Plotkin, "Veblen's Localism and Its Ambiguities," in *The Anthem Companion to Thorstein Veblen,* ed. Sidney Plotkin (London: Anthem Press, 2017), 221.

15 Harlan Paul Douglass, *The Little Town: Especially in Its Rural Relationships* (New York: Macmillan, 1919), 244.

16 Nicole Godek, "About Love Small Town America," http://www.lovesmalltownamerica .com/aboutus.php.

17 SteelCityRising (blogger) post, City-Data.com forum, February 15, 2008, http://www .city-data.com/forum/general-u-s/257149-most-popular-subdivision-names-plantation -suburban-3.html#ixzz4NprpLzLP.

18 Page Smith, *As a City upon a Hill: The Town in American History* (Cambridge, MA: MIT Press, 1966), 3. The first eight chapters of John Reps, *The Making of Urban America: A History of City Planning in the United States* (Princeton, NJ: Princeton University Press, 1965) provide a good overview of the early Puritan settlements and how these differed from European towns, other colonist groups, and the Southern plantation tradition.

19 From John Winthrop's famous 1630 sermon "A Model of Christian Charity," preached while he was still aboard the *Arbela* on its way to the New World. Winthrop was alluding to Jesus's "Sermon on the Mount" in Matthew 5:14 which contains these lines: "You are the light of the world. A city that is set on a hill cannot be hidden."

20 David Handlin, *The American Home: Architecture and Society, 1815–1915* (Boston: Little Brown, 1979), 96.

21 Sinclair Lewis, *Main Street* (New York: Harcourt, Brace and Howe, 1920), 325.

22 Sinclair Lewis, *Main Street*, 265.

23 Thomas J. Campanella, *The Republic of Shade: New England and the American Elm* (New Haven: Yale University Press, 2003).

24 Lynn Nesmith, "The Power of Place," *Southern Living,* September 1997.

25 "Front Porch Fosters Neighborly Charm," *Boston Globe,* August 18, 1996, 1; "Front Porch Shooting Kills One," *Boston Globe,* August 19, 1996, 15.

26 New Urbanists gradually began to address the broader categories of their charter, including involvement with existing cities and environmental stewardship. Proponents now feature vernacular aesthetics somewhat less, and measurable data more. A good example is Jeff Speck, *Walkable City: How Downtown Can Save America, One Step at a Time* (New York: Farrar, Straus and Giroux, 2012).

5 The Company Town Away from Town

Thomas Bender, *Community and Social Change in America* (Baltimore, MD: Johns Hopkins University Press, 1978), 78–79.

Stanley Buder, *Pullman: An Experiment in Industrial Order and Community Planning, 1880–1930* (New York: Oxford University Press, 1967), 42.

Oliva Allen-Price and Mina Kim, "A Sneak Peek at Apple's New Cupertino Headquarters," KQED News, last modified February 15, 2015, https://www.kqed.org/news/10430660.

1 Seth Fiegerman, "Facebook's Glamorous New Headquarters Will Make You Hate Your Cubicle," Mashable website, March 31, 2015, https://mashable.com/2015/03/31/facebook-new-headquarters-photos.

2 Alexander Hamilton, *The Papers of Alexander Hamilton,* ed. Harold C. Syrett (New York: Columbia University Press, 1966), vol. 10, 230–340.

3 Excellent overviews of the American company town include: John Coolidge, *Mill and Mansion: A Study of Architecture and Society in Lowell, Massachusetts, 1820–1865* (New York: Columbia University Press, 1942); Margaret Crawford, *Building the Workingman's Paradise: The Design of American Company Towns* (New York: Verso, 1995); John S. Garner, *The Model Company Town: Urban Design through Private Enterprise in Nineteenth-Century New England* (Amherst: University of Massachusetts Press, 1984); John W. Reps, *Town Planning in Frontier America* (Columbia: University of Missouri Press, 1980).

4 Barbara M. Tucker and Samuel Slater, *The Origins of the American Textile Industry, 1790–1860* (Ithaca, NY: Cornell University Press, 1984). Historians tend to honor Slater and Lowell as the fathers of the American Industrial Revolution. Tucker and Slater also describe how, while cotton came from southern plantations, much of the coarse cotton fabrics produced in places like Lowell returned to the South to clothe slaves, who tended to call their coarse cottons "Lowell."

5 Alexander Hamilton, "Report on the Subject of Manufactures," December 5, 1791, https://founders.archives.gov/documents/Hamilton/01-10-02-0001-0007.

6 Ella, "The Window Darkened," in *The Lowell Offering,* Vol. 5 (Lowell, MA: Misses Curtis and Farley, 1845), 265.

7 John W. Reps, *The Making of Urban America: A History of City Planning in the United States* (Princeton, NJ: Princeton University Press, 1965), 415.

8 Quoted in Charles Cowley, *A History of Lowell, 1868* (North Charlestown, SC: Createspace, 2017), 134.

9 For more on Lowell since its postindustrial era, including its designation as the first urban national historic park, see Cathy Stanton, *The Lowell Experiment: Public History in a Postindustrial City* (Amherst: University of Massachusetts Press, 2006).

10 Theodore Weicker, *A Practical Journal of Pharmacy, Materia Medica, and Chemistry,* vol. 6 (New York: Merck and Company, 1897), 393.

11 For a thorough account of the events and preceding and following the Pullman riots see Lindsey Almont, *The Pullman Strike* (Chicago: University of Chicago, 1942).

12 Buder, *Pullman,* 42–43.

13 "Greenstone UMC History," Greenstone United Methodist Church, https://greenstoneun itedmethodistchurchchicago.wordpress.com/history/. The minister, the Rev. William H. Carwardine, is quoted in "The Parable of Pullman," Illinois Labor History Society, http:// www.illinoislaborhistory.org/labor-history-articles/the-parable-of-pullman. A Pullman employee is also quoted: "We are born in a Pullman house, fed from the Pullman shops,

taught in the Pullman school, catechized in the Pullman Church, and when we die we shall go to the Pullman Hell."

14 Raymond A. Mohl and Neil Betten, "The Failure of Industrial City Planning: Gary, Indiana, 1906–1910," *Journal of the American Institute of Planners* 38, no. 4 (1972): 203–214.

15 "General Motors Technical Versailles," *Architectural Forum* 104 (May 1956), 122–129.

16 "General Motors Technical Center," *Architectural Forum* 101, no. 5 (November 1954), 100, http://www.usmodernist.org/AF/AF-1954-11.PDF.

17 Louise A. Mozingo, *Pastoral Capitalism: A History of Suburban Corporate Landscapes* (Cambridge, MA: MIT Press, 2011), 72–86.

18 A full account of greater Boston's Route 128 has yet to be written, but an excellent brief history is found in Yanni Tsipis and David Kruh, *Building Route 128: Images of America* (Portsmouth, NH: Arcadia Publishing, 2003).

19 Deere & Company's chairman in the mid-1950s, William Hewitt, requested that the headquarters "should be thoroughly modern in concept but should not give the effect of being especially sophisticated or glossy. Instead, they should be more 'down-to-earth' and rugged." Mozingo, *Pastoral Capitalism,* 122.

20 The article continued: "the so-called Spheres will serve as a haven of carefully tended nature geared to letting Amazonians break free from their cubicles and think disruptive thoughts. It's an internet-era, Pacific Rim answer to the architecturally astounding gardens set up by European monarchs during the Enlightenment era." Angel Gonzalez, "Amazon's Spheres: Lush Nature Paradise to Adorn $4 Billion Urban Campus," *Seattle Times,* January 3, 2017. I am a principal in NBBJ, the architectural firm that designed Amazon's new headquarters, though I was not personally involved with the project.

21 Eliot Brown, "Casualty of Cities' Resurgence: The Suburban Offices Left Behind," *Wall Street Journal,* January 13, 2016.

22 Nelson D. Schwartz, "Why Corporate America Is Leaving the Suburbs for the City," *New York Times,* August 1, 2016.

23 In November of 2018, Amazon announced its decision to split the much promised HQ2 into two, the locational winners being Arlington, Virginia bordering Washington, DC, and the Queens Borough of New York City. By February 2019, Amazon reversed its decision to locate in New York following protests from citizens and political leaders about the extent of promised public subsidies to Amazon.

6 "Grace Dwelling in It"

Virginia McAlester, Willis Winters, and Prudence Mackintosh, *Great American Suburbs: The Homes of the Park Cities, Dallas* (New York: Abbeville Press, 2008), 15.

1   Yi-Fu Tuan, *Topophilia: A Study of Environmental Perception, Attitudes and Values* (Englewood Cliffs, NJ: Prentice-Hall, 1974), 225.

2   James Howard Kunstler, *The City of Man: Notes on the Urban Condition* (New York: Simon and Schuster, 2001), 11.

3   David Schuyler, *The New Urban Landscape: The Redefinition of City Form in Nineteenth-Century America* (Baltimore: Johns Hopkins University Press, 1986), 152.

4   Richard Guy Wilson, "Idealism and the Origin of the First American Suburb: Llewellyn Park, New Jersey," *American Art Journal*, 11, no. 4 (1979): 79–90, 83.

5   F. L. Olmsted and Calvert Vaux, *Preliminary Report upon the Proposed Suburban Village at Riverside, Near Chicago* (New York: Sutton, Bowne and Co., Printers, 1868), 262.

6   James L. Machor, *Pastoral Cities: Urban Ideals and the Symbolic Landscape of America* (Madison: University of Wisconsin Press, 1987), 171.

7   Adna F. Weber, *The Growth of Cities in the Nineteenth Century* (New York: Macmillan for Columbia University, 1899), 475.

8   Weber, *Growth of Cities,* 474.

9   Ebenezer Howard, *Garden Cities of Tomorrow,* ed. with a Preface by F. J. Osborn and Introductory Essay by Lewis Mumford (1898; Cambridge, MA: MIT Press, 1965).

10   William E. Smythe, *City Homes on Country Lanes: Philosophy and Practice of the Home in the Garden* (New York: Macmillan, 1921), 58–59.

11   Lewis Mumford, *The City in History: Its Origins, Its Transformations, and Its Prospects* (New York: Harcourt Brace Jovanovich, 1961), 485–486.

12   J. K. Galbraith, *The Age of Uncertainty* (Boston: Houghton Mifflin, 1977), 316.

13   David Handlin, *The American Home: Architecture and Society, 1815–1915* (Boston: Little Brown, 1979), 11.

14   Daniel J. Boorstin, *The Americans: The Democratic Experience* (New York: Random House, 1973), 267.

15   Robert Fishman, *Bourgeois Utopias: The Rise and Fall of Suburbia* (New York: Basic Books, 1987), 3–38.

16   Kenneth T. Jackson, *Crabgrass Frontier: The Suburbanization of the United States* (New York: Oxford University Press, 1985), 12; John R. Stilgoe, *Borderlands: Origins of the American Suburb, 1820–1939* (New Haven: Yale University Press, 1988).

17   Robert A. Stern, David M. Fishman, and Jacob Tilove, *Paradise Planned: The Garden Suburb and the Modern City* (New York: Monacelli Press, 2013).

18   Stern, Fishman, and Tilove., *Paradise Planned,* 957.

19 Andrew Jackson Downing, *The Architecture of Country Houses* (New York: D. Appleton, 1852), v.

20 Letter of Edward D. Page, March 24, 1916, quoted in Mrs. Herbert Barry, ed., *Pageant in Honor of the One Hundredth Anniversary of the Birth of Llewellyn S. Haskell, Founder of Llewellyn Park* (Orange, New Jersey, 1916), 18. Cited in Wilson, "Idealism," 85. A few years later, Sinclair Lewis put the phrase "all these long-haired men and short-haired women" into his *Main Street* character Kennicott's mouth, railing against their antiwar sentiments and general lack of patriotism.

21 Olmsted and Vaux, *Preliminary Report,* 27–28.

22 Julius K. Hunter, *Westmoreland and Portland Places: The History and Architecture of America's Premier Private Streets, 1888–1988* (Columbia: University of Missouri Press, 1988), 9.

23 Waldon Fawcett, "Roland Park, Baltimore, Maryland: A Representative American Suburb," *House & Garden* 3, no. 4 (1903), 180.

24 Fawcett, "Roland Park," 190–191.

25 Samuel Howe, "Town Planning on a Large Scale," *House Beautiful,* October 1914, 135.

26 Quoted in Susan L. Klaus, *A Modern Utopia: Frederick Law Olmsted Jr. and the Plan for Forest Hills Gardens* (Amherst: University of Massachusetts Press, 2002), 31.

27 Frederick Law Olmsted, Jr., "A Suburban Town Built on Business Principles," *New Boston,* January 1911, 395. See two contemporaneous articles by Grosvenor Atterbury, the principal architect of Forest Hills Gardens: "Forest Hills Gardens, Long Island: An Example of Collective Planning, Development and Control," *The Brickbuilder* 21 (January–December 1912), 317–318; and Grosvenor Atterbury, "Model Towns in America," *Scribner's Magazine* 52, no. 1 (July 1912), 20–35.

28 John Keats, *The Crack in the Picture Window* (New York: Houghton-Mifflin, 1957). Reviewers of the novel saw shades of George Orwell's dystopian *1984* in its depiction of suburbia's "little boxes" fronted by picture windows as easy to peer into as to gaze out of.

29 Robert D. Putnam, *Bowling Alone: The Collapse and Revival of American Community* (New York: Simon and Schuster, 2000). Putnam postulates several causes for an increase in civic disengagement, and concludes that sprawl "cannot account for more than a small fraction of the decline, for civic disengagement is perfectly visible in smaller towns and rural areas as yet untouched by sprawl" (215).

30 David Brooks, "For Democrats, Time to Meet the Exurban Voter," *New York Times,* November 10, 2002, 3.

31 The first Earth Day was held in 1970. See also Rachel Carson, *Silent Spring* (New York: Fawcett Crest, 1962); Ian McHarg, *Design with Nature* (New York: National History Press, 1969); Donella H. Meadows, Jorgen Randers, and William W. Behrens III, *The*

Limits to Growth: A Report for the Club of Rome's Project on the Predicament of Mankind (New York: Signet, 1972). Real Estate Research Corporation, *The Costs of Sprawl in Detailed Cost Analysis* (Washington, DC: US Government Printing Office, 1974).

32 A good primer is Howard Frumkin, Lawrence Frank, and Richard Jackson, *Urban Sprawl and Public Health: Design, Planning and Building for Healthy Communities* (Washington, DC: Island Press, 2004).

33 Three recent, and premature, predictions about the demise of the suburb can be found in Leigh Gallagher, *The End of the Suburbs: Where the American Dream Is Moving* (New York: Penguin Books, 2013); Joel S. Hirschhorn, *Sprawl Kills: How Blandburbs Steal Your Time, Health and Money* (New York: Sterling and Ross, 2005); and Alan Ehrenhalt, *The Great Inversion and the Future of the American City* (New York: Vintage Books, 2013).

34 Lawrence A. Herzog, *Global Suburbs: Urban Sprawl from the Rio Grande to Rio de Janeiro* (New York: Routledge, 2015).

7 Seeding Settlement

Hamilton S. Wicks, "The Opening of Oklahoma," *The Cosmopolitan: A Monthly Illustrated Magazine,* Vol. 7 (May–October 1889), 465–468.

1 Richard L. Lingeman, *Small Town America: A Narrative History, 1620–The Present* (New York: Putnam, 1980), 103.

2 Historians now tend to credit another editor, John Babsone Lane Soule, with coining the famous phrase. "Go West, Young Man, Go West" appeared in his *Terre Haute Express* in 1851. Horace Greeley's use of it, in the *New York Tribune* in 1865, is certainly what made it famous. See Coy F. Cross, *Go West, Young Man: Horace Greeley's Vision for America* (Albuquerque: University of New Mexico Press, 1995); and Henry Nash Smith, *Virgin Land: The American West as Symbol and Myth* (Cambridge, MA: Harvard University Press, 1970). Smith's widely read and cited book tended to cement the attribution to Greeley.

3 William Gilpin, *Mission of the North American People, Geographical, Social and Political* (Philadelphia: J. B. Lippincott, 1873), 125. Also see Smith, *Virgin Land,* 35–43.

4 John O'Sullivan, "Annexation," *United States Magazine and Democratic Review* 17 (1845), 5–6, 9–10; and John L. O'Sullivan, "The True Title," *Morning News* [New York], December 27, 1845. See also Julius W. Pratt, "The Origin of 'Manifest Destiny,'" *American Historical Review* 32, no. 4 (1927), 795–798.

5 Edward T. Price, *Dividing the Land: Early American Beginnings of Our Private Property Mosaic* (Chicago: University of Chicago Press, 1995).

6 Charles A. Grymes, "Acquiring Virginia Land by Headright," *Virginia Places* (website), http://www.virginiaplaces.org/settleland/headright.html.

7   Roy M. Robbins, *Our Landed Heritage: The Public Domain, 1776–1936* (Lincoln: University of Nebraska Press, 1976), 3. Also see Adam Smith, *An Inquiry into the Nature and Causes of the Wealth of Nations,* ed. S. M. Soares (MetaLibra Digital Library, May 29, 2007), 442, https://www.ibiblio.org/ml/libri/s/SmithA_WealthNations_p.pdf.

8   Heather Cox Richardson, *The Greatest Nation of the Earth: Republican Economic Policies during the Civil War* (Cambridge, MA: Harvard University Press, 1997); Charles Plante and Roy H. Mattison, "The 'First' Homestead," *Agricultural History* 36, no. 4 (1962), 183; and Robbins, *Our Landed Heritage.*

9   Allen Ray Billington, *The Frontier Thesis: Valid Interpretation of American History?* (New York: Holt Rinehart and Winston, 1966), 121.

10 Trina Williams Shanks, "The Homestead Act: A Major Asset-Building Policy of American History," in *Inclusion in the American Dream: Assets, Poverty, and Public Policy,* ed. Michael Sherraden (New York: Oxford University Press, 2005), 20–41.

11 Smith, *Virgin Land,* 165–200.

12 John T. Schlebecker, *Whereby We Thrive: A History of American Farming, 1607–1972* (Ames: Iowa State University Press, 1975).

13 Smith, *Virgin Land,* 171–194.

14 Newton Everett Dick, *The Lure of the Land: A Social History of the Public Lands from the Articles of Confederation to the New Deal* (Lincoln: University of Nebraska Press, 1970), 216–217.

15 Justin Smith Morrill, "The Educational Fund" (speech, United States Senate, Washington, DC, April 26, 1876), Congressional Globe Printing Office, 10.

16 Stephen E. Ambrose, *Nothing Like It in the World: The Men Who Built the Transcontinental Railroad, 1863–1869* (New York: Simon and Schuster, 2000), 17. Ambrose further concludes: "Next to winning the Civil War and abolishing slavery, building the first transcontinental railroad from Omaha, Nebraska to Sacramento, California was the greatest achievement of the American people in the nineteenth century."

17 The actual amount of land granted to railroads continues to be debated. According to one account, "The acreage to which the railroads actually received title appears in the annual reports of the Commissioner of the General Land Office, the latest such report showing a total of 131,350,534 acres. . . . In addition to Federal land grants, it is estimated that railroads received from the states grants totaling 48,883,372 acres." Robert S. Henry, "The Railroad Land Grant Legend in American History Texts," *Mississippi Valley Historical Review* 32, no. 2 (1945): 171–194.

18 Ambrose, *Nothing Like It in the World,* 377. Written as popular history, Ambrose's account has been criticized for some inaccuracies by other historians.

19 David Schuyler, *The New Urban Landscape: The Redefinition of City Form in Nineteenth-Century America* (Baltimore: Johns Hopkins University Press, 1986), 24.

20 Richard C. Wade, *The Urban Frontier: Pioneer Life in Early Pittsburgh, Cincinnati, Lexington, Louisville and St. Louis* (Chicago: University of Chicago Press, 1972), 1.

8 Making Nature Urbane

Olmsted, Vaux & Co., "Observations on the Progress of Improvements in Street Plans, with Special Reference to the Parkway Proposed to Be Laid Out in Brooklyn" (1868), in S. B. Sutton, ed., *Civilizing American Cities: A Selection of Frederick Law Olmsted's Writings on City Landscape* (Cambridge, MA: MIT Press, 1971), p. 40.

Edward Kern, Edward. "He Saw Democracy in Dirt: America Rediscovers Frederick Olmsted, the Genius Who Designed Our Greatest Parks," *Life,* December 8, 1972, 80–87.

1 George William Curtis, "Editor's Easy Chair," *Harper's New Monthly Magazine* 11, no. 61 (June 1855): 123–132, 125, https://archive.org/details/harpersnew11harper/page/n137.

2 Frederick Law Olmsted, "The Beginnings of Central Park: A Fragment of Autobiography 1877," in Olmsted, *Landscape into Cityscape,* ed. Albert Fein (Ithaca, NY: Cornell University Press, 1967), 52.

3 Albert Fein, *Frederick Law Olmsted and the American Environmental Tradition* (New York: George Braziller, 1972). Witold Rybczynski, *A Clearing in the Distance: Frederick Law Olmsted and America in the Nineteenth Century* (New York: Scribner, 1999), covers Olmsted's earlier career as a journalist in the pre–Civil War South and his role in the establishment of the US Sanitary Commission.

4 Before the germ theory of disease became generally accepted in the 1880s, "miasmas" were believed to be induced by a range of moral, climatic, and environmental factors, especially in urban contexts.

5 Frederick Law Olmsted, *Public Parks and the Enlargement of Towns* (Cambridge, MA: American Social Science Association / Riverside Press, 1870), 22.

6 Olmsted, *Landscape into Cityscape,* 8; Geoffrey Blodgett, "Frederick Law Olmsted: Landscape Architecture as Conservative Reform," *Journal of American History* 62, no. 4 (1976), 875.

7 Richard E. Foglesong, *Planning the Capitalist City: The Colonial Era to the 1920s* (Princeton, NJ: Princeton University Press, 1986); "Parks and Park Planning," 89–123.

8 There have been skeptics—including, surprisingly, Jane Jacobs: "And once people begin looking at nature as if it were a nice big St. Bernard dog for the children, what could be more natural than the desire to bring this sentimental pet into the city too, so the city might get some nobility, purity and beneficence by association? . . . It is no accident that we Americans, probably the world's champion sentimentalizers about nature, are at one and the same time probably the world's most voracious and disrespectful destroyers of

wild and rural countryside." Jane Jacobs, *The Death and Life of Great American Cities* (New York: Random House, 1961), 445–446.

9   Jane Addams, *Twenty Years at Hull House 1910* (New York: New American Library, 1960), 27.

10 Frederick Law Olmsted, *Forty Years of Landscape Architecture: Central Park 1928*, ed. Frederick Law Olmsted, Jr., and Theodora Kimball (Cambridge, MA: MIT Press, 1973), 46.

11 Olmsted, *Civilizing American Cities*, 80.

12 Francis R. Kowsky, *The Best Planned City in the World: Olmsted, Vaux, and the Buffalo Park System* (Amherst: University of Massachusetts Press, 2013); Cynthia Zaitzevski, *Frederick Law Olmsted and the Boston Park System* (Cambridge, MA: Harvard University Press, 1982).

13 Andrew Jackson Downing, *Rural Essays* (1853; repr. Miami: Hard Press, 2017), 157.

14 F. L. Olmsted, "The Little Parks," (letter to the editor), *Express*, October 17, 1886. Quoted in Kowsky, *The Best Planned City in the World*, 134.

15 As Boston's Emerald Necklace was being completed, advocates for a regional necklace of parks and an open space conservation program, led by Charles Eliot and Sylvester Baxter, persuaded the Massachusetts legislature to establish the Trustees of Public Reservations in 1891. Land assembly around the periphery of Boston ensued, with the Olmsted firm, then led by Olmsted Jr. and Eliot, leading the planning for a metropolitan park system. Today, the Boston Metropolitan Park System oversees more than ten thousand acres of park, recreation, and conservation areas, while the present Trustees of Reservations—the world's oldest regional land trust—holds twenty-seven thousand acres (and counting) open to the public.

16 Olmsted's colossal stature often overshadows other important contemporaneous planners, designers, collaborators, rivals, and champions. One of these was George Kessler. For more on Kessler, see Kurt Culbertson, "George Edward Kessler: Landscape Architect of the American Renaissance," in *Midwestern Landscape Architecture*, ed. W. H. Tishler (Urbana: University of Illinois Press, 2000).

17 William H. Wilson, *The City Beautiful Movement in Kansas City* (Columbia: University of Missouri Press, 1964).

18 George E. Kessler, "The Kansas City Park System and Its Effect on the City Plan," in *Proceedings of the Ninth National Conference on City Planning, Kansas City* (1917), 106–116.

19 Kessler, "Kansas City Park System."

20 Horace W. S. Cleveland, *The Public Grounds of Chicago: How to Give Them Character and Expression* (Chicago: Charles D. Lacky, 1869), 6.

21 Charles Waldheim, *The Landscape Urbanism Reader* (New York: Princeton Architecture Press, 2006); and Waldheim, *Landscape as Urbanism: A General Theory* (Princeton, NJ: Princeton University Press, 2016). Among other prominent practitioners / theorists of the movement are James Corner, Nina-Marie Lister, Chris Reed, and Mohsen Mostafavi.

22 William N. Pierson Jr., *American Buildings and Their Architects: Technology and the Picturesque, the Corporate and the Early Gothic Styles* (New York: Doubleday, 1980), 15.

23 George G. Byron, *The Poetical Works of Lord Byron with Memoir and the Original Explanatory Notes* (London: Frederick Warne and Co., 1891), 211.

24 Aaron Betsky, "The High Line Effect: Are Our New Parks Trojan Horses of Gentrification?" *Metropolis* 36, no. 5 (December 2016): 76–79.

9 Utopians and Reformers in a Cauldron of Urbanization

Edward Bellamy, *Looking Backward: 2000–1887* (New York: New American Library, 1960), 43.

William Dean Howells, *The Altrurian Romances* (Bloomington, IN: Indiana University Press, 1968), originally published as "A Traveller from Altruria" in a series of essays for *Cosmopolitan* magazine in 1892–1893 and first assembled in book form by Harper and Brothers in 1894.

1 Richard Guy Wilson, *The American Renaissance: 1876–1917* (New York: Pantheon Books, 1979).

2 Kenneth M. Roemer, *The Obsolete Necessity: American in Utopian Writings 1888–1900* (Kent, OH: Kent State University Press, 1976), 2–3.

3 Henry George, Jr., *Progress and Poverty: An Inquiry in the Cause of Industrial Depressions and of Increase of Want with Increase of Wealth* (New York: E. P. Dutton and Company, 1879). Henry Demarest Lloyd, *Wealth against Commonwealth* (New York: Harper and Brothers, 1894). Helen Campbell, *Prisoners of Poverty: Women Wage-Workers, Their Trades and Their Lives* (1887; New York: Leopold Classic Library, 2015). John L. Thomas, *Alternative America: Henry George, Edward Bellamy, Henry Demarest Lloyd and the Adversary Tradition* (Cambridge, MA: Harvard University Press, 1983).

4 Elisabeth Hansot, *Perfection and Progress: Two Modes of Utopian Thought* (Cambridge, MA: MIT Press, 1974).

5 Richard L. Lingeman, *Small Town America: A Narrative History, 1620–The Present* (New York: Putnam, 1980), 312.

6 The US Census determined that the population in 1890 was 62,979,766 and grew to 76,212,168 by the 1900 Census.

7   Carl S. Smith, *Chicago and the American Literary Imagination 1880–1920* (Chicago: University of Chicago Press, 1984), 141.

8   "A Plan to Put All the World's Fair Exposition Exhibits under One Roof," *Chicago Tribune,* March 9, 1890, 11; reproduced in Titus M. Karlowizc, "D. H. Burnham's Role in the Selection of Architects for the World's Columbian Exposition," *Journal of Architectural Historians* 23, no. 3 (1970): 247–254, 250.

9   William Dean Howells, "Letter II," *Letters of an Altrurian Traveller, 1893–94* (Gainesville, FL: Scholars' Facsimiles & Reprints, 1961): 20-34, 34.

10 Henry Adams, *The Education of Henry Adams: An Autobiography* (Boston: Houghton Mifflin, 1918), 343.

11 Quoted in David F. Burg, *Chicago's White City of 1893* (Lexington: University Press of Kentucky, 1976), 342.

12 Bellamy, *Looking Backward,* 165.

13 Bellamy, *Looking Backward,* 53.

14 Bellamy, *Looking Backward,* 71.

15 Bellamy, *Looking Backward,* 220.

16 Quentin Fotrell, "America's 20 Richest People Have More Money Than These 152 Million People," MarketWatch, December 5, 2015.

17 William H. Jordy, *American Buildings and Their Architects: Progressive and Academic Ideals at the Turn of the Twentieth Century* (New York: Doubleday, 1972), 373.

18 Robert Fogelson, *The Fragmented Metropolis: Los Angeles 1850–1930* (Cambridge, MA: Harvard University Press, 1968), 138–139.

19 Charles Mulford Robinson, *Modern Civic Art: Or the City Made Beautiful* (New York: G. P. Putnam's Sons, 1903), 3.

20 Loring Underwood, "The City Beautiful the Ideal to Aim At," in *The American City* 2, no. 5 (May 1910): 214–218, 214.

21 Jacob A. Riis, *How the Other Half Lives: Studies among the Tenements of New York* (New York: Charles Scribner's Sons, 1890; New York: Penguin Books, 1997).

22 Much of what was called muckraking during the Progressive Era would be hailed today as investigative journalism; it was the work of skeptical writers willing to expose and criticize corruption in governance, industry, and other institutions. The muckrakers found especially eager buyers for their work among popular periodicals such as *McClure's Magazine,* published from 1893 to 1929.

23 Jane Addams, "The Subjective Necessity of Social Settlements," in *Philanthropy and Social Progress: Seven Essays,* with an introduction by Professor Henry C. Adams (New York: Thomas Y. Crowell and Company, 1893), 7.

24 Jane Addams, *Twenty Years at Hull House* (New York: New American Library, 1960), 88.

25 Addams, *Twenty Years,* 92.

26 W. D. Howells, "A Traveller from Altruria: XII," *Cosmopolitan* 15, no. 6 (October 1893): 738–749, 739. As in Bellamy's future Boston, the ambiance throughout Altruria is pastoral, almost suburban. In a later Howells series, called "Through the Eye of the Needle" (1907), the same emissary to America describes village life as the actual Altrurian ideal. In a premonition of post–World War II urban America, the Altrurians often hear "that the population of such or such a capital has been reduced so many hundreds or thousands since the last census." A further dispersion of the population was always welcomed by the Altrurians, who were lovers of the simple life.

27 Howells, "A Traveller from Altruria: XII," 739.

28 Howells, "A Traveller from Altruria: XII," 739–740.

29 Howells, "Letter II," *Letters of an Altrurian Traveller,* 22.

10 Washington

Hugh T. Taggart, *Old Georgetown: District of Columbia* (Lancaster, PA: New Ear Printing, 1908), 98. I owe my introduction to the history of Washington, DC, to my first planning teacher, John W. Reps, who had then recently published *Monumental Washington: The Planning and Development of the Capital Center* (Princeton, NJ: Princeton University Press, 1967). He soon followed with *Washington on View: The Nation's Capital since 1790* (Chapel Hill: University of North Carolina Press, 1991). The following account owes a debt to Professor Reps, and his still invaluable studies of our nation's capital, and American cities overall.

1 Eric H. Monkkonen, *America Becomes Urban: The Development of U.S. Cities and Towns, 1790–1980* (Berkeley: University of California Press, 1990), 1.

2 Anne Mackin, *Americans and Their Land: The House Built on Abundance* (Ann Arbor: University of Michigan Press, 2006), 74.

3 Mackin, *Americans and Their Land,* 73–75.

4 Saul K. Padover, ed., *Thomas Jefferson and the National Capital* (Washington, DC: Government Printing Office, 1946), 42–43.

5 Reps, *Monumental Washington,* 4–5.

6 Debate over the location, scale, and prominence of the capital is found in Andrea Wulf, *Founding Gardeners: The Revolutionary Generation, Nature, and the Shaping of the American Nation* (New York: Alfred A. Knopf, 2011), 124–153.

7 Reps, *Washington on View,* 18–19. Thomas Jefferson to George Washington, April 10, 1791, National Archives Founders Online, https://founders.archives.gov/documents/Washington/05-08-02-0058.

8   Reps, *Washington on View,* 16.

9   Fredrick Gutheim and Antoinette J. Lee, *Worthy of the Nation: Washington DC from L'Enfant to the National Capital Planning Commission,* 2nd ed. (Washington, DC: National Planning Capital Commission, 2006), 78.

10 James L. Machor, *Pastoral Cities: Urban Ideals and the Symbolic Landscape of America* (Madison: University of Wisconsin Press, 1987), 109.

11 Wikipedia offers quite an exhaustive overview of Benjamin Banneker's life and impact, including the *Almanac* that he published between 1792 and 1797. With regard to Jefferson's complex relationship to slavery and the "negro race" see Annette Gordon-Reed and Peter S. Onuf, *Most Blessed of the Patriarchs: Thomas Jefferson and the Empire of the Imagination* (New York: Liveright Publishing, 2016).

12 Reps, *Washington on View,* 20. *Celebration of the One Hundredth Anniversary of the Establishment of the Seat of Government in the District of Columbia,* comp. William V. Cox (Washington DC: Government Printing Office, 1901), 240.

13 Thomas Moore, "To Thomas Hume, Esq. MD, from the City of Washington." The stanza is as reproduced by Ainsworth R. Spofford, in "The Coming of the White Man, and the Founding of the National Capital," in *Celebration of the One Hundredth Anniversary of the Establishment of the Seat of Government in the District of Columbia,* comp. William V. Cox (Washington DC: Government Printing Office, 1901), 240. Moore's poem was repeatedly revised and published in different forms after he sent his initial hundred-line version to Hume.

14 Thomas Twining, *Travels in America 100 Years Ago: Being Notes and Reminiscences* (1894; New York: Hard Press Publishing, 2013), 100.

15 Reps, *Monumental Washington,* 41.

16 Arthur S. Hardy, "Last Impressions," *The Cosmopolitan* 16, no. 2 (December 1893), 195.

17 The group was formally titled the Senate Park Commission, and generally known as the McMillan Commission. Its recommendations were published in 1902 as *The Improvement of the Park System of the District of Columbia,* with Part I being the Report of the Senate Committee on the District of Columbia and Part II being the Report of the Park Commission. Charles Moore is credited as "editor" but is likely the primary author.

18 Gutheim and Lee, *Worthy of the Nation,* 116.

19 A brief overview of the McMillan Plan process is found in Norman T. Newton, *Design on the Land: The Development of Landscape Architecture* (Cambridge, MA: Harvard University Press, 1971), 400–412.

20 Thomas E. Luebke, ed., *Civic Art: A Centennial History of the U.S. Commission of Fine Arts* (Washington, DC: U.S. Commission of Fine Arts, 2013). In particular see the essay by Pamela Scott, "The Improvement of Washington City: Charles Moore and Washing-

ton's Monumental Core," 84–93. The work of the Commission of Fine Arts continues. In 2012 I was appointed by President Obama to serve on the seven-member commission.

21 *Report of the Senate Park Commission* (Washington, DC: Federal Printing Office, 1902).

22 Kermit L. Hall and Kevin T. McGuire, eds., *Institutions of American Democracy: The Judicial Branch* (New York: Oxford University Press, 2005).

23 Reps, *Monumental Washington,* 136.

24 *Extending the Legacy: Planning America's Capital for the 21st Century* (Washington, DC: National Capital Planning Commission, 1997); *Anacostia Waterfront Framework Plan* (Washington, DC: District of Columbia, Office of Planning, 2003). My firm, at that time called Chan Krieger Sieniewicz, Architecture & Planning, was commissioned by the Office of Planning to undertake the plan and was one of the coauthors of the Anacostia Waterfront Framework Plan.

11 Chicago 1910

Carl Sandburg, "Chicago," (1914), Poetry Foundation webpage, https://www .poetryfoundation.org/poetrymagazine/poems/12840/chicago.

1 James Gilbert, *Perfect Cities: Chicago's Utopias of 1893* (Chicago: University of Chicago Press, 1993). In addition to the Columbian Exposition and the town of Pullman, Gilbert presents a third Chicago "utopia" at the nineteenth century's end, which he calls the "Evangelical Metropolis," 169–207. Led by preacher Dwight Moody, founder of the Moody Bible Institute, a town called Harvey was modeled on Pullman but intended to be an Evangelical haven and a model for Christian values.

2 Sandburg, *Chicago.*

3 Lincoln Steffens, *The Shame of the Cities, 1904* (Mineola, NY: Dover, 2004), 163–165.

4 Upton Sinclair, *The Jungle* (1906; New York: Penguin Classics, 1989).

5 Eugene Debs, *What's the Matter with Chicago? His Life, Writings, and Speeches* (Chicago: Charles H. Kerr and Company, 1908), 319–324.

6 Mark Twain, *Life on the Mississippi* (1883), quoted in Scott Cohn, *It Happened in Chicago* (Guilford, CT: Morris Book Publishing, 2009), 133.

7 Kenneth T. Jackson, "The Capital of Capitalism: The New York Metropolitan Region, 1890–1940," in *Metropolis,* ed. Anthony Sutcliffe (Chicago: University of Chicago Press, 1984), 312.

8 William Cronon, *Nature's Metropolis: Chicago and the Great West* (New York: W. W. Norton, 1991).

9 John Brinkerhoff Jackson, *American Space: The Centennial Years: 1865–1876* (New York: W. W. Norton, 1972), 86.

10   Harold M. Mayer and Richard C. Wade, *Chicago: Growth of a Metropolis* (Chicago: University of Chicago Press, 1969); Constance Green, "Chicago, the Railroad Center," in *American Cities in the Growth of the Nation,* 100–128 (London: John DeGraff, 1957); Theodore J. Karamanski, "People and the Port," The Encyclopedia of Chicago website, n.d., http://www.encyclopedia.chicagohistory.org/pages/300010.html.

11   For a concise account of the fascinating, complicated, and controversial history of the demise of LA's early twentieth century transit system, see Cecilia Rasmussen, "Did Auto, Oil Conspiracy Put the Brakes on Trolleys? *Los Angeles Times,* March 23, 2003, https://www.latimes.com/me-2003-los-angeles-streetcar-history-story.html.

12   Paul Johnson, *A History of the American People* (New York: HarperCollins, 1997), 571.

13   Dominic A. Pacyga, *Chicago: A Biography* (Chicago: University of Chicago Press, 2009), 139.

14   Union Stock Yard and Transit Company of Chicago, *History of the Yards, 1865–1953* (Chicago: Chicago Union Stock Yards, 1953), https://babel.hathitrust.org/cgi/pt?id =uiuo.ark:/13960/t6rx9d37p;view=1up;seq=9; J'Nell L. Pate, *America's Historic Stock-yards: Livestock Hotels* (Fort Worth: Texas Christian University Press, 2005); Robert A. Slayton, *Back of the Yards: The Making of a Local Democracy* (Chicago: University of Chicago Press, 1986).

15   Jackson, *American Space,* 72.

16   Harold M. Mayer and Richard C. Wade, *Chicago: Growth of a Metropolis* (Chicago: University of Chicago Press, 1969), 92–97.

17   Donald L. Miller, *City of the Century: The Epic Chicago and the Making of America* (New York: Simon and Schuster, 1997), 125.

18   Henry Ward Beecher, *Eyes and Ears* (Boston: Ticknor and Fields, 1862), 99–100.

19   James Parton, *Triumphs of Enterprise, Ingenuity, and Public Spirit* (New York: Virtue and Yorston, 1871), 55.

20   Cronon, *Nature's Metropolis,* 310.

21   Horace William Shaler Cleveland, *The Public Grounds of Chicago: How to Give Them Character and Expression* (1869; London: Forgotten Books, 2018), 11–15.

22   Bonj Szczygiel and Robert Hewitt, "Nineteenth-Century Medical Landscapes: John H. Rauch, Frederick Law Olmsted, and the Search for Salubrity," *Bulletin of the History of Medicine* 74, no. 4 (2000), 708–734.

23   Lois Wille, *Forever Open, Clear and Free: The Historic Struggle for Chicago's Lakefront* (Chicago: Regnery, 1972; Chicago: University of Chicago Press, 1991). The "Map of Chicago and Additions, 1836" is in the possession of the Chicago Historical Society and can be viewed at http://www.encyclopedia.chicagohistory.org/pages/10636.html.

24   Wille, *Forever Open,* xxi.

25 Daniel H. Burnham and Edward H. Bennett, *Plan of Chicago* (Chicago: Commercial Club, 1909), 90.

26 Burnham and Bennett, *Plan of Chicago,* 121.

27 Burnham and Bennett, *Plan of Chicago,* 2.

28 Burnham and Bennett, *Plan of Chicago,* 119.

29 Burnham and Bennett, *Plan of Chicago,* 121.

30 Charles W. Eliot, "A Study of the New Plan of Chicago," *Century,* January 1910, 417–431.

31 Carl Smith, *The Plan of Chicago: Daniel Burnham and the Remaking of the American City* (Chicago: University of Chicago Press, 2006), 34.

32 Walter D. Moody, *Wacker's Manual of the Plan of Chicago, Municipal Economy: Especially Prepared for Study in the Schools of Chicago* (Chicago: Chicago Plan Commission, 1913), 133–134.

33 Moody, *Wacker's Manual,* 18.

34 Miller, *City of the Century,* 17. In a terrific history of twentieth-century Chicago, Thomas Dyja writes: "As New York positioned itself on the global stage and Hollywood polished the nation's fantasies, the most profound aspects of American modernity grew up out on the flat, prairie land next to Lake Michigan." Thomas Dyja, *The Third Coast: When Chicago Built the American Dream* (New York: Penguin Press, 2013), xxiii.

35 Walter J. Marshall, *Through America: Nine Months in the United States* (London: Sampson Low, Marston, Searle, and Rivington, 1882), 93.

12 Autopia: The Drive to Disperse

William H. Whyte, "Urban Sprawl," one of Whyte's final essays in *Fortune,* reprinted in *The Exploding Metropolis,* ed. Editors of *Fortune* (Garden City, NY: Doubleday, 1958); and in Whyte, *The Essential William H. Whyte,* ed. Albert LaFarge (New York: Fordham University Press, 2000), 123. Whyte is credited with the popularization of the word "sprawl" as a pejorative description of the suburban landscape.

Dr. Seuss, *Oh, the Places You'll Go* (New York: Random House, 1990).

1 John Keats, *The Insolent Chariots* (Philadelphia: J. P. Lippincott, 1958), 13. The title was apparently inspired by a Lewis Mumford phrase.

2 John Keats, *The Crack in the Picture Window,* illus. Don Kindler (Boston: Houghton Mifflin, 1956), 3.

3 Alan Trachtenberg, *Brooklyn Bridge, Fact and Symbol* (New York: Oxford University Press, 1965), 21.

4   Walt Whitman, *Songs for the Open Road,* ed. Paul Negi (Mineola, NY: Dover, 1990), 1. I recalled Whitman's famous poem while listening to a 2016 Volvo commercial that begins with a baritone narrator reciting these very lines.

5   Seuss, *Oh, the Places You'll Go!*

6   James Howard Kunstler, *The Geography of Nowhere: The Rise and Decline of America's Man-Made Landscape* (New York: Simon and Schuster, 2001), 216.

7   Frank Lloyd Wright, *Modern Architecture: Being the Kahn Lectures for 1930* (Princeton, NJ: Princeton University Press, 1931), 101.

8   Wright, *Modern Architecture,* 91. Wright would also quip: "The outcome of the cities will depend on the race between the automobile and the elevator, and anyone who bets on the elevator is crazy."

9   Frank Lloyd Wright, *The Disappearing City* (New York: William Farquhar Payson, 1932), 30.

10 Frank Lloyd Wright, *When Democracy Builds* (Chicago: University of Chicago Press, 1945), 61. This is the second of three virtually identical texts published between 1933 and 1958 in support of his Broadacre plan.

11 Stephen Grabow, "Frank Lloyd Wright and the American City," *Journal of the American Institute of Planners* 43, no. 2 (1977), 118.

12 Robert Fishman, *Bourgeois Utopias: The Rise and Fall of Suburbia* (New York: Basic Books, 1987), 123.

13 Jonathan Barnett, "Rethinking Wright," *Architectural Forum,* 136, no. 5 (1972): 42–46, 45.

14 Martin Meyerson, "Utopian Traditions and the Planning of Cities," in *The Future Metropolis,* ed. Lloyd Rodwin (New York: George Braziller, 1961), 245.

15 Henry George, *Progress and Property* (1879; New York: Robet Schalkenbach Foundation, 1981), 451.

16 John Adolphus Etzler, *The Paradise within the Reach of All Man, without Labor, by Powers of Nature and Machinery: An Address to All Intelligent Men* (London: John Brooks, 1833).

17 H. G. Wells, "The Diffusion of Great Cities," *Population and Development Review* 34, no. 4 (2008): 769–775. Wells wrote an admiring review of the New York World's Fair and particularly its City of 1960 Futurama Exhibit. H. G. Wells, "World of Tomorrow," *New York Times,* World's Fair Section, March 5, 1939, 4–5.

18 Kelly Kazek, "Could Muscle Shoals Have Been a Hub Rivaling Detroit? Henry Ford Thought So," Alabama.com website, January 17, 2013, http://www.al.com/living/index .ssf/2013/01/post_89.html. See also Alvin Rosenbaum. Usonia: Frank Lloyd Wright's Design for America (Washington: Preservation Press, 1993); Muscle Shoals Commission, *Muscle Shoals: A Plan* (Washington, DC: U.S. Government Printing Office, 1931).

19 Frank Lloyd Wright, *The Essential Frank Lloyd Wright: Critical Writings on Architecture* (Princeton: Princeton University Press, 2010), 247. George R. Collins, "Broadacre City: Wright's Utopia Reconsidered," in *Four Great Makers of Modern Architecture: Gropius, Le Corbusier, Mies van der Rohe, Wright* (New York: Columbia University Press, 1963), 71.

20 Today's comparison may be the greater use of drones by farmers to survey large agricultural acreage.

21 James J. Flink, *The Car Culture* (Cambridge, MA: MIT Press, 1975), 39. Thomas Conyngton, "Motor Carriages and Street Paving," *Scientific American* 48, no. 1266 suppl. (1899).

22 Flink, *Car Culture,* 12–13. Another good source is Tom Lewis, *Divided Highways: Building the Interstate Highways, Transforming American Life* (New York: Penguin Books, 1997).

23 Owen D. Gutfreund, *20th-Century Sprawl: Highways and the Reshaping of the American Landscape* (New York: Oxford University Press, 2004), 9.

24 Katharina Fullerton Gerould, "San Francisco Revisited," *Harpers Monthly,* July 1924, 187–202.

25 Gutfreund, *20th-Century Sprawl,* 26.

26 Stephen B. Goddard, *Getting There: The Epic Struggle between Road and Rail in the American Century* (New York: Basic Books, 1994), in particular Chapter 7, "Derailing the Trolleys."

27 Ludwig Hilberseimer, *The Nature of Cities; Origin, Growth, and Decline, Pattern and Form, Planning Problems* (Chicago: Paul Theobald, 1955), 192.

28 "From 1955 to 2015: Disneyland's Autopia in *The 'E' Ticket,*" Walt Disney Family Museum blog, posted July 8, 2015, reprint of article "Autopia," *The "E" Ticket* 27 (Summer 1997), https://waltdisney.org/blog/1955-2015-disneylands-autopia-e-ticket.

29 National Academy of Engineering, *The Competitive Status of the US Auto Industry* (Washington, DC: National Research Council, 1982), 10. In 2017, Bureau of Labor statistics showed that slightly over seven percent of American jobs were linked in some way to the manufacturing and retailing of automobiles.

30 Sigfried Giedion, *Space, Time and Architecture: The Growth of a New Tradition* (Cambridge, MA: Harvard University Press, 1941), 826–827.

31 Reyner Banham, *Los Angeles: The Architecture of Four Ecologies* (Berkeley: University of California Press, 1971), 213. See also David Brodsly, *L.A. Freeway, An Appreciative Essay* (Berkeley: University of California Press, 1983).

32 Joan Didion, *Play It as It Lays* (New York: Farrar, Straus and Giroux, 1972), 98.

33 Jane Holtz Kay, *Asphalt Nation: How the Automobile Took Over America and How We Can Take It Back* (New York: Crown, 1997), 13.

34   Gutfreund, *20th-Century Sprawl,* 7.

35   "There is a thrill in meeting a demand with a product no one else can meet." William Levitt, quoted in his obituary in the *New York Times,* January 29, 1994, 26.

36   To be sure, these postwar benefits were far more accessible for whites than nonwhites. By one recent account, "of the first 67,000 mortgages secured by the G.I. Bill for returning veterans in New York and northern New Jersey alone, fewer than 100 were taken out by non-whites." Brandon Weber, "How African American WWII Veterans Were Scorned By the G.I. Bill," *The Progressive,* November 10, 2017.

37   Ernest B. Furgurson, "The Highway 'Trust' Fund," *Baltimore Sun,* March 21, 1973. Beginning in the 1970s with our nation's capital committing to its Metrorail, over twenty American cities with little transit history, including Dallas and Phoenix, have invested in some form of public transit.

38   Robert Bruegmann, *Sprawl: A Compact History* (Chicago: University of Chicago Press, 2005).

13 Communitarian Journeys

David Grayson, "Adventures in Contentment," *American Magazine* 63, no. 1 (November 1906), 29–36, 31.

1   Stephen Diamond, *What the Trees Said: Life on a New Age Farm* (New York: Delacorte Press), 6.

2   Martin Dobrow, "Marshall Bloom's Liberation Search Ended Alone in a Field," *Daily Hampshire Gazette,* 2016, https://www.gazettenet.com/Looking-for-liberation-finding -loss-2432454.

3   Many histories have been written of America's communitarian journeys. For example, see: Donald E. Pitzer, ed., *America's Communal Utopias* (Chapel Hill: University of North Carolina Press, 1997); Dolores Hayden, *Seven American Utopias: The Architecture of Communitarian Socialism* (Cambridge, MA: MIT Press, 1976).

4   Quoted in Richard L. Lingeman, *Small Town America: A Narrative History, 1620–the Present* (New York: Putnam 1980), 483.

5   David Grayson, "Adventures in Contentment," *American Magazine* 64, no. 6 (October 1907) : 646–650, 647. The work was serialized across a number of issues.

6   The passage is from the Mormon Doctrine and Covenants. Charles L. Sellers, "Early Mormon Community Planning," *Journal of the American Institute of Planning* 28, no. 1 (1962): 24–30, 24.

7   Thomas Jefferson, letter to Constantin François de Chasseboeuf Volney, February 8, 1805, Papers of Thomas Jefferson, National Archives, https://founders.archives.gov

/documents/Jefferson/99-01-02-1123. Jefferson was specifically referring to a plan he had outlined for the expansion of New Orleans, recently acquired in the Louisiana Purchase. For discussion, see John W. Reps, "Thomas Jefferson's Checkerboard Towns," *Journal of the Society of Architectural Historians* 20, no. 3 (1961): 108–114, 109.

8 Pitzer, *America's Communal Utopias,* 153.

9 Karl J. Arndt, *George Rapp's Harmony Society, 1785–1847* (Rutherford, NJ: Fairleigh Dickinson University Press, 1965); Arthur E. Bestor Jr., *Backwoods Utopias: The Sectarian Origins and the Owenite Phase of Communitarian Socialism in America, 1663–1829* (Philadelphia: University of Pennsylvania Press, 1950); Carl J. Guarneri, *The Utopian Alternative: Fourierism in Nineteenth-Century America* (Ithaca, NY: Cornell University Press, 1991); John F. C. Harrison, *Quest for the New Moral World: Robert Owen and the Owenites in Britain and America* (New York: Scribner's, 1969); John Humphrey Noyes, *History of American Socialisms, 1870* (New York: Dover, 1966).

10 For a good overview of Owen's "Vision for Society" see Harrison, *Quest.*

11 For more on Fourier, see Noyes, *History of American Socialisms.*

12 Albert Brisbane, *Social Destiny of Man or Association and Reorganization of Industry* (Philadelphia: C. F. Stollmeyer, 1840).

13 Sterling F. Delano, *Brook Farm: The Dark Side of Utopia* (Cambridge, MA: Harvard University Press, 2004).

14 Quoted in Ralph Borsodi, *Flight from the City: The Story of a New Way to Family Security* (New York: Harper and Brothers, 1933), xiv.

15 Ralph Borsodi, Oliver Edwin Baker, and Millburn Lincoln Wilson, *Agriculture in Modern Life* (New York: Harper and Brothers, 1939), 191–192.

16 Ralph Borsodi, *Flight from the City.* Toward the end of the book, Borsodi quotes a person who wrote to him in admiration of his writing: "In some respects our situation is ideal. Although it takes less that fifteen minutes to reach the city, we are far enough out to hear the coyotes now and then. We enjoy (more than I thought possible) the attractions of the city along with the peace and freedom of the desert. I think this type of community will be more and more popular in the future. As yet no house is closer than a quarter mile to us, yet we have all the essential conveniences of the city such as electricity for light, power, and heating; telephone, daily newspaper services, all kinds of city delivery such as ice, coal, milk, laundry, and the like" (130–131).

17 "Dr. Ralph Borsodi," The Plowboy interview by Carolyn Kimsey, *Mother Earth News,* #26, March / April 1974, https://soilandhealth.org/wp-content/uploads/0303critic/Brsdi .intrvw/The%20Plowboy-Borsodi%20Interview.htm. See also Edwin C. Hagenstein, Sara M. Gregg, and Brian Donahue, *American Georgics: Writings on Farming, Culture, and the Land* (New Haven, CT: Yale University Press, 2011), 204.

18 Helen and Scott Nearing spent decades living simply, first in New Hampshire and then at their Good Life Center in rural Maine. Via numerous publications and by welcoming many visitors to the Good Life Center (which continues to be operated by volunteers) they championed the "Back to the Land" and "Simple Living" movements. See Helen Nearing and Scott Nearing, *The Good Life: Helen and Scott Nearing's Sixty Years of Self-Sufficient Living* (repr. New York: Schocken Books, 1990).

19 Joni Mitchell, "Big Yellow Taxi," on *Ladies of the Canyon* (Burbank, CA: Reprise, 1970).

20 Hayden, *Seven American Utopias,* 321.

21 Arcosanti was Paolo Soleri's effort to achieve "Arcology," an architecture and urbanism based on ecology. See the feature-length biographical documentary *The Vision of Paolo Soleri: Prophet in the Desert,* dir. Lisa Scafuro, Mona Lisa Film Productions, 2013.

22 Noyes, *History of American Socialisms,* 26. This was one of the earliest histories written about socialist communities. Noyes was the founder of the Oneida community, which operated from 1848 until 1881. Among its unusual practices was the idea of complex marriage. Because raising children was considered a communal responsibility, members of the community could engage in consensual, nonmonogamous sex, but only for the purpose of bearing children. While Noyes is credited with coining the term "free love," his meaning was not the same as those using the term in the 1960s.

14 Misguided Renewal

42 US Code Section 1441, Congressional Declaration of National Housing Policy, July 15, 1949, accessible at Legal Information Institute, Cornell Law School, https://www.law.cornell.edu/uscode/text/42/1441.

1 Jane Jacobs, *The Death and Life of Great American Cities* (New York: Random House, 1961), 4.

2 Frederick Jackson Turner, *The Frontier in American History* (New York: H. Holt and Company, 1920), 200.

3 Historians have debated the virtues of Turner's frontier hypothesis for much of the twentieth century. Regarding the American West, see Ray Allen Billington, *Land of Savagery, Land of Promise: The European Image of the American Frontier* (New York: W. W. Norton, 1981).

4 Joel Garreau, *Edge City: Life on the New Frontier* (New York: Doubleday, 1991).

5 Jacobs, *Death and Life of Great American Cities,* 310. For more on Tugwell, see Bernard Sternsher, *Rexford Tugwell and the New Deal* (New Brunswick, NJ: Rutgers University Press, 1964), 337.

6 Tracy Campbell, *The Gateway Arch: A Biography* (New Haven: Yale University Press, 2013). Campbell argues that the primary motivation of city leaders was not to celebrate

Jefferson, the Louisiana Purchase, or westward expansion, but rather to eliminate what was seen as a blighted area. It was believed that a park and monument, funded and maintained by the federal government, would increase nearby property values and limit the spread of slums.

7   Richard Rothstein, *The Color of Law* (New York: Liveright / Norton, 2017).

8   Rothstein, *Color of Law,* 78.

9   John F. Kennedy, "News Release on Conference on Urban Affairs, from the Democratic National Committee Publicity Division, Washington, DC," October 20, 1960, American Presidency Project, https://www.presidency.ucsb.edu/documents/news-release-conference-urban-affairs-from-the-democratic-national-committee-publicity. For discussion, see Jennifer S. Light, *The Nature of Cities: Ecological Visions and the American Urban Professions, 1920–1960* (Baltimore: Johns Hopkins Press, 2009), 1.

10   Eliel Saarinen, *The City: Its Growth, Its Decay, Its Future* (1943; Cambridge, MA: MIT Press, 1965), 147–149.

11   Russell Baker, "The Great Paver," *New York Times,* February 7, 1963.

12   Marion Massen, David Engel, Sone A. Takahara, Elleen Kelly, Hope Marindin, Joseph L. Falkson, and Ray Hay, eds., *Building the American City: National Commission on Urban Problems* (Washington, DC: US Government Printing Office, 1969), 81.

13   A vast literature critical of urban renewal exists. Two excellent sources are Martin Anderson, *The Federal Bulldozer* (Cambridge, MA: MIT Press, 1964); and John F. Bauman, Roger Biles, and Kristin M. Szylvian, *From Tenements to the Taylor Homes: In Search of an Urban Housing Policy in Twentieth Century America* (University Park: Pennsylvania State University Press, 2000).

14   "A Handbook on Urban Redevelopment for Cities in the United States," Federal Housing Administration, Washington, DC, November 1941, https://catalog.hathitrust.org/Record/000341192, v.

15   Martin Millspaugh and Gurney Breckenfeld, *The Human Side of Urban Renewal,* ed. Miles L. Colean (New York: Ives Washburn, 1958), ix.

16   Marshall Berman, *All That Is Solid Melts into Air: The Experience of Modernity* (New York: Simon and Schuster, 1982), 294.

17   Robert A. Caro, *The Power Broker: Robert Moses and the Fall of New York* (New York: Random House, 1974). Chapter 25, "Changing," summarizes the various highway, recreation, and housing projects undertaken under Moses's direction, and includes a gallery of photographs, 499–575.

18   Marshall, *All That Is Solid,* 294.

19   Walter Gropius, *Rebuilding Our Communities* (Chicago: Paul Theobald, 1945), 26.

20 Michelle Young, "Lincoln Center: From Dutch Enclave and Notorious San Juan Hill to a Thriving Cultural Center," *6SqFt* website, November 9, 2016, https://www.6sqft.com /tag/history-of-lincoln-center. See also Edgar B. Young, *Lincoln Center: The Building of an Institution* (New York: New York University Press, 1980).

21 The section on Boston's urban renewal era is largely based on Alex Krieger, "Experiencing Boston: Encounters with the Places on the Maps," in *Mapping Boston,* ed. Alex Krieger and David Cobb with Amy Turner (Cambridge, MA: MIT Press, 2001), 147–172. The "omelet" quote, often attributed to Joseph Stalin, has been traced to the eighteenth century.

22 Boston City Planning Board, *General Plan for Boston: Preliminary Report* (Boston: City of Boston Printing Department, 1950), 42–43.

23 Martin Wagner, "Der Neubau Der City," *Baurundschau* (Germany), no. 17/18, September 1948; William B. Greeley, ed., *The Boston Contest: A Master Program in the Metropolitan Area* (Boston, 1944).

24 Herbert Gans, *Urban Villagers: Group and Class in the Life of Italian-Americans* (New York: Free Press, 1982). This remains a definitive account of the West End transformation.

25 Robert Tayler, "The Roving Eye," *Boston Herald,* July 31, 1962. "It used to be easy with all the low life there, the crooked and noisome alleyways, the confusing clatter of tattoo parlors, gin mills and girlie shows, the human wreckage of the city washed onto its grimy shores. . . . Well that was the Scollay Square we knew and, if not precisely loved, put up with. Its death knell did not find us throbbing with nostalgia. Despite the yeasty vigor of its raffish throngs, the place was also mean-spirited, sour, brutish and nasty."

26 Krieger, *Mapping Boston,* 147–172.

27 John F. Bauman, Roger Biles, and Kristin Szylvian, *From Tenements to the Taylor Homes: In Search of an Urban Housing Policy in Twentieth Century America* (University Park: Pennsylvania State University Press, 2000). See also Lawrence L. Vale, *Purging the Poorest: Public Housing and the Design Politics of Twice-Cleared Communities* (Chicago: University of Chicago Press, 2013).

28 Vincent J. Cannato, "A Home of One's Own," *National Affairs* 3 (Spring 2010): 69–86, 72.

29 William M. Rowe and Harry L. Watson, *Chasing the American Dream: New Perspectives on Affordable Homeownership* (Ithaca, NY: Cornell University Press, 2007).

30 .William H. Whyte, Jr., ed., *The Exploding Metropolis* (Garden City, NY: Doubleday, 1958).

31 Glenn V. Fuguitt and James J. Zuiches, "Residential Preferences and Population Distribution," *Demography* 12, no. 3 (August 1975): 491–504, 493. Gallup has repeated the poll

since, most recently in 2018: Frank Newport, "Americans Big on Idea of Living in the Country," Gallup, December 7, 2018. https://news.gallup.com/poll/245249/americans -big-idea-living-country.aspx.

15 Walt Disney's EPCOT and the New Town Movement

Ralph Waldo Emerson, letter to Thomas Carlyle, October 30, 1840, in Charles Eliot Norton, ed., *The Correspondence of Thomas Carlyle and Ralph Waldo Emerson, 1834–1872, Vol. I* (London: Chatto and Windus, 1883). Emerson was referring to the scores of communitarian socialist communities being founded at that time.

1 Press Conference on the "Florida Project," Walt Disney's original E.P.C.O.T, November 14, 1965, State of Florida Archives Library, https://www.youtube.com/watch?v =PrGH84BvoNY.

2 Housing and Urban Development Act of 1970 (subsequently renamed National Urban Policy and New Community Development Act of 1970), Public Law 91–609, December 31, 1970, 84 Stat. 1770–1817, 42 U.S.C. § 4501. The phrases here are in Title VII: Urban Growth and New Community Development, 1796. For an overview of Federal housing policies see Richard Rothstein, *The Color of Law: A Forgotten History of How Our Government Segregated America* (New York: W. W. Norton, 2017); Lawrence J. Vale, *Purging the Poorest: Public Housing and the Design Politics of Twice-Cleared Communities* (Chicago: University of Chicago Press, 2013); Frederick Steiner, *The Politics of New Town Planning: The Newfields, Ohio Story* (Columbus: Ohio University Press, 1980).

3 Eleanore Carruth, "Private Developers Are Making the Big Move to New Towns," *Fortune*, September 1971.

4 Ann Forsyth, *Reforming Suburbia: The Planned Communities of Irvine, Columbia, and The Woodlands* (Berkeley: University of California Press, 2005), 161. For the ideological roots of the American New Town Movement see Clarence Stein, *Toward New Towns for America* (Cambridge, MA: MIT Press, 1966).

5 Robert Mack, "This Disney Town Does Not Get Close to Walt's Dream of Utopia," *The Guardian,* January 7, 2011.

6 Neal Gabler, *Walt Disney: The Triumph of the American Imagination* (New York: Knopf, 2006), 627.

7 *Disneyland USA* [EPCOT, Florida Original Film], The Walt Disney Company, 1966, https://www.youtube.com/watch?v=sLCHg9mUBag. Produced for use with project partners and community leaders, the film was later made available to consumers as part of a DVD collection: *Walt Disney Treasures vol. 4: Tomorrow Land: Disney in Space and Beyond* (Walt Disney Studios Home Entertainment, 2004), Disc 2.

8 "History of Irvine Company," Irvine Company webpage, https://www.irvinecompany .com/about/history/.

9 *Celebration Chronicle* 1, no. 1 (Summer 1995), published by the Celebration Company, a subsidiary of The Walt Disney Company.

10 Kristina S. Alcorn, *In His Own Words: Stories from The Extraordinary Life of Reston's Founder, Robert E. Simon, Jr.* (GreatOwlBooks.com, 2016), 83.

11 Ian L. McHarg, *Design with Nature* (New York: Natural History Press, 1969). This is arguably the most pioneering planning publication of the 1960s, a passionate case for why quantifiable environmental factors should come first in the planning of any new community.

12 Kenneth T. Jackson, *Crabgrass Frontier: The Suburbanization of the United States* (New York: Oxford University Press, 1985), 33.

13 James Bailey, "Only in Columbia, the Next America," *Architectural Forum,* November 1967, 44–47. $5,000 in 1967 equals $38,000 in 2018.

14 William E. Smythe, *City Homes on Country Lanes: Philosophy and Practice of the Home in the Garden* (New York: Macmillan, 1921).

15 W. H. Whyte, Jr., *The Last Landscape* (New York: Doubleday, 1968), 256–257.

16 Fabulous and Commonplace

Time (cover headline), January 10, 1994.

Kathryn Hausbeck, "Who Put the 'Sin' in 'Sin City' Stories?" in Hall K. Rothman and Mike Davis, eds. *The Grit beneath the Glitter: Tales from the Real Las Vegas* (Berkeley, CA: University of California Press, 2002), 336.

Lewis Black, "Miami and Las Vegas," track 4, *White Album*, Stand Up! Records, 2000.

1 Hal Rothman, *Neon Metropolis: How Las Vegas Started the Twentieth-First Century* (New York: Routledge, 2003), xviii, xxviii.

2 Among the earliest admirers of the city's uniqueness were architects Robert Venturi and Denise Scott Brown. They set off with their Yale students to identify the innovations in form and symbolism of the architecture of the strip, and how these were heralding popular, commercial culture. Robert Venturi, Denise Scott Brown, and Steven Izenour, *Learning from Las Vegas: The Forgotten Symbolism of Architectural Form,* rev. ed. (1972; Cambridge, MA: MIT Press, 1977).

3 D. J. Waldie, *Holy Land: A Suburban Memoir* (New York: Norton, 1996), v.

4 The Culinary Union, with some 57,000 current members, has since 1935 helped over 750,000 hospitality workers and their families, many of them immigrants, achieve

middle-class lifestyles; the union has served an essential role in Las Vegas's becoming a gateway to the American Dream for many. Culinary Workers Union, Local 226, "History," http://www.culinaryunion226.org/union/history.

5 J. R. Moehringer, "Las Vegas: An American Paradox," *Smithsonian,* October 2010.

6 Lynn M. Zook, Alan Sandquist, and Carey Burke, *Las Vegas 1905–1965* (Charleston, SC: Arcadia Press, 2009), 9.

7 Michelle Ferrari and Stephen Ives, *Las Vegas: An Unconventional History* (New York: Bulfinch Press, 2005), 11.

8 Jeff Burbank, *Las Vegas Babylon: True Tales of Glitter, Glamour and Greed* (New York: M. Evans, 2005), 1–2.

9 "Las Vegas Visitor Statistics," Las Vegas Convention and Visitors Authority, https://www.lvcva.com/stats-and-facts/visitor-statistics/.

10 David Hickey, "Dialectical Utopias," *Harvard Design Magazine,* Winter / Spring 1998, http://www.harvarddesignmagazine.org/issues/4/dialectical-utopias.

11 Trip Gabriel, "From Vice to Nice: The Suburbanization of Las Vegas," *New York Times,* December 1, 1991. For an overview of the fascination / revulsion with Las Vegas during the 1960s in the writings of Hunter S. Thompson, Tom Wolfe, and others, see Marianne DeKoven, *Utopia Limited: The Sixties and the Emergence of the Postmodern* (Durham, NC: Duke University Press, 2004).

12 Gabriel, "From Vice to Nice."

13 Kurt Anderson, "Las Vegas: The New All-American City," *Time,* January 10, 1994, 42–51.

14 Interconnect Worldwide, "CityCenter Las Vegas" YouTube video uploaded by ARIA Resort and Casino Las Vegas, https://www.youtube.com/watch?v=hbnY2hx5zmM.

15 Paul Goldberger, "What Happens in Vegas: Can You Bring Architectural Virtue to Sin City?" *New Yorker,* October 4, 2010.

16 Michael Sorkin, *Some Assembly Required* (Minneapolis: University of Minnesota Press, 2001), 63.

17 Herbert Croly, *The Promise of American Life* (New York: Macmillan, 1911), 7.

17 New Orleans and Attachment to Place

Reuben Gold Thwaites, ed., *The Jesuit Relations and Allied Documents* (Cleveland: Burrows Brothers, 1901), Vol. 69, 205–217. See also Richard Campanella, *Bienville's Dilemma: A Historic Geography of New Orleans* (Lafayette: University of Louisiana at Lafayette, 2008), 79.

Captain J. E. Alexander, *Transatlantic Sketches, Comprising Visits to the Most Interesting Scenes in North and South America, and the West Indies, with Notes on Negro Slavery and Canadian Emigration, Vol. II* (London: Richard Bentley, 1833), 237.

Tom Piazza, *Why New Orleans Matters* (New York: HarperCollins, 2005), xx.

1 Albert Camus, "The Myth of Sisyphus" (1942), in Camus, *The Myth of Sisyphus and Other Essays,* trans. Justin O'Brien (New York: Vintage, 1955).

2 Ari Kelman, *A River and Its City: The Nature of Landscape in New Orleans* (Berkeley: University of California Press, 2003), xii.

3 Pierce L. Lewis, *New Orleans: The Making of an Urban Landscape* (Cambridge, MA: MIT Press, 1976), 17.

4 "Mississippi River Flood History 1543–Present," National Weather Service, https://www .weather.gov/lix/ms_flood_history.

5 John Schwartz, "New Orleans Is Fortified but Still in Peril from Floods," *Boston Globe,* February 25, 2018, A12.

6 See, for example, Timothy M. Kusky, "Time to Move to Higher Ground," *Boston Globe,* September 25, 2005, D12.

7 Richard Campanella, *Bienville's Dilemma: A Historic Geography of New Orleans* (Lafayette:, LA: University of Louisiana at Lafayette, 2008), 79. Campanella writes: "Frank assessment of the city's situation—geographic, economic, social or otherwise—leads some observers to conclude that, a century or two hence, historic New Orleans may end up a deltaic Harpers Ferry, occupied only by park rangers and concessionaires who tend to daily waves of tourists then lock up the visitors' center after the last shuttle boat leaves." (178).

8 Lewis, *New Orleans,* covers this topic well, noting that blacks typically occupied the swampy rear areas of blocks.

9 Campanella, *Bienville's Dilemma,* 333–334.

10 Bettina Aptheker, "Katrina and Social Justice," in *Hurricane Katrina: Response and Responsibilities,* ed. John Brown Childs (Berkeley, CA: North Atlantic Books, 2008), 48.

11 John M. Barry, *Rising Tide: The Great Mississippi Flood and How It Changed America* (New York, NY: Simon & Schuster, 1997) is the best historical account of the 1927 flood and its repercussions.

12 Bill Morrison, *The Great Flood* (New York: Icarus Films, 2013).

13 Haroon Siddique, "South Asia Floods Kill 1,200 and Shut 1.8 Million Children Out of School," *Guardian,* August 30, 2017.

14 David Wallace-Wells, *The Uninhabitable Earth: Life After Warming* (New York: Tim Duggan Books, 2019). Nathaniel Rich, *Losing Earth: A Climate History* (New York: Far-

rar, Straus & Giroux, 2019). See also a review of these by John Lanchester: "World on Fire," *New York Times Book Review*, April, 28, 2019.

15 Thomas Paine, *Common Sense,* ed. with an intro. by Issac Kramnick (1776; New York: Penguin Books, 1986), 43.

16 Hal Rothman, *Neon Metropolis: How Las Vegas Started the Twentieth-First Century* (New York: Routledge, 2003), 233.

18 E-topia: Smart Cities for the Creative Class

Anthony M. Townsend, *Smart Cities: Big Data, Civic Hackers, and the Quest for a New Utopia* (New York: W. W. Norton, 2013), 8. For a counterpoint see Edward Tenner, *The Efficiency Paradox: What Big Data Can't Do* (New York: Alfred A. Knopf, 2018). Tanner argues that the mistake being made by big data proponents is over-promoting efficiency algorithms as a substitute for human skill, intuition, and experience.

1 Readers may wish to follow the progress of a smart city project called Quayside in Toronto, a neighborhood under development to be equipped with sensors to monitor a broad array of systems. At this writing, the project is mired in controversy with citizens raising concerns about data privacy issues: Who will manage and control the data? (At present, the answer is a Google sister company called Sidewalk Labs.) Most important, who will have access to the data?

2 "MIT Faculty Approves New Urban Science Major," *MIT News,* June 5, 2018, http://news.mit.edu/2018/mit-faculty-approves-new-urban-science-major-0605.

3 Michael Batty, *The New Science of Cities* (Cambridge, MA: MIT Press, 2013).

4 William J. Mitchell, *E-Topia: Urban Life, Jim—But Not as We Know It* (Cambridge, MA: MIT Press, 1999), 155.

5 A veritable library has emerged promoting the triumph, genius, and happiness to be found in the city—and, oh, yes, predicting the end of the suburbs, too. For example: Leigh Gallagher, *The End of Suburbia: Where the American Dream Is Moving* (New York: Penguin Press, 2013); Leo Hollis, *Cities Are Good for You: The Genius of the Metropolis* (New York: Bloomsbury Press, 2013); and Charles Montgomery, *Happy City: Transforming Our Lives through Urban Design* (New York: Farrar, Straus and Giroux, 2013).

6 For an argument that the Millennial generation will not prove as committed to city life as many assume, see David Z. Morris, "Why Millennials Are About to Leave Cities in Droves," *Fortune,* March 28, 2016.

7 Katia Hetter, "Death of the Hipster, Rise of the 'Yuccie,'" CNN, June 10, 2015, http://www.cnn/2-15/06/1-/living/death-of-hipster-birth-of-yuccie-feat/index.html; Larry Finley, "The Ruppie Realm," *Chicago Sun Times,* September 10, 2006.

8   According to the US Census, by 2010, the number of households with children under eighteen was down to 20.2 percent. US Census Bureau, decennial censuses 1900–2010. See also US Census Bureau, State and County QuickFacts. A revealing account of various demographic shifts may be found in Alan Mallach, *The Divided City: Poverty and Prosperity in Urban America* (Washington, DC: Island Press, 2018).

9   International versions of suburbia are growing as rising middle classes are eager to emulate the American suburban experience. See Lawrence A. Herzog, *Global Suburbs: Urban Sprawl from the Rio Grande to Rio de Janeiro* (New York: Routledge, 2015).

10 Aristotle, *The Politics, Foundations of Political Thought,* ed. Steven Michels (New Haven, CT: Alden Ave. Press, 2015), 53.

11 Richard Florida became the foremost popularizer of this idea, exploring it across three books: *The Rise of the Creative Class* (New York: Basic Books, 2003); *Cities and the Creative Class* (New York: Routledge, 2004): *The Flight of the Creative Class: The New Global Competition for Talent* (New York: HarperCollins, 2007).

12 Richard Florida, *The New Urban Crisis: How Our Cities Are Increasing Inequality, Deepening Segregation, and Failing the Middle Class—and What We Can Do about It* (New York: Basic Books, 2017).

13 A mind-bending statistic appeared on the front page of the December 25, 2015, *Boston Globe*: "America's 20 wealthiest individuals are today worth as much as the bottom 152 million." Regarding growing inequality, see Joseph E. Stiglitz, *Rewriting the Rules of the American Economy: An Agenda for Growth and Shared Prosperity* (New York: W. W. Norton, 2015); and Stiglitz, *The Great Divide: Unequal Societies and What We Can Do about Them* (New York: W. W. Norton, 2015).

14 Lawrence J. Vale, *Purging the Poorest: Public Housing and the Design Politics of Twice-Cleared Communities* (Chicago: University of Chicago Press, 2013), 30.

15 Henri Lefebvre's *Le Droit a la Ville* was first published in 1968. Lefebvre sought a real and metaphysical access to urban life and the power to participate in its social changes. It remains a rallying cry for many urban theorists. See Don Mitchell, *The Right to the City: Social Justice and the Fight for Public Space* (New York: Guilford Press, 2003).

16 "Boston by the Numbers 2017," Boston Redevelopment Authority Research Division, December 2017, http://www.bostonplans.org/getattachment/ff4bf0fa-64ec-4b31-a417-044460018798.

17 Perry Stein, "City Adding 1,000 Residents per Month," *Washington Post,* December 24, 2015. Stein reports from the local census that, between 2010 and 2011, some ten thousand newcomers were in the Millennial age bracket, but only 2,662 Millennials arrived between 2013 and 2014.

18 Emily Badger, "Happy New Year! May Your City Never Become San Francisco, New York or Seattle—or Portland, Denver, Boston, Dallas, Houston or Los Angeles," *New York Times,* December 26, 2018.

19 Amanda Kolson Hurley, "Does America Still Want the American Dream?" *Atlantic,* October 9, 2015; Jonathan Hilburg, "Take That Amazon: New Jersey's Megamall Prepares a Water Park, Ski Slope, and *VICE* Food Hall for Launch," *Architects Newspaper,* August 23, 2018.

20 James Truslow Adams, *The Epic of America* (Boston: Little Brown, 1931), 214–215.

21 Joel Kotkin, "The People Designing Your Cities Don't Care What You Want. They're Planning for Hipsters," *Washington Post,* August 15, 2014.

22 Tom Toles, "The Plan." First published in the *Buffalo News* in 1998, this cartoon brilliantly captured the phenomenon of gentrification. He cast the "conspiracy" in terms of race, but the trend he describes has equal relevance to inequality. There is a wealth of research and critical discussion about the issues of urban gentrification and displacement, including in the mainstream press. For example, Aaron M. Renn, "Blue Politics, Black Exodus," *Dallas Morning News,* May 22, 2016; and Alan Mallach, *The Divided City,* which also discusses the shift of working-class and middle-class African American families from cities to suburbs (285).

23 Peter Moskowitz, *How to Kill A City: Gentrification, Inequality, and the Fight for the Neighborhood* (New York: Nation Books, 2017), 74, 181.

24 Stiglitz, *The Great Divide:* "An economic system that does not deliver for most citizens is one that is not sustainable for the long run" (299). Or, as Edward Luce puts it: "When groups fight over the fruits of growth, the rules of the political game are relatively easy to uphold. When those fruits of growth disappear, or are monopolized by a fortunate few, things turn nasty." Edward Luce, *The Great Retreat of Western Liberalism* (New York: Atlantic Monthly Press, 2017), 13.

19 Postscript

Joseph Priestley, *An Essay on the First Principles of Government, and on the Nature of Political, Civil, and Religious Liberty* [1768] (London: J. Johnson, 1771).

1 David Riesman, "Some Observations on Community Plans and Utopia," *Yale Law Journal,* 57, no. 2 (1947), 174. Also see Martin Meyerson, "Utopian Traditions and the Planning of Cities," in Lloyd Rodwin, *The Future Metropolis* (New York: George Braziller, 1961), 233–250.

2 David Riesman, with Nathan Glazer and Reuel Denny, *The Lonely Crowd: A Study of the Changing American Character* (New Haven, CT: Yale University Press, 1950). A comparable argument is found in Tyler Cowen, *The Complacent Class: The Self-Defeating Quest for the American Dream* (New York: St. Martin's Press, 2017). Cowen finds current Americans with a lower work ethic, decreased interest in interacting with those outside their immediate circle, and reduced desire to explore or innovate.

3 Lizabeth Cohen, *A Consumer's Republic: The Politics of Mass Consumption in Postwar America* (New York: Knopf, 2003).

4 Ashley Dawson, *Extreme Cities: The Peril and Promise of Urban Life in the Age of Climate Change* (New York: Verso, 2017), 306.

5 Rene Dubos, *So Human an Animal* (New York: Charles Scribner's Sons, 1968), 1.

6 Alexis de Tocqueville, *Democracy in America,* trans. George Lawrence, ed. J. P. Mayer (New York: Doubleday Anchor, 1969), 558.

7 Lester J. Cappon, ed., *The Adams-Jefferson Letters: The Complete Correspondence between Thomas Jefferson and Abigail and John Adams* (Chapel Hill: University of North Carolina Press, 1959).

8 Joseph J. Ellis, *American Dialogue: The Founders and Us* (New York: Alfred A. Knopf, 2018).

9 Frederic Jameson, "An American Utopia," in Jameson et al., *An American Utopia: Dual Power and the Universal Army,* ed. Slavoj Zizek (New York: Verso, 2016): 1–96, 95.

10 Bill Moyers, "We, the People versus We, the Wealthy," *The Nation,* September 12, 2016. Judge Brandeis's statement is often quoted in the growing literature about inequality. Three other examples: Andrew Sayer, *Why We Can't Afford the Rich* (Bristol, UK: Policy Press, 2016), 237; Erik Reese, *Utopia Drive: A Road Trip through America's Most Radical Idea* (New York: Farrar, Straus and Giroux, 2016), 328.

11 Langston Hughes, "Let America Be America Again," *The Collected Works of Langston Hughes: The Poems, 1921-1940* (Columbia: University of Missouri Press, 2001), 131–132.

12 George Perkins Marsh, *Man and Nature,* ed. David Lowenthal (1864; Seattle: University of Washington Press, 2003). Scientists have confirmed that humanity has entered the geological age of the Anthropocene as human activity has become the primary impact on the environment. See Joseph Stromberg, "The Age of Humans: Living in the Anthropocene," *Smithsonian Magazine,* January 2013; Andrea Wulf, *The Invention of Nature: Alexander von Humboldt's New World* (New York: Vintage Books, 2015). Wulf pays homage to this polymath and ecological visionary (1769–1759) and how his voluminous research and publications influenced the thinking of many Americans, including Jefferson, Thoreau, and Marsh. Von Humboldt is considered to be the first to have suggested that human action would eventually affect the planet's climate.

13 "Is Monetizing Waste the Secret to Ending Plastic Pollution?," United Nations Environment Programme, March 28, 2018, https://www.unenvironment.org/news-and-stories/story/monetizing-waste-secret-ending-plastic-pollution.

14 Candace Jackson, "Drink in the Good Life," *New York Times,* December 24, 2017. The median US home size is about 2,100 square feet, while in urbanizing China it is 600, having nearly doubled in size over the past two decades.

15 Myra Jehlen, *American Incarnation: The Individual, the Nation, and the Continent* (Cambridge, MA: Harvard University Press, 1986). Jehlen urges us to question the assumption "that each man is an independent entity, that total self-definition is his right, and

that therefore he defines himself in a dichotomy with society, so that freedom is free-dom from it and from others" (229).

16 Jed Kolko, "The Myth of the Return of Cities," *New York Times,* May 22, 2017; "New Home Construction Hits Prerecession Levels," *USA Today,* December 20, 2017, 1B; Wil-liam H. Frey, "US Population Disperses to Suburbs, Exurbs, Rural Areas, and 'Middle of the Country' Metros," Brookings Institution, "The Avenue" (blog), March 26, 2018, https://www.brookings.edu/blog/the-avenue/2018/03/26/us-population-disperses-to -suburbs-exurbs-rural-areas-and-middle-of-the-country-metros/.

17 Oscar Wilde, *The Soul of Man under Socialism* (Boston: J. W. Luce, 1910), 27.

ILLUSTRATION CREDITS

I.1   Princeton.edu.

I.2   Courtesy of Supperretro.com.

I.3   *The Plantation*, c. 1825: The Metropolitan Museum of Art Gift of Edgar William and Bernice Chrysler Garbisch, 1963.

I.4   Serenbe Community, Atlanta.

I.5   Library of Congress Prints and Photographs Division, Washington, DC #20177559593.

I.6   Francis Loeb Library Special Collections, Harvard Graduate School of Design, Martin Wagner Collection.

I.7   Alex Krieger.

1.1   Alex S. MacLean, *Landslides*.

1.2   Alex Krieger.

1.3   Alex S. MacLean, *Landslides*.

1.4a   Ohio Digital Map Library.

1.4b   Published by J. H. Colton, 1866.

1.5   Alex Krieger.

1.6   Jonathan Lucas, Wikipedia.

1.7   Library of Congress Prints and Photographs Division, Washington, DC #96514600.

1.8   Thomas Jefferson Foundation at Monticello.

1.9   Library of Congress Prints and Photographs Division, Washington, DC #97684108.

1.10   Alex Krieger.

2.1a   Crystal Bridges Museum of American Art, Bentonville Arkansas, 2010.106.

2.1b   Alex Krieger.

2.2   Collection of the National Academy of Art.

2.3   New York Historical Society, 1851.1. Gift of the New York Gallery of Fine Arts.

2.4   Chicago Public Library Special Collections.

2.5   New York Historical Society, 1858.2. Gift of the New York Gallery of Fine Arts.

2.6   National Park Service, Frederick Law Olmsted National Historic Society.

2.7   New York Historical Society, 1858.3. Gift of the New York Gallery of Fine Arts.

2.8   Chicago Historical Society.

2.9   New York Historical Society, 1858.4. Gift of the New York Gallery of Fine Arts.

2.10   Chicago Historical Society.

2.11   New York Historical Society, 1858.5. Gift of the New York Gallery of Fine Arts.

2.12   Alex Krieger.

2.13   Getty Images #615299338.

3.1   Library of Congress Prints and Photographs Division, Washington, DC #90708413.

3.2   Library of Congress Prints and Photographs Division, Washington, DC #2016800172.

3.3   Library of Congress Prints and Photographs Division, Washington, DC #96512563.

3.4.   Getty Images #97287201.

3.5   Alex Krieger.

3.6   Ernest Braun, Photographer.

4.1   Alex Krieger.

4.2   Alex S. MacLean, *Landslides*.

4.3   Alex Krieger.

4.4   Alex S. MacLean, *Landslides*.

4.5   Alex Krieger.

4.6   Alex Krieger.

4.7   Alex Krieger.

4.8   Alex Krieger.

5.1   Francis Loeb Library Special Collections, Harvard Graduate School of Design.

5.2   Jeff Hall Photography.

5.3   Alex S. MacLean, *Landslides*.

5.4   Library of Congress Prints and Photographs Division, Washington, DC #2018673849.

5.5   Flickr.

5.6   The Pullman State Historical Society.

5.7   National Archives and Records Administration. NARA record: 8464471. Paul Sequeira, photographer.

5.8   Courtesy of General Motors.

5.9   Courtesy of NBBJ © Architects and Planners.

5.10   Every effort has been made to identify copyright holders and obtain their permission for the use of copyright material. Notification of any additions or corrections that should be incorporated in future reprints or editions of this book will be greatly appreciated.

6.1   Alex Krieger.

6.2   Wikipedia.

6.3   Getty Images #50324702.

6.4   Courtesy of the Stockon School.

6.5   Alex Krieger.

6.6   Riverside Historical Museum, Village of Riverside, Illinois.

6.7   Alex Krieger.

6.8   Library of Congress Prints and Photographs Division, Washington, DC #12015515. From a Book of Pictures in Roland Park, Baltimore, Maryland, 106.

6.9   Alex Krieger.

6.10   Alex Krieger.

6.11   DPZ Architects and Planners.

6.12   Alex Krieger.

6.13   Lisa (the author's niece) and Eliot Hamlisch, family photo.

7.1   Library of Congress Prints and Photographs Division, Washington, DC #97507547.

7.2   Oklahoma Historical Society.

7.3   Oklahoma Historical Society.

7.4   Wikipedia.

7.5   Division of rare and Manuscript Collections, Cornell University Library #RMC2003.0018.

7.6   Norman B. Leventhal Map Center at the Boston Public Library, #15415.

7.7   Norman B. Leventhal Map Center at the Boston Public Library, #060111344.

7.8   Norman B. Leventhal Map Center at the Boston Public Library. #0r96fp272.

7.9   Tennessee State Library and Archives.

8.1   Alex Krieger.

8.2   New York Historical Society, # 60701 Geographic File.

8.3   Every effort has been made to identify copyright holders and obtain their permission for the use of copyright material. Notification of any additions or corrections that should be incorporated in future reprints or editions of this book will be greatly appreciated.

8.4   Alex Krieger.

8.5   Google Earth.

8.6   Olmsted Archives Frederick Law Olmsted National Historic Site.

8.7   Alex S. MacLean, Landslides.

8.8   Francis Loeb Library Special Collections, Harvard Graduate School of Design.

8.9   Photograph from the 1909 Report of the Board of Park Commissioners, Kansas City, Mo. Courtesy of Francis Loeb Library Special Collections, Harvard Graduate School of Design.

8.10   Vitruvius Britannicus Vol.1, 71.

8.11   Vitruvius Britannicus Vol 1, 71.

8.12   Alex Krieger.

8.13   Alex S. MacLean, *Landslides.*

9.1   Francis Loeb Library Special Collections, Harvard Graduate School of Design.

9.2   Norman B. Leventhal Map Center at the Boston Public Library, #19878.

9.3   Courtesy of Museum Syndicate.

9.4   Library of Congress Prints and Photographs Division, #2018677059.

9.5   Library of Congress Prints and Photographic Division, #20133651553.

10.1   Alex Krieger.

10.2   Library of Congress Manuscript Division, Microfilm reel 057.

10.3   Library of Congress Prints and Photograph Division, Washington, DC Andrew Ellicott, 1792-76696408.

10.4   The National Archives Catalogue, 529253, 111-8-5147.

10.5   Courtesy of the US Commission of Fine Arts, Washington, DC.

10.6   Courtesy of the US Commission of Fine Arts, Washington, DC.

10.7   Library of Congress Prints and Photographs Division, Washington, DC #2017716837.

10.8   Courtesy of NBBJ© Architects and Planners.

10.9   Randy Santos Photography, DowntownDC714344.

11.1   Chicago Historic Society, Traffic on Dearborn and Rasdolph, 1909.

11.2   Chicago History Museum ICHI-05776.

11.3   Chicago History Museum Rand McNally Graphics maps 1893.

11.4   Library of Congress, Prints and Photographs Division, Washington, DC John Vachon photographer #2017812612.

11.5   Library of Congress, Prints and Photography Division, Washington, DC George R. Lawrence photographer #2007663982.

11.6   Chicago Historical Society.

11.7   Ninecloudsblog.

11.8   Alex Krieger.

11.9   Chicago History Museum ICHI-068656.

11.10   Alex Krieger.

12.1   Courtesy of General Motors.

12.2   Library of Congress, Prints and Photographs Division, Washington, DC #20122649800.

12.3   Frank Lloyd Wright Foundation, Scottsdale, Arizona.

12.4   Alex S. MacLean, Landslides.

12.5   Library of Congress, Prints and Photographs Division, Washington, DC #2015645804.

12.6   Digitized by Google Images.

12.7   The City of Los Angeles Digital Archives.

12.8   David Rumsey Map Collection.

12.9   Getty Images #92931377.

13.1   Peter Simon, Photographer.

13.2   Alex Krieger.

13.3   The Joseph Smith Papers Archive.

13.4   California History Room, California State Library, Sacramento, California. C. C. Curtis photographer.

13.5   Bibliotheque Nationale, Paris, France / Bridgeman Image, XIR167545.

13.6   Lisa Law, photographer.

13.7   Peter Simon, photographer.

14.1   Jefferson National Memorial Archives, V106–4838.

14.2   Library of Congress Prints and Photographs Division, Washington, DC #2017765036.

14.3   Peter Simon, photographer.

14.4   Advertisement in National Geographic August 1962.
Every effort has been made to identify copyright holders and obtain their permission for the use of copyright material. Notification of any additions or corrections that should be incorporated in future reprints or editions of this book will be greatly appreciated.

14.5   Alamy Stock Photo/Michael Dwyer photographer, A68F97.

14.6   Alex S. MacLean, *Landslides.*

14.7   Courtesy of the Boston Planning & Development Agency.

14.8   Francis Loeb Library Special Collections, Harvard Graduate School of Design. Martin Wagner Collection.

14.9   Francis Loeb Library Special Collections, Harvard Graduate School of Design.

14.10   Originally published by the US Department of Housing and Urban Development, Office of Public Research, and is reproduced with the Department's Permission.

14.11   Alex Krieger.

14.12   Brighton Allston Historical Society.

15.1   DISNEY © Disney Enterprises, Inc.

15.2   DISNEY © Disney Enterprises, Inc.

15.3   DISNEY © Disney Enterprises, Inc.

15.4   DISNEY © Disney Enterprises, Inc.

15.5   Alex Krieger.

15.6   Alex Krieger.

15.7   Pars International/Times.

15.8   Robert Hanson Photography.

15.9   Sam Kittner, photographer.

16.1.   Alex Krieger.

16.2   Alex Krieger.

16.3   Courtesy of the Mob Museum, Las Vegas.

16.4   University of Nevada, Las Vegas.

16.5   Alex Krieger.

16.6   Daniel Hernandez, photographer.

16.7   Photo Courtesy of the Howard Hughes Corporation.

16.8   Tristan Surtel—Wikipedia.

16.9   Alex Krieger.

16.10   Alex S. MacLean, *Landslides.*

17.1   Getty Images—Mario Tama.

17.2   Federal Emergency Management Agency News Photo.

17.3   Coastal studies Institute, Louisiana State University.

17.4   AP Images/Bill Haber photographer #070310044675.

17.5   AP Images/Luigi Costantini photographer #413558486319.

17.6   Rob Rogers Cartoon, 2005 Pittsburgh Post Gazette.

17.7   University of Chicago Photographic Archive, Special Collections Research Center. apf12345.

17.9   Alex Krieger.

17.10   Alex S. Maclean, *Landslides.*

18.1   Michael Oko/World Resources Institute.

18.2   Alex Krieger.

ACKNOWLEDGMENTS

The genesis of this book dates back quite some time. Undoubtedly I will fail to acknowledge many who have influenced me in various ways in this endeavor. My apologies to all I have overlooked.

Among my academic colleagues at Harvard, I am grateful for the support of Deans Alan Altshuler, Jerald McCue, Mohsen Mostafavi, and Peter Rowe. Discussions across time with colleagues have always brought insight, so I thank Anita Berrizbeitia, Eve Blau, Joan Busquets, Harry Cobb, Diane Davis, Richard Forman, Ann Forsyth, David Gamble, Tony Gomez-Ibanez, Stephen Gray, Toni Griffith, Daniel D'Oca, Gary Hilderbrand, Jarold Kayden, Rahul Malhottra, Rick Pieser, Moshe Safdie, Andres Sevtsuk, John Stilgoe, James Stockard, Alexander von Hoffman, and Michael Van Walkenburgh. I much regret that Bill Saunders, former associate dean and my coeditor of a prior publication, will not see the product of his long years of encouragement to undertake such a book. Johanna Kasubowski, Design Resource Librarian at the Loeb Library, was always helpful in locating elusive but important documents and images.

Over decades of teaching at the Graduate School of Design, and visiting stints at other institutions, the students and faculty who have directly or indirectly influenced my thinking are also too numerous to recall. But I thank them all. I've enjoyed collaborating with exceptional teaching fellows over the years, and three deserved special notice: Garreth Dorethy, now a valued faculty colleague; Justin Stern, for an incredibly faithful four-year run as Head TF while completing his PhD, and Benjamin Bolger, who has for many years directed the students taking the course online through the Harvard Extension School. Three research assistants helped in multiple ways: Carlo Urmy, Christina Shivers, and Charles

Smith. Charlie was absolutely indefatigable in locating and acquiring rights to illustrations and fact-checking many references.

From my professional practice, I want to acknowledge the support and friendship of Larry Chan, Fran Henderson, Alan Mountjoy, Tom Sieniewicz, Patrick Tedesco, Will Voulgaris, and Kathryn Firth, among many others at Chan Krieger Sieniewicz, and now at NBBJ. I thank Staci Liu, who has recently helped manage a complex schedule of teaching, practice, and writing. I much appreciate my colleagues at NBBJ putting up with a bit of "book time" even during the proverbial office hours.

I extend a special gratitude to Molly Howard, my administrative assistant and good friend over a two-decade-long period, first at Harvard, then at Chan Krieger Sieniewicz, and then at NBBJ. Matthew Kiefer, another good friend, I thank for innumerable great conversations about many things, including some of the themes of the book.

I am grateful to Ian Malcolm, whose exacting and very wise editing has improved both my thinking and my writing immeasurably. I would wish the good fortune to any author of having Ian as editor. Julia Kirby, while copyediting, provided much more, especially with her uncanny ability to substitute or intersperse several words to make a sentence that much more worth reading. And of course, appreciation for my agent, Albert LaFarge, who introduced me to the wonderful people at the Harvard University Press who, in addition to those above, include Director George Andreou, Tim Jones, Lisa Roberts, Stephanie Vyce, and Olivia Elizabeth Woods. Melody Negron of Westchester Publishing Services provided tireless and exacting attention during the prepress production process.

A fortuitous collaboration occurred with Ron Grim, curator at the Norman B. Leventhal Map and Education Center at the Boston Public Library, and fellow board members Larry Caldwell and Richard Brown, as Ron was developing the exhibition *America Transformed: Mapping the Nineteenth Century*. A natural overlap of themes ensued between the book and the exhibition. The catalog accompanying the exhibition contains an essay, "Seeding Settlement: Homesteads and Federal Land Grants Late in the Nineteenth Century," which is based on Chapter 7.

I thank Beth Clevenger, an editor at MIT Press, for providing valuable early encouragement and insight about the process of developing a manuscript for publication. A special thanks goes to the University of Massachusetts Club, where early mornings on the thirty-second floor of 1 Beacon Street were spent writing while overlooking Boston, that original American city upon a hill.

One doesn't just resolve one day to write such a book. Essays and papers written over the years have served as testing grounds and preparations. I would like to acknowledge a number of publications for allowing me to introduce ideas to their audiences. The Introduction to this book builds on themes first outlined in "The American City: Ideal and Mythic Aspects of a Reinvented Urbanism," in *Assemblage: A Critical Journal of Architecture and Design Culture*, no. 3 (July 1987) 39–59. Chapter 1 revises and expands on "Thomas Jefferson's Blueprint for an Egalitarian American landscape," in *Street Works: Patterns in Urbanity* (Amsterdam: Amsterdam Academy of Architecture, 2010) 42–50. Portions of Chapter 2 were first published as "Civic Lessons of an Ephemeral Monument, Monumentality and the City" *Harvard Architecture Review* 4 (Spring 1984), 149–165.

Chapter 6 expands on ideas I first presented in "The Costs–and Benefits–of Sprawl." *Harvard Design Magazine* 19 (Fall/Winter 2003–2004). Chapter 8 relies in part on "Nature for an Urbanizing Society: The Paradigm of the Boston Park System" written with Anne Mackin, and on "Il Sisema dei Parchi di Boston" *Casabella* 527, September 1986, 42–53. Chapter 14 revisits material I wrote about in "Experiencing Boston: Encounters with the Places on the Maps," in Alex Krieger and David Cobb, eds., *Mapping Boston* (Cambridge, MA: MIT Press, 1999), 146–172.

Finally. every effort has been made to identify copyright holders and obtain permission for the use of copyrighted material. Notification of any additions of corrections that should be incorporated in future reprints or edition of this book would be greatly appreciated.

INDEX

Note: Page numbers in italics refer to figures.